Authority and Markets

Authority and Markets

Susan Strange's Writings on International Political Economy

Edited by

Roger Tooze
Visiting Professor of International Political Economy
Bristol Business School

and

Christopher May
Senior Lecturer
Faculty of Economics and Social Science
University of the West of England

First published 2002 by
PALGRAVE MACMILLAN
Houndmills, Basingstoke, Hampshire RG21 6XS and
175 Fifth Avenue, New York, N.Y. 10010
Companies and representatives throughout the world

PALGRAVE MACMILLAN is the new global academic imprint of
St Martin's Press LLC Scholarly and Reference Division and
Palgrave Publishers Ltd (formerly Macmillan Press Ltd).

ISBN 0–333–98720–9 hardback
ISBN 0–333–98721–7 paperback

This book is printed on paper suitable for recycling and
made from fully managed and sustained forest sources.

A catalogue record for this book is available
from the British Library.

Library of Congress Cataloging-in-Publication Data
Authority and markets : Susan Strange's writings on international political
economy / edited by Roger Tooze and Christopher May.
      p. cm.
   Includes bibliographical references and index.
   ISBN 0–333–98720–9 — ISBN 0–333–98721–7 (pbk.)
      1. International economic relations. I. Tooze, Roger. II. May,
   Christopher, 1960–

   HF1411 .A97 2002
   337—dc21
                                                         2002025211

10   9   8   7   6   5   4   3   2   1
11   10   09   08   07   06   05   04   03   02

Printed and bound in Great Britain by
Antony Rowe Ltd, Chippenham and Eastbourne

Contents

Section V: Conclusions?

Acknowledgements

We are grateful for all the support and encouragement we have received in the course of this project, particularly from Nicola Viinikka at Palgrave who has been all, and more, that we could have asked from a publisher, from our four academic referees who each in their different ways was so enthusiastic about the prospect of a 'Susan Strange Reader' and from our colleagues in International Political Economy who, as Susan would have called them, are our 'kindred spirits' – they know who they are.

Every work by Susan Strange included in this volume has been published previously, in some form or other. We are enormously grateful for the ready permission that copyright holders gave us to reproduce the items collected here. It is testimony to the high regard that Susan Strange was held in that we had such an immediate and enthusiastic response from the vast majority of these copyright holders.

We would like formally to acknowledge the following permissions to reproduce the work included in this Reader:

Chapter 2: 'I Never Meant To Be An Academic' , first published in J. Kruzel and J.N. Rosenau (eds) *Journeys Through World Politics: Autobiographical Reflections of Thirty-four Academic Travellers* (Lexington: Lexington Books, 1989) pp. 429–36. We are grateful to Lexington Books for permission to reproduce this work.

Chapter 3: 'Prologue: Some Desert Island Stories', first published as pages 1–6 of *States and Markets* (London: Pinter Publishers, 1988). We are grateful to the Continuum International Publishing Group for permission to reproduce this work.

Chapter 4: 'A New Look at Trade and Aid', first published in *International Affairs* Volume 42, No. 1 (January 1966) pp. 61–73. We are grateful to the Editor of *International Affairs* for permission to reproduce this work.

Chapter 5: 'Protectionism and World Politics', first published in *International Organisation* Volume 39, No. 2 (Spring 1985) pp. 233–59. We are grateful to MIT Press Journals for permission to reproduce this work.

Chapter 6: 'Finance, Information and Power', first published in *Review of International Studies* Volume 16, No. 3 (July 1990) pp. 259–74. We are grateful to Cambridge University Press for permission to reproduce this work.

Chapter 7: 'The Structure of Finance in the World System', first published in Sakamoto, Y. (editor) *Global Transformation: Challenges to the State System* (Tokyo: United Nations University Press, 1994) pp. 228–49. We are grateful to the United Nations University Press for permission to reproduce this work.

Chapter 8: 'Finance in Politics: An Epilogue to *Mad Money*' was written right at the end of Strange's life and was unfinished. Various versions have been published. Copyright lies with the Estate of Susan Strange.

Chapter 9: 'The Persistent Myth of Lost Hegemony', first published in *International Organisation* Volume 41, No. 4 (Autumn 1987) pp. 551–74. We are grateful to MIT Press Journals for permission to reproduce this work.

Chapter 10: 'Towards a Theory of Transnational Empire', first published in Czempiel, E-O. & Rosenau, J.N. (editors) *Global Changes and Theoretical Challenges: Approaches to World Politics for the 1990s* (Lexington: Lexington Books, 1989) pp. 161–76. We are grateful to Lexington Books for permission to reproduce this work.

Chapter 11: 'States, Firms and Diplomacy', first published in *International Affairs* Volume 68, No.1 (January 1992) pp. 1–15. We are grateful to the Editor of International Affairs for permission to reproduce this work.

Chapter 12: 'Who Governs? Networks of Power in World Society', first published in *Hitotsubashi Journal of Law and Politics* Special Issue (1994) pp. 5–17. We are grateful to the Editors of the Hitotsubashi Journal of Law and Politics for permission to reproduce this work.

Chapter 13: 'International Economics and International Relations: A Case of Mutual Neglect', first published in *International Affairs* Volume 46, No. 2 (April 1970) pp. 304–15. We are grateful to the Editor of International Affairs for permission to reproduce this work.

Chapter 14: 'What is Economic Power and Who Has It?', first published in *International Journal* Volume 30, No. 2 (Spring 1975) pp. 207–24. We are grateful to the Editors of the International Journal for permission to reproduce this work.

Chapter 15: *'Cave! Hic Dragones:* A Critique of Regime Analysis', first published in *International Organisation* Volume 36, No. 2 (Spring 1982) pp. 479–97. We are grateful to MIT Press Journals for permission to reproduce this work.

Chapter 16: 'Territory, State, Authority and Economy: A New Realist Ontology of Global Political Economy', first published in R. W. Cox (editor) *The New Realism: Perspectives on Multilateralism and World Order* (Basingstoke: Macmillan Press – now Palgrave Macmillan/United Nations University Press, 1997). We are grateful to Palgrave Macmillan for permission to reproduce this work.

Chapter 17: 'The Westfailure System', first published in *Review of International Studies* Volume 25, No. 3 (July 1999) pp. 345–54. We are grateful to Cambridge University Press for permission to reproduce this work.

1
Authority and Markets: Interpreting the Work of Susan Strange

The re-emergence of political economy into the mainstream of academic study has been a feature of the world's intellectual and political terrain of the last thirty-five years. Increasingly such study is driven by and takes place within the domain of what is constituted as the 'international'. Therefore it is hardly surprising that 'International Political Economy' (IPE)[1] has become a major focus of policy, writing, research and teaching, particularly with the contemporary focus on 'globalisation'. There are a number of 'pathways to IPE', but within the field owing its origins to the academic discipline of International Relations (IR), the work of Susan Strange is one of the most significant individual contributions. Her ideas, her published work (including her journalism), her teaching, her professional activities (not least, her very distinctive form of personal interaction and intervention), all came together to make a real difference to the way that we now think and write about the international and global political economy.

Many of the core ideas and concepts that both mainstream and critical scholars now use as 'common sense' elements of IPE incorporate, or are drawn indirectly from, the analysis Susan Strange developed over a period of nearly fifty years of thinking and writing. Our acceptance of the fundamental necessity to link politics and economics in order to understand either and both partly stems from her early and continued insistence on this link, despite the prevailing conventional wisdom.[2] Indeed, the core IPE concept of 'structural power' is derived from her thinking on money initially and subsequently from her more general analyses. Even the fact that the field of study we now designate as 'IPE' is known by this name is partly down to her. She insisted, from an early stage in the development of her arguments (Strange 1970a), that the study of the international political relations mediated by national governments, that is intergovernmental relations between and among national economies, did not and does not adequately capture the whole of what she saw as a different reality. In the complex structure of international political economy there was and is so much more than what was then labelled 'The Politics of International Economic Relations'.[3]

1

This book only samples Strange's extensive and wide-ranging academic writings. However we are all too aware that this necessary focus has had some costs. The conventions of academic writing and publishing, as well as the limitations of the medium of print itself, mean we cannot include some of the other contributions and interventions that made her work so immediately powerful, so accessible, and sometimes, so very personal. With this important caveat, the purpose of this introduction is to provide a framework (one of many possible frameworks) for making sense of the central ideas and arguments that Susan Strange developed through a long and intensive process of intellectual and personal engagement with the study of what has become known as IPE.

Making sense of Susan Strange's contributions to IPE

Susan Strange's work does not fit easily within the mainstream methodology and assumptions which govern knowledge production in IPE, and she frequently criticised aspects of this methodology, particularly the application of rational choice models to political economy. Although she was a thoroughgoing empiricist, she did not accept many of the claims made by those in IPE who sought to discover law-like generalisations; she always had a deep suspicion of 'grand theory', its claims and its devotees. This was very much a part of her insistence upon 'grounding theory', most importantly in a detailed knowledge of particular sectors of the global political economy (Strange 1976a/b).

Conventional IR/IPE understanding of the process of academic knowledge production sets the academic researcher/writer in a specific relationship to her/his work, in line with its particular epistemology. Hence, the academic writer (subject) is separated from the international political economy (object) which she researches, and from this position engages in a process of knowledge creation, of discovering testable reality via a discipline legitimised form of empiricism.[4] But, as one of us has previously shown, her methodological eclecticism more closely resembled the view of science articulated by Feyerabend's 'anything goes' approach (May 1996). This was a view of her work she was happy to accept as she recognised that Feyerabend's argument could provide her with an acceptable (to others!) epistemological grounding (Strange 1996a).[5] Thus, it is inappropriate to locate and understand her work using the mainstream approach to knowledge. She was deeply sceptical of the assumptions and the claims embedded in this approach, although she seldom engaged directly with the philosophical underpinnings of established IPE (Palan 1999). Therefore, the standpoint we use from which to review Strange's work is not fixed, it is itself historically and politically situated. And, crucially, it *already* incorporates past and current theorisations of IPE, including, of course, Strange's own.

As IPE scholars, the assumptions we bring to the task of making sense of Strange's work are part of a deeper set of assumptions governing the philosophy and production of knowledge. Significantly, the acknowledgement of a historically constituted context of evaluation means rejecting the conventional model based upon the philosophical assumptions of empiricism, whereby the categories of evaluation and historical location are themselves ahistorical (MacLean 2000; Tooze 2000). The conventional view of knowledge production is based upon, and reproduces, a methodology which seeks to construct an understanding of a global political economy (including the production of knowledge about global political economy) that is external to society. Additionally such a methodology is limited by being made up only of those elements that can be empirically measured. As well as allocating a specific and non-constitutive role to academic knowledge, the conventional view produces a misrecognition of the nature of the global political economy, and most importantly, a misrecognition of the character and distribution of power (MacLean 2000; Tooze 2000).

These considerations lead us to a more complex context-based analysis of Strange's work. While this includes the conventional notions of academic production, it crucially takes account of the processes of engagement and communication that are central to Strange's (and all our) academic knowledge production. Strange herself was clear as to the influences driving the development of IPE, and, by implication, her own work. For her, 'The boom in international political economy as an area of specialisation has reflected, not ideas, but events' (1998c: 5): IPE was and is 'the echo of events'. Typically, she confounded mainstream notions of how academic knowledge develops (and her own methodology) by stressing that IPE is driven by *interests* and as such always serves particular purposes; 'the need to fight the Cold War justified an intellectual investment both in the diplomacy of trade and money and in the academic analysis of the economic issues that threatened to divide and therefore weaken the affluent capitalist alliance' (1998c: 8). The rationale for and the analytical focus of IPE was (and continues to be) determined by US political interests.

The pervasive late 1970s/early 1980s focus of US IPE on regimes, which she criticised at length (1982a), was for Strange an expression of the most pressing of US political needs to manage international economic order: 'IPE was thus just one more weapon in the contest between capitalism and socialism' (1998c: 8). But having made this political purpose/political context argument she also accepted that individuals do matter, albeit within the overall context of interests: discussing the analyses of 'hard-core neo-functionalist scholars' she argued that 'it was not the US government nor the CIA but their own idealistic belief in the potential of international institutions to undermine the wayward self-serving behaviour of nation-states that inspired their work' (1998c: 9). Such personal values and commitments have an important role in academic knowledge production, as Strange's own work clearly illustrates.

Thomas Biersteker provides a useful schema for the analysis of academic knowledge in his 'Evolving Perspectives on International Political Economy' (Biersteker 1993).[6] Here he argues that theories (and therefore for us, *all* knowledge of IPE) 'are contingent upon, and reflect substantial portions of the context in which they were formulated'. Moreover, 'theory is context bounded and emerges either consciously or unconsciously in the service of (or driven by) particular interests' (1993: 7). As we have indicated, this is exactly Strange's view of the development of IPE. For Biersteker 'context' ordinarily has at least three different components: intertextual, social and individual. Hence, over time, 'the direction of theoretical research tends to be the outgrowth of the dialectical relationship between theory and social context, combined with the nature of the reaction of a given theoretical undertaking to its predecessor (given the intertextual nature of theoretical reflection)' (1993: 8). Knowledge, then, 'is socially constructed, and the investigators and their intellectual tools are part of the social context of their investigation and reporting' (1993: 8). Each of Biersteker's three components of context are mutually constituted by the other two, in a continuous process over time, and merge into each other. Yet, these categories of context do provide a focus, and, as we shall see, are particularly appropriate for making sense of Strange's work.

Susan Strange and IPE: predispositions, themes and issues

While resisting the temptation to impose a retrospective order and coherence on Strange's work which might produce a teleological account of its development, there are clearly themes around which her work clusters. These themes provided us with a means of making sense of over one hundred academic contributions she published, and reflect Strange's deep personal value commitments and predispositions. These themes developed over time through her reflections on, and engagements with, the events of the twentieth century as well as her own and others' attempts to make sense of these events.

Some of these themes are present throughout almost all her body of work and act as overarching, 'framing' ideas, some evolve as part of her thinking and others are specific to particular time periods or particular issues. But most of her writings manage to bring together the whole range of questions that she was concerned with at any particular time. This partly explains why it is so difficult to categorise her work according to the problem or issue it nominally deals with: for example, her discussion of money and finance becomes an arena for, and empirical evidence in support of, the development of her argument on structural power; this in turn allowed her to move away from the classical 'Realist' view of the state and eventually argue for the 'Retreat of the State' (Lawton and Michaels 2000). Nevertheless, we have identified four overarching framing themes in Strange's thinking, each related but distinct. The first two are more in the nature of dispositions tending to prefigure her analysis of IPE, but are constantly developed through that analysis.

Framing dispositions and themes

Strange's distinctive approach to analysis

Susan Strange was, above all, concerned to make sense of the myriad changes and developments in the global political economy in ways that could be communicated and shared. One strand of this is her insistence on making academic writing accessible and free from 'jargon'. She was fiercely contemptuous of jargon believing that it is mainly used to hide inadequacies of understanding and the limitations of theory. This is not merely a matter of individual style or preference derived from the social context of her career as an experienced journalist, or her personal dislike of academic pomposity. It is an intellectual and political statement which reflects her views that one of the principal social responsibilities of academics is to speak to as many people as possible, and that academics do not communicate sufficiently between, among and often within disciplines. Both these crucial activities are greatly hindered by the prevalence of theoretical pretension and discipline-specific language. This belief in the necessity of widespread and clear communication through simple and interesting writing makes Strange's work wonderfully readable and accessible when compared to most academic outpourings. This desire to communicate is also one of the reasons she continued to write as a journalist until a few years before her death.

Her concern for accessible writing, as well as her experience of journalism, is allied to her insistence on 'getting one's hands dirty' in the details, the raw material, the technologies and the 'lived experiences' of international political economy. For Strange, it is never sufficient to remain at the level of abstraction and generality if one wants really to understand the subject of IPE. This predisposition provided a strong push towards her development of the idea of sectoral political economy (the 'nitty gritty' of IPE) as a necessary and prior part of a structural analysis which she developed from the 1970s onwards (1971c; 1976a/b; 1982b). It also helps to explain her fundamental distaste for and disavowal of abstract, general theory, what she called 'grand theory', the all singing, all dancing single explanatory framework beloved (in her view) by both Marxists and US political science IPE academics alike.

Fundamental social values

The second of our framing themes is Strange's commitment to embed her analysis and understanding of IPE within fundamental social values. But as she cautioned the main aim 'is to make the study of international political economy value-sensitive, not to make it value laden' (1983c: 210). What she means by this is twofold. Linked to her belief that all academic knowledge is interest driven and thus not 'value free', she argued that all analysis of IPE is based upon someone's values and, usually implicitly, attempts to achieve, legitimate or defend a particular trade-off of these values to benefit a particular group of people at a particular time (what she referred to as 'ideological' analysis). Additionally, unless those who study IPE recognise that political economy and society start from, and are fundamentally concerned with, these values then any analysis will be partial and limited.

The earliest articulation of this commitment in terms of what these values consist of and how they relate to IPE (1983c) built on her empirical work on money, transnationalism and sectors of political economy in the previous decade (particularly, but not exclusively: Strange 1971c; 1972c; 1975a; 1976a/b; 1976d; 1981b; 1982b) and drew from her seminal work on the relationship between IR and international economics (1970a). However this commitment is perhaps best articulated in her 'Desert Island Stories' from *States and Markets* (1988e: 1–6). For Strange there are four fundamental values which are the basis of all contemporary societies, no matter what their formal political economy. Crucially these values apply equally at the international or global level. The values are: the provision of wealth and the meeting of material needs; the provision of security and order; the provision of justice; and the provision of liberty and freedom of choice. Hence, for Strange, the study of IPE is *necessarily* grounded in these values; they are not merely added on to a (supposedly) objective, value-free 'science' of IPE.[7] She insists that 'Who gets how much of each of these values and by what means *are the basic questions, the starting point of all else*' (1983c: 211, emphasis added). And accordingly she identifies the subject-matter of IPE on the basis of these values as 'the social, political and economic arrangements affecting the global systems of production, exchange and distribution, and the mix of values reflected therein' (1988e: 18).

The relationship of politics and economics

The central analytical element, and third framing theme of all of her work, from her earliest academic writings in the *Year Book of World Affairs* to her very last journal article, is the necessary relationship between politics and economics, and the failure of contemporary social sciences (primarily International Relations, Economics, Political Science) to conceptualise, or even to acknowledge, that relationship. This concern is evident in the earliest of her writings (1950a), it was the basis of one of her most influential articles (1970a), and became the core of her extended interaction both with events and with other writings on international relations.

Her insistent focus on this relationship led her towards the conceptualisation of its contemporary form as that between 'authority' and 'markets'. Although in 1988 she had called her seminal intervention 'States and Markets' she later admitted that she should have called it 'Authority and Markets' (1994b: fn. 4; 1996b: xv) (hence the title of this present book). She wanted to include all forms of authority, whether located in the state, international institutions, corporations or the markets themselves, and not just the state. She rejected the implication that the state is the sole source of authority in global political economy. Her focus on the fundamental relationship of politics and economics, on authority and markets, became the springboard for her continuing critique of both mainstream economics and IR for their respective failures to include the other in their conceptualisations of the world (1988e: 12–22; 1996b: xiii–xvi), as well as her call for the creation of a study of international political economy where the boundary between politics and economics, and that between the domestic and the international, were both effectively dissolved.

From the 1970s onwards she was continuously engaged in intertextual initiatives and critique, which informed the analysis in all her books (Strange 1971c; 1976d; 1986f; 1988e; Stopford and Strange 1991; Strange 1996b; 1998f). This critique was also the starting point for what might be regarded as the essence of her work in constructing a theoretically grounded and 'realist' study of IPE, the three books which mounted an extensive campaign against conventional knowledge in IPE: *States and Markets* (1988e); *Rival States, Rival Firms* (with John Stopford, 1991); and *The Retreat of the State* (1996b). Revealing both the power of the established order over the development of academic knowledge, and her disappointment at the resistance to change among academics, the complex relationship between politics and economics remained one of the key themes in her final works (1999; 2000).

The continual spur to the development of a new IPE was also partly provided by Strange's early observation of the international and systemic consequences of the relationship of politics and economics in that 'the pace of development in the international economy has accelerated ... in consequence, it is outdistancing and outgrowing the rather more static international political system' (1970a: 305). The analysis of this systemic dysfunction and its consequences was a major concern of much of her analysis, although as Claire Cutler indicates, ultimately she never achieved her goal of reintegrating politics and economics (Cutler 2000).

Power in political economy

Our final framing theme is Strange's insistence on the centrality of power to any explanation of the character, structure and dynamics of IPE, and her consequent search for an understanding of power in the global political economy. In one sense this provides the intellectual cutting edge to all her work: if a question or analysis does not illuminate who or what has power in the global political economy she thought it neither interesting nor relevant. For her, the key question in IPE is '*Cui bono?*', 'Who benefits?' and power is what explains, and suggests answers to, this question. It was her search for an appropriate and adequate understanding of power, especially in the form of her critique of conventional IR analysis, that led her to develop the conceptualisation of 'structural power' which is the basis of the distinct structural analysis that became one of her major contributions to the study of IPE (1988e).

The question of power informs and directs not only her own analysis but her intertextual engagement with other work in IPE. From an early stage in her career, Strange became convinced of the inadequacy of mainstream IR attempts to explain power, and was deeply critical of the absence of power in (international) economics. In her view the failure correctly to analyse power, specifically the failure to recognise the incidence of structural power, leads directly to a serious misrecognition of the 'reality' of the global political economy, primarily by US scholars, which had and still has serious political consequences and implications. This misrecognition of power was manifested in the overwhelming US IPE concern for regimes during the 1970s and early 1980s, and in the claims of declining US hegemonic power that dominated US IPE/IR in the 1980s. It was also evident in the questions regarding the role and policies of the US in maintaining and directing the structure of global capitalism, particularly in the realm of finance and credit, all of which she addressed, considered and criticised (particularly, but not only: Strange 1982a; 1982c; 1986f; 1987; 1988a; 1990c).

This concern also informed her directly related work on the ontology of IPE, although this was also driven by her analysis of the deepening complexities of the global political economy: who or what are the significant and powerful entities in the global political economy, and how can the interactions between them be characterised? Again, for Strange, the misrecognition of power both derives from, and contributes to, the fact that American IPE continued to be based more on a notion of 'politics of international economic relations' (that is, a state-based ontology), than a more 'realistic' ontology of international political economy (1997b). The 'real' world political economy has changed and with it the nature of the state and the distribution of global authority but, Strange charged, those in IR and most of those in IPE had failed to recognise these changes.

The development of this ontological argument eventually took her, over a period of some twelve years, from a position where she argued that the necessary starting point of IPE was within the state-based study of International Relations (Strange 1984e) to the rejection of mainstream IR as too state-centric to be able to capture the nature of contemporary global political economy, and therefore unsuitable as the disciplinary 'home' of a 'realistic' study of IPE. Referring to IR's claim that the state always remains at the centre of the world stage, she concluded: 'It is the *always* that I now find unacceptable, and which leads me to feel that perhaps I have at last reached the final parting of the ways from the discipline of international relations' (1996b: xv). This is the core argument of her last published works (1999, 2000):

> We have to escape and resist the state-centrism inherent in the analysis of conventional international relations. The study of globalisation has to embrace the study of the behaviour of firms no less than of other forms of political authority. International political economy has to be recombined with comparative political economy at the sub-state as well as the state level. (1999: 354)

International Political Economy needed, Strange concluded, to be about political economy, not about the central concerns of International Relations.

Debates, issues, concepts and theory

Susan Strange's work covers a wide range of issues, debates, concepts and theories. Here we identify four strands of this work, each interacting and informing the others, that reflect her major contributions to IPE. These are: her development of structural power as a basis of conceptualising global political economy; her analysis of international and global money, finance and credit; her analysis of US policy and power; and her distinctive approach to theory and methodology. Each of these strands are developed and articulated within the broader framing dispositions and themes we have discussed above.

Structural power

We regard Strange's development of structural power as her most significant contribution towards IPE, although, as Palan suggests, it is also ultimately probably her most problematic (Palan 1999). Her notion of structural power and the analysis of IPE it inspired, was an intellectual and political response to the problems and growing complexity of the international political economy of the mid-1970s onwards, not least the formal US repudiation of Bretton Woods on 15 August 1971. This was linked with an intertextual critique of conventional notions of power based on her growing conviction that such analyses were unable to capture the reality of power in international political economy. Addressing her own rhetorical question 'What is economic power, and who has it?' she noted that her enquiry was 'prompted by the growing dissatisfaction with the apparent inability of most conventional theories of international politics and economics to offer any coherent explanation of certain recent events and developments' (Strange 1975a: 207), specifically the power of multinational oil companies, US–European monetary relations and possible shifts in US power. Scepticism regarding power seen as only material capabilities, and her earlier work on finance, encouraged her to suggest that the US's key role in the global political economy was as supplier of the world currency and thus, as framer of the rules of the world economy.

This key conceptual shift led Strange to conclude that the conventional IR notion of power was inadequate for IPE. This notion considers power to be relational and is defined as 'the power of A to get B to do something they would not otherwise do' (Strange 1988e: 24) and is usually 'measured' and assessed by physical capabilities. However, she argued, there are two kinds of power in a political economy – relational power *and* structural power – and furthermore structural power had become much more important in the post-1945 world political economy. For Strange, structural power was

> the power to shape and determine the structures of the global political economy within which other states, their political institutions, their economic enterprises and (not least) their scientists and other professional people have to operate … .
> Structural power, in short, confers the power to decide how things shall be done, the power to shape frameworks within which states relate to each other, relate to people, or relate to corporate enterprises. (1988e: 24–5)

As we have indicated, for some time Strange had been having difficulty with the dominant analysis of the role of America in the global system, and perhaps most famously, the arguments in the early to mid-1980s, that the US was losing its hegemony (Strange 1982a; 1987). Having been largely vindicated by subsequent events, during this period Susan Strange strove to develop an IPE analysis that would allow her to present analytically what she believed about the power of America; that its 'decline' was illusory. This work was not popular in the US not least of all because Strange (never one to hold back) peppered her analysis with an assault on the myopia of her American colleagues. Her translation of the concept of structural power into an analysis based on four structures of power was in this sense a direct response to short-sighted arguments that proposed that the global system was entering a period After Hegemony (Keohane 1984). Hence, her structural analysis had been percolating in her work for a few years before its final formulation in the mid-1980s.

In 1968 Strange had acted as a rapporteur for the Social Science Research Council Advisory Group on International Organisation (chaired by Geoffrey Goodwin) and in her report (Strange and Goodwin 1968) she emphasised certain key themes, prominent among which were the impact of structures of power and the impact of technical change. Seven years later, these ideas had started to solidify into the approach which would be set out in *States and Markets*. In 'What is economic power and who has it?' (Strange 1975a), she linked the (to her, already apparent) error in American self-perceived decline to an emerging idea of structures of power (although the final shape of this argument was not clearly articulated at this stage). The problem for her was not so much lack of power, but the lack of will to exercise it, or to recognise the latent possibilities such power encompassed (1975a: 224). American protestations of declining power were not completely without foundation, however they emphasised only one aspect of power, the relational, when in fact, in the realm of international regulation and rule making, that is the realm of structural power, America remained dominant. But by the early 1980s, this tentative structural account of power had become more developed. At the end of her forthright critique of regime analysis (1982a), Strange presented an 'outline of a better alternative' which set out, without developing it at any length, the basic framework she developed over the next six years.

Finally, in 'The Persistent Myth of Lost Hegemony' (Strange 1987), and in considerably more detail in *States and Markets* (1988e), Strange laid out the four structures of power which she had settled on as being the key to understanding both the global system itself, and the role of the US within this system. After some indecision, she had fixed on four key structures: security, finance, production and knowledge, which then related to secondary structures like international trade, welfare or transport. Within these primary structures, the role of agenda setting and its impact on the decision-making (or bargaining processes) was the key issue. The structures set the realm of possibilities, or more clearly the 'rules of the game'. But despite her grounding in the financial sector, Strange refused to accord priority to any one of these structures, rather they continually interacted with each other. As Strange put it:

> [Each structure] security, production, finance and knowledge-plus-beliefs is basic for the others. But to represent the others as resting permanently on any one more than on the others suggests that one is dominant. This is not necessarily or always so. (Strange 1988b: 31)

One or other structure may be dominant, may ground the others, in a particular instance, but this can never be assumed; it is part of the purpose of IPE analysis to reveal at certain points how and which structures are prevalent at particular moments.

Having laid out her new approach at some length, Strange started to deploy it to further her critique of the supposed decline in American power in the global system. For instance, in 'Finance, Information and Power' (1990a) she outlined the differences between the relational power of Japan, and the more important structural power of the USA, linking both with regulatory ability in the financial structure and issues of communication in the knowledge structure. She also developed a notion of an American-based empire, ruled by a new global business civilisation (1989b; 1990c) which allowed her to further develop a non-territorial understanding of power. While not sharing the pessimistic or fatalist view of many writers, Strange started to argue that states were in decline because they were choosing not to act for a number of political reasons, linked partly to changes in the knowledge structure (changes in the presumptions about the possibility for government action and regulation) (1994b). However, at the very end of her life, Strange herself had slipped into the pessimistic frame of mind she had often decried in others, the state it seemed was in decline (1996b), and if governments refused to act perhaps it was not so much a lack of will but the irresistibility of the structural changes that her framework put at the centre of analysis.

Money, finance and credit

Strange's focus on money, finance and credit served a number of purposes. Initially it allowed her to develop a political analysis of international money, at a time when economists were only concerned with the seemingly 'technical' aspects of 'managing' the system. This involved developing a political economy conceptualisation of international money (initially: Strange 1967c; 1970b; 1971a; 1971c; and especially 1976d) and much detailed empirical work. She drew a number of conclusions from her continuing analysis of finance. These related not only to US power, because of the role of the dollar and the power of American banks and investment houses, but also to the 'lead role' that financial structures had come to take in the globalisation of this power and the transformation of the international political economy. Moreover, her lifelong research in this area was the empirical grounding for almost all of her conceptual and theoretical work: finance and credit was *her* sector of specialisation, enabling her to ground her broader analysis of IPE.

Having established her reputation with work on post-war international monetary politics at *The Economist* and then as the Washington correspondent of the *Observer* in the aftermath of the Second World War, Strange moved back to London to teach at the London School of Economics. After a period in the 1950s when her family took precedence (although she began to produce articles for the *Year Book of World Affairs* and continued to work at the *Observer*), she joined the Royal Institute of International Affairs in 1964, and the work for which she is now best known started to appear. Andrew Shonfield had asked her to join his staff at Chatham House and write a book on the contemporary sterling crisis.[8] As Strange later noted: 'The connections between power, influence, and the reserve currency role, and the national economy were an enticing subject and there was very little that was political written about it' (Strange 1989c: 433). For Strange 'money [was] *always* political at any level of community from the family upwards' (1976d: 354, emphasis in original), and bringing a political analysis to the subject-matter of international economics was already one of the core themes of Strange's work. Indeed, her reputation was largely built on a series of analytical studies of the upheavals in the global financial system of the 1960s and 1970s.[9]

In her work on the financial sector, Strange emphasised two crucial arguments. Firstly, political considerations played a major role in international monetary relations, and thus only by looking at political affairs could a feasible analysis of international finance be constructed. This argument was conducted on two fronts: she produced a number of works which developed a political economic analysis of international finance (Strange 1967c; 1971c); and on the basis of this empirical work in international finance as we have already noted, she also wrote two seminal pieces laying the groundwork for the 'new' discipline of IPE which she regarded as crucial for studying the global system (1970a; 1972c). Her second central argument regarding the financial sector was that the internationalisation of money markets (now more often termed globalisation) meant that not only were national financial markets increasingly interdependent, but that the political analysis she was calling for needed to be conducted at the systemic level rather than merely within or between specific states or regions (1970c). Drawing these arguments together required Strange to develop an IPE of International Finance which led her to produce her first major book, *International Monetary Relations* (1976d).

In this book Susan Strange concentrated on the policies and practices that the lack of a fully functioning central bank in the international system led states to adopt. This sometimes prompted emergent collective agreements or management (utilising international organisations like the World Bank or the International Monetary Fund) but also often lapsed into conflict, disruption and various forms of financial crisis. In the end this left the world with only two alternatives. Countries could continue to struggle to maintain their own financial interest in the absence of any legitimate authority. This struggle would lead to 'financial and monetary anarchy and disorder, with political consequences to the security, self-confidence, and stability of the social fabric that can hardly be imagined'. Conversely governments could 'submit to a measure of tyranny by the most powerful and ruthless member of the affluent alliance – the United States' (Strange 1976d: 358). However, given the accelerating interdependence of international financial markets, and the imminent explosion in the Eurodollar market, even this solution (unpalatable for many, and certainly for Strange, given her analysis of the 1930s and the decade's impact on her thinking, only acceptable in light of the chaotic and dangerous alternative) would become less plausible. In Strange's later work, the difficulty of even this second-best strategy for relative monetary stability would lead her to suggest that actually states were no longer able effectively to mobilise authority (1986f).

By 1986 Strange was characterising the international monetary system as a casino (Strange 1986f). She accorded a central role to credit creation and management, which given the ability of banks to work within generous (which is to say, low) capital sufficiency ratios in an international political economy awash with petro-dollars, led her to identify the financial markets' increasing dislocation from state authority as a major problem. In *States and Markets* she berated other analysts for their failure to see how the globalisation of the financial markets had had a major effect in shifting effective authority in the international political economy (1988e: 88ff). The creation of credit, having been largely ceded to the private sector had become one of the major causes of continuing disruption and crisis in the financial sector (and by extension the international political economy as a whole) (1998f). Even in 1994, Strange was still astounded to see how little analytical interest was accorded credit creation, rather than international currency exchange (1994i: 230), and this concern was repeated in her last book, significantly entitled *Mad Money*

(1998f), and in her posthumously published paper on theory and international finance (1998g). Thus, much of Strange's work on international monetary relations was an extended attempt to link the analysis of the financial sector with a wider and deeper analysis of power in the international political economy. As her own work developed, finance therefore became analytically embedded within an inter-penetrated structural understanding of the global system, alongside issues of security, production and knowledge.

The US in the global political economy

We have already indicated that one of Strange's principal analytical and intertextual concerns was the role of the US in the global political economy, and particularly US academic IR/IPE views of that role. This, of course, was largely a reflection of their structural power. Many of her arguments, as well as the longer-term direction of her analysis, were prompted by her desire to explain and to understand the role and policies of the American government. Through her criticism of what she considered the misguided and inadequate analyses provided by conventional IR and mainstream IPE, she strove to highlight the American government's misrecognition of its power and appropriate policies. In this effort to understand it seems likely that she was greatly influenced both by her understanding of the history of the 1930s and by her lifelong personal, political and academic ambivalence towards the global role of the US. As Jonathan Story points out, 'Strange's writings are haunted by memories of the 1930s, the breakdown of the world economy, the slide to war, and the disasters that ensued' (Story 2000: 20). But, however much she thought that their policy was misguided, selfish or just plain wrong, she always accepted the reality of American hegemonic power and hence focused her analysis on understanding the basis of that power. She exposed the inconsistencies of policy that undermined the responsibility she considered America to have towards the peoples of the world. However, she was to remain disappointed by American policy (and, indeed, by much of US IPE) throughout her life.

It is impossible to understand Strange's thinking, writing and arguments without taking account of this engagement with the role of the US; because of the hegemony of the US in knowledge production, especially in academic social science, this role was necessarily also reflected in the intertextual debate that she enthusiastically participated in. Her concern with American power, policy and responsibilities is manifest throughout the whole body of her academic writing (particularly, but not exclusively: Strange 1963; 1972b; 1974b; 1976c; 1982c; 1989d; 1994f; 1995d; 1996b; 1997b; 1998f). Two aspects are particularly important. Making sense of US power in the face of the many analysts who claimed that America was in decline remained an abiding concern. The 'hegemonic decline' debate that occupied so much time and energy in the 1980s (not to mention space in journals) spurred her thinking towards a coherent articulation of structural power, and then an analysis of IPE based on her four structures of security, production, finance and knowledge. Using this analysis she concluded that the US still remained dominant, and, indeed was increasing its power over outcomes in the global political economy (Strange 1982c; 1987; 1988a; 1988b; 1989b; 1990a; 1990c).

Secondly, recognising the reality of power in the global political economy, alongside her claim to 'realism' (Strange 1997b), meant that she saw no plausible alternative to the enaction of American power. In her first major work on the global financial sector (later, structure) Strange had concluded 'that some new political framework must be devised to fill the vacuum [left by the dissolution of the Bretton Woods rules] and to take care of the neglected problems and that the United States must take the initiative in proposing it to its associates' (1976d: 357). Into the 1990s, Strange was still looking in vain for this leadership from the Americans, coupled with her fierce critique of American power. In 1994 in reference to US international economic policy, she wrote that the 'American response, since the late 1960s, was to act – not as the benevolent, self-denying hegemon that the system ... required – but as an irresponsible, self-serving malevolent one when it came to "punishing" the Asian countries it blamed for its own troubles' (1994b: 16). Yet, in the same article she makes explicit her still underlying prescriptive belief in the need for American leadership.

Her analytical approach, which emphasised the structural elements of power alongside the more usually recognised relational elements, was explicitly intended to criticise the political position that America could not effectively act because in the last quarter of the twentieth century it had lost its hegemonic status. Strange argued conversely, that American power was now carried into the global system, not by the attributes of territorial resources but rather by the structural power of knowledge and the activities of multinational corporations (Stopford and Strange 1991; Strange 1989b). This power could, she believed, be used for good. But she remained frustrated that it was not, nor the possibility even recognised in much mainstream writing on the global system.

The continuing failure of US governments to act appropriately pushed her to develop an alternative analysis, emphasising the need for non-state authority to be accorded much more importance in IPE. She had always been sensitive to non-state authority, but now rather than being a problem which state authority needed to address, she increasingly focused on non-state authority as the potential location of a non-state, non-US political will which could resolve the problems of inequality that bedevilled the modern world. Her realism accordingly focused on where she perceived real power lay, with multinational companies (MNCs), and also on the multilateralism she had previously sometimes maligned. However, her concern remained the failure of the states system, and particularly the US, to govern these competing authorities in the political interest of all (1999). Unlike much of the contemporary anti-globalisation movement Susan Strange did not necessarily see the MNCs as the causes of the inequalities of the world; for her it was the lack of political will to modify the effects of unfettered market relations which was the problem. A key part of this lack of political will was the pronouncement of the inevitability of globalisation, which assails us still.

Strange's approach to theory and methodology

Perhaps the most distinctive aspect of all of Strange's work is her view of what kind of understanding she considered IPE *ideally* to be, and how she would construct that understanding. She defined IPE in a way that was very different from other political economists and, indeed, other social scientists. Having explored the limitations of existing 'doctrines' of IPE, in *States and Markets* she characterises the study of IPE in the following way: 'What we need is different. It is a framework of analysis, a method of diagnosis of the human condition as it is, or as it was, affected by economic, political and social circumstances' (1988e: 16). This, as Ronen Palan argues, is unique, and quite startling in its intention and scope:

> IPE is not a discipline or a sub-discipline, nor is it an approach or a theory. IPE is none of the above but a *particular way of looking at the world, a framework of analysis and a method of diagnosis*. (Palan 1999: 125–6, emphasis added)

But the method of diagnosis is not confined to states, or even to authority–market structures; it applies to '*the human condition*'. Hence, for Strange, IPE became a continuing, constantly debated and negotiated, but never fixed, interpretation of the human condition; essentially a study in global hermeneutics.

This explains why she was not concerned to locate and justify her work in 'conventional' philosophical and epistemological terms. She was not trying to develop a full theory of IPE, but a way of thinking, a framework for thinking. She makes this clear, again in *States and Markets*, asserting that the book

> is going to suggest to you a way to think about the politics of the world economy, leaving it to you to choose what to think. It will leave you free to be an arch conservative or a radical Marxist, to think about the world problems from a strictly nationalist point of view or, more broadly, as a citizen of the world. ... Before you there is not a set menu, nor even an *a la carte* menu, but the ingredients for you to make your own choice of dish and recipe. (1988e: 8)

This is a clear statement of Strange's position, in both epistemological and pedagogic terms. Importantly, this helps make sense of some of the other elements of her analysis: her uncomfortable relationship with social science theory; her attitude to her empirical research; the eclecticism of her analyses; and her distrust of abstraction. In this sense, her notions of structural power are not abstract theoretical generalisations, but concepts made concrete and given meaning by contact with historical situations, which could and would change if the concrete world itself changed. It is the claimed universality in space and time of much IR theory, which always hides purpose and interests under 'objectivity' and 'universality', and the implied rejection of historical change contained within 'classical' Realism (and its restatement by Waltz in the early 1990s) that she found impossible to accept (i.e. Strange 1994b).

In this sense also we can understand her normative commitments, her identification of fundamental values as the basis of IPE. These values are the starting point (as we have discussed) of her framework for thinking about IPE. They are necessary diagnostic tools, necessary ingredients for hermeneutic understanding.

The structure of this book

We have structured this volume on the basis of the analytical categories we have used to make sense of Susan Strange's work in this Introduction. Hence, Section I concerns her individual values and normative preferences and has two short pieces which illustrate and consider her personal values, professional concerns and political and intellectual commitments, which as we have argued, have a significant bearing on what she wrote, and how she responded to both events, and other work in IR and IPE.

Sections II and III relate to the social contexts of her work: the events, politics, economics, ideology and language that influenced her writing. Section II concerns Money, Finance, Credit and Trade, while Section III contains four pieces on Authority and Markets in Theory and Practice. Section IV is broadly intertextual, covering the context of other theoretical and academic analyses to which she responded. Finally, Section V: Conclusions? (the question mark is deliberate) contains her last journal article. Each Section of the book has a short 'Introduction' which puts the items in that Section in context, historically and intellectually.

We have chosen not to include, apart from 'Some Desert Island Stories', chapters or sections from any of her books. It is not that the books are unimportant – they are crucial to understanding her contribution to IPE – but all are still readily available. Indeed, *Casino Capitalism* was reprinted in 1997, ten years after it was first published and still sold more than most contemporary academic texts. Susan Strange's books should be read, and read again: this collection is in no way intended to replace her major works, rather it is intended to complement them and introduce her wide-ranging work to a new audience.

Section I
Personal Values   N A

Introduction and Commentary

In many ways Susan Strange's career was a particularly personal odyssey. She never liked to be called an academic, regarding her early career as a journalist an integral element in the development of her approach to the study of the global system. Our first selection is a fragment of autobiography which appeared in 1989, in a little-known book of 'autobiographical reflections' published in America. As this reveals, many of the themes of her work were driven not by scholarly and secluded reflection, but rather reflected both the circumstances of her life, and her political views. Although sometimes criticised for her lack of academic rigour, Strange was more interested in understanding the real international political economy, than constructing elegant theoretical models. This often led her to present her most profound challenges to the study of the international political economy as merely the products of common sense. However, driven by a personal vision of what was important in life, Strange was also aware of the importance of thinking clearly about the world. She was no methodological or theoretical naïf, but rather felt arguments over method and theory obscured the real issues.

In the second piece, the prologue from *States and Markets*, Strange presents the choices and values that she regarded as crucial for understanding the various ways social settlements (and political programmes) in the international political economy emerged. Strange always regretted calling this book *States and Markets* preferring the formulation 'authority and markets' which figures throughout her 'desert island stories'. Importantly, Strange stresses: 'Theories of international political economy are rooted in personal preferences, prejudices and experience.' While seldom prepared to explore or develop explicit and extensive epistemological arguments about the character of social scientific knowledge, Strange also was unprepared to accept the possibility of value-free social science. Indeed, in 'The Persistent Myth of Lost Hegemony' (Section III), and *Cave! Hic Dragones'* (Section IV) as well as elsewhere, Strange was at pains to point to the hidden importation of values into American IPE.

Both of these very personal pieces help those fresh to Susan Strange's work to understand how her approach was rooted. And for those more familiar with her work, it is always as well to remind ourselves of the values and commitments that made her work both iconoclastic and down-to-earth at the same time.

2
'I Never Meant to Be an Academic', 1989

I never meant to be an academic. If I had had the talent, I would rather have been an actress, preferably a comedian, or a painter. Next to that, and if I had had the chance – and no children – I would also have dearly liked to be an independent newspaper columnist.

Moreover, I have to confess that luck and coincidence, more than planning and purpose, have shaped my career. I have certainly never thought that by teaching students about international relations (which I have been doing now for nearly forty years) I was going to change the world or alter the course of history. I am a woman and an ex-journalist. Women seem to me to tend to be more realistic about life and people than men – who are often incurable romantics. Journalism too brings home the truth that politics is the art of the possible – and a good many things are just not possible. We can do a lot in personal relations. Beyond that we can expect only to change things at the margin, to move ideas a little further along one path rather than another.

My first lucky break was getting to a university at all, and specifically the London School of Economics. At school, if you were bright you hoped to get to Oxford or Cambridge. (Misguidedly, British boys and girls still nurture this curious ambition.) But to do so in my pre-war days you still needed both money and Latin, and I had neither. But the father of another girl at my school was the LSE careers officer and my head teacher arranged for me to go and see him. He persuaded me to enter for an LSE scholarship. I won it, to my amazement, and the school came up with another one.

The second lucky break was getting out of France in 1940, a day after my elder brother in the British Army escaped from the dunes of Dunkirk. Having six months to fill in before the university term started, I had found an au pair job as 'secretary' to a French professor of English at the University of Caen in Normandy. I was happy there and saw no reason to leave despite the advancing tide of wretched refugees – until we could hear the German guns shelling Rouen and I began to get furious telegrams from my father, then flying somewhere over France with the RAF, telling me to come home.

19

To cut a long story short, I finally joined a troop ship at Cherbourg carrying three thousand weary British soldiers who had fought in vain to hold the line of the Somme, the four other civilians – 'Uncle Dick' of the commercial Radio Normandy and his wife from Rouen, and a Belgian lady and her daughter who had come along the coast from Boulogne by fishing boat. But for the British Army, I would have spent the rest of the war in France, or a German concentration camp.

I had a great, rackety time at the LSE, then evacuated to Cambridge. Cambridge girls were locked firmly into their colleges every evening. We LSE girls were free and could go to the local pubs or stay up late in a friendly Greek cafe singing, arguing and eating plates of eggs or baked beans and chips. The fact that London was being blitzed and that most of the boys would be drafted sometime in their second year and some would never come back sharpened our appetites for life and love. The only problem was what to study. We had to choose from a broad social science menu. My preference was for politics, but I found the Department dominated by a cliquey set of disciples of Harold Laski. I found Laski an entertaining lecturer but I couldn't agree with some of his rather simplistic ideas, nor did I want to be anybody's disciple.

International relations seemed the answer. The professors had all gone to fight the war in Whitehall. We were a small bunch of students of several nationalities, supervised by one kindly but ineffectual old diplomatic historian. It was the ideal solution though I must say, in fairness to Laski, that he was invariably accessible, kind, and helpful to students. When I left the LSE, he gave me excellent advice to take the job with *The Economist* rather than work for twice the money as David Mitrany's research assistant.

That came about through a third lucky break – though it didn't seem at the time that getting pregnant at nineteen and in my third undergraduate year was so very lucky. I was at least married – but to a penniless medical student. As soon as the baby was born, I had to get a job. The good luck was that motherhood spared me being drafted into the armed forces or the Foreign Office or some other branch of the British government. *The Economist*, then edited by Geoffrey Crowther with Barbara Ward as foreign editor and Isaac Deutscher as special writer on Russia and Eastern Europe, was as good as any graduate course at a university. I was taught to write clearly, concisely, and to the point. I have to say too that I only got the job by luck; my brother picked up a girl in a London bar on his last leave before shipping out to fight in Burma. Her mother sat on some committee with Crowther. Knowing I was desperate for a job, she persuaded Crowther to give me an interview. The job was great, though the pay was terrible. In fact, to make ends meet I had to moonlight with *Time Life* and the now defunct *March of Time* documentary film team. They paid twice as much for half the work – but were apt to murder truth without a qualm.

The Economist led to an irresistible offer in 1946 from the prestigious British Sunday paper, the *Observer*, to go to Washington as a correspondent. At twenty-three, this was an offer I couldn't refuse even though it meant temporarily parting from my husband and baby. I was the youngest White House correspondent by about ten years – even though, again, the pay was terrible. But, as my mentor and guide to American politics, the great historian Denis Brogan (also employed from time to time by the *Observer*), used to tell me, 'The higher the morals, the lower the pay!' He told me many other things besides in long one-to-one tutorials on the old Baltimore and Ohio trains between Washington and New York. He was a great scholar and a great liberal – a great drunk sometimes too, but that was less important.

If I have dwelt quite a bit on this apprenticeship in serious journalism, it has been conscious and deliberate. Journalists are often despised by the academics. 'Journalistic' applied to a book is often a derogatory adjective; 'no more than a journalist' means that the writer has failed in analysis, and has been purely descriptive.

Such judgments are unfair as well as offensively arrogant. Some of the best academics I know have been, or have learned to be, journalists. And in my experience, the best journalists are every bit as intelligent, as diligent and hardworking, as much concerned with the pursuit of truth as the best academics. They gain in breadth what they lose in narrow specialization. They have their faults, but few of them inflict on their readers the sort of stodgy, long-winded, pretentious, jargon-ridden writing that too many academics inflict on their unfortunate students. Nor, contrary to what might be supposed, does competition stop the journalists from being ever ready to help a colleague, particularly one in trouble.

It is also arguable that academic theorists have less impact on events and on the processes of policy formation that do the journalists. Like the eccentric who explained that he was throwing lavatory paper out of the window of the London-to-Manchester train to keep the elephants off the track, the academics are often prone to think that it is *their* powerful arguments that have convinced policy-makers. More often, the truth is that the politician has 'rented an economist' – or a political scientist, or a version of history – in order to justify and legitimate a course of action already forced on him by the pressures of power and events. It is not he, or she, who is keeping the elephants off the track.

Journalists and newspapers do, however, sometimes alter the course of history – or at least nudge it strongly along one path rather than another. In *Marshall Plan Days* (1987), Kindleberger recollects that it was the BBC correspondent in Washington at the time who, through his dispatches, focused official thinking on the problems of European reconstruction and expounded ideas later formulated by Acheson and Marshall. And everyone is familiar with the *Washington Post*'s exposures of Watergate and the consequences. More recently, the television crews who risked their lives to get pictures of Israeli conduct on the West Bank and in the occupied territories may well have had more effect on American policy-making in the long run than all the academic literature on Lebanon and the PLO.

On my return from the United States at the end of 1948, I took my first teaching job, thinking I would stick to it for a couple of years and use it as a learning device to broaden my reading and deepen my understanding. I owed the chance to Georg Schwarzenberger, a German international lawyer at University College in London. He had taught me at Cambridge and taught me well. He was a realist writer on international relations even before Morgenthau was ever heard of. But though he had fled Nazi Germany, like many of his generation, his ideas of the role of the professor had been formed in his native country. He tended to be overbearing and intolerant of contradiction, especially from his students. When the *Observer* followed up a summer assignment to cover the first meeting of the Council of Europe in Strasbourg with an offer to come back part-time to be their economic correspondent, I jumped at the chance. I could slip away from Gower Street at the end of the week to join an editorial conference that was lively, informed, and open to new ideas. In the 1950s, the paper had a small staff and a radical reputation. We had to be ready to tackle other jobs besides our own. I wrote editorials, stood in for the political correspondent when he was ill, for the diplomatic correspondent when he was abroad – and even sometimes for the man who covered labour relations and strikes. Even that was instructive; I only got to talk to some striking railwaymen by explaining that the *Observer* was the Sunday equivalent of the *Daily Worker*! Mostly, I got to talk to senior officials at the Foreign Office or the Treasury and to most of the leading politicians, Labour, Liberal, and Conservative.

I can't say any of them impressed me as intellectual giants. Most of them seemed perversely blind to Britain's changed position in the world. They overrated the importance of the Commonwealth, which I came to think of as a kind of methadone to the heroin addict, softening the withdrawal symptoms of a postimperial role. They also overrated the 'special relationship' with the United States. As I had seen in 1949 at Strasbourg, neither party really saw the country's future as part of a European union of states. Change at home and in foreign policy was needed but they were not really ready to make it. Much as I loved the green hills and valleys of England – indeed, because I did, and because I thought we still had brains, and enterprise, and an unquenchable love of liberty – I was increasingly impatient of The Establishment and all it stood for. Even the Royals with all their flummery served to sustain a class system that belonged to a past age. Academic life at least gave the freedom to teach and write independently.

Sadly, I had to leave the *Observer* when, with a second marriage, I started another family, adding three more sons and a daughter to the boy and girl from my first marriage. The pregnancies made me vulnerable to Schwarzenberger's bullying ways, and when he tried to take away my tenure on a technicality, I felt it was time to go. One of my colleagues in the law faculty offered to help by proving that if the real grounds were that I had had too much maternity leave, he could prove that the chances of heart disease striking any of the middle-aged teachers in the college was hundreds of times greater than my getting pregnant for the seventh time. But twenty years ago the feminist case in the professions still had to be made, and with four young children at home I didn't relish a fight.

Moreover, there would have been two battles to fight. While my last son, Adam, was being born, John Burton had appeared on the Gower Street scene, and like Laski, was more interested in recruiting disciples than teaching students to think for themselves. Nor could I accept his unrealistic notions that all conflicts could be resolved with better analysis and rational discussion. (I remember asking him once if he had ever quarrelled with his wife or his mother-in-law!) My view of international relations was that it was an arena in which there was, inevitably, *both* conflict and cooperation – and wishing it otherwise was not going to change that fundamental fact of life. All reports suggested that Burton wasn't an easy man to get along with if you didn't agree with everything he said. I thought it better to leave him to it.

As it turned out, falling out with University College over the number of children it was reasonable for a lecturer to have turned out to be another lucky break. Andrew Shonfield had taken my job at the *Observer* when I left. Now he had moved on to be research director at Chatham House, the British equivalent of the New York Council on Foreign Relations. It was 1964 and Harold Wilson's Labour government had just been elected. There had been a crisis for sterling, and Andrew asked me if I would like to come and write a book on the subject. The connections between power, influence, the reserve currency role, and the national economy were an enticing subject and there was very little that was political written about it.

I stayed on at Chatham House after the book was finally written – and stayed with the politics of monetary relations as a still largely unexploited subject. I found that writing the second monetary volume for a study edited by Andrew on international economic relations in the 1960s wasn't easy. But it raised some new questions and made me challenge some of the neofundamentalist ideas about the relation between governments and international organizations. For instance, even Shonfield – who understood the economics well enough – misunderstood the significance of the issue of Special Drawing Rights at the beginning of the 1970s. Like many economists he welcomed it as the embryo of a world currency, an acorn to be welcomed and cherished as the seed of a great oak tree. He could not see that *supplementing* the dollar as a reserve asset was not the same politically as *substituting* for the dollar and replacing it as the prime component in monetary reserves. Another thing that came out strongly from the story was the enormous structural power of the United States under the Bretton Woods arrangements, and its even greater power after the dollar devaluation of 1971 and the floating rate regime after 1973. That power enabled the United States to shift the burdens of adjustment on to others, and to choose when, for its own reasons, it preferred inflation to deflation or vice versa, and when it preferred a strong dollar to a weak dollar and vice versa.

That insight into structural power was reinforced by my last assignment before I left Chatham House in 1976. This was to direct a project funded by the Ford Foundation on transnational relations. My colleagues were a distinguished Italian economist, Marcello de Cecco, and a British writer on multi-national corporations, Louis Turner. We made a good team and though (to the mild annoyance of the foundation and the institute) Louis was the only one to produce a full-blown book out of it, we all wrote articles and conference papers and held many meetings of people from the far left to the far right to explore the same issue of structural power and to discuss the problems of both research and teaching in international political economy.

I had been interested and puzzled by this for some time. Before leaving University College, my colleague and predecessor at the LSE, Geoffrey Goodwin, and I had put on an intercollegiate course we called the Politics of International Economic Relations. That was in 1963 and was quite an innovation in its day. But the work at Chatham House made me think that this – still the title of two or three leading textbooks in the field – was not really the same as international political economy. Surely, if transnational relations meant anything, it involved more than the topics that governments saw fit to discuss and negotiate over. That hunch had led me as a visiting teacher to start a course at the LSE in the early 1970s on International Business in the International System.

About the same time, I had started a working group of academics drawn from several British (and sometimes, one or two French) universities and polytechnics to meet and argue about the theory and substance of international political economy. Mostly young and enthusiastic, the International Political Economy Group got some modest supporting funds for the British Economic and Social Research Council and though we did not have the resources available to Keohane and Nye in America, we too were convinced that this was the coming new wave in international relations, a wave that would make the arid debate between the behaviouralists and the traditionalists seem outdated and uninteresting. Indeed, I increasingly came to think that the study of international (that is, intergovernmental) relations was only a branch of international political economy, as diplomatic history had been a branch of international history. International relations was concerned (sometimes almost obsessively so) with questions of order, with the problematic of war and peace. International political economy was concerned with that too, but also with problematics of wealth and poverty, of justice and freedom, not only for states but for other social groups in the increasingly integrated world economy and society.

The symbiotic, conflictual and cooperative, asymmetrical and inconsistent, relationship between states and markets, markets and states, seems to me to contain the key to the perennial political question, who gets what?

The 1970s also gave me a chance to get to know about the International Studies Association, as a vice president when Ken Boulding was its president. ISA had – and, if I am right, still has – grave financial problems unless heavily subsidized by some kindly American university. But it seemed to me lively, democratic, liberal and, in a peculiarly American way, friendly and unstuffy. Its proceedings were much more stimulating than the dreadfully constipated and hierarchical Bailey conferences that Charles Manning used to run at the LSE. When I got the chance, I resolved to get something similar started in Europe, or at least in Britain. I wrote to every vice chancellor in the country asking for the modest sum of £2 ($4) as start-up funds for a British ISA. My old colleague on the *Observer*, Alistair Buchan, had started the International Institute of Strategic Studies and had just moved to Oxford as the professor of international relations. He used his good transatlantic contacts to get us some funding and we held the first conference in Oxford in 1974. Money is power and as treasurer of BISA I saw to it that we provided the members with a service, and lived frugally and carefully within our means, offering equal opportunities to the young lecturer as to the established professor, to the provincial polytechnics as much as to any of the older universities. Getting BISA going was a job worth doing.

Unfortunately, I think both ISA and BISA have failed to live up to their names. They are not associations of people engaged in international *studies* but of people engaged in international *relations*. A few historians, a few lawyers, a few sociologists, and more than a few political scientists have joined in from time to time – indeed the International Political Science Association could hardly function without its IR participants. But the lawyers and even more the economists have their own professional associations and they bar the door to outsiders. Both operate a one-way system: we are welcome to try and learn from them, but they cannot see that they have much to learn from us, more's the pity. International relations stands as the one social science with barriers to entry so low that anyone can jump them. It has been and will remain the richer for keeping those barriers low. Today, one of the most promising avenues of cooperation seems to me to lie with the business schools. They are more involved with the real world, less hidebound by conventional theories, and increasingly aware of the international political dimension within which business enterprises must function. My own experience of collaboration with Professor John Stopford of the London Business School in a research project on bargaining between governments and foreign enterprises suggests that we have a lot to learn from each other.

Looking back I am not sorry now, that instead of two years, I have spent nearly forty teaching – and learning – about international relations. Next to having a large family, having students to teach at all levels is a great way to stay mentally alert and alive. I am doubly lucky to have had both – and both have taught me a great deal. In return, I have tried to teach both students and children not to expect justice in life – but to try hard to get it; to work hard – but to question authority, whether political or academic; to distrust ideologies – but to respect the evidence; to avoid following the crowd – but to trust your own judgment and to stand up for your own ideas. The freedom to do so is one of which, in free countries, the universities should be the most jealous guardians. That and not the service of the state is the true justification for their existence.

3
'Prologue: Some Desert Island Stories', 1988

It was a dark and stormy night. A ship was steaming laboriously through mountainous seas whipped by gale-force winds. Suddenly there is a terrific explosion amidships. All the lights go out. Whatever the cause, it has wrecked the power system. On board there is panic. People rush about in all directions, shouting and screaming and bumping into one another. Everyone is trying to get to the lifeboats. The deck begins slowly to tilt to one side. The explosion must have torn a hole in the side. Panic gets worse. Some of the lifeboats, clumsily handled, get stuck in the davits. Some capsize in the heavy seas. Only three get safely away before the ship, with one last shuddering lurch, sinks beneath the stormy water. This is the story of what happened to the people in the three lucky lifeboats.

In one of the lifeboats, there is a group of people who, by accident, all followed Martin, one of the ship's officers. He kept his head and took charge of the launching, helped by three of the crew, Mike, Jack and Terry. Among the handful of passengers with them are two lovers, John and June; and a mother, Meg, and her children, Ken and Rosy.

For three days and nights, blown by the storm, they have a fearful journey. For some reason the radio won't work. They have no idea where in the wide ocean they are. Water's getting short when, well into the third night adrift, they hear breakers. Miraculously escaping the reef, they land exhausted on a beach, and all fall asleep on the sand, happy to be alive.

In the morning, they explore the shore of their desert island. They find fresh water, coconut palms and fish in the lagoon. Martin, still in charge, sees that the lifeboat is safely pulled up the beach and organizes the building of a rough shelter. After some days Martin gets everyone together one evening and tells them he has been exploring the hills behind. He says he has seen tracks that look human. 'Friends,' he says, 'we may be in danger. We must cut down some trees and build a stockade. We must fashion some spears, organize a watch and send out some patrols.'

There's a bit of discussion about that. John and June, happy in a lovers' idyll, don't much want to work on the stockade. They have other ideas. Meg would rather hunt for fruit and nuts and start a garden for vegetables. But the crew are used to taking orders from Martin and their agreement carries his plans. Gradually, the little group gets used to doing as they're told.

Meanwhile, the second lifeboat to get away from the ship also reaches the island – but lands in another part. They do not meet. So far as each group knows, they are the only survivors. This boat has a very different group aboard. It's a bunch of young students, led by Jerry, a bit older than the rest. It's he who got them together, organized the launch and managed to get the lifeboat safely away. As it happened, there were no officers or crew in the boat – and no professors either. In the three days and nights at sea they are being blown about, as ignorant as the first group about where they are. They talk endlessly, as students will, about their predicament and what they'll do if they ever find land. Idealistically, they agree with Jerry that it would be a great idea to organize a commune. To each according to their needs, from each according to their ability. Equality in taking decisions; the same rules for everybody.

When they wake on the beach that first morning ashore, they set happily to work gathering coconuts and fishing in the lagoon. After a few days, the first problems start to arise. Two lovers, Bob and Betty – just like John and June in the first lifeboat – are apt to wander away from their allotted jobs and go off together hand-in-hand into the woods. The others feel they are slacking. Then there are other long arguments about who is to fish and who is to work on the coconuts and the shelter. Joe, a practical fellow who brought along a toolbox, claims he ought to get extra rations or extra free time because, with his saw and axe, he can do as much in an hour as the others in a week. Amos is big and hefty and likes to work. Should he be rewarded? Meanwhile, the camp site not only has no stockade, it has no latrines. No one wants that particular job, so it begins to get a bit squalid and smelly. But everyone still believes the commune is a good idea.

The people in the third lifeboat land on yet another part of the same island. They too think they are the only survivors. This time the group includes some old people and many more mothers and children, as well as members of the crew. These include some of the ship's cooks, Jack the head steward, and the ship's purser, a silent, tough character who says 'Call me Mac'. But, at first, with this group, there is no one who takes charge. Everyone cracks their own coconuts and catches and cooks their own fish.

After some days, the mothers are complaining that a diet of coconuts upsets the kids' stomachs but they can't leave them to go fishing. The older people sit around looking lost and miserable. No one's building a shelter, let alone latrines. Then Jack has a suggestion. Instead of the bartering of fish for coconuts that's growing up, why not use the bag of nails that somehow was found among the lifeboat's stores as money? To start with everyone will be given an equal share of nails and they can be used to buy or sell fish, coconuts, fruit and personal services, like hut-building or mending clothes. To make life easier until rescue comes, he suggests, everyone ought to contribute two nails a week to Mac who will act as guard and take care of security and sanitation, and one nail a week to old Uncle Tod, who's lame and not too well but offers to organize a sort of school for the kids so the mothers can fish or hunt.

The market starts out well, though some problems do arise. The price of fish in nails is so good, everyone wants to go fishing. But how to decide who uses the lifeboat? A bargain about who has first claim, when and for how long, has to be negotiated among them. The diet of grilled fish and coconuts begins to pall. It would be good to grow some crops, but how can the growing period be financed? Someone kills a wild goat. Should it be divided equally or sold to the highest bidder? Aunt Jane falls ill. Who's to look after her? How are these collective decisions going to be taken? But at least the group is sheltered and fed, and even the old people believe that, though rescue may be slow to come, they'll be able to manage.

*   *   *

The next part of the story is about what might happen if, and when, the three groups find out that they're not, after all, the sole survivors from the sinking ship. This is where the reader joins in, and the desert island stories become an allegory of political economy. We have three groups, each dominated by a different social value. Martin's group gives priority to order and security; it is a fortress society. Jerry's group of students gives priority to justice and equality; it is trying hard to work as a community. Jack's group gives priority to wealth, to efficiency in production; it is a market society. 'Ah, I see,' says the sophisticated reader at this point, 'you are setting up three competing models. The fortress society is a realist model; the commune is an idealist model and the market society is an economic model. The economists would find that most familiar. Students of politics would recognize the realist model and the sociologists would be more familiar with the idealist model.' In simpler terms, you might say that the three represented the nationalist, the socialist and the liberal approaches to the authority–market relationship that is at the heart of political economy.

There are two games, both quite instructive, that we can play at this point. One is to ask people what they think will happen when the groups encounter each other. How will each group react to the others? How, you ask, would they carry on and finish the story – always assuming that it really is a conventional desert island and that it's some time before the castaways are 'rescued'? That game can tell you something about other people's perceptions of reality, of their own experience of the real world, their particular interpretation of history and human nature. You will find, I think, that not everyone agrees about what is most probable.

They will do so even less if you play a different game and ask, not how people think the story really would end, but how they would *like* it to end. Honestly played, that should tell you something about their normative preferences, their aspirations, their idea of what constitutes a 'happy ending'. People do in fact attach different values to order and security, to wealth and to social harmony and the search for a just society.

Let me suggest a few alternative scenarios. One is that, as Martin's fortress group has put security first and organized itself for defence against a real or imagined enemy, so it is their patrols that first find out about the others. 'We can't afford to let Jack's lot get too rich, and we can't risk the mothers and the lovers slipping away to join the students', says Martin, 'We have to act first.' Catching both unprepared, Martin issues an ultimatum: 'Join us, or else ...'. From then on the story depends on whether either or both give in and accept the military authority, or whether either or both resist, even to the point of fighting if necessary. The story can also take different turns according to whether, after the takeover, the other two groups are treated magnanimously as equals, albeit in an authoritarian but secure and orderly society, or whether the victors are corrupted by power and treat the others as servants or exploit them as 'colonies'.

A different scenario starts with the students one day hunting wild goats. Venturing far from the camp, they accidentally catch sight of Martin's stockade. They figure out what they think is going on and decide they had better prepare for the worst. Freedom and equality have to be compromised. Socialism has to wait. Once organized, though, they are strong enough to issue *their* ultimatum: be liberated or we attack.

Yet another scenario lets one of the market group accidentally make the same discovery that they are not alone on the island. A meeting is called and, reluctant to lose their evidently higher style of living, they decide to double their 'security tax', appointing Mac to organize an army of paid volunteers. This team plans and carries out a surprise night attack on Martin's stockade when the watchman is asleep. So, in this scenario it is they who liberate the group from Martin's iron rule, at once increasing the size of the market and the opportunities for specialization in the division of labour. Easier still would be a second takeover of the commune, increasingly squalid and ideologically divided among themselves.

All three scenarios contemplate the possibility of violence, even among people who – literally – were once in the same boat. Is that realistic, or pessimistic? Is a peaceful co-existence among the three groups a possibility? And if so, in this miniature society of states, do the leaders begin to play a primitive game of diplomacy – making alliances, and perhaps subsequently breaking them – with one or other groups? Will they make promises of mutual defence? Will they go in for discriminatory trading?

One obvious lesson is that different societies, in ordering their political economy, will give different values priority over others. One, perceiving an external threat and/or under militaristic authority, will put security before the creation of wealth and will give a low priority to freedom for individuals or opposition groups. Even democratic states at war restrict the citizen's freedom in all sorts of ways. We can represent this crudely in Figure 3.1 as Model A. It also follows that, in the see-saw nexus between authority and market, market will tend to take the lower position.

Another society will value the creation of wealth above security and freedom (using a broad definition that includes economic freedom from the pinch of poverty and want). In Model B we see the see-saw tipped the opposite way, with the state (or other authority) interfering as little as possible with market forces. The use of money in this model enhances wealth through the division of labour and has in it the seed of a financial power structure through the creation and use of credit.

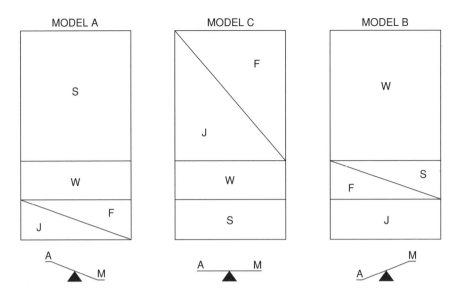

(where A = authority, M = market)

Figure 3.1   Value preferences of three lifeboats (where S = security, W = wealth, J = justice and F = freedom to choose)

In yet another (as in the students' commune where freedom and justice for the individual are given joint priority) both market and authority are shrunk in importance and more evenly balanced, and the pursuit of security and wealth are given secondary importance. I have represented this equally crudely in Model C.

In an international economy in which authority is diffused and not centralized, and in which power is unequally distributed among states, the dominance of a state basing its political economy on any one of the three models naturally will, if it is able, try to bias the global political economy towards the same pattern. Capabilities, in military power in pursuit of security, in production power in pursuit of wealth, in the ability to appeal for the compliance of others on the basis of ideas and beliefs, will affect outcomes. But, the tales are trying to say, the judgement of outcomes, as of goals, is a subjective matter. Theories of international political economy are rooted in personal preferences, prejudices and experience. It is all up to the reader. My stories are like Lego, the little Danish-made building blocks that fit together in endless variation to make whatever you will. Like toys, you can learn something from them even if you do not take them very seriously.

Section II
Money, Credit and Trade

Introduction and Commentary

The five pieces in this section illustrate Strange's often repeated dictum that before anyone can understand the international political economy at a general level, they need to understand the workings of particular sectors. Although she wrote about other areas of the international economy, throughout her career Strange frequently returned to international finance and international trade. Indeed, the politics of international finance and credit furnished her with many of her key insights, and was the area in which her work is best known. Earlier in her career she had balanced this interest with many articles on the politics of trade, which have sometimes been overlooked in posthumous assessments of her contribution to the development of IPE.

The first selection examines the problems of the declining optimism over foreign aid and the unfavourable terms of trade for developing states. At this stage she still regarded the state as the agent of its own development. This is partly reiterated by the second selection's discussion of protectionism but by then Strange had moved to make more explicit her understanding of the underlying structures of the global system. This piece was the first time that Strange fully articulated the relationship between the four central power structures she wanted to focus on and the secondary structures which were too often regarded as independent of other aspects of the global system. This new approach was further developed in *States and Markets* where the basic analysis presented here is elaborated although not altered.

In the third selection, Strange mobilises this analytical approach to discuss the different sorts of power that America and Japan enjoy in international finance. While including issues of technology, here Strange is also concerned to identify the structural underpinnings of American power (which the selections in Section III explore at greater length). This is underlined in the fourth selection in which Strange foregrounds the creation of credit in the global system as a key mechanism by which the United States is able to maintain its domination. In this phase of her career, Strange was developing an account of American power which saw it not only as a form of imperialism but (in a clear link with neo-Gramscian critical theorists) built on the control and shaping of knowledge (through the knowledge structure she had first identified ten years earlier).

The last selection is published for the first time here in this form, although some sections of the text were edited to form 'World Order, Non-State Actors, and the Global Casino: The Retreat of the State?' (Strange 2000). Partly a response to her critics and partly a drawing together of the themes of this volume, this reveals Strange still developing her approach to understanding the international financial system, and still arguing for its centrality to analyses of global political economy.

4
'A New Look at Trade and Aid', 1966

In the course of 1964 there developed a new and plainly perceptible plateau in foreign aid. The upward trend of recent years in help for the economic development of the poorer countries came to an end and began to flatten out. In most of the richer, industrialised countries, aid programmes came up against political resistance and experienced a mild set-back.

This aid plateau was less immediately apparent in Britain than elsewhere. The sincere and earnest concern among the rank and file of the Labour Party for the problem of world poverty led the new Labour government to take steps that seemed to point towards increased, and not diminished, emphasis on the foreign aid programme. A new Ministry of Overseas Development was set up, and Mrs Barbara Castle – an old Bevanite and a favourite of long standing in party executive elections – was chosen to head it, with Cabinet rank. British contributions to the United Nations Special Fund and Technical Assistance funds, it was announced, would be increased.

Yet the White Paper (Ministry of Overseas Development 1965), produced in August 1965, carefully avoided any commitment about the total volume of future British aid. The costs of its new measures were all minor, and all in sterling. Significantly, British aid which had risen 100 per cent, in the last four years of the fifties, rose only 25 per cent, in the first four years of the sixties. Already there has been a decrease since 1963 in British loans to developing countries outside the Commonwealth. But in the figure for total British aid this is disguised by a sudden jump in loans to independent Commonwealth countries – a jump partly balanced by a corresponding fall in bilateral aid to the (shrinking) dependent territories. The rather uneven pattern of British aid suggests that the deciding factor in the past has been the need to award golden handshakes to departing colonies, and that, in the future, the overriding concern to protect the balance of payments will tighten the tap still more.

Meanwhile, President Johnson's foreign aid programme for 1965, it will be recalled, was the lowest requested of Congress since 1948 – less than half the size of the 1951, 1952 or 1953 programmes. France, too, has put a ceiling on aid to her client-states in Africa, and on the proportion of national income going to overseas investment. Rather disillusioned sounds of resistance to pleas for more aid are now heard from most of the other European countries. New loans commitments by the Soviet Union have also declined, and there has been markedly less enthusiasm for foreign aid, even for the Moscow-favoured few, since Mr Khrushchev departed. The United Nations Secretary-General in his midway report on the UN Development Decade speaks openly of a set-back – and also of the widening gap that needs to be financed by external capital.

His warnings are borne out by the latest available UN figures. These show that the net flow of international assistance and capital has now virtually ceased to increase – certainly in terms of the percentage of national incomes of the rich countries. The average in 1956–59 was 0.6 per cent. By 1960–61, it had risen to 0.7 per cent – and there it has stuck. (The latest British figure of 0.67 per cent, is also no higher than in 1960–61, and is still somewhat below the average.)

The latest OECD figures confirm the levelling-off of government loans and grants to the poorer countries. Bilateral official loan and grant disbursement rose from £1,167m in 1956 to £2,154m in 1961, but the last four years have stayed practically static, varying only slightly between £2,000m and £2,250m. Export credits (not mainly designed for aid purposes) show a gentle rise, and so do gross disbursements by the international agencies, though official contributions to the international agencies have significantly retreated from their 1961 peak of £301m.

Altogether, there is no longer much doubt about the evidence. We have come to the end of an era of optimism so far as aid is concerned. The warmer-hearted spirits who for years have been arguing, in earnest conferences and draughty village halls, the moral compulsions of a common humanity, will find it hard to abandon their hopeful visions. For some of them, liberality (like prosperity in the thirties) will always be just around the corner; some little crumb of news will feed their optimism. But wilful myopia does no good. The facts no longer allow the rest of us to assume – as many people have done hitherto – that when the rich countries become more affluent, they will increasingly help the poor countries to share their affluence. The old difficulties are gone. The necessary machinery and institutions are all there. There has been no lack of publicity about the problems. It is clear that the whole concept of aid has run into a barrier of resistance. While the great mass has stayed, as always, indifferent, the antis – the Raymond Cartiers who say that charity begins, and ought to stay, at home – have become noticeably more vocal.

*   *   *

It is not the aim of this article to argue the case for helping the poor countries with their economic development. Rather, taking the aid-plateau as a starting point, it is to take a new look at the most important alternative approach to the problem – trade. This is not to say that other possibilities do not deserve more attention than they have lately been getting. Practical, material help with family planning, for instance, through some new international organisation which would be less inhibited by a dissident minority than the WHO or the UN bodies, is one outstanding one. Another is the devising of fiscal incentives to private investment in manufacturing industry in developing countries (OECD 1965) – another field in which a fairly small carrot could help move quite an important donkey. There are still other possibilities such as using food surpluses as aid, international monetary reform, commodity agreements – or at least more orderly marketing of primary products, compensatory insurance against sudden falls in export earnings due to market fluctuations, and so on. But, whereas the giving of aid from government to government has now come up against political barriers very much *stronger* than was widely anticipated, the approach I have chosen seems to me, at least, to be barred by political barriers which are, on the contrary, actually very much *weaker* than is widely believed. A fresh push against them, therefore, might have useful results.

It has this further asset, that it manages to avoid the two outstanding things about foreign aid programmes which, to my mind, are mainly responsible for arousing antagonism and resistance. One is the too-close involvement of governments, and the other is the sickly aroma of charity which clings to every aid transaction (and which the Cartierists rightly detect). The result, every time, is that gratitude is expected for the charity. And every time the claim to gratitude is violently rejected, and the politician of the developing country (to prove his self-respecting nationalism) spits at the venerable Aunt Sallies of neo-imperialism and Western capitalism, the Western taxpayer cannot help feeling his resistance stiffen. Both politician and taxpayer are far too closely and directly involved, emotionally, in the transfer of aid. The further both can be removed from the scene the better.

* * *

For many of the developing countries, the aid plateau would not be so serious a matter, were it not coinciding with both a slow-down of new private investment (exacerbated in Commonwealth countries by Mr Callaghan's blunderbuss measures against capital outflow) and a singularly poor outlook for export earnings of foreign exchange. Even to maintain their present earnings from foreign trade is proving very difficult, and overall these earnings are still four or five times as important to them as the gross flow of aid.

Briefly, the situation is that the prices of the commodities the poorer countries export to the richer countries have been carried, as if on an inexorable 'down' escalator, lower and lower. Average unit prices of these exports were 12 per cent, lower in 1962 than in 1955, while average unit prices of their imports from the rich countries rose over the same period by 16 per cent. Prices for primary products showed a temporary upturn in 1962–63 – due chiefly to sugar, wool and coffee. But in the last year or more, food and fibre prices (according to *The Economist* Index) have fallen again quite alarmingly, and only metals have done better. Reporting last autumn to the UN's Trade and Development Board, the Committee on Commodities said that the position of cocoa, sugar and coffee 'gave cause for immediate concern', and that the markets for ten other primary products, including cotton, rubber, tea, tobacco and copper, required 'close attention'.

Nor is it possible for most of the poor countries to compensate for lower prices by selling increased quantities. The demand for food products and natural fibres is very slow-growing; but even if it were not, the growth in population and rising consumption in the poor countries has outrun increasing agricultural production in every underdeveloped region of the world except Central Africa. In short, as the British White Paper puts it, 'the second half of the 1960s may show, therefore, as did the second half of the 1950s that the developing countries cannot increase their export earnings enough to support even moderate growth rates'. Certainly, as things are, the prospects of reaching the UN Development Decade's goal for 1970 of a 5 per cent, annual economic growth through either aid or expanded trade look extremely slim.

Two years ago, it will be remembered, many hopes were raised in the poor countries at the prospect of a United Nations Conference on Trade and Development (UNCTAD) which it was thought might seek, and find, a way out of this confining *impasse*. At the conference held in Geneva, March–June 1964, the Group of Seventy-Seven (underdeveloped countries) enthusiastically supported the Prebisch thesis which pin-pointed dependence on the export of primary products as the besetting economic weakness of them all. To break out of the vicious circle which this dependence entailed, it was emphasised, they must somehow diversify their economies, expand industry and export manufactures, as well as food and raw materials. From among the rich, developed countries, the only serious support came from the British delegation led by Mr Edward Heath. He proposed that the rich countries should not only remove all barriers to imports from the poor countries but should actually give them preferential treatment. The Conference's Final Act, however, was much more non-committal, a mixture of long-term aspirations and compromise formulae.

Practical results in the subsequent eighteen months have, moreover, been disappointing. All the leading Western governments, including the British, have been distracted by other problems. The Trade Board set up by UNCTAD became sidetracked in a squabble about its future site. And even the economists have been busy pouring cold water on the Prebisch thesis by calculating that the infant industries of the poor countries would still not be able to break into export markets because, as constituted at present, only a very few of them are able to compete with the manufactures of developed countries in terms both of quality and price.

Just possibly, though, UNCTAD was unlucky in its timing, and 1966 could conceivably produce a more auspicious moment for a second and more constructive look at the trade problems of the poorer countries.

In 1964, the United States still had high hopes of the Kennedy Round of trade negotiations to lower trade barriers among the industrialised countries, especially between the US and the EEC. This was regarded as a major national economic interest of the United States and took priority over all other problems of trade policy. It also followed in the established conventions of the GATT tariff-cutting conferences. Now, however, the Kennedy Round has been more or less becalmed for almost a year. Hopes are dwindling of recovering its lost impetus before the Trade Expansion Act of 1962 (allowing the President to negotiate exceptionally generous tariff cuts under certain conditions) expires in two years. It may now be too late, therefore, for the Kennedy Round to recover its lost impetus before the Act is about to expire, and the question once more becomes subject to the winds of Congressional opinion.

Similarly, in Europe, it has become clear over the past year that the Economic Community is also suffering from lack of momentum and that internal disagreements will enforce a pause. This pause might be the right moment for a fresh initiative.

*   *   *

The proposal which follows is likely to be dismissed with scorn by a good many of the experts in government and industry as wildly impractical and nonsensical. But it is based on the belief that if it is true that the infant export industries of under-developed countries cannot compete with ours on equal terms, then the answer might be to increase the incentive for them rather than to abandon the problem of their economic development altogether as insoluble and hopeless. The proposal is simply that the rich countries should not only drop existing tariff barriers, but should also either allow the poor countries to offer substantial export subsidies to their manufacturers; or, better still, that they should organise a system of import bounties which would be payable on the value of every shipment of manufactured goods from a poor country to a rich one. The import bounties, which could be quite substantial, would be financed by a purchase tax levied *equally* on domestic manufactures and on those imported from other rich countries.

(The point about this equal taxation is that it removes what seems to be a major objection to the Prebisch and Heath proposals and to any measure – such as an improved International Textile Agreement – which seeks to remove barriers against poor countries but to retain them for their trade competitors in other rich countries, thus incidentally offering protection to the domestic industry. Such equal taxation would put all the rich countries on an equal footing, and would leave open and unaffected the question of further tariff reduction as between rich countries.)

What is striking is that although economists and statisticians have spelt it out in considerable detail (UN 1963: chapter 7), very few people have realised how relatively easy and painless it could be for the rich countries to make a quite substantial impact on the economic frustration and stagnation of the poor countries. Because the latter are so many, and often so large, it is difficult to remember how small their manufacturing output is in relation to the consumption of what the statisticians call the 'developed market economies'. In world trade in manufactures, the combined share of *all* the poor countries amounts to no more than 4 per cent.

The volume of manufactures imported by the developed countries from the developing countries has recently amounted to about $1.4 billion. By comparison, the developed countries have been importing manufactures from each other to the value of $33.8 billion. Even if imports from the developing countries were to be instantaneously doubled, they would still amount to only 1/12 of the current trade among the developed countries in manufactures. (UN 1963: chapter 7)

*   *   *

The arguments behind the import bounty proposal, however, are not primarily economic or technical, but political and psychological. They are based on some simple observations about political attitudes and behaviour which seem to have been overlooked by the experts.

The first concerns the special interests who will immediately claim that such a system would be unfair and ruinous. They do this without inhibition because to argue that 'coolie labour', paid on 'rice-bowl standards', is not fair to the high-minded and progressively-inclined Western employers paying out decent wages to their loyal employees casts no aspersion on themselves as efficient managers. It is much more difficult for them to make the same loud complaint about unfair competition from, for example, imports of American cotton manufactures, based on wages two or three times as high, because it strongly invites criticism of the quality of management in the importing countries. Yet, in fact, 'the problem of domestic adjustment in the richer to an expansion of imports from the developing (poor) countries could only be minor in comparison with that which might be engendered by the enlargement of trade among the developed countries' (UN 1963).[1]

The special interests involved are, in any case, only paper tigers. They can quite safely be ignored by any determined Western government. We have all for a long time been so taken in by the pretensions, of the so-called pressure groups that we have allowed them – or rather, the politicians have allowed them – much more influence than they need have. In fact, in only comparatively rare cases does a government have to bother about sectarian squawks. One occasion is when the special group is in a position to enlist the sympathy of the rest of the community. Whether the sympathy is deserved or not does not matter, so long as the special group can use it to blight the image of the party in power. This they can best do when they are already regarded as unfairly treated.

It is on these grounds, perhaps, that there has been some shred of excuse for the softness shown by both British and American governments in the past towards the textile industry when it has appealed for protection against foreign competition. In both countries, for reasons of economic history, a good deal of the old textile industry has been concentrated in one region, where obsolete housing and social amenities combined with debilitated management to produce a depressed area. Times, however, are changing. The excuse that the textile areas merit special tenderness is losing its validity as other industries grow up alongside and as the textile industry itself is rationalised and re-capitalised. The outlook for the British cotton industry, for instance, has been greatly changed by the injection of £70m from outside the industry, from the man-made fibre producers. Thanks to new investment, cotton mills can become capital-intensive like the chemical industry and therefore less affected in their overall costs of production by the level of wages.

Nor, in fact, does British experience with free entry from Commonwealth textile producers bear out the prophecies of disaster due to 'unfair competition' from less developed countries. It is true, as spokesmen for the Lancashire pressure group are fond of pointing out, that imports of cotton cloth and garments from 'low-cost' (that is, poor) countries are equal to 36 per cent, of British home consumption, while in the United States they are only 7 per cent, and in the EEC only 5 per cent. But if, under this stimulus, the British industry has been revitalised, the moral is not that Lancashire 'deserves' some protection, but rather that it has in the long run greatly benefited from competition. The advantages of greater competition in a larger market were, after all, one of the chief economic arguments in favour of Britain joining the EEC.

Nevertheless, it might still be felt that some areas in the developed countries ought not to be subjected all at once to foreign competition aided by import bounties, because they themselves were depressed – like Northern Ireland, or under-developed – like Southern Italy. In that case, an import bounties system could be made flexible enough so that, in addition to other state aid, the area could be exempted from the sales tax applied everywhere else to pay for the import bounties.

*   *   *

So much for the special interests likely to be affected. The second objection to the proposal is – inevitably – that opinion generally among the voters is not prepared for such a step. The counter-proposition here is, in the first place, the general one that it is for governments to govern and to lead, and not to wait until they have been left far behind by the opinion polls. It is arguable that, on the contrary, public opinion is much readier than Western governments have credited to see positive and constructive action on the problem of world poverty. The very sensitivity of the Labour Party to keep up appearances on the aid question suggests this. And if the pinch is put on the taxpayer as consumer rather than on the taxpayer as wage-earner, more than half the sting is removed. The weakness of aid programmes hitherto – as argued earlier – has been that they too directly involved both Afro-Asian nationalists abroad and the wage and salary earners at home who pay out income-tax for foreign aid – a process which in any case is always resented because it cannot legally be avoided.

Specifically, therefore, the counter-proposition is that it would be very much easier to get political acceptance for a system which taxed the voters as consumers. The incidence of a tax to pay for import bounties would in any case be very small. In Britain, for instance, total imports of manufactures in 1963 amounted to some £1,397m, of which 12.3 per cent came from the developing (poor) countries. If a bonus equal to one-fifth, or 20 per cent, of the value of these imports from developing countries had been paid out, the cost would have been some £34m only. Since total consumer expenditure in Britain is of the order of £20 billion, and specifically on manufactures about £4½ billion, a purchase tax on the latter of ¾ per cent would cover the bill. Britain is, in fact, the country already taking the biggest percentage of her imports of manufactures from the developing countries.

UN figures estimate these at 12.3 per cent of all imports of manufactures, compared with 11.3 per cent in the United States, 3.9 per cent in Australia, 3.8 per cent in Germany, 3.2 per cent in France and under 1.5 per cent, in Canada, Sweden, Italy and others. And in the United States, of course, the domestic market is so large that even textiles imported from developing countries (by far the largest category) amounted to only 1.4 per cent of total domestic supplies in 1960. It must be obvious that a tax to expand this tiny fraction need not be onerous. From an economic or fiscal point of view, therefore, the means are immaterial. It is just that in an industrial country it is psychologically easier to bear a tax on things bought than on hard-earned income. British experience with the import surcharge imposed after the sterling crisis in 1964 is illuminating. This added substantially to a number of consumer prices. But it was quietly accepted, and it was foreign, not domestic, protests that urged its removal. British taxes on petrol and on tobacco, heavy as they are, have never yet been proved to have had any effect on voting patterns. To the ordinary person, the relative prices of things appear highly arbitrary and disorderly anyway; and a tax which is paid as part of the price of things bought rapidly comes to be accepted as part of this disorder. It certainly is not particularly resented, in the way that income-tax may be, because it is not so inexorable. In theory, at least, it can be avoided by not buying.

*   *   *

These are the objections to a policy of import bounties for manufactures from developing countries. The counter-propositions are admittedly subjective and open to dispute. Less so the arguments in favour of import bounties from the point of view of the developing (or poor) countries, and as an alternative to aid. Politically, if they are paid direct to the exporters, bounties avoid the humiliations to receiving governments of direct grants; economically, they do not carry the inherent and increasingly heavy financial burdens of interest-bearing loans. Still more important, from the point of view of the pattern of economic development in poor countries, import bounties would deliberately load the dice in favour of manufacturing industry and against the less rewarding and less predictable primary production.

At present, as the Seventy-Seven complain, the dice are loaded the other way round. The result is that, as the gap widens between export earnings and necessary imports, the governments of poor countries are forced to adopt every policy which saves imports (and, therefore, foreign exchange). This not only means restricting imports from other poor countries as well as from the rich ones; it means deliberately encouraging home industries to produce substitutes for goods previously imported. Such policies multiplied throughout the poor countries means that they are all forced to duplicate a long list of infant import-substituting industries, few of which can ever hope to be run economically by Western standards. To quote from a brilliant survey of economic problems in Latin America by Mr Norman Macrae,

The present total market for passenger cars in Latin America seems to be between 300,000 and 400,000 a year. In Western Europe, the desirable economic level for production by a single big firm is often estimated to be over 250,000 units a year. This suggests that there might at present be ideal scope for only one or two integrated Latin American car producing concerns ... But in fact local manufacture of passenger cars is now divided between some forty plants owned by a dozen or more foreign companies operating in six Latin American countries and all of them running hopelessly below the really economic level of production.[2]

Thus, not only does the economic integration desired by the poor countries become more difficult to negotiate, but production costs are kept high and uncompetitive, and the difficulties of breaking into export markets, and, indeed, of attracting foreign capital are increased. Any encouragement or incentive given to export industries would help to break this vicious circle. Compare, for example, the record of India and Argentina in expanding exports of manufactures. Argentina is in many ways the more 'advanced' of the two and has fewer of the social handicaps of an underdeveloped country. But thanks to Commonwealth preference,[3] India has been able to expand her exports of manufactures where Argentina has not. It is certainly a striking fact that 47 per cent of all exports of manufactures from developing countries originate in Hong Kong or India.

As an alternative, or supplement to direct aid, import bounties would have several other advantages. Aid programmes, it is generally observed, face an awkward and invidious choice between the claims of the most needy and those of countries best able to make good use of outside assistance. Import bounties would unashamedly give help to those most capable of developing export industries – and these would be just those countries who are closest to the economic take-off; those who are also most acutely aware of the burden of debt-servicing on their limited resources of foreign exchange (e.g., Brazil, Chile, Pakistan, Turkey). Thus, aid programmes, especially technical assistance programmes, would be left freer to favour the poorest and least advanced.

A further weakness of most aid programmes, and one increasingly apparent, is that both donors and receivers of aid are tempted to prefer the grandiose and impressive 'development project' to the more humble and workaday. The result too often is a monument to economic wishful thinking, standing isolated and half-crippled in a vast hinterland of underdevelopment.[4] Here again, import bounties would escape these unfortunate pressures and exert a contrary influence on the patterns of development.

This point raises the question of methods. It may be suggested that if the aim is simply to expand export industries in the poorer countries, this could be done much more simply and directly. Why not save administrative complications just by giving aid on condition that the receiving government uses it to subsidise export industries? The objection to this apparent short-cut, however, is that it would lead back again to the familiar problems of aid-with-strings. One great advantage of the import bounty system is precisely that it by-passes the political end, as it were, of both the giving and receiving government. It appears to relieve them of the invidious responsibility for deciding who gets how much, and on what terms.

General agreement to allow developing countries to offer export subsidies, as suggested by Norman Macrae in the survey already quoted, would certainly be better than nothing. But the weakness of national subsidies – as almost every developed country has discovered – is that they are extremely easy to begin and extremely difficult to end. This is mainly because the group receiving the subsidy immediately importunes and threatens the government if it ever seems to contemplate cutting off the subsidy. This pressure is much less likely to be effective if the source of the subsidy lies outside the country, and therefore largely beyond the political reach of local special interests. This is an important point in the long term, because the time would come when it might be necessary to take a semi-developed country off the bounty list and add it to those intermediate countries who would neither receive bounties nor pay them out.

Yet another administrative short-cut would be a differential exchange rate, which would apply to exports of manufactures from developing countries and which would automatically make them cheaper in terms of the importer currencies. This would be rather similar to the differential tourist exchange rates which, in some countries, in effect subsidise the foreign visitor. This, however, would be very open to abuse and political pressures and would certainly be frowned upon by the monetary mandarins. (Some abuse and some fraud – the odd cargo 'Made in Asia' but originating in Birmingham or Düsseldorf – is probably unavoidable; but on the whole the system of certificates of origin devised for Commonwealth preferences and for the EFTA imports has worked pretty well and could be extended.)

* * *

So far, the scheme has been discussed as a multilateral one, in which all the developed countries of North America, Western Europe, Australia and Japan would offer comparable bounties, although, clearly, the method of taxing domestic manufactures and those produced in each other's territories could be left somewhat to each government to decide. The only essential international agreement for a multilateral scheme would be on the rate of bounty, the list of qualified developing countries and the short list of intermediate countries excluded from the bounty system.

There are good arguments for trying an early start with a multilateral system even if, at the outset, it were only applied to a partial list of manufactures. Already the pressures from the developing countries are creating a series of special preferences and agreements which has not yet got very far, but could easily and quickly proliferate into a tangled patchwork of special commercial relationships which would be the negation of the United Nations aims in trade, and, in the long run, in the best interests of none.

Already the trend of policy in the EEC towards the African associates is not only putting new emphasis – and properly so – on industrialisation and diversification, but it also gives free access within the Community to their exports of manufactures as well as of commodities. This free entry is now to be extended to Nigeria. There is also the Australian proposal for a waiver of GATT rules to give similar preferential entry to her poorer northern neighbours. In the United States, the idea has been heard of offering preferential terms to manufactured imports from Latin America. This could be the time when a determined lead by one of the developed countries would reveal that resistance was much less than has been supposed. Official opinions on trade policy have in practice proved much more flexible than they pretend. Surely, on no other issue in world politics has there been so great a shift of opinion as that on the principles of world trade which has taken place between the Havana Charter and the Final Act of UNCTAD. In smaller groups, too, the Ottawa agreements and the European Common Market have shown how quickly, in all but the tenderest spots defined earlier, the unthinkable in trade policy becomes the acceptable.

If the multilateral approach failed, it is still conceivable that a unilateral, or perhaps even a Commonwealth, initiative on these lines would suit British interests. Suspended in a sort of economic limbo outside the European door, the British economy has missed the stimulus of European competition and the sense of any alternative direction. It has been still further feather-bedded by the import surcharge. Meanwhile, a chronic balance of payments situation is bound to frustrate British aid programmes, no matter how good the new Ministry's intentions. The offer of import bounties – which, at a pinch, could always be paid into special non-convertible accounts, so that they were in turn spent on British goods – might be the means of salvaging some self-respect from a humiliating situation.

5
'Protectionism and World Politics' / 1985

(selected countries)

F13

F14

Much public debate and speculation in many Western countries today – in political parties and government circles, in the business community and among academics – is about international trade. It concerns both the prospects for the future and the policies that governments should, or should not, adopt in their own interest or for the general welfare of world society.

In this debate it is high time students of international relations and international political economy finally threw off the intellectual bondage of liberal economics and began to think for themselves about international trade and its part in the international system. This cultural dependence has led them to accept too easily the liberal assumption that the connection between international trade and international relations works both ways, that not only do better trade relations result from better political relations but that better political relations result from better trade relations. Historical experience does indeed sustain the contention that more and freer trade improves political relations. However, the second, Cobdenite assertion, that restricted trade damages political relations, is much more doubtful.

Yet its wide acceptance has led to a further assumption. Positive corrective measures have to be consciously taken, its proponents hold, to secure international trade against the shortsighted tendency of states to interfere with it – to the detriment not only of efficiency and wealth in the economic system but of peace in the political system. These measures, it has been widely supposed, must be either imposed by the power of a hegemonial strong trader with a self-interest in freer trade or else engineered on the basis of negotiated rules strong enough to restrain the perverse and misguided nationalist impulses of states to obstruct commerce.

The gloom and despondency of liberal economics notwithstanding, trade experience in the early 1980s tells us that protectionism in fact poses no great threat to the world's trade system. On the contrary, the only really serious disorders in the system result from ten years' mismanagement of money and credit and to some extent from an interrelated instability in the world oil market.

The explanation for this gulf between theory and experience, I shall argue, is to be found in a changing world production structure and its effects both on the decisions of governments and on the decisions of corporations. Because national wealth, and eventually power, depend on success in a world market, the argument goes, governments have a natural resistance, widespread and growing, to protectionist pressures from special interests. And because a corporation's survival also depends on success in a world market, trade between countries in goods and services will be, and is being, sustained by a complex network or web of transnational, bilateral bargains – bargains between corporations and other corporations, between corporations and governments, and between governments. The interest of both parties to these bilateral exchanges is (and will continue to be) a far more powerful influence on the level, the direction, and the content of international trade than the puny efforts of states to interfere with market forces.

It follows that the collapse of the system of rules which people (still, alas) refer to as a regime is of little moment – except to those with a vested professional or ideological interest in it. The alleged decline of the hegemonial power is also irrelevant to this particular issue, except insofar as it may lead to war or civil disorder.

The argument has both policy implications and intellectual implications. Politicians and officials need to know what the real choices are in trade matters; yet they are still apt, as Keynes remarked, to be the mental prisoners of defunct economists. And some academics, at least, seek a better understanding regardless of ideology of what is going on. The analytic implications of the argument are clear: trade in the international system has to be seen as a *secondary* structure. It is subsidiary to four primary structures of the international political economy: the security structure; the production structure; the money and credit structure; and the knowledge structure. The security structure includes both external security and internal security; it determines whether there is war or peace in the international political system of states and whether and how governments within states are able to maintain domestic order. Trade is obviously highly vulnerable to both. It is also responsive to the production structure, which together with the knowledge structure decides what is to be produced, how (i.e., with what technology), where, by whom, and for whom; and it is vulnerable to the money and credit structure, which decides who can pay for traded goods or services and how.

It follows that if war and civil disorder can be avoided in the security structure and if (a big if) the money and credit structure can be even moderately well managed, the production and knowledge structures, between them, will take care of the future of world trade. If we abandon both the hegemonial and the multilateral regime model as inadequate approximations to reality in trade matters, and if we adopt instead a web-of-contracts model, we may begin to hope that trade will satisfy more basic values of political economy than either of the other two models leads us to expect. Trade, we might realize, is more stable and durable than we had thought because it is better able to sustain growth in the face of technical and economic change. It may be more equitable because it may redress some of the asymmetry between North and South. And it may ease the coexistence of a unified world economy with a political system of divided authority, allowing states more leeway to choose freer trade or protection – or both at the same time for different sectors – without risking damage either to world peace or to world prosperity.

A first step in the argument must be to rehearse, for the benefit of those still in bondage to them, the myths of liberal economics and the reasons, derived from a study of international history, why they need no longer be taken too seriously.

The myths of liberal doctrine

The main tenet of liberal economics regarding international trade is that the less governments intervene to obstruct the flow of trade, the better. The more generally liberal policies are adopted toward foreign competition, the better the national welfare and global welfare will be served. Free trade, it is held, allows the most effective allocation of resources to the production of goods and services and thus maximizes the production of wealth for the community. Protection, conversely, encourages inefficiency and impoverishes both individual consumers and the society as a whole.

Much conventional liberal opinion goes on to argue that protectionism adopted by one country provokes retaliatory protectionism in others, setting off a vicious spiral. To avoid this vicious spiral, it is held essential to maintain the momentum of multilateral diplomacy aimed at the reduction of trade barriers. The more protectionist policies multiply, the more imperative for world order it becomes that the states that have signed the General Agreement on Tariffs and Trade (GATT) should make a 'new joint initiative', in the words of the 1983 GATT report, to stop the rot (GATT 1983). Moreover, it is sometimes argued, the economic effects are apt to spill over into politics, poisoning international relations and contributing if not actually leading to conflict between allies and to war between states that might otherwise have been content to coexist.

Like most other simple doctrines, liberal economics is held with enormous passion but with rather less than unassailable logic or strict regard for historical facts. The chief fallacies, false premises, and historical misrepresentations that sustain the liberal doctrine can be fairly briefly stated, since most of them have already been perceived and identified (Block 1977; Cox 1981; Finlayson and Zacher 1981; Sen 1983; Tooze 1984).

The basic premise that state policy should, or even can, be based on the single criterion of maximizing efficiency in the production of goods and services for the market is demonstrably false. Efficiency never has been, *and never can be*, the sole consideration in the choice of state policies. Given an international political system in which the world is divided territorially among states over whom there is no reliable higher authority to prevent conflict among them, security from external attack and the maintenance of internal order are and always have been the first concern of government in each state. Efficiency can be given priority only if the provision of security, internally and externally, is taken for granted – as indeed it is by many if not most liberal economists.

Some, it is true, have acknowledged that guns must sometimes take priority over butter. Adam Smith himself saw that the defence of the realm and security from invasion had to be an objective of political economy for the state. Some modern liberal economists will admit that military production can count as part of the national product, even though it is not exactly consumable or productive in the usual sense. They may even concede, if reluctantly, that it is rational for the state in the interests of national security to adopt a 'second-best' strategy, maintaining a less than fully efficient agriculture or coal-mining or textile industry to make the country less vulnerable in wartime to the cutting-off of imports of food, fuel, or clothes.

Where liberal economists are reluctant to follow the logic of the admission that security is a basic value is where internal order and the security of government are concerned, for it is no more irrational to sacrifice efficiency in the allocation of resources to the need for social cohesion than it is to do so to the need for national security. An inefficient group of producers might constitute a potential group of revolutionary dissidents. It would be cheaper and quicker to pay the price of keeping them in business than to pay the police to quell their rioting.[1] To maintain the loyalty of its citizens – a necessary condition of political security – the state in wealthier societies is also called on to provide economic security. Economic security may mean setting up a welfare or social security system for all. It may also mean making special provision for groups considered to be disadvantaged, whether the physically handicapped or those like steelworkers most acutely afflicted by the rapid rate of change in the international division of labour. From a politician's point of view there is no essential difference between the two. Both are claiming a measure of justice as the price of their continued support of and loyalty to the politician at the polls or even to the state itself. A political order within the state cannot be stable without the consent and support of major groups in society.

Efficiency, in short, is only one of four basic values that any politically organized society seeks to achieve for its members. Wealth, order, justice, and freedom; these are the basic elements of political compounds just as hydrogen, oxygen, and carbon are the essential elements of some chemical compounds. And just as chemical elements can be combined differently to produce oil, wood, or potatoes, so basic values will be combined differently in all politically organized societies to produce, for example, fast-growing authoritarian states or slow-growing democracies, or conversely, fast-growing democracies or slow-growing police states. Wealth and efficiency in the production of wealth will seem the most important objective of government only if the safety of the state and civil order within it can be taken for granted, either because consent is freely given because the existing order is thought to be just or because potential dissidents are coerced and frightened into silent compliance. It is no coincidence that the two strongest champions of free trade – nineteenth-century Britain and mid-twentieth-America – were both states secure and confident in the basic justice of the social order. They did not normally need to fear revolution from within or invasion from without. Both were so strong that they could afford to have relatively limited government. Others whose societies were actually less secure, both internally and externally, paradoxically required strong central government in order to protect their society from internal division, external attack, or both.

Freedom, too, is a basic value, and one that market economies enshrine and liberal economists extol. But it is precisely the freedom to choose to be governed differently from others, to be governed by those with whom people identify as 'us' rather than 'them', that is the sustaining reason for the continued existence of a society of states as prone as is the present international political system to destructive and debilitating internecine conflict and war. If history has not shown that men and women do from time to time choose freedom and justice rather than the most efficient allocation of resources, it has shown nothing. Individuals the world over, for all the superficial concessions they may make to internationalism, do tend to identify themselves with a particular national group and do give their loyalty to one particular nation-state.

Government, consequently, is a matter of finding an appropriate trade-off between these four basic values – security (or order), wealth, justice, and freedom – when it comes to making state policy. On occasion it may be necessary to sacrifice some freedom and accept binding rules (as under the GATT), if it is thought the rules are just and that greater wealth through faster economic growth will thus be attained. At other times it may be necessary to assert independence over efficiency in order to preserve the order of national unity. The French did so in the 1880s, as Alan Milward has argued, when the National Assembly voted to protect peasant farmers against cheap imported grain. That decision he characterizes as a de facto extension of democracy, 'a set of stages in the widening participation of different groups in that body politic'. In this sense, 'the transition from mid-nineteenth century liberalisation of trade to late nineteenth century protectionism was not a regressive atavistic response by conservative agrarian pressure but a progression in political participation' (Milward 1981: 63). After the peasants have come the steelworkers, the textile workers, and the shipbuilders, and to the needs of each important social group the policy-making process has – in order to maintain national unity in a democratic society – become more attentive.

So much for the first myth, the pursuit of economic efficiency. It raises all sorts of enticing questions of political philosophy, but exploring them is not my present purpose.

The second myth is almost a rider to the first. Liberal economists believe that the individual pursuit of private gain is consistent with the general welfare of the society, since the hidden hand of the market ensures that the producer will make what the consumer wants and at the lowest price, or else he will go out of business. Transposing the coincidence of individual and collective interest from the national to the international level produces a corollary myth. It holds that the pursuit of national interests by individual states is consistent with the general welfare of international society – or, in short, that the world economy will be well served if each individual government or state observes the law of comparative costs and sells on the world market what it produces best.

The fallacy here is that the political or economic security of the state may *not* in fact be best served by observing the law of comparative costs. The supposed coincidence of national and global welfare objectives, moreover, assumes the absence or unimportance of adjustment costs and risks. In theory, states can freely adapt either to the changing prices of factors of production or to the changing demands and conditions of the world market. In reality, the political as well as material costs of having to chop and change from one production sector to another are by no means inconsiderable, especially for poor countries or ones that do not share the high degree of conformism, respect for authority, and adaptability of, for instance, Japanese society. These costs, moreover, are probably higher now than they used to be as the pace of technical change accelerates and the cost of capital investment in the latest technology appreciates. Prompt adjustment may be in the collective interest, but it will not always be in the interest of the individual state. The law of comparative costs is an essentially static concept, ever more open to question as the world economy becomes more dynamic.

All this is not to say that political choices are always rational and always made in the best general interest. The point is simply that the choices involve a difficult trade-off among different values and value-laden objectives; and the discounting of time – that is, the weighing of certain present discomforts against uncertain future benefits – is not an easy and certainly not a scientific business. Economists are apt to complain that politicians are irrational because they make 'political' choices, but what is politically rational, how one takes political values into account is not that simple to define and cannot be assessed by quantitative methods.

The next three myths of liberal economics all concern the interpretation of twentieth-century economic history. Everyone knows that two different bystanders may give totally conflicting accounts of a road accident. Similarly, two quite unbiased witnesses of a world depression may give entirely different versions of the sequence of cause and effect. But when, as I believe is the case with protectionism in the last great world depression in the 1930s, almost all those who have spent most time studying the evidence have come up with one conclusion while those liberals who have a political axe to grind have come up with a quite different one, the latter conclusion must be doubted even though it may be widely accepted as the 'true' version of what happened.

Regarding the world depression of the interwar years, the conventional wisdom of liberal economics is that though it may have started with financial crisis, a main cause of shrinking markets was the raising of trade barriers. The major problem was protectionism; the system was trapped in a vicious spiral of beggar-thy-neighbour policies, in which each country retaliated against the others for barriers raised against its own products. The result was that all suffered and no one benefited.

But this is not what the economic historians say – or rather, what they said when, a few years later, they finally got around to sifting the evidence and looking at the figures. Unfortunately, that was just the time when all over the world people's attention was already turning to the impending outbreak of another world war, or when that war had actually started, threatening the very survival of states and political systems. The result was that the economic historians' verdict on the Depression was little heeded and soon forgotten. What they said was that tariffs, though substantially raised, had made surprisingly little difference either to the volume of world trade or to its direction. (Even Frank Taussig concurred with this view.) Nor had retaliation been the significant motive. There was not much tit for tat. It was just that as markets shrank, politicians were everywhere under pressure to handicap foreign producers against domestic ones, to keep jobs open at home if it could be done. Yet the handicaps actually did little to alter the pattern of trade flows. Instead, as Arthur Lewis concluded, 'The decline of trade in manufactures was due neither to tariffs nor to the industrialisation of new countries. The trade in manufactures was low and only because the industrialised countries were buying too little of primary products and paying so low a price for what they bought' (Lewis 1970). They were buying too little not only because commodity prices had tumbled long before tariffs had been raised but also because credit had dried up in London and New York, especially credit for foreign borrowers. By comparison, the effects of tariffs (and that other bogey of the historical imagination, competitive devaluation of currencies) were minimal (Ashworth 1962; Kindleberger 1973).[2]

Why, then, did the myth gain such popularity that it persists to this day? The answer is simple. Americans correctly perceived themselves as the strong traders of the post-war world, both because they were technologically more advanced and because American corporations were better organized to produce for and to sell to a mass market of consumers (Chandler 1977; Melman 1970). They also regarded British and other Europeans' sheltered colonial markets as obstructing their conquest of the world market after the war, and the destruction of preferential barriers against American exports was the first target of US commercial policy. The myth that protectionism had been the main cause of the pre-war Depression, propagated by economists led by Clair Wilcox (1949), was echoed by US policy-makers (Gardner 1980; Harris 1948; Milward 1984; Patterson 1966). The Europeans, including the British, accepted the argument, recognizing that whether or not trade barriers had done much harm, they certainly had done little good, and that a fresh start at the end of the war would probably be in everyone's interest.

Another historical myth holds that the post-war recovery of Europe and the unprecedented growth of all industrialized countries' economies in the 1960s was primarily the result of multilateral tariff reduction conducted under the aegis of the GATT – and perhaps of the earlier cuts in quotas and quantitative restrictions which the Americans demanded of the Europeans as a condition of Marshall Plan aid. That these tariff-bargaining rounds were an important innovation in economic diplomacy and that they helped make business more confident about expanding markets for most capital and consumer goods is not in doubt. But were tariff reductions the *main* cause of post-war prosperity? No one can ever prove conclusively which of two factors was the more decisive. Correlation can be demonstrated, but causation in either direction can only be implied, never proven.

In this case it seems to me far more probable that prosperity permitted liberalization. Trade revived after the war, and continued to grow, because the United States injected large doses of purchasing power into the system at a rate that pretty well matched the physical ability of enterprises to increase production. Impelled by a perceived national interest in holding the line against Soviet expansion, in Europe and elsewhere, the United States came up first with UNRRA aid and the British Loan, then with the European Recovery Program, and finally with military aid to NATO and other allies (which even financed British wheat imports) and with dollars to pay for the stationing of US troops abroad. By that time the US private sector was able to take over from the government a share of the task of maintaining an outflow of dollars to the rest of the world. Americans bought up foreign companies or invested in new plants for foreign affiliates, allowing their allies and associates to rebuild their monetary reserves (composed largely of dollar IOUs) to the point where most of them – Britain excepted – no longer needed to fear the political consequence of a temporary deficit on their balance of trade. Eventually, of course, and especially after the mid-1960s, the injection of dollar purchasing power became increasingly inflationary as the US government also took on the financing of social welfare. But that it was instrumental for a generation in spreading purchasing power more widely throughout the whole economy is hardly in doubt.

When it comes to more recent history and the present state of the world economy, one must be careful not to overstate what the liberals say. There are, of course, substantial differences of emphasis both in their analyses of past events and in their prescriptions for future policy. But three general observations crop up again and again, observations that do not always accord well with the analysis that precedes them. One is that the main problem afflicting the world economy is the deterioration in the trade system. Sometimes this is explicitly stated, sometimes it is implicit in recommendations for governments.

Another is that if the drift toward protectionism is not arrested, things will get a lot worse. We might call it the 'bicycle theory' since it says that if you do not keep up the momentum of trade liberalization, disaster will follow. For instance, Miriam Camps and William Diebold wrote recently for the Council on Foreign Relations in New York that 'Doing nothing will lead to trouble.' 'Hanging on' – by which they meant protesting devotion in principle to the GATT and its rules while in practice giving in to protectionist pressures – is a 'prescription for deterioration' (Camps and Diebold 1983). Similarly, a recent experts' report written for the Commonwealth Secretariat in London stated flatly, and apparently without any supporting evidence, that recent expansionary trends in the exports of developing countries 'cannot continue even if world expansion is soon resumed unless the drift toward protectionism is arrested and reversed' (Commonwealth Secretariat 1982: 5, para. 1.29).

The final historical myth is the unwarranted but very widespread assumption that the only hope lies in multilateral agreement, negotiated through international organization. This assumption rests, of course, on that biased interpretation of post-war history which ascribes so much importance to multilaterally negotiated reductions in trade barriers and so little to other factors. It greatly underrates the importance of some key bilateral relationships within the American alliance, specifically those of the United States with Britain, with Canada, with Germany, and with Japan. Each of the four had its own reasons for complying with American policy objectives. It also underrates the steady creation of credit first by the US government, then through the investment of dollars abroad by US corporations, and finally, after the first oil price rise of 1973, by international bank lending through the Eurodollar and the Eurocurrency markets.

By contrast with these rather dogmatic assertions, the analysis that leads up to them often gives far more importance to the disorder of the monetary and financial system than it does to the state of trade. (World trade fell only in 1982, after nearly a decade of mounting protectionism, and by 1 per cent, a trivial amount compared with the 28 per cent fall in world trade in 1926–35. The inflation-adjusted increase in world trade in 1973–83 has been of the order of 6 or 7 per cent.) Camps and Diebold, for example, begin by describing the financial problems of the world economy before going on to assert that a 'solution' of trade problems is a necessary condition of economic recovery. And it is even more true of the analysis made by Jan Tumlir, the research director of the GATT, in a British bank review. He begins his analysis with the statement that 'the key issue of the moment is the precariousness of all financial structures'. Neither debtors nor creditors, Tumlir thinks, 'would go along indefinitely with patchwork rescheduling arrangements'. The overloading of the financial system with bad debts – loans for which creditors claim an inflated book value far above their marketable value – calls for a comprehensive plan for the stabilization of the world economy (Tumlir 1983).

Several economists point to the slower growth of the great industrialized countries as the major problem and the proximate cause of the trend toward protectionism. Perhaps prematurely, Max Corden has written that 'the developed world has just emerged from a major recession created essentially by tight monetary policies designed to squeeze inflation out of the system. During this period there has been a great increase in protectionist pressures and also some increase in actual protection' (Corden 1984). Corden is careful, however, to note that there is no unambiguous evidence that this new protectionism has had a significant effect on trade. Yet he hesitates to conclude that it does not much matter, saying that the effects may come later, *or* the distortion will work through exchange rates and an overvalued dollar to handicap exports, *or* trade would have expanded faster had it not been for these restrictive measures.

These three afterthoughts, or riders, indicate a reluctance to admit that protectionism has not, after all, had very much effect. They tally with an apparent disinclination to look beyond tighter US monetary policies to the deeper causes of the recession of the early 1980s. Such inhibitions are fairly common among liberal economists, for example, and are to be found in British explanations of the slower economic growth of recent years (Matthews 1982). Except for a few academic economists particularly interested in international finance, and for people engaged with financial markets whether as central or commercial bankers, there is a curious distaste for acknowledging the tremendous structural changes that have taken place in financial markets and thus the reason why tighter monetary policies in the United States should have had such enormous worldwide consequences. The relation between monetary disorder and either the commodity boom of the early 1970s or the commodity slump of the early 1980s (the worst in 15 years according to the World Bank) is thus glossed over. And so is the coincidence of the slackened demand that accompanied recession with the major structural changes in the international division of labour, which have in fact buoyed up the exports of manufacturers from developing countries even in the face of mounting protection.

Why should there be this widespread reluctance to face up to the financial and monetary factors contributing to present difficulties or to the structural changes in production resulting from the internationalization of business? There are several possible explanations. At the lowest possible level there is the institutional interest of international bureaucracies in preserving their role and their importance. Ever since the fiasco of the trade ministers' meeting at Geneva in November 1982, the GATT secretariat, for instance, has had to face the uncomfortable fact that the road to further progress in trade liberalization was firmly closed by yawning gulfs of disagreement between the Americans and the Europeans, between the Europeans and the Japanese, and between all the industrialized countries and the Group of 77 developing countries. No wonder the GATT reports sound so full of doom and gloom. The truth is that if the whole organization were wound up, and its tax-exempt officials made redundant with a golden handshake, the world's trade would be remarkably little affected. At a somewhat higher level, there is a natural preference among many academic economists for an interpretation of economic change that allows them both to ignore politics and to be rather self-righteous about it. They can thus condemn politicians or their lack of moral fibre while telling their students that all would have been well if only their priestly advice had been heeded. That is much easier and a lot more fun than trying to come to grips with the complexities of a monetary and financial conundrum to which no one has a sure or simple answer.

At the political level there is, I think, an ideological explanation. The ideology of free trade, private enterprise, and competition unimpeded by the interference of government still has a strong appeal for the business community in most cities of the world. It is an ideology that tends to persist long after the material interest reflected in government policy and in business behaviour has turned from open competition to protection, cartelization, and restrictive practices. Well into the 1940s and 1950s, British government officials continued to believe and advocate the ideology of free trade even though by that time only a few in British industry were still able to win in open competition with Americans, Germans or Japanese. I suspect the same thing is now true of the United States, where the rhetoric of free, non-discriminatory trade still strongly persists in Washington long after the reality of US policy in some sectors is pointed in quite an opposite direction (Destler 1979; Hudson 1977: chapter 16; Walters 1983).[3]

So strong is this ideological hangover that the quite unwarranted belief still also persists among a few economists and politicians that protectionism jeopardizes peace and that world order at the political level may be directly threatened if the multilateral trade order is allowed to crumble. The Commonwealth Secretariat, for example, commenting on the wider effects of protectionism, declares that 'resentments may build up and issue in aggressive exchanges and a breakdown of peaceful relations when opportunities of fruitful effort are cut off by arbitrary and discriminatory acts on the part of foreign powers' (Commonwealth Secretariat 1982).[4] Historical examples of deliberate trade wars being pursued by countries engaged in commerce with each other or even competing for shares of third markets are extremely hard to find, but the difficulty does not stop the myth persisting. Nor does the fact that political and military conflicts have seldom if ever grown out of commercial rivalry. The competitors in pre-1914 Britain most feared, curiously enough, were Japan – then a newly industrializing country undercutting Britain with cheap manufactures of china and textiles – and the United States, already beginning to buy up British companies and set up affiliates across the Atlantic. But it was Germany that Britain fought. And of all the many international conflicts either since 1914 or before, it is hard to think of one that was provoked or exacerbated by the protectionist policies of one or both contestants. How much has protectionism had to do with the Cold War, with the recurrent Arab–Israeli conflicts, the tension between India and Pakistan, the Iraq–Iran war, or the battle of the Falklands?

Recent trends in trade

Even the most cursory examination of recent trends in world trade shows that while world trade, as pointed out earlier, declined only a trivial 1 per cent, growth rates, output, and employment suffered a much more severe setback. In the early 1980s the world passed through quite a severe recession, and indeed it may not yet have fully emerged from it. Yet recession did not have nearly so violent an effect on the volume of international trade as the Depression of the 1930s. The reasons for this paradox are not at all well understood, but one plausible explanation implicates the growth of what Judd Polk first described as *international production* – that is to say, production for a world market by large corporations that operate with a global strategy and not only sell abroad but actually produce in more than one country (Polk, Merster and Veit 1966). Charles-Albert Michalet has made a further useful distinction between two kinds of international production. One takes place in a 'relay affiliate', which merely reproduces abroad the production process developed at home – a practice that fits with product-cycle theory. The other takes place in 'workshop affiliates', where one stage of a production process is farmed out, as it were, to another country where labour is cheaper or more docile or taxes are lower (Michalet 1976).

Whatever the reason, trade in manufactures has grown very much faster than trade in primary products. Moreover, there is far more trade between industrialized countries than trade between them and the developing countries. The conventional notion holds that trade is determined by differences in resource endowment. But, as Fred Meyer has argued, technology and the accelerating rate of technical change has a lot more to do with the drive to produce for the world market. For, as technology becomes more complex, and expensive, each new plant or process a company installs is dearer and is destined to more rapid obsolescence than the one it replaces (Meyer 1978). In most industries it becomes impossible to recoup the investment fast enough by selling on only a local or national market. One result is that trade in semi manufactures – half-finished goods – has also grown faster than the average rate of growth. Thus a totally Swedish Volvo car or a totally American Boeing aircraft, even a totally South Korean ship, no longer exists. Components are put together from all over, and the figures on trade collected by international organizations tell only half-truths inasmuch as they allow us to continue to think in these obsolete terms of trade as an international exchange of national products.

A second point is that developing countries' penetration of industrialized countries' markets has been faster in manufactured goods in the 1970s than ever before and faster than the general rise in trade in manufactures (see Table 5.1). Though textiles, shoes and electrical goods are the sectors where Third World exports are best known, they are by no means the only ones. Exports of paper, paper products, and printed matter, for instance, increased by 26 per cent in the 1970s, those of chemicals, petroleum, coal, rubber, and plastic products by 25 per cent, and those of all fabricated metal products, machinery, and equipment by nearly 33 per cent.

Table 5.1   Share of developing country imports in the apparent consumption of manufactured goods in eleven industrial countries, 1970–80 (percentages)

| | Share in Apparent Consumption | | | | Growth of Import Shares | |
| | 1970 | | 1980[a] | | 1970–80[b] | |
	All Imports	Imports from Developing Countries	All Imports	Imports from Developing Countries	All Imports	Imports from Developing Countries
Australia	22.3	2.1	25.9	5.5	2.6	11.0
Canada	27.0	1. 3	31.1	2.1	1.7	5.0
European Community	20.4	2.5	31.8	4.6	4.8	6.7
Belgium	57.5	5.7	80.1	6.2	3.2	1.4
France	16.2	1.9	23.1	3.8	3.6	7.8
Germany	19.3	2.3	30.8	4.8	4.9	8.1
Italy	16.3	2.2	31.6	5.2	6.8	9.3
Netherlands	52.3	3.9	62.1	7.5	2.0	6.7
United Kingdom	15.8	2.8	26.6	4.1	5.8	3.8
Japan	4.7	1.3	6.2	2.4	2.4	5.8
Sweden	31.3	2.8	37.9	3.8	2.5	3.9
United States	5.5	1.3	8.6	2.9	4.5	8.6
Industrial Countries	11.6	1.7	17.6	3.4	4.3	7.2

a.   Preliminary data subject to revision.
b.   Average annual rate of growth estimated by an ordinary least square regression: growth rates are of the share of market growth wherever possible, to avoid deflation problems.

Source. H. Hughes and A. Krueger, 'Effects of Protection on Developing Countries' Exports of Manufactures', mimeo, January 1983.

It is clear from these figures that protectionism does not work as a check on the industrial development of developing countries. Very precise arrangements, bilaterally negotiated between industrialized countries such as Japan and the United States, for well-defined products, do apparently check market penetration. Quota restrictions and tariffs, and even voluntary export agreements reached with developing countries, apparently do not. As Table 5.2 shows, the only export markets where LDC manufactures did take a knock in 1982 (and probably in 1983 too) were the OPEC countries, then suffering from the falling oil price and the other LDCs, then suffering from falling commodity prices (and therefore earnings of foreign exchange) and the shrinkage of credit associated with debt problems. But no one has suggested that the drift toward protectionism has been most marked in either of these groups of countries. They may perhaps have been protectionist, but it is the developed countries that have become markedly more protectionist in the last decade.

Table 5.2   NOPEC/LDC exports of manufactures ($ billion)

	1973	1980	1981	1982
DCs	15.10	58.70	63.0	63.0
OPEC	1.40	9.80	11.40	10.80
LDCs	5.20	26.50	28.90	27.50
CMEA	6.70	2.70	3.40	3.60
World	23.15	99.80	110.55	107.50

Source. GATT annual report, *International Trade, 1982/3* (Geneva, 1983).

Throughout the period of the so-called new protectionism the developed countries have continued to lose their share of total market and of other countries' markets. In an analysis conducted for the World Bank, H. Hughes and A. Krueger concluded that 'the rate of increase of LDC market shares was sufficiently great that it is difficult to imagine that rates would have been significantly higher in the absence of any protectionist measures' (Hughes and Krueger 1983: 37). Welfare losses, presumably therefore, fell not on the developing but on the developed countries.

The new international division of labour appears to be unstoppable. The move of manufacturing industry to the Third World is structural, not cyclical. Though more visible in the export-oriented economies of South Korea and Taiwan, it is also happening in India and Brazil where an expanding mass market – for clothes, radios, even computers – is increasingly satisfied by domestic production rather than by imports from the old industrialized countries. (No one would deny that this is so, though statistics on consumption in such countries are sometimes so scanty that it is hard to find statistical evidence.)

The progress of the newly industrialized countries that are the main targets of protectionism is indicated by the figures in Tables 5.3 and 5.4 on South Korean exports and in Table 5.5 on the exports of Taiwan – a country arbitrarily excluded from most UN statistics because of its anomalous legal status. Though the value of Korean exports to the United States of primary products (fruit, vegetables, and tobacco) took something of a knock between 1981 and 1983, Korean exports of most manufactures continued to grow rather substantially. In the space of two supposedly bad recession years Korean exports of textiles to America grew by 60 per cent, of machinery and transport equipment by 140 per cent, of steel by 20 per cent, of rubber by 24 per cent, and of clothing and shoes by 27 per cent. Overall, the growth in US imports from Korea was 43 per cent.

Table 5.3   Korean exports to the United States, 1981–83 ($ million)

	1981	1982	1983[a]
Fish & products	81,618	78,642	90,212
Fruit & vegetables	12,816	8,898	2,877
Tobacco & manufactures	46,165	26,809	20,485
Chemicals	42,165	52,987	55,553
Rubber manufactures	120,716	106,669	150,748
Wood manufactures	131,304	75,241	32,631
Textile yarn, cloth & manufacture	162,230	176,842	260,013
Iron & steel	488,774	405,336	584,084
Metal manufactures	328,816	328,301	253,155
Machinery & transport equipment	1,046,377	1,257,996	2,512,651
Clothing & footwear	1,825,718	2,141,810	2,318,602
TOTAL (including other items)	5,140,727	5,636,822	7,351,300

a. January–November.

Source. Economist Intelligence Unit and Korean Trade Centre, London.

Table 5.4   Korean exports to Japan, 1980–82 ($ thousand)

	1980	1981	1982	1983[a]
Fish, meat & products	102.076	118,191	629,880	556,822
Oilseeds	12,329	12,858	1,285	924
Crude minerals & fertilisers	8,586	8,113	28,807	21,243
Mineral fuels	9,804	32,673	n.a.	n.a.
Chemicals	47,468	48,734	72,236	60,528
Wood & manufactures	17,952	5,731	5,585	11,784
Textiles fibres & manufactures	105,718	91,494	388,480	270,716
Iron & steel & manufactures	68,945	87,121	585,826	482,780
Machinery & transport equipment	68,087	70,659	75,140	351,687
Clothing	91,606	121,417	594,623	387,385
TOTAL (including other items)	681,218	748,074	3,314,444	3,018,095

a. January–November.

Source. Economist Intelligence Unit and Korean Trade Centre, London.

The figures for Korean exports to Japan in Table 5.4, though on a smaller scale, show equally striking growth rates. Over four years clothing textile exports more than quadrupled, iron and steel exports increased seven times, and machinery and transport equipment increased by more than five times. Exports of textile fibre and manufactures were up in some years and down in others, but they were in any case not as important as any of the other categories of manufactures.

In Table 5.5 a similarly strong upward trend can be seen in Taiwan's exports of manufactures until 1982, the last year for which figures are available. Here, the only hiccup is from 1981 to 1982 (and from 1974 to 1975, when slack demand interrupted the upward trend) except in transportation equipment – mainly container ships, of which Taiwan is now the second most important producer in the world.

The conclusion is surely clear: protectionism is far less important to LDCs than the rate of growth in the world economy as a whole. Although it may well be, as Corden has suggested, that these exports would have been greater still had it not been for the barriers they encountered, the rate of growth remains astonishing. It is far beyond anything anticipated by economic forecasts made in the 1960s. The record of the four leading East Asian NICs (South Korea, Taiwan, Hong Kong, and Singapore) is of course streets ahead of the ASEAN group and still further ahead of the Latin American countries. Nevertheless, the point is still valid that if protectionism has not effectively held back the leaders (those whose products pose the greatest threat to the domestic industries of the developed countries), then protectionism cannot be the main problem.

Table 5.5   Taiwan: exports of manufactures, 1973–82 ($ million)

Year	Metal Products	Electrical Machinery	Transportation Equipment	All Industrial Products
1972	56	531	63	2,489
1973	91	788	105	3,794
1974	145	1,000	132	4,766
1975	132	782	114	4,441
1976	243	1,277	198	7,154
1977	324	1,489	329	8,189
1978	504	2,009	427	11,310
1979	696	2,775	446	14,581
1980	862	3,899	643	17,990
1981	1,052	4,171	864	20,859
1982	1,019	3,910	1,092	20,523

Source. Ministry of Finance, Republic of Chine (Taiwan), Statistical yearbooks.

Such at least is the conclusion of Bela Belassa. He has pointed out that despite the industrialized countries' protection of their domestic textile producers against Third World imports, the latter rose from 7.3 per cent of domestic consumption in 1973 to 17.4 per cent in 1981. Despite US protection of American steel producers, imported carbon steel took 26 per cent of the American market in 1982 against 5 per cent in the 1960s. The 1 per cent decline in the volume of world trade in manufactured goods in 1982, he concluded, was attributable to a 2 per cent fall in production rather than to increased protection in the developed countries. 'Quantitative restrictions have not substantially limited the expansion of the imports of manufactured goods into the developed countries' (Belassa 1983).[5]

All the evidence, in fact, points to volatility in the availability of credit as the dominant factor. Here, the Latin American experience differs vastly from the East Asian, and mainly because it was the Latin Americans who borrowed most heavily in the Eurocurrency markets, led to do so by the big US banks. (South Korea was also a big borrower but mostly from Japanese banks. The same sort of difficulties that brought Brazil, Mexico, Venezuela, Indonesia, and the Philippines to the door of the IMF were resolved for Korea by a quietly negotiated bilateral agreement with Japan, extending by $4 billion the credit line linked to a long-standing post-war reparations agreement.) When credit ran out and the mounting burden of interest rates made it necessary to reschedule Latin American debts under IMF surveillance, an immediate consequence of what the Fund refers to primly as 'good housekeeping' was a drastic cut in imports. The GATT noted that in 1982 the total deficit in LDCs fell from $74 billion in 1981 to just over $60 billion in 1982 – an 'improvement' of $14 billion and one achieved largely by *not buying abroad*. Argentina, Mexico, and Chile all cut their imports by half, according to the GATT (GATT 1983: 5). And, as a recent study for the Federal Reserve Bank of New York observed, 'The initial effect of the Latin American debt crisis has been felt most severely in the United States by exporters.' Between 1978 and 1981, US exports to Latin America had grown over 50 per cent faster than US exports to the rest of the world, presumably as a result of loans. But as the loans dried up, so did US exports, reversing the trend and accounting for as much as 40 per cent of the total decline of US exports in 1982 over 1981. By the first half of 1983, US exports were less than two-thirds of what they had been a year earlier (Dhar 1983). As Lewis observed about the 1930s, trade declined primarily because of a lack of purchasing power.

Significantly, this lack has affected LDC trade with the industrialized countries more than it has their trade with each other. More than one-third of their exports of manufactures now go to other LDCs , and in some cases even more than that. Over half of South Korea's growing exports of cars and trucks – now nudging the half-million mark – go to other LDCs, even though ten years ago the industry did not exist. The explanation for this expanding trade in manufactures within the Third World may lie in the growing number of regional and bilateral trade arrangements between the countries concerned.

Finally, there is no doubt that other, domestic factors have heavily affected the divergent experience of trade which marks the Third World scene in the 1970s and early 1980s. World Bank studies have shown, for example, that though wages in Colombia were no higher than in East Asia, labour productivity was much lower. Because of government policies, moreover, imported raw materials were often dearer and management less prompt in executing orders and making deliveries. It was neither quotas nor tariffs that was holding Colombia back (Morawetz 1981). Mexico, which in its border zones long enjoyed preferential treatment from the United States over other developing countries, was yet unable to compete with less favoured LDCs, mainly because its own import-substituting, protectionist policies kept its prices high and the quality of its products low (Cline 1984; Odell 1986).

By about the mid-1980s, however, in Mexico and in several other previously protectionist countries, a change was beginning. It was due less to the exhortations of liberal economists or the urging of international organizations than to the urgent need to earn foreign exchange. Governments of all political kinds began to perceive the handicap that protection imposed on national competitiveness in world markets and to extol the advantages of opening the home market to more competition. The South Koreans, for examples, declared that they would learn by Japan's mistakes and allow in many more foreign firms to compete with local enterprise in the home market. Bob Hawke, a Labour prime minister of Australia who might have been expected to be under pressure from unions to protect jobs, not only liberalized restrictions on foreign banks but declared his government's intention of dismantling the defensive barriers surrounding (and, he argued, choking) the Australian car industry. In these and other instances governments were responding to the imperative need to be competitive in at least some sectors in a world market.

Their need is one very strong reason why protectionism is not such a great threat, why the bicycle theory is unconvincing, and why the fear of retaliatory trade wars has even less foundation today than in the past. It is even possible that governments in some industrialized countries – the United States, for instance – are shadowboxing with their protectionist lobbies. Ostentatiously appearing to respond with quotas or other barriers to foreign competition, they succeed in quelling the clamour of protest. But at the same time they are well aware that the barriers (e.g., against LDC clothing or shoes) will soon be breached. They may even think that the broad national interest will be better served if they are.

Another reason is that the developing countries are getting much better at finding ways to wriggle around the barriers raised against them. In the well-known case of Hong Kong, quotas on low-cost textiles and clothes forced exports to go up-market, where barriers were fewer, thus actually increasing the total value of exports. Provenance and final destination in trade are always tricky matters, as those running blockades or strategic embargoes soon find out. There are always third-party go-betweens ready and willing to pass on consignments above the producers' quota as their own exports.

Most important of all in explaining why protectionism is not working to keep out LDC manufactures is the connivance of the transnational corporations. Between them and the governments of developing countries there is a strong symbiotic relationship that accelerates the shift of manufacturing industry from North to South. It is this symbiosis that leads TNCs to negotiate complex bargains with other corporations and with state enterprises and governments around the world. Some estimates of the proportion of world trade which is actually trade between different sections of transnational corporations suggest that intrafirm transfers account for as much as half of some countries' total imports.

Many developing countries, in consequence, recognize that the bargaining which the government conducts with the private sector – foreign banks and foreign corporations – is a good deal more important than ordinary diplomacy with other states. Ecuador's negotiations with Gulf Oil in recent years, for example, have probably been more important to the country than its diplomatic relations with its neighbours. In this new form of diplomacy the state's control of territory gives it control over access to its markets as well as to its natural resources, its work force, and its financial resources and borrowing capacity. The corporation, on its side, can be taxed for revenue and often has new technology based on its R&D capacity;

it has managerial experience and the capacity to market products in other countries, all of which it can exchange for the access that the state alone can give or withhold. A mutuality of interest exists which both parties acknowledge when they bargain with each other but which both often deny in public.[6]

Yet the extent of these trade-creating agreements between states and corporations is unknown. No one has a vested interest in collecting the figures comparable to the interest that governments have always had (originally for tax and revenue reasons) in collecting statistics about the volume of goods entering or leaving their territory. Though most government–corporation agreements are probably with developing countries, there are quite a few well-publicized ones with the developed countries. Both Britain and the United States, for instance, have concluded agreements with Japanese car companies to invest in new plants. Moreover, it is probable that most Western trade with Soviet bloc countries and China has been negotiated by companies rather than governments. Under a 1984 Franco–Soviet commercial agreement, French exports of capital goods to the Soviet Union will rise from Fr. 2 billion to Fr. 10 billion in the first year along, and French exports of steel will triple; but the important negotiations will be those with French companies. Most of the Soviet–West European gas-pipeline arrangments were negotiated over a long period between the Soviet government, the oil companies (notably Shell), and major engineering firms (such as John Brown). Although in their commercial relations with Saudi Arabia the South Koreans have negotiated with the government (arranging, for instance, first to build hospitals and later to staff them with doctors, nurses and technicians), in other bilateral relationships negotiations with governments are often only a preliminary to more detailed bargaining with foreign companies.

Such spotty and uncoordinated evidence as we have, chiefly from the financial press, strongly suggests that this bilateral network of contracts is not only sustaining – despite the financial disorder – the continued expansion of world trade but is actually doing a great deal more than debates in the United Nations to achieve the much-discussed New International Economic Order. This quiet commercial diplomacy produces more tangible results in the shape of new investments, new jobs, and new production in the South than all the resolutions, codes of conduct, guidelines, and declarations on which so much offcial time has been spent. Meanwhile the GATT reports on international trade make a great deal of those bilateral arrangements which restrict trade, notably the market-sharing arrangements for steel between the United States, Japan, and the European Community. They are, however, curiously reticent about trade-creating agreements, even those between governments, such as the Australian–New Zealand Closer Economic Relations agreement of 1983, let alone those between governments and corporations or corporations and other corporations.

One partial indicator of how important these agreements are is the rapid growth in recent years of countertrade, a new elaborate form of barter in which exchange takes place without the use of money. Sometimes the goods concerned are part of the output of a plant in which a foreign corporation had made the initial investment. They can also be goods that are totally different from those which the receiving corporation normally markets. Countertrade by one estimate now accounts for $500 billion a year, about one-quarter of world trade and ten times as much as existed ten years ago. Quite recently the United States decided that countertrade was important enough to warrant changing the law so that US banks could finance countertrade deals.

That such energetic attempts should be made by firms and governments to overcome the economic uncertainty that has characterized the past decade should not surprise us. In the 1930s the first reaction of governments to economic depression and the shrinkage of trade that followed was to seek trading partners with whom special deals could be done, to restore confidence and reopen markets for exporters. The Roosevelt administration, armed with the Reciprocal Trade Agreements Act of 1934, signed 16 bilateral agreements covering one-third of American trade before concluding the 1938 agreement with Britain. The Latin Americans were particularly active in building a continental cobweb of bilateral arrangements, abandoning them only reluctantly after the war under pressure from Washington. Though Hjalmar Schacht's bilateral arrangements with Germany's southeastern neighbours are the best-documented set of commercial arrangements of that time, and are notorious for their 'exploitation' of primary producers, they were in most respects not at all unusual.

From an international relations perspective, moreover, it does not seem strange that a commercial system should be made up of an interlocking network of bilateral arrangements and relationships. All the talk of an 'international system' notwithstanding, that is what most international relations actually consist of – relations between particular pairs of states. The Western alliance, for instance, boils down to a set of bilateral relationships between the United States and certain key countries, first Britain, latterly Germany and Japan, but also Canada, Australia, and other minor allies. The biggest issue of world politics – nuclear arms control – is generally acknowledged to be a matter of bilateral relations by the superpowers. And when the future of Hong Kong has to be settled, no one finds it surprising that it should be negotiated bilaterally between the British and the Chinese.

What has happened between the 1930s and the 1980s is that international corporations have taken over in large part from governments in arranging trade deals across frontiers. This bilateralism is regarded with disdain in international organization circles and by liberal economists, but their attitudes are more than a little biased, by self-interest in the first case and by ideology in the second. It seems at the least arguable that the model of a web of bilateral contracts is capable of producing a more durable and generally satisfactory trade-off among the basic values of political economy than any other. It would appear capable – always given the necessary monetary management – of sustaining growth and efficiency in the production of wealth. By aiding the changing international division of labour to benefit the NICs, it is also bringing about some more just and equitable distribution of the benefits of economic integration. And it is certainly giving greater freedom to states to be openly inconsistent (instead of covertly, as before) in their trade policies. For political security reasons they may choose to be protectionist in one sector (German shipbuilding) while open and competitive in others (German automobiles). The choice is theirs, and there is no reason why governments should not change their mind in either direction.

In any case, the next few years will show whether world trade can continue to survive despite the deadlock in the GATT and despite a certain amount of increased protectionism. My contention is that a combination of political and economic interests, reinforced by structural change in the international division of labour brought about by the mobility of capital and technology, is preventing a world depression from seriously arresting or reversing the steady growth in world trade.

Theoretical implications

If this conclusion is correct, it undermines some of the basic assumptions of liberal economic doctrine about the political economy of trade. Liberal doctrine assumes that there is something inherent in the nature of the state which biases its decisions toward protectionism and other interventions in the market, and that this bias ought somehow to be corrected. It needs to be corrected, so the argument goes, for economic reasons, so that wealth will be maximized through international specialization. It needs to be corrected for political reasons, so that beggar-thy-neighbour trade policies will not start a vicious spiral of retaliation ending in open violence.

Liberal doctrine leads in two directions, to the hegemonial model and to the multilateralist model. The first says that the best way to correct this regrettable tendency is to depend on the coercive and persuasive power of a dominant economic and military power, a hegemon, to restrain the other states in the system. The second says that if all major trading countries can agree on a binding set of rules, the benefits reaped by each of them from expanding trade will far outweigh the inconvenience of obedience to the rules.

It was Charles Kindleberger who first argued that the integrated world economy of our times requires a hegemon at its centre to function in an orderly and productive way. He also defined the basic requirements of such a hegemonial system (Kindleberger 1973). A capitalist or market system is apt, as experience has shown, to suffer cylical booms and slumps and to fail periodically to match its demands and supply. The hegemon thus has to function in three ways in order to preserve order in the system. Whenever necessary it must offer a vent or outlet for surplus production; it must act as a lender of last resort to maintain monetary liquidity; and it must generate an outflow of capital or credit to keep the system expanding. Kindleberger argued (and many people have accepted his argument) that Britain played this role more or less successfully in the three or four decades before World War I, and the United States played it in the two decades following World War II. Between the wars, however, Britain was unable and the United States was unwilling to do so. The result was that the world suffered the worst depression in its history.

Most Americans believe that the United States today, like Britain 50 years ago, has suffered a decline in power that no longer permits it to play this hegemonial role. Most non-Americans are highly sceptical about this decline in US power and would agree with Hedley Bull that 'The problem America presents for us is not, as so many Americans appear to think, the relative decline of its power, but the decline of its capacity for sound judgment and leadership' (1983). Bull was referring more to matters of security and defence, but the observation applies equally to money and trade. In these matters it is not so much that the United States is unable as that it is unwilling. It is not so much that it has lost power to Japan, Germany, or any other state as that the private sector has grown so large that its regulation has been allowed to go (or seems to have gone) beyond the power of any government.

In the version of the hegemonic model developed by Robert Gilpin and later Stephen Krasner, the political and economic decline of the hegemon inevitably brought about the collapse of the liberal trade order (Gilpin 1975; Keohane and Nye 1977; Krasner 1978).[7] Arthur Stein (1984) recently went on to argue that this decline was itself inevitable, inherent in what he called the 'hegemon's dilemma'.[8] Both Britain in the nineteenth century and the United States in the twentieth century adopted economic policies that undercut their own dominant position. The hegemon's dilemma was to reconcile the national interest with maintenance of the system. The crucial question, according to Stein, was 'whether the hegemon, now facing economic collapse, will be able to forgo retaliation' when others act illiberally.

The point Stein misses is that the trade system is secondary to the security system and the monetary and credit system. Therefore it is not what the hegemon does or does not do in trade that matters, but what it does or fails to do to maintain the peace and what it does or fails to do to keep the monetary system stable and credit flowing in a steady fashion. Kindleberger was right to emphasize that the basic hegemonic tasks in the interwar period were all monetary – that is, stabilizing the flow of purchasing power through the issue of credit, stabilizing the price of goods in terms of money, and keeping the exchange rates of the major currencies in some sort of rough equilibrium. Neither of the alternative trade policies that Stein suggests might have allowed the hegemon to keep its dominance, and thus save the system (according to his argument) from collapse, was ever feasible. Britain could never have kept a monopoly of the secrets of the Industrial Revolution, and the United States could not have prevented the eventual recovery of the major industrial powers. Rather, it was the failure to maintain peace in 1914 and the failure to maintain monetary order in 1929 and 1979 that caused the decline in trade in each case. At no significant point, as Stein's own narrative makes clear, was the system threatened by the hegemon resorting to retaliation.

Hegemonic leadership may have been useful in accelerating and maximizing the dismantling of trade barriers. Given the structural changes outlined above, however, it is not essential now even if it was in the past. It is worth remembering that trade liberalization in the 1950s, the 1960s, and the 1970s continued just as long as the credit system was expanding. It stopped when credit and purchasing power ran out. At no point did it depend on a clear, consistent, and uncompromising lead from the United States. Trade liberalization continued despite all the contradictions of US trade policy, such as the waiver for agricultural trade in the 1950s, Buy American and tied-aid policies, subsidized shipping, and featherbedded defence industries. The contraditions and inconsistencies (in favour of freer trade in services and of managed trade in manufactures) have changed, but they are hardly new. Perhaps the reason that the hegemonic model has been so appealing, however, is that it claims the status of a law of nature. In the face of such *force majeure*, failure to be consistent or to deal with the underlying monetary problems can be more easily excused.

The same can be said of the second, multilateralist model in which all the major participants in the trading system accept a standard body of rules and neither cheat nor change the rules too frequently. It is the model preached by the GATT and championed by liberal economists. Both are apt to confuse correlation and cause and to make exaggerated claims for trade liberalization as the major cause of trade expansion and growth in the world economy. It is very likely that the agreement on rules boosted confidence. Confidence probably assisted other factors – political alliance and peace between the Western allies, credit expansion and the internationalization of production through the TNCs – which were powerfully contributing to the growth of trade.

But to say that standard rules are an *essential* prerequisite for expanding trade goes too far. In the first place, standard trade rules mean little if combined with an asymmetric monetary system. The GATT was originally designed to work in tandem with a system of fixed exchange rates between currencies, one in which the rules would apply to all. But the Bretton Woods system diverged from the model from the very start. The development of the dollar-gold exchange system allowed the United States, by exercising its 'exorbitant privilege' of paying its debts with IOUs, to escape the discipline imposed on other deficit countries. Since 1973 floating rates have created what Robert Triffin called a 'paper dollar standard', imposing even less discipline than ever on the United States. Thus it has been free to restore a weak trade balance by allowing the dollar to depreciate – a more effective method of boosting exports and repelling comercial invaders than any tariff policy. At other times, when domestic pressures called for a strong dollar, it could compensate for any handicap this put on American industry by insisting on involuntary export restrictions or by borrowing heavily abroad to make up on the financial side what it lost on the trade balance.

And in the second place, there is no correlation between rules and growth. World trade in food has grown substantially without rules to restrain agricultural protection. So has world trade in services, from tourism and shipping to banking and insurance. By now, moreover, the deviation from the standard achieved through nontariff barriers, subsidies, quota agreements, and preferential purchasing are so great that the overnight disappearance of the GATT beneath the water of Lac Leman would hardly be noticed in the world of commerce.

As with the hegemonic model, the multilateral 'regime' (as it is inaccurately still referred to) appeals to academics in search of tidy models and general rules. The reality of hegemonic domination and multilateral surveillance was far messier and more full of contradictions than the intellectual bystanders appreciated.[9] The degree of order achieved in the system, whether by Britain as hegemon in the nineteenth century and America in the postwar decades or thanks to the GATT and its rule making, was always very relative. Only in ideal form is either model inherently truer to life than the complex web of contracts and bilateral deals on which we now depend.

6
'Finance, Information and Power' 1990

[handwritten notes: US, Japan; related countries; F30; G21]

The point of this article can be quickly made: it is just that there is a big difference between the financial power exercised by the United States and that exercised by Japan, and that the difference is partly explained by the role of information in the global financial structure. It also happens that this difference is a rather good illustration of the difference between structural power and relational power.

What I am comparing is the structural power to extend or restrict the range of options open to others which has been, and still is, exercised by the United States in the postwar decades, in this case specifically in the field of finance, with the relational power which Japan exercises in the same field of finance by virtue of its position as the world's major creditor country and aid donor.

By the field of finance, I refer particularly to the system by which credit is created, bought and sold and by which the direction and use of capital is determined. Although it is hard to separate this entirely from what might be called the field of money   that is, the exchange rates between currencies – on account of the key role in both fields played by the rate of interest, I shall try to leave exchange rates aside as unnecessary to my argument, although broadly supportive of it.

The first step in the argument will be an analytical description of the present global financial structure as it has developed over the past twenty or thirty years, and of the part played in recent changes by changes in communication systems together with the ways in which these comparatively recent changes have shifted options available to borrowers and lenders, to financial operators and to governments. The second step will be a backward-looking account of how it became like that and of the consequences in terms of the distribution of structural power in and over the global financial system.

A third part will consider the financial position of Japan in the system and the extent of its power to influence others – essentially, in my opinion, a kind of relational power combined with some specific vulnerabilities to exogenous changes in the system. The conclusion merely points up the differences in power to be deducted from the foregoing analysis.

The financial structure described

It is not just, as Gilpin says, that 'international finance is a major force in integrating the world economy' (1987: 206). It is more than that. The integration of the world economy has been achieved through the bringing together of national financial systems into one global system. Instead of a series of national financial systems linked by a few operators buying and selling credit transnationally, across national frontiers and across the exchanges (i.e. from one national currency to another) and by a few national asset markets (e.g. stock exchanges) so linked that they respond to each other, we now have a global system in which the national markets, physically separated by distance, actually function as if they were one. And this global financial system, instead of being a minor appendage to the various national financial systems, is now both larger than any of them and more influential. The balance, in short, has shifted from being a predominantly state-based system with some transnational links to being a predominantly global system with some local differences.

The unification of national financial systems into one global system has had several important consequences. Firstly, there are the consequences for the customers, whether they want to put funds into the system (i.e. sell) or whether they want to borrow from it (i.e. buy), or whether they want to exchange one asset or liability for another (e.g. debt/equity swaps). Then there are the consequences for the banks and other kinds of operators in the financial markets. And, finally, there are the consequences for the governments on whom the responsibility rests for managing the national economy, regulating the money supply to it and thus to the banks and other credit-creating institutions, whether private or public. To identify in each case what these consequences are is quite a good way of describing the changes in the financial structure.

For savers who want to deposit money in a bank, these changes have offered more options – a wider choice and the opportunity to escape some of the restrictions on the rewards for saving (i.e. the price for deposits, otherwise known as the rate of interest). This broadening of options applied particularly to savers in countries like the United States where very strict regulations, like the Fed's Regulation Q, were imposed during the 1930s as a means of protecting the financial system against any tendency by the banks to use short-term deposits to invest long term, thus reducing their potential liquidity and even perhaps their solvency in any crisis. Escape from these restrictive regulations came about first through the licensing of the Eurodollar market outside the United States – and subsequently other offshore Eurocurrency markets; and secondly, through the effects of inflation on the banks, leading to the invention of new methods of attracting depositors with higher interest rates sufficient to compensate for the eroding effects of inflation on their saving.[1]

For borrowers, too, change brought new options and opportunities. But it also brought new risks through the way in which interest on bank loans in the Eurocurrency market were charged at a price related to LIBOR – the London Inter Bank Offer Rate – which varied with the state of the market. Instead of borrowing by the issue of bonds, in which the risk of change in the current market rate of interest is carried by the bondholder, Eurocurrency loans imposed that risk on the borrower. The result, therefore, of a change in the monetary strategy of the United States at the beginning of the 1980s from a loose inflationary policy to a tight deflationary strategy of monetary targeting immediately resulted in a restriction of the supply of credit and a rise in its price – the real rate of interest. Everyone is familiar with the consequences this had for heavily indebted Latin American and East European governments who found both that the servicing of their Eurobank loans cost them more dearly and that the available supply of new credit had shrunk dramatically. The price, in short, of an extended range of options at the hands of the financial system turned out to be increased vulnerability to the volatilities of capital markets over which they had little control. Integration in one global Eurocurrency banking system also meant that the opportunity, as one might say, to 'take their overdraft across the street' that is, to look to another source of credit when the usual one dried up was taken away from them. Equally, however, the changes in the international financial system from one in which official inter-government loans predominated for developing countries to one in which bank loans predominated meant that the borrowing countries were freed to some extent from politically determined financial vulnerability to the whims of one creditor country. This had been the plight of Tsarist Russia in the nineteenth century and was true in the post-1945 period of such dependents of the United States for official aid as Taiwan or the Philippines. Yet freedom was still not theirs. Instead of the chains to particular national creditors, most developing countries who wanted foreign credit now found themselves chained to the decisions of the International Monetary Fund, without whose seal of approval the commercial banks were unwilling to give them new credit.

For other would-be borrowers, notably large economic enterprises whether publicly or privately owned, the globalization of banking and the innovation of new credit instruments by the banks greatly enlarged the choices they had for the financing of new investments, including investments in the assets of other corporations. The typical business enterprise was freed from dependence on the say-so of banks in its own home state, or to some extent on the state of the stock market in its own home state. Not only was there the Eurobond market through which funds could be raised, there was also the possibility of syndicated Eurocurrency loans, or of innovations like junk bonds which could be marketed on the often dubious promise that the merger or acquisition so financed would be profitable enough to carry the financial costs involved in the bond issue.

For the operators, the big change brought about by the globalization of the financial structure has been the wholesale disappearance of cosy, national cartel arrangements in which governments, in an essentially political bargain, exchanged a measure of protection against unlicensed competition for the acceptance by the operators of restrictions on what they could and could not do, and how they could do it. In some countries like the United States, the restrictions were statutory and legal. In others like Britain they were predominantly customary and unwritten, self-administered by the members of the protected group, whether discount houses or stockbrokers. In yet others, they were a mixture of both forms of regulation. In either case, the system relied on functional fences between the different groups of operators who were not allowed to poach on each other's territory.

The result, obviously, has been a great increase in competition between the operators, raising the stakes for all players of staying in the game. Syndication was one strategy adopted by banks to minimize the risks consequent on their vulnerability to competition. Another was the development, for their own benefit and for that of their customers of markets in all types of futures – forward markets for foreign exchange, futures in commodities, in stock indexes for particular stock markets or for a basket of multinational markets. On the whole, over the last fifteen years or so, such changes have increased the profits made by banks – and the salaries and perks they offer – far above the kind of money made in banking in the 1950s and 1960s. The price of higher profits has been higher risks – to those employed in banking, to the banks as corporate enterprises and, not least, to the governments responsible for their regulation. In the last resort, this has meant that the taxpayers (and holders of government bonds and treasury bills) have had to stand prepared to bail out banks that took risks in the pursuit of profit that they were not really in a position to sustain. As shown by the US government's handling of the Continental Illinois crisis of liquidity in the mid-1980s and more recently of the troubled Savings and Loans, for example, this had had the consequence for governments of making it more difficult to keep to their role of impartial ring holders, applying standard rules to all and avoiding intervention in the market processes so far as possible. Just as borrowing governments found that they had to take over the liability for debts incurred by local authorities, state enterprises and national companies when these were denominated in foreign exchange, so the governments of creditor banks have had to assume new liability for the activities of banks within their jurisdiction which had acted rashly beyond it.

The system was marked in the 1970s and early 1980s by increased volatility of exchange rates, interest rates, oil and other commodity prices. This led both, as already mentioned, to evasive, risk-avoiding action by the operators, and to a preference on their part for short-term transactions or where long-term ones were in demand for the transfer to others or a limitation of their own liability for the consequences of unforeseen developments. Reflecting this risk aversion, the system lowered the transaction costs of short-term operations, and these came to occupy greater prominence in it than long-term ones. A necessary condition for the proliferation of all kinds of short-term transactions has been, of course, the improvement in the systems of communication by which information about the wishes of the parties could be communicated to each other. A large number of short-term deals across frontiers and exchanges requires better systems of communication than a smaller number of long-term deals, even though the total sums involved might be the same. Since the system had changed from a national one with international links added on to a global one with minor local variations in market conditions and state regulations, the communication system necessary and appropriate to the change also had to be swift, efficient and low-cost. It is to the changes in the system of communicating information that we now turn.

Systems of communication

Systems of communications between human beings are differentiated on three levels, or in three ways: by the *mode* of communication; by the *means* of communication; and by the *channels* of communication. The three main modes of communication are by signs, by literate modes, using language and words; and by the numerate mode using numbers. The means of communication can be employed for either literate modes or numerate modes. They include speech, both face-to-face and at a distance as by telephone, and writing both by hand and by various kinds of machine beginning with printing presses and going on to typewriters and computers. The channels of communication are the systems by which speech or writing are transmitted from person to person when these are not face-to-face – whether by pony express or mail coach, by telegraphy cables, by radio transmission, or by geo-orbital satellite. Just listing these leads to a realization of the rapid changes in modes, means and channels which have compressed the globalization of financial markets into such a short space of time.

In the modes of communication, there have been two revolutionary changes: the expansion of the numerate mode over the literate mode through the use of digital systems used in computers; and the spread of one international common language – English – alongside all other national and sub-national languages, as the prevailing mode of communication for international commerce, business, government, science and the professions. In the means of communication, costs have been drastically cut and opportunities enormously expanded by the spread of telephones (and television), of telex and fax machines, and by data networks and other systems by which computers physically distant from each other can communicate, even without the intervention of human operators. These new channels of communication have been so much faster, so much cheaper in terms of unit costs of messages, and so much more reliable and accessible that they have made possible the functioning of global financial markets in which, potentially, all operators are in touch with each other all over the world at all hours of the day or night. Since a market is defined by the possibility of buyers and sellers (and intermediaries) communicating information on demand, supply and price to each other by whatever modes, means or channels, we can see why a leading banker like Walter Wriston has observed that, today, money is information. That is to say, it is not gold, silver or copper, nor yet banknotes, cheques, letters of credit or bills of exchange. It is electronic messages crediting or debiting accounts in computerized recording systems operated by financial institutions. The changes have been made possible only in part by technological progress in means and channels. The willingness to adopt them – to learn English or to operate the new machines – has been powerfully motivated by the demands of commerce and the desire to exploit new opportunities for profit on the part of bankers and financial brokers.

But it would be wrong to suppose that these opportunities opened up by chance. They were opened up by a combination of conscious policy decisions by governments, especially on the regulation of financial markets and banking institutions, and by a production structure – itself, in turn, the creation of politically determined laws and administrative decisions – which was predominantly 'capitalist' (i.e. pro-market) and which therefore was so organized as to encourage and reward technical innovation. The most significant of these policy decisions were those taken by successive postwar governments of the United States. This was because the US was the authority in control of the dominant Top Currency in the world market economy. Despite much mismanagement in the 1960s and 1970s the US managed to hang on to this position in which the dollar was the preferred international medium of exchange and the preferred store of value for governments and for many foreign investors.

It would take too long to describe these decisions in detail. Nor is it necessary to do more than list the main ones since there is an extensive literature in international monetary history that can be referred to (Block 1977; Calleo 1982; Moffitt 1984; Parboni 1981; Strange 1976d; 1986f; Versluysen 1981). One of the first and most important – and deducible more by inference than by reference to any specific act or document – was the decision to liberalize international capital movements by putting pressure on America's allies and dependents to make their currencies freely convertible, to lift exchange controls as soon as possible and to allow free entry to foreign investors. This pressure was exercised generally on the Europeans through the IMF, through the OEEC, and also in bilateral relations, as with Japan. Although inconsistent with the Bretton Woods Articles of Agreement which only provided short-term IMF assistance for deficits on current account, it was part of a much broader US postwar strategy of creating a more open, liberal world market economy than that of the post-depression 1930s. Within this broad strategy, an important complementary non-decision was surely the refusal to take any inhibiting steps against the flight of capital from distressed developing countries when these found themselves caught in difficulties over debt in the 1980s. In the United States, it was implicitly and unthinkingly assumed that the prevention of tidal waves of capital flight was exclusively a problem for the exit countries and that there was no need for the entry countries to take action (Lessard and Williamson 1987; Naylor 1987).

A second, supporting policy decision, for which British consent and connivance was necessary, was to allow the development of London as an alternative location for US banks dealing in Eurodollars that were not counted as part of high-powered money in the US and were therefore not subject to Federal Reserve System rules and restrictions regarding the holding of reserves and the payment of interest on short-term deposits. London then became a kind of adventure playground for British and other European banks as well as American ones to profit from uncontrolled intermediation between dollar depositors and corporate or public borrowers of large Eurocurrency loans. If London had not shown the way for other financial centres, there would be no global network of markets for short-term financial transactions on the vast scale that exists today.

Thirdly, there was the area of domestic bank regulation where state and federal regulators proved unable and/or unwilling to check the slow erosion of New Deal statutes like the Glass–Steagall Act banning interstate banking. This was the protective wall within which banks enjoyed protection against competition from outsiders. This erosion allowed some little local banks to get into dealing in London and New York; the ill-fated Franklin Bank from Long Island that failed in 1974 was such a one (Spero 1980). It also allowed non-banks and investment houses to cross functional frontiers dividing the business they did from that done by others.

A fourth landmark was the US decision in 1975 to allow competitive fixing of fees by stock market dealers. The increased competition for business on Wall Street, both between the established stock exchange members and others, cut profits but also gave an incentive to insider dealing and other practices that once would have been regarded as unprofessional, and which opened the way to the Boesky/Milken affair and other scandals. It also pushed dealers into trying to invade other stock markets, like London, a process of internationalization that not only integrated other stock markets with Wall Street but made it almost impossible for other regulatory systems to avoid change. 'Liberalization' was often a euphemism for unregulated competition in which margins were cut so fine that banks were tempted to take on the risks in financing dubious mergers and takeovers, and highly illiquid property deals. They were motivated to look for any business from rescheduling to consultancy services for which they could charge corporate clients high fees. As one commentator remarked, 'The basic business of banking – borrowing and lending – has become a loss leader for more marginal financial activities.[2]

One of these marginal activities is known by the seemingly anodyne name of 'securitization'. It means that companies now go direct to the market to raise funds without necessarily issuing new shares. Their commercial paper – which is really no more than a short-term IOU – has made them, alongside banks, into creators of credit instruments, and on a very large scale, running into hundreds of billions of dollars in the US alone. Over none of this have the regulatory authorities tried seriously to set limits. And because financial markets worldwide are open to big transnational companies, a Dutch auction of deregulation is set in motion which is clearly going to be hard to stop. Like the abandonment of the fixed exchange rate system it is going to be harder to put Humpty Dumpty together again than it was to let him fall.

What this adds up to is the dissolution of a series of national banking cartels – in the United States, in Britain, in Australia and to a lesser extent in other countries like Germany, France and Italy. In each country, the banks 'paid' the national monetary authorities for their sheltered market with obedience to prudential rules limiting how much credit they could create, in what form and for whose benefit. Having conceded the principle of freedom for capital movements under pressure from the United States – the Europeans in the 1950s and the Japanese, more reluctantly, in the 1960s – neither found it so easy by the 1980s to insulate their systems of bank regulation and control over credit creation from the competitive influence of the American system. Moreover, because financial innovations like CDs (Certificates of Deposit) or junk bonds are not like new machines or new pharmaceuticals which can be patented or otherwise protected against imitators, there was nothing to stop these financial innovations spreading from one financial centre to another where many of the same major banks were also players.

In all these changes, the improvement and standardization of modes, means and channels of communication have played an enormously important part. Although not a sufficient condition for the rapid creation of a globally integrated financial structure, it is abundantly clear to all the operators that they were a very necessary condition. They confirm that none of the changes would have happened so fast, nor would the integration of national economies into one interdependent financial structure have been completed so quickly without the improvements in the communication links between players and between physically distant markets.

Structural and relational power

So much for the contributory causes of financial integration. As to the consequences, it seems fairly obvious that the structural power of the United States to change the options open to other governments, to foreign banks and trading corporations has been vastly increased. This is so whether or not on any specific issue the power has been exercised with the intention of producing particular effects. In the United States, this consequence has been somewhat obscured by the quite corect perception by Americans that their options, too, have been restricted and that market forces have on certain issues become more powerful than the wishes of policymakers. While this is not untrue, the fact is that they are hoist with their own petard: the liberalization, privatization and deregulation that brought about this vulnerability to market forces was in large part of their own doing.

Conversely, it is logical to conclude that it is they – US presidents and Congress – who have the power if anyone has to reverse the process and tip the balance of power back again from market to state.

By far the most important consequence of financial integration for other governments has been the accelerated change in the nature of the competitive game between states. Every one has become aware in the space of little more than a decade of the imperative necessity of acquiring a more or less secure share in one or another sector of the world maket without losing too large a share to others of its own domestic market. The freedom produced by the open, relatively unregulated financial system for national residents to shift wealth out of the country or to incur debts in foreign currencies has landed national governments with increased vulnerability to balance of payments deficits for which they, and not the private persons or enterprises who may have create the problem, are held politically responsible. The responsibility is both to the foreign creditors and trade partners and politically to the voters or political groups in the country who will object by any means available to the consequences of govenments' failures to correct such deficits. There may be increased inflation if currency depreciation raises the price of imported goods without a corresponding expansion of exports. Or there may be a reduction of government spending on welfare or subsidies in accord with recommendations of the IMF. Or there may be a tightening of bureaucratic controls over industry and trade which is held to slow and hinder enterprise and growth. To avoid all these unpleasant pressures, governments cannot help but adjust the order of political priorities – their agendas, or policy targets – in pursuit of world market shares. Instead of competing for the security gained by possession of territory or of access to supplies of raw materials, sources of energy or basic industrial outputs like steel, chemicals or textiles (preferably by having all these located within the territorial frontiers of the state), the state's need for foreign exchange forces it to compete for market shares. It can rarely succeed in this game by itself as a direct participant in the market. Hence, the wholesale privatization of state enterprises in many countries. A state is obliged to seek allies in the world of enterprise, whether local or foreign, who will help achieve this new priority objective. Politicians fomerly bitterly critical of foreign multinationals have everywhere swallowed their prejudices and suspicions and stood ready to negotiate deals with them which will either save on imports or add to exports.

This almost universal shift in attitudes to foreign investors which has marked the middle years of the 1980s in countries as far apart as Tunisia, Malaysia, Ecuador, Turkey and Canada has not taken place in response to the preaching of monetarist economists. It has taken place mostly because of the changes in risks and opportunities consequent on the globalization of finance. The same process has made the economies of many more countries much more vulnerable than they were in the 1960s to slower growth in the world economy. The caveat, 'provided there is no recession in the world economy' has been the constant refrain of every economic report by the major international economic organizations in recent years. That is one heightened vulnerability to which all are susceptible. Another, of course, is vulnerability to the competitive efforts of others to take market shares for themselves. In the summer of 1988, for instance, it was reported that tourist numbers in the Greek islands were down by about 30 per cent on the previous year. Coincidentally, Turkey reported a payments surplus for 1988 largely thanks to a 40 per cent rise in foreign exchange earned from tourism. Again, in South-east Asia, the competition for help from Japanese companies engaged in electronics pits the efforts of the Malaysian government against that of Thailand or Singapore. The market-share game is necessarily a zero-sum one at any given moment of time. More jobs for auto workers in Sao Paulo or Tijuana means fewer for workers in Detroit or Wolfsburg.

Here, of course, is the paradox: that US strategies for global financial integration have pulled other states and their economies further into involvement with the world market economy. This has enlarged opportunities for American providers of financial and other services; but at the same time, the deliberate creation of a open world economy in the image of the USA has inadvertently restricted opportunities for bluecollar workers in the United States.[3] The fact that national strategies, as in war, sometimes have consequences unforeseen by their creators does not mean that the latter are powerless, only that they cannot always see into the future, or forecast the full costs as well as the benefits of their chosen strategies.[4]

Similarly, the power to exploit others, whether the exploitation is primarily economic or political, is not inconsistent with the possibility that taking advantage of that power will ricochet back on its possessors to their ultimate disadvantage. If the British had not had the privileges of a reserve role for sterling in the 1960s, they would have devalued earlier, been less tempted to play stop–go with the economy and adjusted better and more promptly to their reduced status. And if the United States had not enjoyed the super-exorbitant privileges of the post-1973 paper dollar standard, free of even the slender restraints of the gold-exchange standard, they would never have been able to increase government spending and the budget deficit to the point where they were impaled on the horns of the dilemma of two deficits – where correcting one was apt to exacerbate the problem with the other.

The point applies particularly to the US budget deficit as an indicator of structural power exercised through the financial structure. The damage which the build-up of this deficit has done must not obscure the fact that no other country was in so favourable a position that it could draw so heavily on other people's savings to finance its own overspending.

Most of these savings have come, as we all know, from Japan. In 1980, 34 per cent of a total capital outflow from Japan amounting to US$10.8 billion went to the United States. By 1987, the outflow had grown by a factor of more than 12 to US$133.4 billion, and 46 per cent of it was going to the United States. If that outflow had gone instead to the high-growth developing countries, whether in the form of loans or direct investment; or to slower-growing less developing countries in the form of grant aid, who can doubt that Third World debtors would have been spared seven very lean, hard years, and that average growth rates for the whole world economy would have been a great deal better. But this global Keynesian solution for the world economy has been prevented primarily by the conscious neglect or indifference of US politicians – and, it would seem, of US voters, to judge by the 1988 election campaigns – to the US budget deficit. Neither Republicans nor most Democrats were prepared even to contemplate such obvious remedies as tax incentives for personal savers – which might at least have financed some government spending by US residents instead of foreigners, thus sparing the balance of payments – or, as suggested by *The Economist* on several occasions, the imposition of a tax on petrol. Even a tax of 50 cents a gallon would have cut the deficit by a third – and, incidentally would have allowed interest rates world-wide to fall.[5]

The high cost of servicing that national debt, in short, must be seen as a self-inflicted burden. International monetary history since the middle 1960s has demonsrated again and again the dominant effect of US policies and the state of the US economy on the upward or downward direction of interest rates world-wide. To take only two examples from the present decade, the changeover in US policy to monetary targeting which was begun under President Carter and completed by President Reagan standing firm behind Paul Volcker at the Fed was a monetary shot that echoed round the world. Interest rates shot up as the global market responded to rising demand from governments and corporations combined with a shrunken supply by raising the price. The second instance was in 1987, when on two occasions, the markets came close to losing confidence in the dollar. Twice, it was calmed by a show of collective central bank determination and market intervention, and reassured when higher interest rates in the US made it unlikely that the private capital inflow would dry up.

Nor, it must be pointed out, are the Japanese under any illusion about the extent of American structural power in matters of finance. I would quote, for instance, the conclusions of two excellent recent volumes on the political economy of Japan by a distinguished team of Japanese and some American scholars (Inoguchi and Okimoto 1988; Yamamura and Yasuba 1988). These make it clear that recent changes in the Japanese financial system were triggered by market responses to US monetary strategies, strongly reinforced by direct government-to-government pressures.

Partly because of economic pressures and partly because of political pressures (which culminated in the US–Japan financial agreement) the Japanese financial system has been, and will continue to be, liberalized more speedily than anyone a few years ago expected. This is especially true of its international aspects (Shinkai 1988: 268).

The same author concluded a detailed account of the internationalization of finance in Japan by noting that the more or less enforced liberalization was bound to have significant effects on the profits of Japanese banks and financial institutions. Increased competition, he thought, would tend to produce increased volatility of interest rates in sharp contrast to their customary (i.e. postwar) stability. This change alone, as noted by Shinkai, had led to a major change in the financial behaviour of Japanese households and enterprises.

The share of firms' portfolios invested in instruments with market-determined interest rates (CDs, bonds, foreign currency deposits) rose from 10 per cent in 1978 and 63 per cent in 1985. In household portfolios, the share of bank deposits whose interest rates are regulated declined from 63 per cent in 1981 to 11 per cent in 1985, when computed in incremental terms (Shinkai 1988: 264).

Precisely the same points about the combined effect of US–Japanese negotiations and market forces giving Japan no option but to adjust to liberalizing trends initiated in the United States is repeated by Koichi Hamada and Akiyoshi Horiuchi in their chapter for the first volume, 'The Political Economy of the Financial Market'. They note the importance of technological progress in electronic communication as a necessary factor facilitating transnational financial transactions. They also conclude that the internationalization of Japanese business finance will promote interest rate arbitrage between domestic and foreign capital markets and that this will make it difficult for monetary authorities to regulate domestic interest rates. It can do nothing else, as they say, 'lest Japanese financial institutions and businesses be barred from foreign capital markets, which will become increasingly important as their spheres of activities broaden'. Since Japanese banks now dominate the list of the Top Ten in terms of assets and turnover, this is an important observation (Yamamura and Yasuba 1988: 256–60).

Japanese relational power

Thus, though Americans may be worrying about their possible vulnerability in future to Japanese investors' taste for, and confidence in, dollar assets, the Japanese have already felt and recognized their vulnerability at the hands of American structural power. Whatever the future may hold, there is little or no evidence that the Japanese as yet share in this form of power. Two important indicators are the international use of the Yen, and the percentages of Japanese trade invoiced in Yen. As of 1986, Yen holdings still amounted to only 7.6 per cent of the world reserves, and of Eurocurrency deposts only 2.3 per cent were denominated in Yen. Even Yen loans constituted only a meagre 5.5 per cent of 1985 totals. And in trade, where many industries in the United States are protected from exchange rate risks by invoicing in dollars both for exports and imports, Japanese industry has minimal protection; in 1986, only 10 per cent of Japanese imports were invoiced in Yen, and only a little more than a third (36.5 per cent) of Japan's exports. Such lack of two important bases of financial autonomy leaves only two remaining ways in which Japan might influence the financial structure. One would be to act through international economic organizations. The other would be to take an independent line on international debt.

Combining the two, Japan did make a tentative move at the 1988 Toronto summit meeting to initiate more positive action on debt. But when this was rejected by the United States, Japan submitted to *force majeure*. Japan has also tried – but unsuccessfully – to use its major creditor status to justify more power for itself in decision-making in the Asian Development Bank. Once again, its initiative was stonewalled by the United States (Ogata 1988). In the larger organizations like the IMF and the World Bank, it may also have been handicapped in building bureaucratic support by a certain unwillingness in Tokyo to see talented Japanese make long-term career commitments outside the country. But that factor alone does not account for the failure of Japan to influence important policy decisions in the IMF, for instance. The Fund officials are convinced of the necessity of increasing its capital base by 50 per cent. The Japanese – and the Europeans – are agreed that this would help put a cushion under the whole financial structure and not just under distressed debtor countries. But Mr Brady, armed with the weighted veto of the United States, blocked the way. It seems generally agreed that the American obstruction was not a little motivated by the fact that, if the expansion were agreed, Japan would move from fifth to second place, behind the US in the weighted voting system.

In principle, there would be nothing to stop Japan using its power as a major creditor and source of finance in the future by diverting part of its surplus to the debtor countries. This it has promised to do in some small measure to Latin America and now in 1990 to Eastern Europe. But it dare not divert more than a fraction of its capital outflow away from the United States for fear of the effect which that might have on the dollar exchange rate. A devalued dollar would mean either increased competition for Japanese industries in world markets or preventive increases in interest rates with unavoidable repercussions domestically affecting the stability of the national financial system. In practice, therefore, this is not a serious option on a scale sufficient to wrest structural power away from the United States. What it confers is the rather double-edged relational power of an aid donor over its beneficiaries. From an economic point of view, this is not insignificant as shown by the 1983 US$4 billion 'reparation' loan by Japan to South Korea. This timely assistance to a country then high on the list of major candidates for default on foreign debt was undoubtedly of substantial interest to the many Japanese enterprises with joint-venture operations in Korea. Now, those same Japanese multi-nationals have extended operations in Malaysia, Thailand, Indonesia and the Philippines, in addition of course to Taiwan. Japanese official support will surely help at least some of these 'little Asian dragons' to expand their world market shares.

In a speech in July 1988, the Japanese foreign minister, Sousuke Uno, made an explicit connection between Japan's decision to massively increase its foreign aid, especially aid to ASEAN countries, and its interest in stimulating and upgrading economic growth in that region. 'In 1987', Uno reported, 'Japan's imports of manufactured goods from the ASEAN countries rose 48 per cent over the previous year'. To encourage this trend, he went on, 'we expanded our GSP quota ceilings for mineral and industrial goods last April. We also intend to continue cooperating on import promotion with the ASEAN Promotion Centre on Trade, Investment and Tourism' (Uno 1988). In June 1988, Japan determined to double its budget for foreign aid for the five years to 1992 as compared with the previous five years, and with an annual aid budget of US$50 billion expected to become the world's largest aid donor as well as its largest creditor. In a pre-election visit to Europe in January 1990 Prime Minister Kaifu promised more aid than the United States – nearly US$1 billion – to Poland and Hungary. As with Korea, there was a strong Japanese interest both for the state and for major Japanese corporate investors in helping the growth of domestic markets as a base not only for local-for-local production but also as an export platform to third countries. Financial resources, in short, could be used to win a circle of friends well-disposed to Japanese companies competing for world market shares. But the aid to Eastern Europe would not gain as much influence over events there as that of either of the two superpowers, although the Asian countries would perhaps constitute a prosperous regional bloc over which Japan could exercise some bilateral leverage when and if that were necessary. It would not

Table 6.1 Japanese aid and investment by area, in 1986 (in million US$)

| | Official aid | Private investment* | | |
		Direct	Indirect	Total
Asia	2.588	526	3.115	3.432
M. East	94	–124	6.9	–114
S. Asia	1.075	10	246	256
E. Asia	1.415	639	2.862	3.289
South America	160	40	421	452
N & Central America	156	2.554	694	3.196
Europe	73	–14	795	765
Africa	593	8.3	433	132
Other	276	–5.8	–1	–13
Total	3.846	3.093	5.457	7.965

* Indirect Investment includes shares in local enterprises bought by Japanese banks and corporations. Total of Private flows also includes export credits.
Source: Japan Statistical Yearbook 1988.

always guarantee their compliance with Japanese national or corporate interests –
as all the history of foreign aid and international relations amply demonstrates.
But on some issues and for some purposes it might help. This sort of limited
influence I would characterize as relational power. Tables 6.1, 6.2, 6.3 and 6.4 show
the increase in Japanese official aid, and in private investment through, particularly,
the purchase of shares in local enterprises and joint ventures, and the concentration of both in East Asia.

Table 6.2   Japanese financial flows to LDCs (in US$ million)

	1970	1980	1986	1987
Total ODA	*458*	*3.304*	*5.634*	*5.248*
Bilateral, of which	372	1.961	3.846	5.076
Grants	121	653	1.703	2.221
Loans	250	1.308	2.143	2.855
Multilateral	87	1.343	1.788	2.207
Other (including export credits)	694	1.478	–724	–1.808
Total Private	*669*	*1.958*	*9.817*	*16.987*
Export credits	387	74	237	n.a.
Foreign direct investment	265	906	2.902	
Portfolio investments	265	660	5.315	13.643
International investments	18	318	1.326	n.a.
Non-profit organizations	3	26	82	n.a.
Total	1.824	6.766	14.808	22.726

Note: The Japanese 1987 total compares with a US gross resource flow to DAC countries of $13,193 million
for W. Germany of $8,843 million.

Sources: Japan Statistical Yearbook, 1988, Kaizai Koho Centre, 1989.

Table 6.3   Net official development assistance from DAC countries to developing countries
and multilateral agencies: net disbursements (1975–87) (US$ million, except as indicated)

	1975–77 Average	1985	1986	Share of GNP (%) 1987	Share of GNP (%) 1975–77	1987	Share of total (%) 1975–77	Share of total (%) 1987
USA	4.401	9.403	9.564	8.776	0.25	0.20	30.9	21.3
Japan	1.226	3.797	5.634	7.453	0.21	0.31	8.6	18.1
France	2.168	5.578	5.105	6.600	0.60	0.75	14.8	16.0
Germany, FR	1.666	2.942	3.832	4.433	0.36	0.39	12.0	10.8
Italy	202	1.098	2.403	2.427	0.10	0.32	1.6	5.9
Netherlands	748	1.136	1.740	2.094	0.79	0.98	4.5	5.1
UK	968	1.530	1.750	1.887	0.40	0.28	6.5	4.6
Canada	919	1.631	1.695	1.880	0.50	0.46	6.3	4.6
Sweden	651	840	1.090	1.337	0.84	0.85	4.0	3.2
Norway	232	574	798	891	0.74	1.10	1.6	2.2
DAC, total	14.519	29.429	36.653	41.219	0.34	0.34	100.0	100.0

Source: OECD, *Development Co-operation, 1987,* Press Release 17 June 1988.

Table 6.4   Comparison of resource flows by type from DAC[a] countries (1986) (US$ million)

	USA	Japan	France	Germany FR	Italy	UK	DAC total
Official Development Assistance (ODA)	9.564	5.634	5.105	3.832	2.403	1.750	36.678
Bilateral ODA	7.602	3.846	4.162	2.642	1.487	1.022	26.228
Grants & grant-like contributions	7.033	1.703	3.177	1.799	1.211	1.102	21.061
Technical Assistance	1.606	599	1.975	1.230	412	405	7,409
Development lending & Capital	569	2.143	985	844	275	−80	5,167
New Developing lending	−226	2.038	876	534	268	−83	3,829
Multilateral institutions[b]	1.962	1.788	943	1.189	917	727	10.450
UN agencies	631	349	109	176	125	116	2,688
Other Official Flows (OOF)	−559	−724	955	1.135	772	333	2.124
Official export credits	−1.787	−858	–	366	−29	−13	−2.228
Grants by private voluntary agencies	1.753	82	84	545	11	191	3.328
Private flows at market terms	1.344	9.817	3.031	2.378	−620	5.080	22.988
Investment	2.722	9.543	2.228	1.852	263	4.912	23.813
Resource flows, total	12.102	14.808	9.176	7.889	2.566	7.353	65.127

[a]   The Development Assistance Committee (DAC) is one of the specialized committees of the OECD: DAC members include Australia, Austria, Belgium, Denmark, Finland, Ireland, New Zealand, Norway, Sweden, Switzerland and the Commission of EC, as well as countries shown above.

[b]   Contributions to ...

Conclusion

This disparity in power in the field of finance between the United States and Japan is one strong reason why what Gilpin calls the *nichibei* solution to global economic disorder (i.e. a US–Japan condominium) is unrealistic (1987: 336–9). Japanese power in finance is relational only whereas that of the United States is structural. The process of equalization if it ever happens will take a long time and would involve radical reform of the international economic organizations over which the US still has constitutional veto power. It would also involve some reassertion of regulatory power over national banking systems which at present seems merely fanciful.

Another equally strong reason takes us back to the question of communications and information. It will be some time, if ever it happens, before the numerate mode of communication totally displaces the literate mode. Within that mode, it seems as though the international use of English as *lingua franca* has now gone too far to be reversed. Japanese, meanwhile, remains a minority language even for Asians. As Kindleberger remarked many years ago, there is much in common between the international use of the dollar and the international use of the English language. Each is even more unassailable today than when he made the comparison in 1967 (Kindleberger 1967).

By way of postscript to the above, I would add my conviction that our priority problematic as students of international political economy for as far ahead as it is possible to see is *not* how to get governments to coordinate their economic policies, nor yet how to reform the international monetary system through regime changes. Rather it is to see how to persuade people and politicians in the United States to use the hegemonic, structural power they still have in a more enlightened and consistent way. To do so, as Jacques Rueff (1972) saw over fifteen years ago, would also be in the long-term interest of the Americans.

7
'The Structure of Finance in the World System', 1994

G-20
F30

Finance – the provision of money in the form of credit – is the life-blood of any capitalist economy. None of the capitalist countries could have grown in wealth as they have done without making use of money. Not only was money needed as a medium of exchange for current transactions; it was also necessary to have it as a store of value, enabling purchasing power to be borrowed, for money to be used as credit. By this means, the savings made in one part of the economy or by one group of people could be temporarily 'bought' by other people who wanted to invest it in other parts of the economy. Only thus could essentially risky but potentially productive enterprises be started up so that the wealth and total product of the system could grow.

A market economy of any kind, including the new worldwide one, cannot exist without a competitive market for capital and credit. Such a market will call into existence enterprises devoted to the competitive marketing of credit – borrowed money in all its forms. Some of this credit will result from the intermediation by such enterprises between the savers and the would-be borrowers. But it will result from their power to *create* credit – something Marxists who use the term 'capital accumulation' (as though they were talking about squirrels storing up nuts) find it hard to conceptualize. Credit is created whenever the ratio between the savers' deposits and the borrowers' loans exceeds 1:1; that is, when the banks lend more than they have taken as deposits on the usually safe assumption that not all their depositors will want their money back on the same day. From the very beginnings of banking in the Middle Ages, this was the essence of banking, that more was lent than was deposited.

This point is important in order to establish the basic fact, central to the argument of this paper, that a capitalist economy cannot function effectively without the aid of banks to create, as well as to allocate, credit. It simply cannot function any other way, even though the governments of market economies may decide not to supplant but to supplement the market for credit with state banks, or with state-financed international organizations that will exist side-by-side with commercial competitive banks.

The essential difference, therefore, between a capitalist economy (in the generally accepted meaning of the word) and a socialist economy is that, although in the socialist economy credit is available, it is available *only* on the say-so of the state (or party) and *only* from state-run institutions, whereas in the capitalist economy it is made available through a market. Thus, it is possible to have industrialization and economic growth through state capitalism; but we have seen the results in the former socialist economies of the former Soviet bloc. The experience suggests that, by comparison with the market system, it is infinitely more wasteful and less flexible and has failed to satisfy the material demands of the people.

In his 1994 book, Professor Sakamoto has correctly identified the globalization of capitalism as a key element in the changing world order. The present essay seeks to explain in simple terms why and how the structure of finance plays such a crucial role in this globalization of capitalism. In order to do so, it was necessary from the first to explain in a rather basic way what is meant by a structure of finance; to explain, in short, that we are talking about a market-based mechanism for the creation of credit and a set of institutions and enterprises set up by governments to monitor and regulate the price relations between national monies, i.e. currencies.

That it has been necessary to do so is the result of some widespread confusion about the close relationship between the *international monetary regime* and *international financial markets*. Together, they may be said to form the international financial structure. The international monetary system – if system it must be called – consists of the arrangements between states for the management of relations between their respective national currencies, in other words, of exchange rates and related matters. Yet even these are not solely within the command of governments; international markets can upset the decisions and agreements of governments. Conversely, international financial markets could not exist without governments, and are subject to whatever rules and restrictions that states may impose upon them. The financial structure, therefore, may be defined as the sum of all the arrangements and institutions governing the availability of credit *plus* all the arrangements and factors determining the terms on which currencies – units of account – are exchanged for one another.

On the whole, it is the latter that has dominated the literature of international political economy. Because there was set up after World War II an institution, the International Monetary Fund (IMF), backed by articles of agreement (usually referred to as the Bretton Woods 'regime'), which aspired to lay down rules about these monetary relations and the management of exchange rates, much more attention has been paid by scholars to this development than to the financial markets. Economists in particular have produced a large literature on the Bretton Woods system and the IMF. And since the early 1970s, when the United States decided it no longer liked the fixed exchange rate rules, they have produced another large set of writings about the pros and cons of fixed and floating exchange rates. In the 1980s, yet another large body of literature has existed on the problems, and the experience, of governments in coordinating their monetary policies so as to stabilize (as far as they can) the movement of exchange rates. In Europe especially, where since the early 1970s there have been repeated attempts to negotiate arrangements among the member states of the European Community (EC) that would bring them closer to a monetary union and permanently fixed rates, the debate about monetary union has engaged a lot of academic work as well as the pages of newspapers and journals.

Clearly, this international monetary system, which is dominated by the major national currencies such as the dollar, D-mark and yen and watched over by the finance ministers of the Group of Seven (G7) major industrialized market economies, cannot be separated from, and is intimately related to, developments in the international financial markets. Obviously, if one of the seven governments decides to borrow – or itself to create – a lot of credit in order to go to war or in other ways to expand its money supply, this will have some impact on the global financial structure. It will also affect its relations with other governments in the G7 and thus may have an effect on the international monetary system. And if market operators (banks, for example) decide to cease lending to an indebted government, then that government's relations with the governments of its creditors, and with international organizations like the International Monetary Fund or the World Bank, are suddenly transformed into relations of greater dependency.

The financial structure in the world economy can thus be visualized as a hybrid of states and markets, a halfway house between, on the one hand, the realist conception of separate national societies, surviving on more or less discrete national economies and governed by the political institutions of nation-states, and, on the other, the financiers' and bankers' perception of a single global market for monies and credit instruments and for financial services. In the former, it is state frontiers that matter. In the latter, the most significant divisions in the market are set by the different times that the sun rises and people start work, and that the sun sets and they go home. Between the international monetary system, where it seems as though national governments are the chief actors, and the financial markets, where the decisions of debtors and creditors and their intermediaries seem more decisive, there is a significant difference in the democratic dimension. National governments may be directly subject to popular interests and pressures, whereas in financial markets democratic principles take second place to supply and demand and the vagaries of the markets. And whereas the monetary system is largely a matter for negotiation between governments – of state–state diplomacy – the financial structure is largely a matter of political authority over markets and market operators – of state–firm relationships and bargaining.

This may be one reason why many scholars in international political economy have found international finance difficult to analyse. Most of them were trained in international (i.e. inter-state) relations. They were brought up to think – and for some it is almost an article of faith – that the state is the basic unit of the international system. Political economy in the world system, for many of them, was therefore taken to mean the study of relations between states with reference to matters of money, trade, and (less often) investment. Only a few scholars for one reason or another have shown much interest in the political economy of inter-national finance (Frieden, 1987; Kindleberger, 1978). Though their number is growing, it has to be admitted that most of the contributions to the literature on the subject have come from journalists (or ex-journalists like Fred Hirsch and Andrew Shonfield) or from expert advisers to banks, governments, or international organizations (most notably Robert Triffin but also Jacques Polak, Robert Solomon, etc.). It is paradoxical that international trade, which has proved extraordinarily vulnerable to the self-defensive policies of states, should have been so exhaustively studied by international political economists, whereas international finance, which is rather exceptionally vulnerable to the decisions, or non-decisions, of national monetary authorities, has been comparatively neglected.

That vulnerability makes all the more necessary an examination of the changes in the international financial structure that have taken place since about 1960. This, together with a brief summary of changes in the international monetary system, will form the main part of this essay. However, I will conclude by considering, from an international political economy point of view, the consequences and implications of these changes, first, for the world system as a whole, rather than for individual nation-states, and for the basic values expressed through that system; and, secondly, for people, for the various social and economic groups in world society. In this way, I hope to have something relevant to say concerning Professor Sakamoto's concern for the democratic aspects of world order.

Changes in world finance

Changes in the global financial structure in recent decades can be considered under five main headings:

(1) the system has *grown* enormously in size, in the number and value of transactions conducted in it, in the number and economic importance of the markets and the market operators;

(2) the *technology* of finance has changed as fast as the technology in any manu-facturing or productive sector in the world economy;

(3) the global system has *penetrated* national systems more deeply and effectively than ever before – though some people are apt to retort that there is nothing new in international banking or international debt, the degree to which both have played a growing part in national economics and societies is quite new;

(4) the provision and marketing of credit have become overall a much less regulated and a much *more competitive* business than it used to be when national systems were less integrated in the global system; and, not least,

(5) the *relation of demand for and the supply of credit* has changed rather radically, with very large implications for the world political economy and for the material prospects of many social groups and social institutions in the future.

Size

No one who knows anything about international finance is in any doubt that it has grown rather phenomenally in the last quarter-century. There is, however, the problem of measurement and, connected with it, the problem of definition. The numbers that are available are only rough indicators, not precise indices. Here are a few of them:

- Transactions in the Eurocurrency markets had risen to over US$1,000 billion – 1 trillion – in the year 1984, compared with US$75 billion in 1970 and only US$3 billion in the nearly 1960s.
- Trading in the foreign exchange markets worldwide in the late 1980s amounted to over US$600 billion *a day*, no less than 32 times the volume of international commercial transactions worldwide.
- Between the mid-1960s and the mid-1980s, international banking grew at a compound rate of 26 per cent a year on average, compared with an average growth rate in international trade of 12.5 per cent and an average growth in output of a little over 10 per cent.
- The issue of bonds is a credit instrument traditionally associated with international finance since the last century. Equal in value to 2 per cent of world exports in 1980, their total value had risen to 9 per cent of world exports by 1985 and they have continued to grow in popularity since. ECU-dominated bond issues, which totalled ECU 1.9 billion in 1982, totalled nearly ECU 17 billion in 1988.
- Transnational trading in shares was comparatively rare even by 1980. Most national stock exchanges dealt only in the shares of nationally registered companies within the state. By 1989, more than 18 per cent of all share trading was in the shares of foreign corporations – only the major multinationals.

Among the significant numbers, we should also note the growth of trading in futures and options in some of the main international financial centres like London, Paris and Frankfurt. For they reflect not only the growing transnational nature of international finance but also the rise in the perceived risks involved in it. Futures and options are the hedging devices that allow traders and investors to offset the risks inseparable from one financial transaction by buying/selling options or futures contracts on the opposite price movement. The London International Financial Futures Exchange (LIFFE), for example, was started only in 1982. Its turnover by 1991 reached over 38 million contracts. Its French rival, MATIF (Marché à Terme Internationale de France), in the same year traded 37 million contracts, and the German Terminborse (DTB), which opened only in 1990, already traded 15.4 million contracts the next year.

These are only rather rough indicators of both change and growth in international finance. To anyone in the business of banking and finance, it is obvious that the international (or global) financial structure coexists with a lot of national financial structures, some parts of which remain more or less unchanged and are affected only indirectly by developments in international finance. Each overlaps to some extent – for example, when commercial 'High Street' banks also engage in international transactions. Thus, there is no clear dividing line between the two, and some national systems remain much more insulated than others (see below).

So much for measurement. As for the definition of what is meant by international financial structure, that, too, is not easy. We cannot identify some institutions as belonging to it while others are outside. Nor can we define some markets as being purely national, while others are integrated in the global structure. So long as people or companies place deposits in foreign banks, or pension fund managers buy shares in foreign companies, the dividing line between the two is blurred. The fact is that the international financial structure is a sort of hybrid, a halfway house between a completely integrated worldwide structure and a totally unintegrated collection of national structures.

What we are analysing though is clear enough. It is the part of the credit-creating mechanism, and the part of the market for financial assets, that is integrated with others across national frontiers. In that structure, market forces are beyond the total control of any single national government. Indeed, with the notable exception of the United States, most governments have very little influence over it. Their vulnerability to its changing character, its volatilities, and the new risks it brings, however, is only too acutely felt.

By way of illustration, we may say that the market for foreign exchange is globally integrated. The price of dollars in yen – and indeed in gold – is virtually uniform everywhere at any given moment. Only where exchange controls have created pockets of black, or illegal, markets for foreign exchange are there local differences. Similarly, the acknowledgement of the London Inter-Bank Offer Rate (LIBOR) for Eurocurrency loans as a standard benchmark for prices worldwide – just as Brent Crude or the Middle East posted price for Saudi Arabian light are benchmarks for oil prices – shows that this part of the mechanism belongs in the global structure. The same is true for the international bond market and for some but not all equities, or shares. The big multinationals' shares are traded on all the major stock markets. The shares in other small firms may be traded only on their local bourses. (The fact that, on most local stock exchanges, the shares of national enterprises are more numerous than those of the multinationals explains why daily movements in the index of share prices are often larger in some centres than in others or even move in opposite directions.)

By and large, the numbers seem to indicate that transactions in the global financial structure are growing faster than are those in local, national structures. They have also tended to be the least regulated ever since the early days of the Eurodollar market back in the 1960s. If trends are extrapolated, this suggests that the unregulated, or underregulated, part of the market will eventually overtake the regulated part.

Technology

The technology of international finance has changed very rapidly in the last two or three decades in two ways; mechanically, and in the nature of the goods and services traded.[1] Banking used to employ hundreds of clerks, entering figures in ledgers by hand. Now, the transactions are registered automatically, through integrated computer systems, communicating with each other by satellites. They are also executed mechanically, by automatic monetary transfer systems (AMTS).

One central clearing system in New York – CHIPS – handles all dollar and Eurodollar transfers between banks in the USA. And whereas markets used to operate by personal contact and negotiation, most deals nowadays are concluded by telephone or telefax or through computers. The London Stock Exchange is being revolutionized by the introduction of TAURUS, an automatic system of share transfers that does away with the need for buyers and sellers to meet face-to-face. By these means, financial transactions are concluded in real time. The pace of change in market moods and trends is accordingly accelerated out of all recognition. October 1987 demonstrated how panic, or near-panic, could spread around the globe in a matter of hours.

Some of this mechanical innovation has had important consequences for the efficacy of national bank regulation. But it has probably been less important than the less visible and less tangible innovations of new credit instruments, new ways in which funds can be deposited with banks, new ways in which funds can be borrowed, or new services provided by financial institutions. All these are the result of looser regulation by authorities over financial operators, and of increased competition between them for profits from banking.[2] The first significant step in deregulation, it is generally agreed, was the permission accorded to US banks to deal in Eurodollars – that is, funds denominated in dollars but held in bank branches outside the territorial United States. The story is well known and need not be repeated here. Although the Eurodollar market looked like – and was – an innovative device thought up by inventive bankers, it could have come into being only with the permission of the US and British governments; the one allowed offshore dealings to go on free of US bank rules, and the other allowed dollar dealings to go on free of British rules and regulations (Strange 1976d).[3]

The same is true of many of the other innovations in financial practice in recent years. In the 1930s, US banks in the Federal Reserve System were not allowed to pay more than nominal interest on short-term deposits. By the 1970s, these rules had been relaxed and customers could put their spare cash on the money market, earning high interest rates for short periods. Similarly in Britain, the old system of a strict separation of function between stockbrokers and stockjobbers, between commercial banks and investment or merchant banks and discount houses, reinforced self-administered rules on banks' behaviour. In the 1970s, from NOW (negotiable order of withdrawal) accounts and Money Market Funds, banks progressed to the creation of 'junk bonds' to finance corporate mergers and take-overs. The practice became well known when one of the US banks that had pioneered the issue of junk bonds, Drexel Lambert, got into trouble with the authorities and was the subject of criminal investigations. After that came the growing practice of 'securitization', which in plain terms really meant the issue by banks of 'commercial paper', i.e. loans to corporations on fixed terms, usually better than those given to shareholders. According to a recent survey of banking, the practice is now spreading to Europe and Japan.[4] As Enkyo (1990) had observed earlier, it is hard for either not to follow a lead in financial innovation in the United States. And the next step in the United States was the creation of a secondary market in what are called C and I (commercial and industrial) loans. Sales of these increased tenfold between 1983 and 1989, when no fewer than US$290 billion were sold in the third quarter of that year. No wonder a Brookings study observed, 'The mass production of credit ... has become the Trojan horse of the American banking system.'[5]

Penetration

The signs of the increasing penetration of national financial markets by the global ones are visible in the financial district of any large city. The passerby can see the nameplates of foreign banks side-by-side with local ones. No major international bank fails to have its offices in at least half a dozen of the biggest financial centres like New York, Tokyo, London, Frankfurt, Toronto, Sydney, Hong Kong, Paris, or São Paolo, not to mention the tax havens in Luxembourg and the Caribbean. Although some countries, especially developing ones, limit the business of foreign banks to foreign trade and investment, the barriers to entry of foreign competitors are gradually crumbling. American banks deal in London in British government securities. Some European banks do business in the United States. More important, perhaps, than this visible sign of penetration is the evidence that local financial markets all around the world market economy are shaken or encouraged by the same world events. This could be seen in their response to such news as the 19 August 1991 coup in Moscow or the start and finish of the Gulf War. The events in themselves may have little direct effect on market conditions, but there is no doubt about their power to affect the mood of market operators. It is proof enough that national financial markets are being invaded, or submerged, by global markets.

Competition

As noted earlier, financial innovation has loosened the grip of national regulatory systems; and interpenetration has brought newcomers in to join local competitors. The point is important because of the difference between financial firms and manufacturing ones. In the latter, more competition generally leads to a shrinking of profit margins, to efforts to cut costs, and eventually to lower prices to the customers. In banking, though, the shrinking of profit margins has historically been followed not only by lower prices so much as by higher risks. The crude fact is that the costs of production for a bank are no greater to organize and service a risky loan than to do the same for a sound one. And if the risky loan is not repaid and has to be written off as a loss, this will happen some time after the profit has been received.

It is true that increased competition from foreign banks will, in many cases, break down the comfortable cartel-like arrangements that have featherbedded local banks in many countries and have kept the price of their services up to consumers. But more competition is not costless. As Toyoo Gyohten, formerly a senior official in the Japanese Foreign Ministry and now adviser to the Bank of Tokyo, observed, the most important question raised by the experience of world finance in the 1980s was 'how do you reconcile the pursuit of security with the efficiency of the market?'[6]

Demand and supply

The fifth change to be noted is the changed relation of demand and supply in these integrated transnational markets for credit. Recall that banks not only intermediate between savers and borrowers but also create credit in the process.

If they are tempted to create much more credit in relation to total savings, the result is likely to be an increase in money supply and therefore in inflation – higher prices all round. To the extent that they resist increased demands for credit, thus failing to match supply with demand, the result is likely to be a high price, i.e. higher rates of interest as the price for borrowing. In fact, in recent years, both consequences can be observed: some increase in the rate of inflation in most of the G7 countries; and a real interest rate that, even in the cheapest markets, has been substantially above the rates ruling in the 1930s or 20 years after World War II. To observe this change is not to blame the banks alone. Their actions are only the end of a chain of factors that begins with an almost philosophical, or even psychological, change in the way people and collectivities of people think about spending and saving, how they choose between the two. The distinguished economist Al Hirschman once speculated that capitalism may have benefited from a mental or philosophical carry-over from pre-capitalist societies in which social and economic behaviour was ruled by such non-materialistic notions as honour (in standing by inconvenient contracts) and prudence, parsimony and self-restraint (in eschewing overindulgence in material consumption and the display of wealth). Whether this is right or not, it is historically demonstrable that well-off people in the rich countries – poor people do not have the choice – have tended in this century to spend more and save less than their grandparents. Their governments, which used to consume a rather small proportion of the gross national product, now spend 40–50 per cent or more of the GNP. And what they cannot finance by raising taxes, they finance by borrowing. Firms, large and small, and smaller entrepreneurs like farmers and shopkeepers, which used to finance their new investments by the accumulated profits of the past, now go to the banks for credit or raise borrowed money on the financial markets. The oil companies are a striking example of enterprises that never used to borrow to finance exploration for new oil wells and now regularly do so. Moreover, the thirst for new corporate capital has led to more and more resort to international financial markets instead of national ones. The latest example of this trend is the decision of Toshiba Corporation to seek additional – and significantly more expensive – finance abroad instead of from the Japanese stock market (Aglietta 1990).

The consequences of structural change in finance

If itemizing the major changes in the international financial and monetary system gives the broad impression of change for the worse, to a more unstable, risky, and volatile system of creating and allocating credit, that is perhaps unavoidable. But these changes should never obscure the salient fact that developed monetary and financial systems *are* engines of economic growth. The creation of credit in a competitive market does enable investment to be made in new products and new, more cost-effective processes, and this raises living standards, if not universally or equally, nevertheless enough to make national economies as units larger and more prosperous. Some economists have been tempted by liberal theories of economic trade to attribute the growing wealth of the world market economy since the 1950s to the reduction of barriers to imports and to more efficient allocation of resources through the exchange of goods and services. Since growth continued, even more in the volume of trade than in output, in the last 10 or 15 years when non-tariff barriers to trade were visibly on the increase, this explanation seems insufficient if not actually wrong. Much more likely, and more consistent with the pattern of economic growth from year to year, is an explanation that finds the cause of growth in the capacity of the financial institutions to create credit and to move it about more freely than ever before. Growth in developing countries was fastest when credit was available to them; and it flagged most dramatically and seriously only in 1983, the year after the onset of the debt crisis – beginning with Mexico and Poland and spreading to other indebted countries in Latin America and Central Europe.[7]

In short, the development of a more sophisticated and integrated world market for finance added to the efficiency of the world market. But, in doing so, it also frustrated the 'pursuit of security' – which, translated into more old-fashioned language, means the stability of money, the value of the currency in which exchanges take place. This certainly is much more vulnerable in the 1990s than it was in the 1960s. It is the Achilles' heel of global capitalism: the one thing that, if confidence in it failed for any reason, would destroy all that the market economy had achieved in this century. Just as the inability of the socialist system to satisfy the aspirations of the people both for a better material life and for a more effective voice in government eventually destroyed the whole economic system – with what long-term political and social consequences we cannot tell – so financial instability, the precariousness of a banking system that sometimes looks as poorly balanced as a house of cards, could do the same for capitalism.[8]

Change in international money

So much for the changes in international banking and finance. The accompanying changes in the international monetary system are much better known and so can be referred to quite briefly.[9] To make an assessment of the consequences of both, we shall have to look first at the outstanding political and social issues that changes in both the monetary and financial systems have raised and that remain – and look to remain for the foreseeable future – unresolved. Identifying these issues will allow us to make some broader comments on the impact of both on the nature of world society and the basic values expressed therein.

Recall that the arrangements agreed upon between the major Western allied governments at Bretton Woods in New Hampshire, USA, before the end of World War II had to wait 15 years or more before they became effective as a system of rules governing the management of exchange rates between the signatory states.

These rules provided for stable rates between their currencies by binding governments first to make their currencies freely convertible into others, and then to maintain the par value of their currencies within narrow limits. (Par value, in effect, meant value in terms of the US dollar. Although, formally, a par value was expressed in terms of gold, in practice the gold price was fixed in US dollars at US$35 an ounce of gold – and had been since the mid-1930s – and, because the US Treasury stood ready to convert on request any dollars presented to it into gold at that price, the system of fixed par values therefore constituted a dollar–gold exchange system.)

Once a member state had made its currency convertible and fixed the par value of its currency, it was entitled to draw on the resources of the International Monetary Fund for short-term help in financing any deficits arising on its current account balance of payments.[10] These drawing rights varied according to its IMF 'quota' – fixed rather roughly by the size of the national economy. This quota also determined the amount of its contribution in local currency and gold or dollars to the IMF's resources, and its weighted vote in the IMF Executive Board. Only in 1959, when for the first time the European governments in concert made their currencies convertible, did the Bretton Woods 'regime' begin to function. Its reign as a system of clear rules for exchange rate management lasted barely more than a decade, until 1971 when President Nixon declared the dollar inconvertible into gold and allowed the market, rather than the US government, to determine the dollar's exchange rate with other currencies.

Thus, although the IMF as an organization had been set up already in 1947 (11 years before the fixed exchange rate regime came into operation), and although it continued to function as an intergovernmental forum and as overseer, or monitor, of the macroeconomic management policies of states – more particularly, of financially weak, indebted states – it cannot be said that in the last two decades it has really fulfilled its original role and purpose in the management of exchange rates.

It is a paradox of this whole story that the dollar's central role as a reserve currency and as the preferred medium of exchange in the private sector of international trade and finance was built up in the four decades or so between 1934 and 1971 when the gold value of the dollar was fixed and stable, but that the dollar continued to enjoy the benefits and privileges of being the world's top currency – the national currency most used in world business (Strange 1970c)[11] – long after it had ceased to have a stable value in terms of gold, or oil, or any basket of goods and services. Although they knew that the real value of dollars accumulated in national or corporate reserves was variable and that some risk attached therefore to holding dollars, or to fixing prices in terms of dollars, its pre-eminence over its rivals in the system has so far never been seriously in doubt (see Parboni 1981).

The result for the international monetary system has not just been that the United States has enjoyed the 'exorbitant privileges' (to quote General de Gaulle) of its pivotal role in the Bretton Woods gold exchange standard. But since 1973, when the dollar was finally floated, the United States has enjoyed even greater asymmetrical – 'super-exorbitant' – privileges. For it has been able to borrow through the international financial system large amounts of money *denominated in its own currency*. With the aid of such credit, it has been able to finance a growing fiscal and balance of payments deficit. No other debtor country has enjoyed this privilege, or the power over the system, for good or evil, that went with such a privilege.

Instead of a fixed system of rules governing foreign exchange rates, therefore, the international financial system has had to live with an international monetary system in which the United States sometimes was content to let the markets decide the value of the dollar, but at other times was inclined to put all sorts of pressure on its affluent allies – to intervene in these markets, or to change their policies, in order to stop the dollar rising too high or falling too low to the perceived detriment of US national interests (see Destler and Henning 1989; Funabashi 1988; Marris 1985). The United States has also been inclined unilaterally to put pressure on some of the newly industrializing countries (NICs) like South Korea or Taiwan to revalue their currencies as a check on the competitive attractions of the exports to the US market.

Although the institution of the Group of Seven summits and regular meetings of finance ministers have seemed to the press and the public like a ruling oligarchy presiding over the international monetary system, the reality behind the bland communiqués issued after every summit reveals much less consensus. America's affluent allies are becoming less compliant. The Europeans, led by the then President of the EC Commission, Delors, agreed to set up their own fixed-rate regime – a European Monetary Union (EMU), making irreversible the commitments under the 1978 European Monetary System – within the undisciplined global monetary system. And the Japanese government, shaken by the political and financial reverberations from its close involvement with the United States, is becoming much less inclined now than in the past to go along so tamely wherever Washington leads.

Yet all is not quite anarchy in the system. Beginning in 1974, when the failures of Bankhaus Herstatt in Germany and the Franklin National Bank in New York brought nightmare visions of the possible consequences of giving too much freedom to operators in financial markets, the governments of the affluent countries, led by the United States, began using the network of central banks organized since 1930 through the Bank for International Settlements in Basle, Switzerland, to tighten the rules on bank supervision. An agreement called the Basle Concordat,[12] supplemented in 1973 by another one, progressively clarified the division of responsibility between national central banks, so that it was clearer who was supposed to see prudential rules observed. The Basle Concordats also sought progressively to harmonize the standards governing the limits on bank lending, as for instance by setting a target ratio between a bank's capital and its outstanding loans. But although progress towards these ends was made, the next collapse of a big international bank, the Pakistani-owned Bank for Credit and Commerce International (BCCI), in 1990 showed clearly that loopholes still existed in the central banks' network of supervision over market operators (see de Cecco 1987).

To sum up, I might quote from an earlier survey of the state of international money and finance written some six years ago.

An orderly, developed monetary system would thus be characterized by steady (and not too jerky) growth, by increasing controls over the credit structure, its markets and its operators; by increasing allocation of financial resources to the welfare system and further provision of public goods.

A disorderly system, contrari-wise, could be characterized by growth, interrupted by periods of failing confidence and unused, idle productive resources; by the threat of inflation due to the creation of credit-money by governments or banks or by both; by the threat of financial crisis and collapse; and by exploitation of the system by political authority for its own particular ends rather than for the general welfare. (Strange 1988e)

The conclusion was that the global financial structure displayed all the characteristics of a developed monetary and financial system, but that it was less stable and orderly than it might be and ought to be if it was not to put the rest of the world economy at risk. In national economies, ways had been found to compensate for the tendency of bankers to over-bank (in Hirsch's words). In a politically divided world, this was more difficult. While the development of sophisticated monetary and financial mechanisms within capitalist economies had led to the rich getting richer and the poor staying poor, national governments, in order to survive and stave off revolution, had used countervailing political power to build welfare systems that compensated for the inherent inequity, but this was more difficult when the financial structures had become globalized. Not only was the political incentive for redistributive welfare lacking, but such foreign aid as there was did not always help the poor. The political system made it too easy for the ruling élites to hijack foreign aid for their own benefit.

Conclusions

Today, it is more vital than ever before to use a political economy approach to global finance and international money. That means to start by asking about *power* in the system: who has it and how do they use it? The main difference between economists and political economists is that most of the economists leave power out of their calculations.

Secondly, it means asking who benefits – '*Cui bono*?' as the philosophers asked in ancient Rome – and also who suffers, who has greater risks imposed on them, and who has the new opportunities, material or otherwise, opened for them? These allocative questions, moreover, should be asked concerning social groups and not just states.

Thirdly, it means asking questions about the basic social values reflected by the working of the system. Does it value the creation of wealth more than the achievement of social justice? Does the maintenance of order come before the assurance of freedom?[13]

The answers to the first set of questions concerning power are already implicit in the outline of recent changes in the financial and monetary structure. In the financial system, the influence of global markets for money and for credit instruments has grown as the power of governments to influence or control these markets has diminished. Within the markets, the power to move the market up or down has gone more and more to the innovative specialists with their sophisticated information system, and less to their customers, whether depositors or borrowers. The banks, for instance, were able to decide that they would extract profit from their operations by 'front-loading' loans with management fees, and the customers could not stop them. They also decide which borrowers must pay so many percentage points above LIBOR for their loans.

In the monetary system, too, the answer is clear enough. For the time being at least, the asymmetric power of the United States to act in monetary affairs unilaterally, and without the constraints imposed on others, is unchanged, whatever weaknesses there may be in the American manufacturing sector.

Answers to the second question have also been addressed from a Filipino point of view in chapter 9 in Sakamoto (1994). Professor Briones makes the valid point that, in the handling of international debt, the debtors have been weak bargainers and have suffered accordingly. Their interests came second to those of creditor banks and creditor governments. Both these were fearful of the consequences of unpaid debts on the stability of the whole financial structure. Banks were therefore told to rebuild their capital base and to be more prudent in lending in the future, and the result, predictably, was to check the outflow of new capital. As debt servicing costs mounted, the reverse flow of funds from South to North increased. This was the reason Professor Robert Triffin (1991), the veteran critic of the International Monetary System (IMS), observed that the letters stood for International Monetary Scandal.

One consequence, relevant to the power questions, is also correctly observed by Professor Briones: that the power that the IMF had lost as a result of the end of the fixed exchange rate regime, it had regained through its key role in the rescheduling of foreign debt. All debtor governments found it harder to resist or reject IMF advice on economic management when IMF approval was a necessary condition for new lending – even though the new loans did not always reduce the total debt burden. The contrast with the last century, when indebted states were able to default on bonds bought by foreign creditors without, in most cases, having to change their internal policies, is worth remarking.

As to the allocation of costs and benefits, risks and opportunities, among other social groups, the mobility of capital created through global finance has certainly weakened the bargaining power of organized labour in the face of the corporate managers of multinational corporations. But while some employees 'at home' may have done less well in wage bargaining than in the past, others in the plants located in developing countries have, in fact, enjoyed higher incomes than they would have done if production had not become international.

We may also observe that the development of this integrated financial structure has benefited big businesses over small ones – but, again, not uniformly so. Some big names have disappeared through bankruptcy or take-over from the lists of top companies – and in part as a result of financial changes. And new names have risen and new fortunes have been made by people and firms that were unknown only a few years ago. There are plenty of new Indian, Chinese, and Latin American 'multinationals' soon to join these prestigious lists.

Changes in the financial structures have also affected two other categories of society not often considered in the literature of international political economy – the old and the young, and the educated (or smart) and the uneducated and unskilled. Whereas the availability of capital has given new opportunities to younger generations, there is a sense in which their parents and grandparents have paid heavily for postwar economic growth. They worked hard. They saved voluntarily or through state pension funds for their old age. And now, in many cases, they find inflation has eroded the real value of their savings or pension rights, or that the fiscal problems of the state may cause governments to alter the rules to their disadvantage. Worst hit of all are the pensioners of the ex-socialist states.

As for the *cui bono* between educated/unskilled social groups, some might see this as a widening gap between office workers and factory workers (white collars and blue collars); or between peasants still toiling in the fields to produce food and computer programmers or foreign exchange dealers producing only 'services' of doubtful value. Both are simplifications. But there is little doubt that financial changes have played a large part in what is referred to as the 'information revolution' and that financial resources have flowed more readily to Wall Street 'yuppies' and those with new skills and knowledge than to the more traditional occupations. Never has it been more true that, in terms of life chances or entitlements, there is a core in the periphery and a periphery in the core.

These allocative consequences suggest that, in answer to the last set of questions concerning the mix of values reflected by the financial and monetary structure, we should not – and cannot – generalize about the results of change for states or nations. As between the four basic social values of wealth, security, justice, and freedom, we have to ask both *how much* of each the system produces and *for whom* – security for whom, wealth for whom, justice for whom, and the freedom to choose for whom.

How much? unfortunately is unquantifiable. Comparison with past periods suggests only that the world political economy today produces more wealth than it did in the past, but while security of some kinds and for some groups is greater, it is not clear how we balance one kind of security (e.g. from nuclear holocaust) against another kind of insecurity (e.g. from financial crisis).

Most difficult of all, perhaps, is the question posed by Professor Sakamoto concerning democracy: what chances does the system give, or not give, to people to decide their own destiny, through the ballot box or through the political rights associated with the concept of democracy, such as freedom of association, freedom of speech, freedom of religion and belief, freedom from official intimidation and coercion? (Do we all also have the freedom to own property, the freedom to choose life or death for unborn children or for ourselves? As the philosophers have always said, the debate over when freedom becomes licence, over the balance between collective welfare and individual freedom, is an endless one.) Absolute, objective answers are impossible, as well as unwise. I can offer only some subjective observations on the consequential impact of the globalization of capital and capitalism on the global preference for democracy.

The financial structures inseparable from capitalism on a world scale are not democratic. Central banks, for example, are secret, élitist, and authoritarian institutions – but necessary for the safe functioning of financial markets and transactions. The shift of power from governments (democratic or not) to markets is a derogation of popular power. The fact that among governments the most powerful in matters of money and finance is the United States, and the United States counts politically as a democracy, does not alter this derogation of popular power over the economy. Not only is the US Congress unconcerned over financial issues, as it is over trade or unemployment, even when it is concerned, its decisions are taken in response to the perceived interests of the United States, and its short-term interests at that. The impotence of the developing countries, through the United Nations or any other multilateral organization, to reform or to moderate in any substantial way the arrangements made by the United States and its affluent allies concerning money and finance can only suggest to us the very strict limits on the expression of world opinion on matters central to the capitalist system. History, unfortunately, suggests that the power of bankers and financial markets is seldom checked until *after* a financial crash.

8
'Finance in Politics: An Epilogue to *Mad Money*' 1998

F 30
G 20

Although analysts readily admit that international trade and investment have important implications for the distribution of wealth and power among nations, no similar agreement exists regarding the significance of the international monetary system.

So Bob Gilpin began the fourth chapter of *The Political Economy of International Relations* (1987) titled 'International Monetary Matters'. He went on to say,

A well-functioning monetary system is the crucial nexus of the international economy ... a prerequisite for a prosperous world economy ... Money and financial flows now dwarf trade flows and have become the most crucial links among national economies. The efficiency and stability of the international monetary system, therefore, are major factors in the international political economy.

That was written more than a decade ago, in 1986. Gilpin argued that the enhanced role of the international monetary system constituted 'a virtual revolution in world politics'. It was a revolution that almost no one else in international relations or even the international studies business recognised or wrote about. A deafening silence followed Gilpin's clarion call.[1] One reason could have been that he did not distinguish clearly between the 'International monetary system' that governed exchange rates between national currencies, and the 'international financial system' that governed the creation, access to and trade in credit. Indeed, only five out of more than fifty pages of the chapter focus on what I have called the 'financial structures' of political economy. Since the public debate since the middle 1960s, and consequently the bulk of the academic writing by economists and others, concentrated on the currency and exchange rate issues and not on the organisation and management of credit, it was hardly surprising that those five revolutionary pages got overlooked both by students and by Gilpin's colleagues in international relations (Gilpin 1987: 118–23).

(A glaring example of this bias was the earlier and influential work of Keohane and Nye, *Power and Interdependence* (1977). Although their comparative study of US–Canadian and US–Australian relations claimed it was focused on the two issue areas of money and oceans, the definition of the money issue area was not only state-centric to a degree but also narrowly confined to currency and exchange rate questions. There was nothing there about capital flows, nor about the informal 'regime' governing the allocation of transnational credit.)

All the same, twelve years is a long time for a challenging pronouncement by an acknowledged leader in an academic discipline like Gilpin to go unremarked. How can we explain this long neglect, this long and deafening silence?

The answer seems to me to lie in the basic assumptions underlying the study of international relations, and in the related problematic that defines the discipline. The basic assumption is that world politics – international relations – are conceptually different from national/domestic politics, and must therefore be studied separately, preferably in separate departments of universities, or in separate courses of study. The assumption is taken directly from the international lawyers who early on argued that international law was different from municipal law in that it was not sustained by established political authority and stable institutions of juridical responsibility. It was fluid where municipal law was much more static. Much of it was 'customary' law. The judgements of international courts, unlike those of national courts, could not always be enforced. If this was not the result of a state of anarchy in world politics, it was certainly the result of the lack of an over-arching political authority sustaining international law.

Today, it is true, this sharp distinction between international law and domestic law, and, correspondingly, between international politics (including foreign policies) and domestic politics is being widely questioned (Keohane and Milner 1996; Rosenau 1997). The evidence of overlap and of reciprocal influence is abundant. What is still generally lacking is any explanatory theory for why this has happened; coining unlovely terms like 'fragmegration' is no substitute for theory (Rosenau 1997).

Even more important in explaining the long neglect of the politics of the international financial system in the IR literature is the central problematic accepted by the great majority of contemporary scholars engaged in studying and teaching international relations/world politics. This central problematic is the prevalence of violent conflict and war between states. The historical background to this choice is important; the coincidence of mass slaughter in two world wars and an academic interest in questions of war and peace highlighted the importance of studying world politics. It also favoured the realists of the 1930s, E.H. Carr (1939), Georg Schwarzenberger (1941), Frederick Schumann (1937) and others (mostly German refugees), and the 1950s, John Herz (1951), Hans Morgenthau (1954) and, most of all perhaps, Ken Waltz (1959) over the idealist of the 1920s.[2]

Search the booklists of standard IR courses today and the absence of any discussion at all of international finance, how it works and is managed or mismanaged is striking. Check out the most used texts – Holsti (1972), Waltz (1979), Ray (1995), Aron (1974), Bull (1977). You will find in some of these texts appended chapters on transnational corporations, environmental and ethical issues, adding secondary actors to the cast-list of the state-centric system. You will not find analysis of the role of credit in the politics of the world market economy nor even of the politics of inter-national financial relations.

Or search the extensive literature now devoted to theories of international relations. There is nothing there about the international financial structure and how it may affect the power and wealth of states. Yet there is the prime example of Japan, once perceived as the leader of a third economic bloc, challenging both the United States and Europe for leadership. What else but international finance accounts for the different perceptions of 1998: Japan as the weak link in the world market economy, dependent on support from the United States, its recovery from deep financial disorder delayed by its own political institutions. In recent months, I have searched this IR theory literature in vain for the slightest hint of concern about finance. There is none.[3]

Even the neo-Gramscians and other critical theorists who are not usually inhibited when it comes to criticising the capitalist system have had astonishingly little to say about the role of finance, and financial policy, in deciding the 'who benefits?' question at the heart of international political economy.

If the myopia of international relations theorists is derived from their obsession with the problematic of war and peace and conflict between states, the equal myopia of Western political theorists is derived from a similar obsession with values of political liberalism. Their current literature focuses a great deal on the nature, extent and promotion of democracy and liberty. Look in vain for any consideration of the structural power in democratic states based on the financial system which – as Polanyi clearly perceived – could directly affect both the international political system – the gold standard – and the relative influence of social classes over domestic politics.

Other social scientists share the general myopia. David Landes, an historian of repute whose recent book *The Wealth and Poverty of Nations* (1998) made a comparative historical study of societies and their success or failure in adopting or discovering new technologies. Much of the detail is fascinating. But the key question of how innovations were financed, and whether access to credit was a deciding factor is totally overlooked. And a social theorist, Francis Fukuyama, identified the key variable in societies as the level of trust developed between its members (Fukuyama 1996). High-trust societies owed their advantage to social capital developed over time. Low-trust societies, lacking such social capital, were conversely handicapped. But he too fails to ask whether the society did or did not develop the trust in the value and stability of money necessary between buyers and sellers, debtors and creditors.

The neglect is the more astonishing because it is contradicted by the everyday experiences of people. What is it that causes most conflict at every level of social interaction, from the family, to the village and the local sports club, up to the management of the city, the state or international organisations? It is the control of money – whether cash or credit. Who gets to spend it and under what constraints. Is it you or I, wives ask, who manages the housekeeping budget, or who signs for the social security cheque? In the sports club, is it the members, or the club secretary and other paid employees, who decides between alternative uses of the funds? In national governments, it is Finance ministries that try to control the spending of other departments, and thus to determine the hierarchies within the national bureaucracy. It is they who govern if anyone does the raising of revenue, the state's access to other people's money by borrowing, and the discharge of debts. International institutions too experience their sharpest clashes over finance – whence it comes and where it goes.

Are these not all highly political issues? Why then are writers on international politics or national politics so perversely oblivious to them?

The answer, as I have suggested elsewhere, is to be found in their narrow and constricting understanding of what constitutes politics, and of how and by whom power is exercised within society (Strange 1996b: chapters 2 and 3). If you start from the assumption that politics is what politicians do, and that corporate politics or university politics don't count, you draw a restrictive line around the questions to be asked and investigated. Similarly, if you start from the assumption that power resides in resources, and overlook the kind of power derived from regimes or structures of political economy, you again draw a restrictive line around the questions to be asked and the methodology to be used in answering them. The conceptual wall that was built to define the study of international relations has become a prison wall putting key questions like the politics of the financial system off-limits in the study of international politics.

This is precisely what Kal Holsti has done in a brave attempt to get to grips with the problematic of change in the international system (Holsti 1998). By defining that system as the way in which states relate to each other and conduct their business, he is unable to explain change, although he concedes that we live today in an era of profound change without having discovered a new way of seeing the world. He agrees with Ruggie that there is no consensus on what constitutes change, nor how to identify it (Holsti 1998: 1–2; Ruggie 1993: 140–4).

Peter Dombrowski is a writer who asserts the contrary: that there is a consensus. He concludes a long and exhaustive survey of the literature by writing, 'researchers have reached a consensus on a number of key questions emerging from the increasing importance of international finance within the global economy' (Dombrowski 1998: 24). One is that though capital mobility has greatly increased since the late 1960s, price and regulatory differentials still separate national financial markets. Since, the extent of regulatory or policy coordination between states 'has been more limited than might be expected', so that despite liberalisation and deregulation, significant regulatory differences remain. Lastly, there is 'some agreement' he finds, on the origins and management of financial crises, the relationship between states and financial markets, the role of finance in economic development and the interaction of financial markets and regulatory change. And the growing literature on international finance, he notes, is cumulative. That is, it slowly adds to our understanding of what is going on and why.

In fact, there is in reality wide *disagreement* on every one of these points. Some believe financial crises – the 1977 Asian crises, for example – were self-inflicted by incompetent and short-sighted national governments; others blame the external factors and actors which brought hot money flooding in and setting off financial bubbles that were bound to burst. Equally, there is disagreement on how such crises should be managed; whether rescue lifeboats are necessary because otherwise the repercussions of say, Indonesian bank failures will spread the contagion throughout the region and possibly to the whole world market economy. And while the IMF and most liberal economists see capital mobility in the system as enhancing competition and therefore efficiency, others argue that it has not been in the interest of developing countries. They would point to the two or three Asian countries that escaped the worst of the turmoil – China, Taiwan and South Korea and find a common factor in their maintenance of exchange controls over financial transactions with the rest of the world.[4]

Hardly surprising, therefore, that the 'lessons' Dombrowski draws from his wide-ranging survey are equally dubious. First, he says the state is not in retreat. 'Even though globalized financial markets now appear beyond the control of individual states, states have not declined in significance.' They have just changed their role to a more permissive one and changed the way they operate in the financial system. That seems to me to be a retreat before the power of markets and financial operators. And if ever there was a description of the structural power of beliefs and ideas in political economy, this is surely it. It was not the power of the US or the IMF that persuaded France or Germany to privatise, to deregulate and to liberalise their financial markets. It was structural change in the world market economy, the imperative of competition for market shares and underlying change in the knowledge structure, reflected then in the power of the financial structure.

Students will find his four-page bibliography useful, even though it is heavily weighted toward economists and US-published books and journals and towards the international monetary system rather than the financial system. Non-Americans – Cerny, Underhill, Corbridge and Strange – however, get credit for their work. Germain's recent seminal book should be added, precisely because it deals in historical perspective with the relations of state authority and financial markets (Germain 1997). These works suggest that the neglect of finance noted earlier has been more marked in the US literature on international political economy than in the European. Perhaps the prevailing ideology of liberal economics in America has something to do with this?

In short, both of Dombrowski's conclusions are complete rubbish. There is no consensus and no clear cumulative lessons to be drawn from the work surveyed about the power of states and other authorities in relation to financial markets.

Keynes, Bagehot and Soros

The most amazing omission in all this is the work of John Maynard Keynes. After all, it was Keynes who developed the only coherent, vigorous and influential theory concerning the conduct of financial markets. His *General Theory* influenced generations of economists, and still does despite the counter-influence of Friedman and Hayek (Keynes 1936). In fact, the *General Theory* is more of a sociological theory than a purely economic one, even though it argues in economic terms and draws on empirical economic data. Keynes' target was not capitalism *per se*; it was the capitalists who ran the system. When financial markets collapsed and profits fell, these capitalists lost their nerve. They lost their 'animal spirits' as Keynes put it. They went, suddenly and disruptingly, from illogical optimism to deepest pessimistic gloom. Drunken sailors one minute; terrified rabbits the next. Market opportunities beckoned, but were ignored. The only remedy for the real economy was state intervention to restore demand and therefore economic growth.

Keynes' work had popular appeal partly because it drew on homely analogies familiar to most of his readers. He explained the illogical behaviour of the markets by drawing an analogy with the competitions run by newspapers in the 1930s to build circulation. Readers were shown pictures of pretty girls. They were asked to pick the prettiest. But the winner was not the best objective judge of beauty or sex-appeal. Nor was it the entry closest to others' judgement of the prettiest. Rather, it was the entry reflecting what other entrants thought other entrants would put down. This, Keynes said, was how financial markets behaved. They did not respond to objective truths, nor to prevailing opinions about objective truth. They reacted to perceptions of how others perceived the likely behaviour of the markets.[5]

A nearly-forgotten elaboration of Keynes' analysis was the work of Hyman Minsky in his 'Financial Instability Hypothesis', written in the 1930s, reprinted in 1982 and rediscovered after the 1987 stock market collapse.

> Prices of capital assets depend on current views of future profits flows and the current subjective view placed upon the insurance embodied in money or quick cash; these current views depend upon the expectations that are held about the future development of the economy. (Minsky 1982: 8)

A source which surely influenced Keynes' thinking but is also ignored in Dombrowski's survey is that of Walter Bagehot, the long-time editor of *The Economist* before the First World War and author of *Lombard Street* (Bagehot 1875). Bagehot closely observed the relations between state authority, as exercised over banks in the City of London chiefly by the Bank of England and the House of Commons. His comments on the fall of Overend Gurney in the aftermath of the American Civil War and the reasons why the Bank of England allowed it to fall highlight the very similar difficult choices faced by regulators today – including the Fed, the European central banks or the Bank of Japan. To let a big bank fail threatens to destabilise the entire financial market; to rescue it, enhances the moral hazard problem, encouraging others to think they can pursue profit at the expense of security.

Bagehot's judgements were not always the conventional ones. These were that the swift rescue of Barings in 1890 was necessary because Barings was not insolvent but merely illiquid and its failure would have had major repercussions for the City and the whole world system of credit. Overend Gurney, however was simply insolvent. It had lent too much and unwisely – even dishonestly and there was no way it could have met its commitments. But while not dissenting from this fundamental point, Bagehot thought there was a bit more to the two cases than met the eye. Baring's Argentine partners had been callously abandoned, sacrificed to City interests, and the rescue had well served the latter's interest by reinforcing the existing structures of power in London and increasing the Bank of England's control over the joint stock banks. Allowing Overend Gurney to go down too was not a simple case of exercising regulatory discipline over a bad bank. Overend Gurney was an inconvenient competitor for commercial business important to the Bank of England; letting it fail while supporting the rest of the system was not simply an impartial regulatory act. In both cases, therefore, motivations were mixed; preferences multiple and complex.[6]

Finally, I would direct Dombrowski's myopic vision to the contribution of George Soros. Like Bagehot, Soros is no professional academic but an observer of – and a successful player in – the financial market game. But his analysis of *why* financial markets behave as they do is actually more profound and radical than Keynes' explanation. Soros claims that it is derived from his studying with Karl Popper at the LSE in the 1950s; I would say it is much more based on direct personal experience and reflection.

The basic concept he calls the 'reflexive principle'. This is what fundamentally distinguishes natural from social science. In (most) natural science, theory is based on objective observation of the subject-matter, which remains unaware and unmoved by the research. The behaviour of variable stars is a good example. But in social science, in Soros' estimation, a reflexive principle is at work, whereby the object of the research – financial markets, say – reacts to the opinions expressed by researchers and other observers; while, conversely, the researchers react to the behaviour of the markets. This cannot be properly described as objective science. An aspiration to scientific objectivity, or at least impartiality between vested interests may still be desirable and achievable. But a truly scientific result is not. Goodbye, social science, and the scientific study of society, national or international. Welcome the necessary practice of multidisciplinary social studies including international studies.

The implicit theories in *Mad Money*

Having briefly justified my preferred sources for the study of international finance, it is time to explain why I think of *Casino Capitalism* (Strange 1986f), supplemented by *Mad Money* (Strange 1998f), as containing within them important contributions to the neglected role of credit and finance in the international political economy. They are rather more than analytical surveys of change in the world's system. Perhaps they are a bit like those children's comic-book puzzles in which the reader had to try to find the cat, the rabbit, the fox and the dog hidden in the foliage of a forest scene. A quick glance may not reveal them. But they are still there for the careful observer.

Some of the theoretical implications of both books are already apparent in *Casino Capitalism*. *Mad Money*, which takes the story on from the mid-1980s, asks the question what changed and what was still the same, and in answering adds further theoretical implications and conclusions. One important one is that both political theory and economic theory have ignored the power of technological change – and have impoverished and crippled all of social science in doing so. In international political economy, the omission is particularly disabling, for technological change, more than anything else, has driven change in the structures of power (Stopford and Strange 1991). It has certainly changed the financial structure, as explained in chapter 2 of *Mad Money*. And it has changed the production structure by shifting power over trade and production from governments to firms. Because it is firms – including financial enterprises – who have developed the new technologies, the knowledge structure (as described in *States and Markets*) has also been changed. In the post-war decades and for much of the Cold War, technology was led and directed by states. By the 1990s, it was led and directed from the private sector – Microsoft, for example. Important for theory here is the tendency of technological change to accelerate, and to spread more easily over economic and political space.

You will not find much about the technology factor either in political theory nor economic theory. Both tend to take it for granted and to ignore the dynamism that produces ripples of change throughout the world economy. What there is, comes from observers of science policy (Freeman, Sharpe and Walker 1991; Freeman and Soete 1995; Pavitt and Soete 1982) and from totally new directions. For example, John de la Mothe and Gilles Paquet both of Universite d'Ottawa are editing a new series, published by Pinter, showing how science and technology are shaping the world economy. Business schools and policy analysts are more aware of this than conventional social scientists.

The other thing that has changed from the earlier period is the involvement of organised crime in the international financial system. Of course, there have always been criminals active in financial markets (Strange 1998f: 134), some of them respected pillars of society. Organised crime is different. Large, rich transnational networks flushed with profits from the international trade in drugs, arms and illegal immigrants emerged during the 1980s as big players in international finance. Their operations were the basis for a boom in the business of money laundering – the conversion of dirty money derived from crime into untraceable, legitimate investment funds. Because organised crime has developed from mafias, especially the US and Italian mafias, it has not functioned like other economic enterprises. Secrecy between its members has protected it from state authority (Paoli 1997). The obligation not to bear witness against fellow-members – the principle of *omerta* – protected the Sicilians against prosecution until in 1993 the Italian law was changed, making membership a criminal offence (Strange 1998f: 128).

The theoretical implication of the closer links between finance and crime, however, go deeper, into the structures of power in the international political economy. *Mad Money* identifies three structural features that not only allowed but encouraged these links. One was the strong demand for hallucinatory drugs in the rich countries. Second was the ready supply from poor ones – Colombia, Burma, Afghanistan. In the 1960s and 1970s, the developed countries had steadfastly refused UNCTAD pleas to apply the principles of agricultural support and protection that they used at home to support and protect export crops produced by developing countries. Poor returns for coffee, tobacco, sugar etc. compared with high returns from growing cannabis and opium and processing the material for the eager market. And third was the amazingly permissive market for transnational banking services, including the laundering of dirty money. *Mad Money* argues that the ideational sources of the permissiveness lie in the ambivalence of capitalist systems toward the 'learned professions'. This permissiveness allowed bankers and accountants to share with priests the privileges of client confidentiality. Banks and tax havens have exploited this privilege, and in doing so have punched a big hole in the governance system of international finance.

Nor was it the only one. A major change, noted in *Mad Money*, has been the change in the role of banks, and the diffusion of financial service business to all sorts of new players. The business of banking used to be what was called intermediation – that is the bank intermediated profitably between the wish of savers to lend money profitably and the interest of borrowers to make use of OPM (Other People's Money). Their profit was the price difference to the savers and the borrowers. Liberalisation of financial markets going back to the Eurodollar story in the 1960s, increased competition between banks and cut profit margins. (Liberal economic theory fell into the error that competition necessarily lowered prices to the customer. Not so in banking; it induced bankers to take bigger risks (Strange 1998f: chapter 8).)

The policy implications of this change are far-reaching. They have been denied by conventional writers. Ethan Epstein, for example, wrote in the mid-1990s that the system was secure because it was regulated both at the national level by central banks and other regulatory bodies, and at the international level by cooperative accords reached through the Bank for International Settlements in Basle, and the International Monetary Fund in Washington. But subsequent research has revealed the fallacies in this comfortable belt-and-braces analysis (Strange 1998f: chapter 9). Globalisation of finance has poked big holes in national regulatory systems and bankers and others have not been slow to use them. Everywhere, these systems have been eroded to the point where they no longer deter nor control (Story and Ingo 1997). As for the international accords, the evidence again suggests that they are no longer effective. The BIS in 1996 abandoned its efforts to impose common capital–loan ratios on banks worldwide, deciding to leave the consequent risk-management to the banks themselves to take care of (Strange 1998: chapter 9).

The theoretical implications are even more far-reaching. Economic and social theories of regulation make the assumption that regulation has a clear purpose – to reduce pollution for example, or to protect consumers against monopoly pricing – and that the market and its operators to be regulated are clearly defined (Majone 1994). These assumptions no longer hold for financial services. Where banking used to be clearly defined and its essence was intermediation of OPM, so that the banker was not himself risking capital, the present competitive market for financial services, in which banks compete with non-banks, and in which they are tempted to bet their own as well as their clients' money, is poorly defined. That, essentially, is why the Basle rules were abandoned and the prudential role left to the managers of banks themselves.

States' role in globalisation

Perhaps least obvious of the theoretical implications of the two studies are those concerning the role of states in liberating the forces of globalisation. A lot of the literature on globalisation has presented the power of states as being under threat from the forces of the market. The alternative view, tenaciously held by realists in IR and some economists, is that the erosion of state power has been exaggerated and that the changes encapsulated in the term globalisation have not been nearly so great as the opposing school asserts.

Although it was never explicitly stated, the resolution of this important disagreement lies in the attention given in both my books to decisions and non-decisions. They are picked out for their longer-term effects on the structures of the world economy. *Casino Capitalism* chose just five decisions or non-decisions that seemed to have contributed to the heightened volatility in financial and other markets that was the leitmotiv of the whole study. They were, first, the refusal of Europeans to accept more equal burden-sharing with the Americans for the costs of Western defence and particularly NATO. Second and third were the rich countries' refusal to undertake redistributive UN aid, and the decision to opt for case-by-case, ad hoc treatment of sovereign debt (Strange 1998f: 5–6; Strange 1986f: 31–58). Fourth, was the failure to make and keep rules about subsidised export credits; and fifth was the British Labour government's decision to reopen the City of London for international financial business.

These were all early post-war decisions. I added five more critical political choices taken in the later period 1971–85. Briefly, these were the US withdrawal from foreign exchange markets in the mid-1970s; the cynical pantomime (as I called it) of continued discussion on international monetary reform in the 1960s; American refusal after the oil-price rise in 1973 to negotiate with the oil-producing states; and the stonewalling strategy chosen by Washington to deal with the French-led Conference on International Economic Cooperation (CIEC) in 1974. The only positive key decision was the US response to bank failures – The Franklin National Bank and Bankhaus Herstatt, both in 1974.

Note that all these key decisions were decisions of state policymakers – mainly but not all, American. That was also true of the key decisions picked out as important in *Mad Money*. In 1987, the stock market crash in October of that year might have led the US authorities to reimpose stricter rules on share dealing, insider trading, entry conditions etc. It did not. The light stayed green for deregulation and liberalisation not just in the US but in competing markets in London, Europe, Tokyo and the markets emerging in the developing world. Second, in 1988, there was a positive decision on the regulation of banks. The BIS, led by the US and supported by Britain, adopted an 8:1 capital–assets ratio. Third, came the decisions following the fall of the Berlin Wall and the collapse of the Soviet rule in central Europe. Germany unilaterally decided to reunite east with west Germany but all the other decisions were negative. Fourth, was the reversal in 1996 of the Basle Accord on capital–assets ratios, already referred to. Fifth, was the response of the US, the IMF and the Group of Ten to the turmoil in Asian currency and investment markets in the summer and autumn of 1997. Even when it meant rescuing insolvent banks in Mexico or in Asia, the security of the system took precedence in policymaking over the principles of bank regulation.

In a nutshell, it was the governments of states – especially that of the United States – that decided in favour of deregulation and globalisation. Sometimes pushed by market forces, they still had freedom of choice, and by and large opted to give way, rather than resist. If this caused problems for them later, it was their own doing, their choice.

We are back, therefore, with the old International Relations question of the national interest. Looking after national interests is the responsibility of national governments. But who decides what policies are in the national interest? History gives us many examples of states choosing policies supposedly in the national interest, but which in fact were chosen to serve the interests of social, political or economic elites, and burdened society in general with high costs and risks that could hardly be avoided. What we have to ask, therefore, is whether, and how far, the decisions and non-decisions taken by the United States were really in the long-term interests of the American people or whether, and how far, they served the vested interests of Wall Street and big business.

This is not a new question. History has many examples of national policies serving special interests. The British government decision in the mid-nineteenth century, after the Indian Mutiny, to take over government from the East India Company might be one example. This clearly served the interests of British traders in India, opened new career possibilities in the army and civil service for the younger sons of an expanding British middle class and added imperial glamour to the monarchy – 'the brightest jewel in the imperial crown'. But the longer-run consequences for the British economy and society generally were negative. The British education system was shaped to produce young colonial administrators, rather than the technologically trained industrial managers produced in Germany (Corelli Barnett, Maurice Zinkin etc.). The Indian tail came to wag the British dog, despite the subordination of Indian trade and production to British interests and the extraction of gold to finance persistent payments deficits (Kenwood and Loughheed 1999; de Cecco 1987).

A comparable case would be the French decision to annex Algeria and to use it as a cheap way of rewarding underpaid French army veterans with land taken from the locals – a policy first practiced systematically by the Romans. Although special state and economic interests benefited, the end result was the creation of the 'pieds noirs' – the settlers who bitterly resisted de Gaulle's decision to give Algeria its independence, cutting the material and human losses to French society.

Another might be the American decision, first taken by Kennedy, to intervene with 'military advisers' in Vietnam. Military and ideological interests were given priority in the name of containment and the US national interest in resisting communism. But the cost and the involvement escalated under Johnson to the point where American society, seeing no national interest worth pursuing, turned against the Vietnam war.

And a more recent one might be Chancellor Kohl's unilateral decision on German unification after 1989. His decision found widespread popular support. But was it really in the long-term national interest of west German citizens? It was certainly very costly for west German taxpayers, particularly when Kohl insisted against the advice of the central bank on an exchange rate of 1:1 between west and east German currencies. And who benefited? German (and some foreign) companies who were given protection and generous state subsidies to expand in the new Lander; a miscellany of administrators, employed east German workers, west German academics and others who climbed on the unification bandwagon. History and sentiment assured popular support. But was it really a rational choice?

One could go back through history collecting more of the same: the British rejection of autonomy for the American colonies, the Spanish and Portuguese invasions of south America in search of gold and silver, and many, many more. Moreover, ideas and ideologies – 'manifest destiny', 'the white man's burden', 'la mission civilisatrice', 'the final triumph of socialism worldwide' – have often served to veil the conflict between special and national interests. In the period covered by *Mad Money*, the concealing ideology has been that of liberal economics and specifically, monetarism and supply-side economic logic. The failures of Soviet planning and the success of US capitalism carried the message to the developing countries and then to the ex-socialist ones.

American decline?

It is hardly necessary, in view of the record since the mid-1980s, to reiterate the point that the power of the US, far from declining as conventional American thinking had it in the 1980s, is greater than ever, and that there is growing asymmetry between the structural power of US decision making over the world economy (and especially the financial system) and that of other states. The US is more powerful; they are less powerful. *The Retreat of the State*, therefore, is imposed on most national societies, but is self-imposed on US society. Joseph Nye's notion of the 'soft power' of the United States in the world is not wrong, but still distorts the truth, which is that there is nothing very soft about the way US administrations can take unilateral decisions affecting others, military or monetary, with immunity (Nye 1990). Most of such decisions, we have seen, have enhanced the power of market forces, increasing volatility and uncertainty. But some have also been consciously system-preserving, imposing re-regulation rather than deregulation, and undertaking new costs and responsibilities in the interests of global financial stability rather than simply the shorter-term interests of the US economy and its taxpayers.

This ambiguity in US policies towards the international financial system, – permissive in some directions, re-regulatory in others – reflects in miniature the continuing but ill-founded controversy over globalisation. Is it real or a myth? The clear conclusion to be drawn from the evidence in *Mad Money* is that globalisation is real. It can be exaggerated, but change there undoubtedly has been. State power, on the other hand, still exists and can be – and has been – used to limit the local consequences of globalisation. The erosion of national controls over banks and non-banks (Strange 1998f: chapter 8) however, shows that this state power is increasingly shared with markets, enterprises and non-state authorities (Strange 1996b).

But the evidence also shows the wide diversity of experience – for states and governments, for enterprises and for social classes. The theoretical implication is clear: the search for general theories is a vain one. Social scientists – and especially economists – have always hoped to find such general theories – theories of economic growth and development, theories of the business cycle, theories of the firm, theories of inflation. A recent study in international political economy by Jonathan Nitzan has explained why such hopes were always vain and exposed the hollowness of theoretical pretensions in economics (Nitzan 1998). Nitzan argues that economists always left the power of capital out the picture. It could not be accommodated in the logic of liberal economics; and no agreed definition of what constituted capital was therefore possible among economists. Without an agreed definition, no general theory could be found. Nitzan, interestingly, draws inspiration from Thorstein Veblen and Lewis Mumford, arguing that the power of capital is not a constant. Rather, the differential power of capital (DPK) and variations in the rate of differential accumulation (DA) help explain the widening rich–poor gap in incomes and the progressively higher returns in the United States to financial business than to manufacturing or agriculture.

In their vain search for general theories, social scientists have for a long time put great faith in the value of quantitative data. The more, the better. Both *Casino Capitalism* and *Mad Money* poured cold water on such hopes. The earlier work introduced the concept of the 'areas of significant ignorance' developing in international finance. As capital became more and more mobile across national jurisdictions, regulatory authorities had less and less reliable information about behaviour in financial markets and about the effectiveness – or otherwise – of government fiscal and monetary interventions. The evidence in *Mad Money* strongly suggests that the areas of significant ignorance are even more extensive today than they were in the mid-1980s.

Bad theory misleads policy

To sum up, the description of change in international finance does not merely show there is very little good theory to discover. It shows that there is a lot of bad theory out there that continues to dominate research agendas and teaching practices. Students should be warned against these bad theories. They may choose to disregard the warnings for career reasons, or they may cling to them in desperation as drowning men clutch at straws. In the United States especially, researchers are told that you must find an hypothesis and proceed to test it against the available data (King, Keohane and Verba 1994). This imperative derives from Karl Popper who defined a theory as a proposition that could be falsified (Popper 1969). The alternative approach to research – generally in contemporary social science – was that of Feyerabend. In *Against Method* (1993), this eccentric writer argued that all you needed for research was a good question. Forget theory. Ibn Khaldun in North Africa in the fourteenth century would have agreed. His question was, simply, 'Why and how are things as they are?'

Two examples of bad theory, leading to counterproductive policy decisions were, first, the theories of declining US power just mentioned; and, second, theories of the beneficent effects of capital mobility.

Belief in the decline of US power dominated American thinking in the 1970s and 1980s. Paul Kennedy's *Rise and Fall of the Great Powers* (1987) and a number of other works promoted the idea that hegemonic power in the international system was fated to be temporary, either because of military over-commitment (Kennedy 1987; Calleo 1987) or because of the economic burdens of maintaining stability in the world trade and finance. Events reinforced academic interpretation: the Americans were shocked by the oil-price rise engineered by OPEC, by the fall of the Shah of Iran, by the depreciation of the dollar, and the loss of export and manufacturing production share to Japan.

But the policies adopted in accord with the theory were often – not always – counterproductive and contrary to US long-term interests. 'Strategic' trade policies designed to promote US exports and protect US industry from Asian competition meant adopting bullying tactics – as in the Super 301 programme – not only toward Japan but generally to Europeans, Latin Americans and other allies. The Cold War had suppressed resentment. When it ended, the legitimacy of US structural power was damaged.

The other example of bad theory leading to counterproductive policy is much more controversial. The theory plays a central role in liberal economics. It holds that the market economy requires the free, unobstructed movement of capital to achieve the efficient allocation of resources, from which all will benefit. In the last decade, country after country has appeared to subscribe to that belief by opening its economy to foreign capital. They did so not only because many of their policymakers came to accept liberal economic theory, but pragmatically to gain and hold market share with the help of foreign firms who brought access to capital, new technology and access to rich-country markets (Stopford and Strange 1991). And they did not always distinguish between opening up to foreign investors in long-term production and foreign investors looking for short-term speculative gains.

The most coherent, radical attack on the theory is to be found in a recent fifty-page UNDP monograph by the British economist John Eatwell. He challenges the validity of every theoretical claim made for the liberalisation of capital as being contrary to the experience of countries that have obediently liberalised (Eatwell 1998). The clear conclusion is that theory has led to bad policy. First, he says, theory argues that markets will efficiently allocate capital from capital rich-economies to capital-poor ones. In fact, capital moves in the opposite direction, from poor countries to rich ones. Second, liberalisation in theory would lower costs to borrowers. In fact, the borrowers have paid and the lenders have profited. Third, the theory praised the market for discovering derivatives and other devices for moderating risk. But in fact, the growth of derivatives has created new systemic risks unforeseen in theory. Fourth, the more efficient allocation of capital and other resources predicted by theory should have resulted in faster growth and more investment. It has not. Fifth and last, theory promised that the discipline of market forces would force states into policies that would promote both growth and stability. It has not done so.

Eatwell points out that none of these theoretical claims were reflected in the Bretton Woods agreement to maintain fixed exchange rates between national currencies. That was conditional on national currencies becoming by the late 1950s freely convertible with each other for current account transactions, not for transactions on the capital account. Thus, it was assumed states would keep exchange controls over capital coming in, and going out of the country. American financial and business interests, however, had other ideas. They sought freedom to produce and sell goods in Europe, and did not want exchange controls to stop them. The result was a revision of Bretton Woods rules to allow convertibility – and therefore IMF help – for countries (like Britain) with problems arising on the capital account as well as on the current account (Strange 1976d).

By comparing the theoretical claims with actual experience over the last two or three decades, Eatwell arrives at the conclusion that the theory, far from producing greater efficiency and stability in the world economy, has resulted in policies that greatly increased its fragility. That fragility, he suggests, is manifest in four ways. The liquidity crises – as in Asia – actually cut GNP, lose jobs and choke food supplies. Second, higher risks in the market sectors increase the bias toward short-term responses rather than productive long-term ones. Third, increased risks to states produce a deflationary bias in policymaking. And fourth, market operators aware of the fragility of local currencies and markets, press for greater ease of exit – flexibility, which in effect relieves them of the costs of their own risk-taking.

The two examples are enough to reiterate Cox's point that theory is always *for* someone. US decline suited interests that wanted US power to be used to open Japan's domestic markets to American competition. Liberal economic theories about the beneficent effects of financial liberalisation for developing as well as developed economies suited Wall Street and its associated financial elites.

The Asian story also reinforces the contention that the pursuit of a general theory is futile. The only common feature in Asia in 1997 was the fatal combination of external pressures on Asian states to liberalise too fast and the weakness of state regulation and supervision of banks. Beyond that, the experience of China and Taiwan was quite different from that of Indonesia or Thailand. Explanatory theory should say why this was.

Eatwell concludes by asking the So What? question: If liberal theory has misled policymakers, what is to be done to save the international financial system from the consequences? It is a question neither economists nor other social scientists should ignore. They have a social responsibility – the price of academic freedom – to enlighten, to explain and to prescribe if they can. Yet, although expectations of a bear market in shares, even of an ensuing decade of world recession, have grown, there has been a curious absence of serious academic discussion of measures that might be taken, even now, to avert or to moderate the downturn. Yet a number of proposals have been made, independently of others. Some, like the Tobin tax on foreign exchange transactions, have been debated. Others, like Soros's idea of a voluntary insurance fund for international banks, have not. Such free and open discussion can only be arranged by academics – national and international officials and market operators both have too many interests and prejudices to protect. And although academic debate by itself rarely changes the basic ideas – whether pro-market or pro-state – that at any time dominate the knowledge structure, academic debate when it takes place against a background of growing disillusion, of doubt and uncertainty can act as a catalyst to action.

Section III
_N A_
Authority and Markets in Theory and Practice

Introduction and Commentary

One of the core themes which runs through Susan Strange's work is the question of how to analyse authority in the international political economy. For Strange, it was not enough to merely look at the resources various states and groups utilised in the global system, rather she insisted the structures of the system were also an integral part of the way power was manifest. In each of the four structures she identified, security, finance, production and knowledge, the ability to set the rules of the game, the ability to construct the agenda from which choices by other actors could be made, was a major if under-recognised element of power. Discussed at length in _States and Markets_ (Strange 1988e) this is perhaps the theoretical innovation for which Strange is best known. However, from her notion of structural power and her earlier work on transnational political economy she was also insistent that much IPE lacked any serious assessment of the role and power of multinational corporations. This drove her to argue for the development of links with business school researchers who she thought had been much less myopic in this regard. This led to one of her most influential books outside the discipline of International Relations: _Rival States, Rival Firms_ (Stopford and Strange 1991).

The first selection uses her analysis of structural power, authority and markets to consider the argument that in the mid-1980s the US was suffering a decline in its power. In typical fashion she attacks conventional (US) academic analyses which support the decline thesis, and argues that far from losing power the US had, in some ways, reinforced its dominance of the global political economy. The problem was not the lack of power but rather the responsible use _of_ power, and the US was sorely lacking in terms of responsibility. The core of her structural analysis is extended in the second selection where she starts to develop a 'theory of trans-national empire'. Significantly she initially delves into the epistemology of international theories, and then uses this as a basis for her analysis of 'non-territoriality'. This chapter therefore represents an important extension and partial reconceptualisation of her notion of structural power to take account of her interpretation of the complexities of globalisation.

In the third selection Strange offers a useful summary of her work with John Stopford, published as _Rival States, Rival Firms_ and a product of her long-held belief that the academic separation of the disciplines of IR and international business hindered the understanding of the global political economy. In this article she outlines the conceptual basis of the analysis of the book: that diplomacy is now triangular, traditional state–state diplomacy has been joined by state–firm, and firm–firm diplomacy in the international political economy. This reflected her view that linking TNCs with specific national economies is increasingly difficult, not least due to the decreasing centrality of territorial considerations of power. The fourth selection is Strange's extension of her structural power analysis to a broader historical and sociological frame. Characteristically, she prefaces her remarks with a broadside against the conventional view of IR, in this case Waltz's famous LSE lecture. She then develops an analysis which argues that the US retains structural power, and that action should be taken to encourage Americans to recognise this (to her, obvious) fact. This should then enable the US to act again as hegemon for the general good rather than for the supposed benefit of their domestic economy.

9
'The Persistent Myth of Lost Hegemony', 1987

The distinguished Swedish economist, Gunnar Myrdal, once commented ruefully on the failure of social scientists in general and economists in particular to apply the methods of social science to themselves. Why was it, he asked, that they so seldom bothered to ask the sort of questions about their own activities and behaviour that sociologists and anthropologists usually asked about tribes and societies remote from the world of the present, either in distance or in time? Why did it apparently never occur to them to investigate the priority given in social science to some issues above others? Why did certain questions absorb the interest of a whole generation or school of academics while others, just as intrinsically puzzling, went unnoticed? Why did academics accept some underlying assumptions, while questioning others? In economics, particularly, the conventional literature taught in thousands of graduate and undergraduate courses shows that most economists tacitly share certain fundamental assumptions about the rationality of buyers and sellers in the marketplace, or about the easy availability of information regarding supply and demand that happen to be convenient for economic argument but which do not always accord with everyday experience (Myrdal 1970).

Myrdal's injunction, which could be summarized in the command, 'Physician, diagnose thyself!' applies equally to the study of international relations and international political economy. I shall argue that it is high time indeed that we pay much more attention to the sociology of international studies, and especially to the reasons why one particular myth – that of America's lost hegemony – took root so strongly in the United States academic community about fifteen years ago and why it has been so generally and unquestioningly accepted since – so much so that it has even gained credence in the world beyond North America. I do so because history seems to show that some speciously attractive myths can be extremely powerful, persistent, and dangerous. Think only of the belief that certain old women had supernatural powers and could cast magic spells or put the Evil Eye on people, or the myth that eating an enemy made one strong and virile. Or, thinking again of virility, consider the consequences for wildlife of the pathetic, but still persistent, myth that rhinoceros horn was an aphrodisiac. More recently, there have been no less destructive myths of a more political, nature – invented, perhaps, but none the less powerful – for example, that German-speaking people came from a distinct Aryan race; or that Iranian boy-soldiers who undertook suicide missions for their country would go straight to heaven.

In its extreme form, the myth that the United States today is just a little, old country much like any other and has, in some sudden and miraculous way, lost its hegemonic power may seem more plausible than do some of these other myths. But when it is subjected to close and searching scrutiny, it is just as far from truth. And unless cool and rational analysis undermines its power to move minds and shape attitudes, it can be every bit as dangerous. In living memory, the optimism of the United States gave Americans and others a vision of a new, better and attainable future for the world; today, the myth of lost hegemony is apt to induce in everybody only pessimism, despair, and the conviction that, in these inauspicious circumstances, the only thing to do is to ignore everyone else and look after your own individual or national interests. Thus, some of the same American contributors to *International Organization* who are personally persuaded of the benefits of more international cooperation and conflict resolution, may paradoxically be contributing to a *less* cooperative environment by subscribing to and perpetuating the myth of lost American power.

Two other fashionable academic notions which have gained rapid popularity, especially in the United States, have multiplied its power and influence. One is the notion, derived from the theory of public goods, that we can explain the lack of international economic cooperation by applying the theory to the behaviour of states in conditions of dispersed political power. And the other is the notion – now, I would guess, at the very peak of academic fashion – that Game Theory can be usefully applied to an analysis of state policies in the face of common transnational social and economic problems, including everything from the control of banking to the stabilization of oil prices. When combined with the conviction that the United States has permanently lost its powers of leadership, both fashionable notions offer a speciously convincing explanation – even an excuse – for the present lack of international cooperation and feebleness of international organizations.[1] Especially in Game Theory, facts are ignored or overlooked; it is all the easier because the vulgar representations of Game Theory habitually deal with situations in which the 'players' are engaged in one game at a time; in which the players are limited to two, or some quite small number; and in which the game is played in *vacuo* and the players are motivated by precise and singular goals. These situations are the very opposite of the reality of international political economy, in which the players (including 'bit players') are engaged simultaneously in a whole series of bargaining games, some domestic and some international, and are motivated by a complex and shifting tapestry of interacting, sometimes contradictory, motivations.

For present purposes, however, I shall confine myself to a critical examination of the two politically important propositions regarding hegemony that these theories supposedly sustain and explain. These are that the United States has lost its hegemonic power over the system, and that this loss is a major reason for the instability and aimlessness of the international political economy. This examination will require attention on the origins of these propositions, a testing of the historical evidence for hegemonic stability theory, and, finally, some discussion of the nature and exercise of power on which the theory implicitly rests. Such assumptions are crucial to explanatory theory because the outcomes in an international society that has no legitimate, overriding authority are necessarily determined by relationships of power and far less by law, custom, or social convention than is the case within national societies.

Contrary to conventional American wisdom, I shall argue that my critique of hegemonic stability theory leads to five quite important concluding propositions. These are:

- The great game of states has changed over the last quarter-century in a very fundamental way, for reasons that are primarily economic, not primarily political.
- In this new great game of states, structural power decides outcomes (both positive and negative) much more than relational power does, and the United States' structural power has, on balance, increased.
- There has always been an inherent conflict in US foreign policy between its goals of liberalism for the pursuit of its commercial and financial interests and the exigencies of realism in the pursuit of political and military national interests. Now, in a world depression, perceptions of US national interests are more apt to be perceived in terms of the short run than of the long, so that 'realism', 'unilateralism', or 'domesticism' in US policy is now much more evident than liberal internationalism.[2]
- The use of hegemonic structural power in ways that are destructive of international order and cooperation has been an important cause of world economic instability and continuing crisis.
- A necessary condition, therefore, for greater stability and cooperation lie within the United States, rather than in the institutions and mechanisms of international cooperation.

These conclusions support, though on somewhat different grounds, arguments made by Bruce Russett (1985), Giovanni Arrighi (1982), and Stephen Gill (1986).

Origins

The theories I shall challenge do not constitute a single body of homogeneous or consistent ideas. Rather, they are a bundle of concepts and explanations centring around the notion of the role of the hegemon or leader, the dominant state in an international system, and the connection between the hegemon and the stability of that system. First of all, the concept of hegemony is loose and ambiguous regarding both its attributes and its application. Opinions differ as to how you can recognize a hegemon, and on how hegemons use their power.

Many contributions to the literature have chosen indicators that are either irrelevant (monetary reserves, trade as a proportion of GNP) or imprecise (share of world trade, share of world GNP, production of raw materials or manufactures). Russett has usefully made the valid distinction between a state's power base and its control over outcomes (1985: 208ff). It follows that while one may look for quantitative indicators of the former, control over outcomes can only be inferred from historical evidence – a more difficult task. Hegemonic stability theory, as it is referred to, has been advanced both as a general law applicable to widely separated periods of world history and as a specific explanation for the difficulties of our own times. The theory takes two forms: a 'strong' version, which says that a hegemon will produce order and stability in the world – and, more specifically, order and stability in an interdependent world economy – when it uses its power to enforce order on others; and a 'weak' version, which says that hegemonic power is a necessary, but not always a sufficient, condition for order. In other words, the presence or absence of a hegemon only partially answers why order and stability have prevailed at some time in the international economic system and disorder and instability at others.

One reason is that we have not clearly understood the alternative ways hegemons exercise power and the alternative uses to which their power may be put. Duncan Snidal has made the useful distinction between hegemony that is beneficent (that is, exercised by example and persuasion); hegemony that is beneficent but exercised by coercion; and hegemony that is coercive and exploitive (Snidal 1985; cf. Gilpin 1975: 34). Russett concludes that the United States at its hegemonic peak did use coercive power to exploit the system, but it also beneficently paid some of the costs to bring about postwar economic prosperity. The notion that international 'regimes' sustain order has also been associated with the role of the hegemon. These regimes are more than the international institutions set up to administer or facilitate multilateral cooperation, though the institutions like the GATT (General Agreement on Tariffs and Trade) or the International Monetary Fund (IMF) often reflect as well as serve the regime. The word 'regime' embraces the customs and habits of behaviour that, together with the formal agreements and institutions, provide a measure of continuity and stability in relations of states and of other transnational actors, such as corporations and banks (Krasner 1983). For many American scholars, it seemed no accident that the decline of order in the world economy and its financial system coincided in the mid-1970s with a time of weakness and humiliation in the conduct of United States foreign policy and, as many of them came to think, of American power.

Thus, the popularity of this set of theories began to grow about the time of the break-up of the convertible dollar and the gold exchange system at the beginning of the 1970s and the publication of Charles Kindleberger's scholarly study, *The World in Depression* (1973). This historical analysis challenged the rather US-bounded interpretation of the causes of economic depression in the 1930s that had been expounded in the monumental study by Milton Friedman and Anna Schwarz, *A Monetary History of the United States* (1963). Friedman and Schwarz had heavily emphasized the weaknesses of US monetary regulation (as in the freedom to deal in shares on margin) and the perversity of US monetary management by the Federal Reserve Board at crucial moments in the crisis years 1929–31. John Kenneth Galbraith, too, in *The Great Crash* (1980) had emphasized the folly of American bankers and the weakness and vacillation of American politicians and officials.

No, said Kindleberger, there was more to it than that. Commodity prices had started falling in 1927 and soon afterwards the flow of funds to primary producing countries had begun to slacken. But instead of acting in a counter-cyclical fashion, the United States had allowed the Wall Street boom to draw US funds back from Europe, had raised protectionist barriers and had failed to support its banking system when panic set in. What such an integrated financial system really needed at such times of crisis, said Kindleberger, was a leader, or hegemon, which would maintain an open market for other countries' surpluses, especially in primary products. The hegemon would also maintain a steady outflow of capital for productive investment and, as an international lender of last resort, would keep an open discount window for distressed banks. These were functions that Britain had fulfilled before World War I and America after World War II. But between the wars, Britain, herself in trouble, was no longer able to take this role and the United States was unwilling to do so. Hence the prolonged depression of the 1930s (Kindleberger 1973: 291–4).[3]

Another contribution to this beguiling edifice of argument was made by Robert Gilpin in a neat study rather misleadingly titled *The United States and the Multinational Corporation* (1975). Setting a trend in academic exposition, Gilpin described and explained the different approaches to world politics taken by liberals, mercantilists (realists, in political terms), and Marxists.[4] He went on to make a realist argument, based on an interpretation of Britain's long decline, that the United States should avoid making the same mistakes of investing heavily overseas to the detriment of its own national economy. Hegemonic power, Gilpin's argument said, brought about its own destruction as the outflow of precious capital sustained the economic development of rival states at the expense of the hegemon's own economic base. The argument (later referred to as the hegemon's dilemma) appealed strongly to American liberals, who are traditionally suspicious of big business and critical of the part played by American corporations in Latin America (Stein 1984).

Gilpin's argument has recently been refined and reinforced by a much more generalized (and thus more susceptible to question) piece of theorizing by American economist Mancur Olson in the grandiosely titled *The Rise and Decline of Nations* (1982). In *The Logic of Collective Action*, Olson had earlier developed an austere line of economic reasoning about free riders and the provision of public goods. He explained how America's allies could continue to act with impunity as free riders on the security provided by the Western alliance, leaving the United States to pay the lion's share of the defence bill (Olson 1965). Encouraged by this success, Olson then embarked on economic history with a new general theory. The enjoyment of hegemonic power, Olson argued, conferred special benefits on certain social and economic groups, which consequently developed a natural resistance to change and a preference for the comfort of their familiar privileges. A kind of economic and social sclerosis was thus apt to set in, clogging the arteries and fatally delaying adaptive change. This would explain why the former hegemon lost, first, its economic leadership, and then its political power, to rivals unencumbered with the same coalition of conservative, self-preserving interests; the successful rivals were therefore in a better position to take advantage of technological advances and the changing demands of the market.

Today, there are variants of hegemonic theory to suit most political tastes. For American radicals, Immanuel Wallerstein has developed an alternative general theory of hegemonic rise and decline, building on foundations laid in his large study, *The Modern World System* (itself following the trail blazed by Fernand Braudel) (Wallerstein 1984).[5] In a series of essays entitled *The Capitalist World Economy*, Wallerstein usefully defines hegemony to mean more than military predominance or capturing the largest share of the world market, yet less than total omnipotence, which he rightly says cannot exist in an interstate system. Hegemony, he asserts, refers to:

> ... that situation in which the ongoing rivalry between the so-called 'great powers' is so unbalanced that one power is truly *primus inter pares*; that is, one power can largely impose its rules and its wishes (at the very least by effective veto power) in the economic, political, military, diplomatic and even cultural arenas.

That power has a simultaneous edge in efficiency in agro-industrial production, in commerce and in finance so great 'that all allied powers are *de facto* client states and opposed major powers feel relatively frustrated and highly defensive vis-à-vis the hegemonic power' (Wallerstein 1984: 37–44).

In Wallerstein's historical perspective, hegemonic power was exercised on three occasions in the modern world system: by the United Provinces in the mid-seventeenth century, by Britain in the nineteenth, and by the United States in the twentieth centuries. In each case, there was a short period in which the hegemon had an edge over all others in all three fields of economic endeavour. In each case, the hegemony was secured by a thirty-year war; and hegemonic decline eroded the alliance system which the hegemon had created.

Meanwhile, for American realists, Stephen Krasner followed Gilpin, closely connecting hegemonic decline and the collapse or disintegration of international 'regimes'. At their peak, hegemons use their power to build frameworks of acceptable rules, institutions, and customary usages that will maintain economic order in money and trade. But as their influence declines, their appetite for international economic order also wanes and they are more concerned with their own particular national interest (Krasner 1983).

The conclusion reached via these post-hegemonic interpretations of recent history, however, are by no means mutually consistent. Wallerstein foresees the break-up of the North Atlantic Treaty Organization (NATO), and a diplomatic reshuffle as a new Kondratiev upswing takes hold in the 1990s. Krasner predicts a return to what he perceives as the normal state of international society – a Hobbesian all-against-all. Keohane comes near to arguing that any international cooperation is always preferable to none. (For instance, he defends the notoriously illiberal Multi Fibre Arrangement on the curious grounds that it is better than unilateral action leading to escalating discord (Keohane 1984: 216). But the fact is that the agreement is only a cover for bilateral agreements between importers and would-be exporters, and that because the latter are powerless to bargain, their discord is, if not silent, at least inconsequential; thus, the action half-legitimized by the agreement *is* in fact unilateral.) Robert Keohane argues, at the end of *After Hegemony*, that without American leadership, America's allies and partners will have to renew their collective effort to rebuild the collapsing framework or order in the international economy. According to Keohane: 'Shared interests and existing institutions make it possible to cooperate but the erosion of American hegemony makes it necessary to do so in new ways' (1984: 244).

Only a very few American voices have questioned the two basic propositions on which all the forms of this conventional wisdom rests. These are, first, the proposition that the United States has lost power in and over the system; and secondly, the proposition that this reason accounts for the disorders in the system. Russett has asserted that the decline of American power, like the premature reports of Mark Twain's death, has been greatly exaggerated (Russett 1985). David Calleo argues in *The Imperious Economy* (1982) that the general disorder was not so much attributable to a decline in American power as it was to the persistent attempt of successive US administrations since Eisenhower to get a quart out of a pint pot, that is, to finance both military supremacy and national welfare programmes with inadequate budgetary resources. Similarly, Henry Nau argued that it was the 'domesticist' tendency in US policymaking that was the root of the global troubles, rather than the decline of American hegemonic power (Nau and Bergsten 1985).

But these minority views have been drowned out by the rest. This is the more surprising since the last few years have seen a small but steady stream of journal articles published in the United States, many of them by younger American scholars, who have tried to test the historical validity of hegemonic stability theory as a general law or axiom of the international system. Their conclusions for the most part have thrown grave doubts on the basic assumptions of the theory.

The record of history

One basic assumption of this literature is that hegemonic powers at their peak of strength and economic leadership are liberal by inclination. The second is that the system benefited because they were able to influence others to be more liberal than they otherwise would have been. The result of both their liberalism and their influence was that the international economy was more stable and more prosperous as a result of their leadership. But much recent American research work – to say nothing of past studies by economic historians in many different countries – has denied the validity of hegemonic stability theory. Searching back in the records of the nineteenth century, American scholars found that Britain as the hegemonic leader of the time had not in fact been consistently liberal in its management of trade. In the three important ports of the Arabian peninsula controlled by Britain

– Aden, Muscat, and Mocha – compelling strategic considerations had led Britain to adopt increasingly restrictive commercial attitudes (Lawson 1983). In West Africa, British leadership is often credited with the agreement reached at the Congress of Berlin to maintain an open door policy in trade but David Laitin (1982) found that political issues had modified British liberalism. In another, much broader study of relative tariff levels in Europe in the nineteenth century, Tim McKeown found that many other factors besides British hegemony had influenced European states towards more liberal trade policies – and, after 1870, away from them (1983). Trade policy tended to be more liberal when business was booming than when it hit a slump (as in the 1870s), regardless of the power or attitude of the leading economic power. Much the same conclusion emerged from a piece of comparative analysis by Peter Cowhey and Edward Long of trade policies in the 1970s, which found that, as economic growth slowed in the mid-1970s, European and American governments responded to distressed industries with subsidies and protectionist trade measures (1983). The crucial factor has not been the decline of American hegemonic power, as Keohane argued, but rather the depressed state of the world economy, as I argued in *The International Management of Surplus Capacity* (Strange and Tooze 1981).

The evidence of postwar history on the basic assumptions of both weak and strong hegemonic stability theory is just as damaging. It is not hard to show that the United States (like Britain before it) has not consistently pursued liberal objectives, nor has it successfully persuaded others to join that pursuit.

In the late 1940s, the United States Senate refused to ratify the Havana Charter so persistently that the Truman administration was obliged to settle for the less extensive regime contained in the GATT. And later, in the mid-1950s, the United States used the agreement's waiver clause to exempt agricultural trade from the processes of multilateral tariff bargaining, thus protecting American farmers from the lower-cost competition of Argentinian beef, New Zealand wool and lamb, Caribbean sugar and citrus, and various other products.

While the Havana Charter was being negotiated, the United States took an initiative – in the Truman Declaration on the continental shelf – extending state jurisdiction, which was far from liberal. This declaration was the first step in a process of maritime enclosure, and was quickly copied by Latin American governments to extend their fishing rights to the same 200-mile limit that the Americans had declared within their jurisdiction for oil exploration. The Soviet Union, the European Community, and every other maritime state followed the American move. Whether in the long run the enclosure of the high seas is regarded as good (because it may help to conserve fishing stocks) or bad (because it is a limitation on free competition for the ocean's resources in the market) is beside the point. The fact is that for reasons of domestic policy and to assert the primacy of federal authority over state authority, the United States took the first illiberal step, extending state power and limiting the old 'freedom of the seas'.

In a recent study on the protection of American shipyards and the subsidization of ships flying the United States flag, Alan Cafruny concluded that only changes in technology had led the United States to oppose the implicitly restrictive system proposed by both the UNCTAD Code of Conduct on Liner Conferences and the Brussels Package, approved by the European Community. At an earlier stage the United States had turned a blind eye to the illiberal cartel arrangements of the conference system and had allowed its own fleet to take part in them just as it allowed its own airlines to join the IATA cartel in air transport (Cafruny 1985; Krasner 1985: chapter 8).

After the war, when the United States used its persuasive powers, backed up by coercive leverage, to get others to help establish liberal economic arrangements, the evidence throws even more doubt on the effectiveness of US hegemonic dominance. The United States could hardly have been in a stronger position to exercise hegemonic power than at the beginning of the European Recovery Program. The American monopoly of atomic weapons gave the West Europeans the only effective barrier to a further spread of Soviet influence and domination. American dollars offered the only hope of maintaining imports of food and capital goods which were necessary to keep up the momentum of economic reconstruction after the damage wrought in war. Another winter of shortage and cold like that of 1946–47 would have threatened the stability of at least two governments, France and Italy. Yet, as Alan Milward's recent study of the negotiations between the Americans and the Europeans has shown in considerable detail, the West Europeans were successful in resisting American attempts to insist on a full-blown customs union between the recipients of Marshall Aid. Wedded by history and sentiment to their particular concept of the role of the state in the economy, the Europeans foiled all the efforts of the United States to set a liberalizing supranational authority over their respective governments (Milward 1984).

Similar successful rearguard actions had been fought over the liberalization of air transport at Chicago in 1945. The Americans were in their strongest position ever: they had the only viable aircraft manufacturing industry in existence; an exceptionally thriving home market as a base for foreign operations; and a worldwide network of bases and operating experience, both acquired through the wartime operations of its strategic air command. Yet the American demand for the five freedoms and an open market was successfully defeated by the other states setting up the ICAO (Jonsson 1987).

Nor did the Europeans cease their resistance to American liberalism in trade. Under Article 35 of the GATT they could individually refuse to extend to any new High Contracting Party the privileges already negotiated on the basis of the most-favoured-nation principles to all the other members. The result was that though the United States could use its hegemonic power in the organization to insist on the admission of Japan, the Europeans could delay for years the moment when they had to admit Japanese competitors on equal terms to their domestic (and their often sheltered colonial) markets. And by 1962, when the Americans, still concerned for strategic reasons to get Japan admitted to the 'rich man's club', proposed first the short-term and then the Long-Term Cotton Textile Agreement, which would assure a steady expansion of market access, it was able to do so with only limited success as far as European Community markets were concerned; even then, it could hardly have succeeded without the support of Britain, which had its own reasons for wanting to share with others the problems of adjusting to price competition from Commonwealth textile producers in India and Hong Kong (Curzon *et al.* 1976). But while some strategic considerations made the Americans act liberally toward Japan at least until the late 1960s, other strategic considerations took precedence over liberal doctrine when it came to American policy towards trade with the communist states. Just as the British had political reasons for preferring restrictive commerce in Arabian ports, so the Americans were convinced that the beneficial influence of trade on politics stopped at the Iron Curtain. After the mid-1950s, the Europeans, especially the West Germans, favoured a more liberal trade regime, and the Americans opposed it.

In short, it is hard to see American liberalism in the twenty-five years after World War II as a genuine doctrine rather than as an ideology, that is, a doctrine to be used when it was convenient and fitted the current perception of the national interest and one to be overlooked and forgotten when it did not. Moreover, if it were a genuine doctrine, it is hard to explain why it should have been quite so summarily abandoned in the space of about five years between 1968 and 1973. The British bureaucracy, by contrast, had clung to the liberal doctrines in which they had been brought up long after British economic dominance had faded away even in finance, let alone in manufacturing and in agriculture (Gardner 1980). The decline of American hegemony could hardly have been so steep that it brought a fundamental shift in the direction of US policy in less than a decade. It would seem that history, both under British and American economic leadership, has been rather more complicated than Gilpin, Keohane, or even Kindleberger suspected.

Liberalism in trade, I would argue, both as an attribute of hegemonic power and as a contributing factor to world economic growth and stability, has been much less important than Kindleberger's other two attributes of hegemony – the outflow of capital for investment and the provision of a stable international currency supported by discounting (that is, lender of last resort) facilities in times of financial crisis. The influence of hegemonic power on the trade policies of other states in the nineteenth century was at best very marginal. It has singularly little effect on the Austro-Hungarian Empire, or on the Turkish and the Tsarist empires, and precious little on the United States. Far more important, perhaps, were the statutory restrictions on the power of every British government from the Bank Charter Act of 1844 up to 1914 to pay its debts by printing money. The result was that relative prices in international trade were little affected by changes in the purchasing power of the currency in which bills of exchange were mostly denominated. Confidence in the value of money, in the political stability of Britain, and in the continued outflow of British capital provided other countries (like Japan) with the necessary confidence to pursue economic growth. The shorter period of American hegemony, though it began with confidence in the same three important factors, proved much more short-lived. It was strongly marked first by acute dollar shortage, soon followed by dollar glut, and in the last fifteen years, by a rapid depreciation of the dollar followed by an equally rapid appreciation. This depreciation resulted from policies producing a credit expansion that was geared, not to trade as in the nineteenth-century British system, but to bank lending through the uncontrolled

Euromarket system. The uncertainty produced by such monetary volatility has provided a powerful incentive for banks and other financial institutions to develop new instruments and operations that shift the consequent risk on to others. But the shift, in turn, has served to complicate and frustrate the efforts of governments to manage so rapidly changing a financial system (Strange 1986f).

Power and wealth

Another important point concerns the divergence between the reality of inter-national relations and its biased representation in hegemonic stability theories. They make the unspoken assumption that there is not much significant difference between the world economy of the nineteenth century, in which Britain was the economic leader (first in industry, later in commerce and finance), and the world economy of our own times, in which the United States is the economic leader. But there are very important differences. While many texts on international relations still portray the international system of sovereign states – or rather, of states claiming still to be sovereign – as a permanent feature, its economic environment has already substantially changed, and will continue to change in the future.

Economic changes integrating national societies with each other are bringing political changes. The nature of the competitive game between states is not what it was. Instead of competing for territory (because land was the prime source of wealth, and therefore wealth and political power for the state could be achieved through control over territory), states are now engaged increasingly in a different competitive game: they are competing for world market shares as the surest means to greater wealth and therefore greater economic security. True, some military security, however provided, is often a necessary condition for economic security. But with today's costly and fast-changing technologies, economic security can no longer be assured by producing for, and selling on, national markets alone. The LDCs who tried import-substitution as a development strategy found this out the hard way. The most successful industrialized countries, too, have been those who have been able to gain, and keep, a larger share of the world market for goods or services, or both. This truth has been obscured for the United States because, in many sectors, the US domestic market was so much larger than other national markets and formed such a large part, by itself, of the world market. In the 1950s and 1960s, moreover, US industry was often the beneficiary of US defence spending. Contracts for the US Defence Department helped companies develop new high-technology products, like computers and integrated circuits, with no downside risks.[6] By the 1980s, it became more uncertain whether technologies developed for military purposes will be so easily adapted to civilian markets, so that the opportunity costs of diverting corporate research efforts may in future be greater than the spillover benefits for US industry.

States, like Japan, which started without the benefits of such defence contracts, were obliged to find other means to apply existing technology and to finance the development of new technology so that national enterprises could enlarge their market shares and adapt flexibly to changing world market conditions.

If this analysis of change in the international system is broadly correct, then it follows that, in the new competitive game between states it is not relational power – described in conventional realist textbooks as the power of A to get B to do something it would not otherwise do – but structural power that counts. It is this power that, I shall argue, the United States still overwhelmingly possesses, and I shall now turn to a brief description of that structural power.

Four aspects of structural power

Structural power is the power to choose and to shape the structures of the global political economy within which other states, their political institutions, their economic enterprises, and (not least) their professional people have to operate. This means more than the power to set the agenda of discussion or to design (in American phraseology) the international 'regime' of rules and customs.

Structural power is to be found, not in a single structure, but rather in four separate but interrelated structures. They are like the four sides of a pyramid. Each is held up and supported by the other three. These four structures are not peculiar to the global political economy or world system. The sources of superior structural power are the same in very small human groups, like the family, or a remote and isolated village community, as they are in the world at large. In each of these, structural power lies:

- with the person or group able to exercise control over – that is, to threaten or to defend, to deny or to increase – other people's security from violence;
- with those able to control the system of production of goods and services;
- with those able to determine the structure of finance and credit through which (in all but the most primitive economies) it is possible to acquire purchasing power without having either to work or to trade it;
- with those who have most influence over knowledge, whether it is technical knowledge, religious knowledge, or leadership in ideas, and who control or influence the acquisition, communication, and storage of knowledge and information.

This breakdown of the components of structural power is only common sense. But it is often obscured by theoretical discussions about the nature of the state or of power that are either far too abstract or far too narrow. Structural power has four aspects, each reinforcing or detracting from the other three. In the international political economy, all four are important, and the state which is dominant in most aspect of structural power is the most powerful.

Take, first, power in the security structure. So long as the possibility of violent conflict threatens personal security, the state which offers protection against that threat exercises power – and does so even though the same defence force that gives protection may itself be something of a threat to security. Today, as in the past three decades, the United States controls the only force of intercontinental missiles carrying nuclear warheads that are any sort of a match for the corresponding force controlled from Moscow. Soviet power in the security structure was once inferior, and is now roughly equal. But among the other countries involved in the NATO alliance, the United States is still pre-eminent, as Table 9.1 shows.

Not only are America's NATO allies so much weaker in nuclear weapons that they are dependent on US protection, their dependence is increased by their inferiority to the Soviet Union and its Warsaw Pact allies in conventional weapons, especially on land and in the air. It need hardly be added that Japan is a negligible force in armaments; it is inferior even to South Korea. And it is this fundamental asymmetry in the security structure of the non-communist world that is often and easily overlooked in contemporary discussion of international economic issues. Always in the background, there is the contrast between the provision of security by the United States defence forces and the dependence of its partners upon them. The preponderant power of the United States in the security structure operates on land, at sea, in the air, and (most markedly) in space. There is no comparison between such a universal basic force and the very limited naval preponderance which was the main backing to British economic power in the earlier period of supposed hegemony.

Table 9.1   Nuclear forces: United States and NATO/Europe

	United States	*NATO excluding US*
Missiles		
ICBM	1,010	–
Intermediate	278	18
Tactical	144	171
Aircraft		
Long range	199	–
Medium range	55	–
Land-based strike	1,182	1,236
Carrier-based strike	666	38
Nuclear submarines	85	16
Total defence budget (1984)	$237 billion	$40 billion

Source: International Institute for Strategic Studies, *The Military Balance*, 1986–87, pp. 200–12.

Almost as important is the continued domination by the United States of the world's production structure. Who decides who shall produce what, how and with what reward, has always been almost as fundamental a question in political economy as who decides what defence shall be offered against security threats. Some American analysts' choice of indicators has misled them into thinking that their country is suffering economic decline. It is not the share of industrial manufactured products made in the United States nor the share of US exports of manufactures to world markets that counts. We should look instead at the proportion of total world production of goods and services produced: (a) in the United States, and (b) by enterprises ultimately headquartered in the United States and responsible to the government in Washington. We should note which corporations lead, rather than the percentage of world output produced in the United States, or the share of world exports produced in the United States. For example, of the largest corporations producing computers, the top six are American, as are twelve of the top twenty. Between them, they produce 62.3 per cent of total world production and have over 50 per cent of world turnover. IBM alone dominated the market with 35.6 per cent of world turnover in 1983, though it is now an open question whether some of the market will go to smaller competitors. The significance of this dominance is underlined by estimates that the present world demand for computers (estimated at $200 billion) will *quadruple* by 1991. It is the same story with integrated circuits. Texas Instruments and IBM are the leading world producers, even ahead of the Japanese. In telecommunications, too, AT&T and ITT are the top two companies in terms of sales. Both are sustained by the great size of the homogeneous domestic market – an asset the Americans are inclined to forget but one of which Europeans are acutely aware. Dr W. Dekker, president of Phillips Corporation, recently warned European governments that if they could not combine to provide a comparably uniform home base, European companies like Phillips, Siemens, Nixdorf, Bell, ICL, Ericsson, and Olivetti would be unable to survive and certainly could not stay based in Europe. 'If Europe does not unite, industrial innovation will pass Europe by', he concluded.[7]

Table 9.2   Percentage of total output produced in the United States

	1970	1980	1985 (est.)	1990 (est.)
Manufacturing	37.7	36.8	36.4	36.9
High tech	4.1	5.7	7.1	8.5
Capital goods	4.0	4.0	3.2	3.3
Consumer durables	4.8	4.4	4.8	4.6
Consumer non-durables	9.4	8.8	8.2	7.6
Basic goods	8.4	7.4	6.6	6.4
Services	48.1	51.5	52.2	52.1
All others	14.3	11.7	11.4	10.9

Source. Data Resources, Inc.; *Business Week*, 14 January 1985.

Broken down into categories, we see from Table 9.2 that, while the US shares of basic products (including steel, chemicals, paper) and consumer goods have declined between 1970 and 1980, the US share of high technology products is actually larger. And, it is estimated that this share will more than double the 1970 level by 1990. Similarly, American service industries will hold their share – 50 per cent or more – of the whole world market (Shelp 1981).

In the oil business, which remains the lifeblood of the world's industries and transport system, the seven American major oil companies dominate the top ten, together outnumbering and overpowering by far even the largest European and Japanese and OPEC enterprises.[8] In the aircraft business, the big names are still American – Lockheed, Boeing, and McDonnell Douglas. Six of the top nine companies, including the two largest, are American. Although there are big Swiss and British names in pharmaceuticals, the corporations with the biggest research budgets are American; and three of the largest five companies are American. Among the big industrial conglomerates, hedging their bets across a variety of sectors, it is again the Americans who lead.

In short, a perusal of any list of the top 100, 500, or 1,000 corporations producing for a world market will quickly bear out the contention that the decision-making power over the world's production structure still lies, not in Europe or Japan, but in the United States. Of the leading 300 enterprises in the world, 142 are US-based.

One reason for this dominance over production is that the United States provided the first mass market for manufactured consumer goods. The laws and policies of US governments therefore shaped the corporations that first exploited that market. They then discovered the managerial techniques for controlling international networks of foreign subsidiaries. The mode of operations and the *mores* of today's business world were first made in America; developments in the United States still influence it more than developments anywhere else (Casson 1983; Dunning and Pearce 1985; Vernon 1977).

The third leg of American structural power is almost as important. America has the ability to control the supply and availability of credit denominated in dollars, and thus to exert predominant influence for good or ill over the creation of credit in the world's monetary system. In this respect, the conventional indicators are all turned upside down. How much gold and foreign exchange the US government holds compared to Germany or Japan is beside the point when the United States is the only government capable of creating dollar assets that are accepted and saleable worldwide. In some sense, a financial system largely operating in dollars has no need of reserves.[9] In most countries, whether the balance-of-payments is in surplus or deficit indicates the strength or weakness of its financial position. With the United States, the exact converse can be true. Indeed, to run a persistent deficit for a quarter of a century with impunity indicates not American weakness, but rather American power in the system. To decide one August morning that dollars can no longer be converted into gold was a progression from exorbitant privilege to super-exorbitant privilege; the US government was exercising the unconstrained right to print money that others could not (save at unacceptable cost) refuse to accept in payment. And in the period 1973–83, when the dollar–deutschmark exchange rate became even more volatile, the power to decide whether or when central banks should intervene to check market trends rested solely with the United States. West Germany alone was powerless. The asymmetry was quite striking, just as it was later in the 1980s for the dollar–yen exchange rate (Feddersen 1986).

The significance of the dollar's predominance has also been well illustrated by the experience of Third World and Eastern European debt in the 1980s. American banks were foremost in lending to Latin America and were bailed out; German banks were foremost in lending to Poland and were not. The great majority of foreign bank loans were denominated in dollars. When first Mexico, then Brazil, Argentina, and the rest were unable to service their debt, the United States possessed two weapons more powerful than those of any other government: it could take advances in dollars to meet an emergency; and it could twist the arms of the largest and most influential banks in the system to follow its example with renewed medium-term credit. The evidence of American domination of the world's financial system is plentiful enough.

Not only were banks in the United States responsible for the lion's share of total bank assets in the industrial world but, more important, something like three-quarters of all these assets were denominated in dollars.[10] The ability of the United States to move this market is unequalled. By its unilateral decision, the International Banking Facilities (IBF) legislation of 1981, which allowed US banks the same freedom to conduct 'offshore' transactions from home, practically halted the expansion of Eurodollar assets in US bank branches abroad. These assets had grown in 1980 by $126 billion. In 1982, the growth was a mere $20 billion. A 1975 decision to deregulate markets (by allowing stockbrokers to compete in their charges) made comparable changes in policy irresistible for Britain, as for Japan.

Finally, implicit in much of the evidence already cited, America continued to dominate the world's knowledge structure. Knowledge is power, and whoever is able to develop or acquire a kind of knowledge that is sought by others, and whoever can control the channels by which it is communicated and the access to stores of knowledge, is able to dominate. In past times, priests and sages often exercised such dominance over kings and generals. The jealousy with which priesthoods guarded their knowledge and restricted access to it has been a common feature of all great religions. Today, the knowledge most sought after by those who pursue power or wealth, military or corporate leadership, is technology – the technology of new materials as well as new processes, new products and new systems of collecting, storing, and retrieving information and new systems of communication. Overall, the United States still leads in the advanced technology sectors – including those at the developing stage, such as artificial intelligence (space, ecology, ocean mining, and biotechnology) and the fast-growing new technologies of microcomputers, microelectronics, telecommunication, robots and factory automation, and data processing. The major flows of data still go to data banks in the United states (UNCTC 1979).

Three factors have combined to give the United States this leadership in knowledge. One is the large home market operating under uniform (or nearly uniform) laws and regulations in standards and performance criteria. The Japanese have this, too, but the Europeans do not. As a result, US companies can more easily specialize, while European corporations of comparable size are tempted to diversify, but in so doing often spread their R&D too thin. Where Europe had a 15 per cent share of the world market in semiconductors as recently as 1977, today it has less than 8 per cent. A recent Office of Technology Assessment report to Congress on prospects in biotechnology concluded that the old world of Europe 'will be outspent by the new, out planned by the rising sun (of Japan), and fragmented by national rivalry'. The same is true of almost all high technology sectors in which United States and Japanese shares have increased while Europe's have declined. The telecommunications field, dominated by procurement by national monopolies (usually state-owned), is a classic example of the political disunity's fatal consequences on economic performance.

The second factor is the stimulus, support, and headstart a large defence budget offers. It is true that IBM gained its lead in computers by developing the marketing techniques necessary to find large numbers of commercial buyers. But the first boost came in 1954 from the US defence programme, which financed 60 per cent of IBM's R&D. Similarly, the first international circuits were built in 1962 and 1963 almost exclusively for defence and the space programme. Even as late as 1968, 37 per cent of US production was absorbed by the National Aeronautics and Space Administration and the Department of Defence. Orders from the government carried much less risk and provided an invaluable beachhead for the conquest of commercial markets.

The third factor is the great size, wealth, and adaptability of American universities. In Europe's political history, the university has been the traditional bastion of political dissidence and opposition. This situation has sometimes produced an arm's length attitude to both government and business, so that European universities have often been slower than their American counterparts to seize the opportunities offered by both to expand research. Gerd Junne of Amsterdam University has found that in biotechnology, as in some pharmaceutical fields, the European multinationals spent more in American universities than in the ones at home in Europe. According to Junne: 'In biotechnology more than in other new technology, European managers have located much of their research in America or pay American researchers to do research for them' (Junne 1985).[11]

One further factor really relates more to the dominance of the United States over access to the largest and most innovative capital markets, both at home in the United States and abroad in the so-called Euromarkets. They are able to finance new development rather more easily than even the Swiss or Japanese corporations. IBM left its competitors behind when it spent $5 billion developing the third generation of computers. New, small enterprises in Silicon Valley find it easier to find venture capital in the United States than they would in Europe.

All in all, therefore, there is little question about the combined structural power the United States derives from the security structure, the production structure, the credit (or financial) structure, and the knowledge structure. Neither Europe nor Japan can equal the Americans' performance across all four structures. Since each of them interacts with the other three, and the European and Japanese are so far behind militarily, it seems likely that America will enjoy the power to act as hegemon for some time to come. How the power is used is a different question.

The alternative explanation

Once American predominance in structural power is conceded, we can look for other explanations of international economic disorder and the proliferation – despite all the summit conferences – of unsolved issues like that of Third World Debt, volatile and unpredictable exchange rates and commodity prices, the precariousness of international banks, the multiplication of protectionist trade measures, and continued conflict over trade in agriculture and services.

A far more plausible explanation for the erosion of so-called international regimes than the decline in American hegemonic power lies within the American political system rather than in the role of the United States in the international system. Stability in these regimes requires, above all, some consistency on the part of the leading participant. The United States is ill-suited to sustaining this consistency in policymaking, partly by reason of its constitutional provisions, and partly thanks to the coalition-building practiced by its dominant political parties. The hallowed doctrine of the separation of powers has been an excellent safeguard against the abuse of executive power. But it has tended to make policymakers in Washington ever mindful of the capacity of powerful lobbies and interest groups operating upon or within Congress to distort, frustrate, or even reverse strategies adopted by the White House towards the outside world.[12]

Take, for example, Henry Kissinger's post-OPEC strategy to strengthen the hands of the oil-consuming countries against the organized power of the oil producers. The International Energy Agency was set up with much fanfare and endowed with an elaborate institutional structure. But all its efforts (save the expansion of oil stockpiles, which would doubtless have taken place anyway) were rendered practically ineffective by the inability of the Nixon and Carter administrations, in the face of Congressional opposition, to raise the domestic price of energy high enough and fast enough to affect the short-term impact of demand on supply.[13]

Again, the disruptive strategy of introducing the voluntary export restriction into the conduct of international trade relations has been most responsible for the decline of a multilateral, non-discriminatory regime based on the GATT rulebook. And this, too, was the direct result of pressure from the Congress on successive administrations.[14]

By all accounts, too, the Reagan administration surprised even its own delegations to the United Nations Conference on the Law of the Sea when, at the very last moment, it decided to reject the draft negotiated text which had consumed so much time and diplomatic effort. This, at least, could not be attributed to the need to placate the Congress so much as to a reassessment of United States' interest in the prospects for exploiting new technology for deep-sea mining.

Cafruny's study of shipping comes to a similar conclusion, even while it notes that technical change and the shifting imperatives of the market exacerbate existing conflicts among domestic interests. Policy, he says, has become ever more incoherent, 'ranging from ruthless anti-trust enforcement to protectionism'. (The quotation is from a British trade minister.) Most industry analysts, Cafruny says, 'refer to domestic politics to explain policy incoherence; indeed, most European and American officials and shipowners reject the proposition that America has a "shipping policy"'. In the same way, the complaint that American trade policy is often contradictory, the left hand playing a protectionist card while the right hand bangs down a free trading trump, is met by the revealing assertion that America neither has nor seeks to have an 'industrial policy'. Americans may believe this, but no one else does. European companies, especially in high technology industries, are acutely aware of the advantages that US corporations have enjoyed as a result of fat defence contracts. Government procurement for advanced technology and government protection for older industrial sectors is not irrational, though in the long run it may not be the best strategy for safeguarding national economic interests.

Besides the inconsistency of American trade policy across sectors, there is the tendency – as in monetary policy – to suddenly reverse the entire policy direction. Here, we must note that the American political system has far less built-in resistance to such political U-turns. No American president has to consider the risk of revolt in the parliamentary party and the consequent prospect of unwelcome early elections. As political scientists have observed, the very certainties of the American system may even encourage a certain cyclical repetition of policy shifts – for instance, to relieve unemployment at one stage or to check inflation at another. In Washington, there are few if any permanent senior bureaucrats, as there are in London, Paris, Bonn, or Tokyo, so firmly ensconced in positions of considerable blocking power that they provide a deterrent counterweight to political whims and fancies.

From outside the United States, it seems fairly clear to non-Americans why this sort of explanation is not very palatable to American academics – and even less so to American policymakers. It is not easy for either to admit that the conduct of American policy towards the rest of the world has been inconsistent, fickle, and unpredictable, and that United States administrations have often acted in flat contradiction to their own rhetoric. While pronouncing the virtues of liberalism for all in trade and investment, they have practiced partiality towards their own and protection and discrimination against successful newcomers like Japan or Taiwan. While preaching the ideals of internationalism and multilateral decision-making, they have never hesitated, as Patrick Sewell (1986) has written, to spring unilateralist surprises on America's friends as well as on its opponents. Nor have they felt any inhibitions about indulging in sudden ventures in bilateralism – with Israel, Mexico, or Canada, for example. They have done so because there is – and always has been   an inherent and unresolved conflict between the two sets of ideas that have influenced American policymakers ever since the end of World War II – between the liberalism preached by neoclassical economists and by internationalist political scientists and the realism practiced by the US Departments of State and Defence.

The conflict has been between the realism necessary to any great power, which leads to unilateralist power politics, and the liberalism necessary to a great economy dependent on world markets, which leads to internationalism (whenever realism and domestic politics permit). Charles Krauthammer has remarked on this inherent conflict, but its implications are unlikely to gain ready acceptance in American intellectual circles (1986). As Holsti observed and documented recently, the trend to parochialism in the American literature on world politics has actually been increasing. Books or articles in foreign languages are almost never read or cited. Only a few non-American writers, even in English, are regularly assigned to students in US universities (Holsti 1985). American awareness of how others see the failure of international cooperation in relation to the continuing power of the United States is actually less now than it might have been a generation ago. This may be because the rising generation are native-born Americans, while many of the older American academics were born and educated in Europe; they occasionally returned on visits, and most read at least two European languages. These old men – there were few women – are now passing from the scene.

It is much easier for Americans to assert with Keohane, Fred Bergsten, and others that the decline of American power means that collective goals require collective collaboration and that, if this is elusive, there is nothing more the United States can do. Their arguments tend to overlook the fact that collective action is still possible but *only* when the United States takes the lead – when, in short, it still chooses to act as leader. The recent history of exchange rate stabilization, after the Plaza accord of September 1985 and after the Group of Seven meeting in Paris in February 1987, easily demonstrates this conclusion. We can also see it in the field of policies on ocean pollution or whaling. After Bhopal, the United States is likely to lead the world in setting standards of corporate liability for chemical accidents. Its leadership was vital to the rescheduling of Mexican and Brazilian debt. The United States initiated – and forced others to follow – action against financial fraud and insider dealing. These examples may be too few and far between, but they are enough to reject the myth of America's lost hegemony.

That is why I think it legitimate to talk of the 'myth' of lost hegemony.

10
'Towards a Theory of Transnational Empire', 1989

The American Empire is one of the most successful inventions in history, and all the more remarkable because no one knows it's there.

– Gore Vidal

In any discussion among academics about the theory, or theories, underpinning their field of study, it is important that each participant should make explicit his or her assumptions about the nature of theory; about how these assumptions are justified. He or she should also give some general indication of his or her general opinions about past theorizing and about desirable directions for future theorizing. Without such preliminary clarification, discussion can easily become confused and incomprehensible to the outsider. I shall start therefore by making my own position on each of these four points as explicit as I can.

There is a great deal of confusion about the nature of theory concerning the working of the international system, political and economic. This has resulted in a lot of 'theoretical' work that is not really theory at all, in the sense in which that word should be used and is defined in dictionaries (for example, 'a supposition explaining something, especially one based on principles independent of the phenomenon to be explained' – *Concise Oxford Dictionary*).

Because of this we cannot proceed to discuss future directions for theoretical work nor can we assess recent contributions to it, whether real or imagined, until we have made some judgement about what is real theory and what is phony theory.

I make four negative assumptions about what is *not* theory and three positive assumptions about what *is* theory. Both are necessary to explain my general pessimism about the current state of theory in international studies, and my own rather tentative explanatory supposition with regard to the current state of the international political economy (which will constitute the second part of this chapter).

Negative assumptions concerning theory in social science

First, a great deal of social theory is really no more than description, often using new terms and words to describe known phenomena, or to narrate old stories without attempting theoretical explanations. Putting one event after another without explaining the causal connection, if any, cannot count as theory. Sometimes, though, there are indeed implicit theories underlying the narrative that are so taken for granted that they are not even mentioned.

Second, some so-called theory in international studies merely rearranges and describes known facts or well-chronicled events in new taxonomies. This is not to say that a fresh taxonomy may not be necessary to the elaboration of a new theory. But the taxonomy by itself does not constitute an explanation and therefore does not qualify per se as a theory. The same is true of using new terms or words to describe known phenomena.

Third, simplifying devices or concepts borrowed from other social sciences or fields of knowledge often have their pedagogic uses in teaching; they can help get across to students or readers a certain aspect of individual social behaviour. Examples are the story of the prisoners' dilemma, or a demand curve, or the graphic presentation of the concept of marginal utility. But none of these by themselves explains the paradoxes or puzzles of the international system. Their current appeal to some teachers, I suspect, is that they offer a politically and morally neutral explanation (indeed, an exculpation) for the recent failures and inadequacies of the international organizations dominated by the United States in which post-war America put so much faith. Their appeal to students lies in their simplicity; it confirms what their common sense already tells them that individuals are apt to act selfishly. But these are simplifying devices, not theories of social behaviour. They do not help to explain the actions of corporations, of political parties, or of states in a global political economy. They do no even constitute evidence that would be relevant to a theory – in the way in which a map of the world might be relevant evidence for, say, a theory of continental drift and the existence of Old Gondwanaland. Moreover, those in the other disciplines who have developed such pedagogic devices are usually under no illusion as to their usefulness to policymakers or the possibilities of their practical application to real-life situations.

Fourth, the development of quantitative techniques applied to international studies has not advanced theory. The choice of what is to be counted is too arbitrary and the determination of what is causal and what is coincidental is too subjective to provide a basis for explanation. For the most part such methods have been used only to substantiate platitudes and to reinforce conventional wisdom concerning historical patterns of state behaviour in relation to other states.

Positive assumptions concerning theory in social science

First, theory must seek to explain some aspect of the international system that is not easily explained by common sense. It must serve to explain a puzzle or a paradox where there is some aspect of the behaviour of individuals, groups, or social institutions for which a simple explanation is not apparent. It is not necessary to look for a theory to explain why people try to leave a burning building. It *is* necessary to find a theory to explain why they patronize shops on one side of the street more than another. International relations started with the puzzling question why did nation-states continue to go to war when it was already clear that the economic gains made in war would never exceed the economic costs of doing so (Miller 1986; Aron 1958). Theories resulted. International political economy today addresses another puzzling question: Why do states fail to act to regulate and stabilize an international financial system which is known to be vitally necessary to the 'real economy' but which all the experts in and out of government now agree is in dangerous need of more regulation for its own safety? Theories result. By contrast, the common use of the term 'information revolution' does not usually reflect good theory. Although it notes rapid technological change, it does not postulate a clear causal connection, supported by logic or evidence, between that technological change and social change – change in political or economic relationships so great as to result in a redistribution of power and/or wealth. It does not, therefore, advance our understanding or add anything to our capacity to make causal connections and to see the consequential effects of certain phenomena.

Second, the theory need not necessarily aspire to predict or to prescribe. This is where social science differs from natural science. Natural science can aspire to predict – though it does not always nor necessarily does so. Much science, from astronomy to microbiology, enlarges understanding of *what* happens without being able to offer conclusive explanation of *why* it happens. Social science can never confidently predict because the irrational factors involved in human relations are too numerous, and the permutations and combinations of them are probably countless. The one social science that has most notably aspired to predict is economics. But its record of success is so abysmal that it should make all those that seek to emulate the economists and to borrow from them try something else. (I think I can explain why their record of success in prediction is so bad but that it is not necessary to my argument.) They are particularly bad at prediction when it comes to the world economy because many of the basic theories regarding international trade and exchange rates are based on assumptions that no longer hold good in the present state of the integrated world market economy.

As to prescription, that is a matter of choice. Whether the theorist chooses to proceed from explanatory theory to policy prescription is up to him or her. He or she need not necessarily apply theory to policymaking, because policymaking necessarily involves value judgements and risk assessments that are exogenous to theory and that are better made by practical policymakers than by irresponsible academic theorists.

And third, theory should be scientific only in the sense that the theorist respects the scientific virtues of rationality and impartiality and aspires to the systematic formulation of explanatory propositions. The title of 'social science' is only justifiably used to remind us that, although our subject lies closer to our emotions than the origin of rocks or the composition of molecules, and although it has to do with subjectively important questions concerning power and wealth, we must nevertheless still try to preserve a 'scientific' attitude in our studies. Indeed, many of the problems regarding theory and social science stem ultimately from the inferiority complex of social scientists towards natural scientists and, more specifically for us, the inferiority complex of political economists towards the apparent rigor of economic 'science'.

A basic proposition

This is that structural power is more important to an understanding of the international system than relational power; and consequently, that because the United States has more actual and potential structural power than any other political authority in the international system, its power in the system is undiminished.

This runs against hegemonic stability theory and the many theoretical (and often conflicting) conclusions about the functioning of the international political economy and of international economic organizations that derive from it. I have explained elsewhere why I think these are wrong and also why they have been so popular in recent years (Strange 1987; 1988e).

The important point here is – as I shall argue more extensively later – that the failure to understand and appreciate the extent of US structural power has led too many writers and teachers to compose premature epitaphs on the American Century and American hegemony (cf. Russett 1985). This conventional – but in my view quite unwarranted – conclusion has foreclosed any debate on how an American empire (which is very different from the empires of the past because it is based on structural power in the world economy and world society) might be improved, maintained, and prolonged. My concluding proposal for further thought and research is that we should reopen such a debate, more particularly because the alternatives to prolonging American hegemony are either demonstrably impracticable, or unattractive, or both.

But first I have to explain why I think the assumption of hegemonic decline is wrong and why we have to look for a new point of departure for theory concerning the international system and the management of the world economy. In short, I am like the man in the story the English like to tell about yokels from parts of the country other than their own. 'Can you tell me the way to get to Norwich (or Dorchester, Wigan, Maidstone or wherever)?' asks the bewildered stranger, lost in a maze of country lanes. 'Ah well,' replies the local, 'if I were you, I wouldn't start from here!'

My starting point in this discussion is that although there is disorder in the world economy and some disintegration of 'regimes' so-called, the reason for this is not to be found in the decline of US power. Rather, the explanation lies in the misuse of American hegemonic power in a unilateralist manner and in pursuit of national interests far too narrowly and short-sightedly conceived. Asymmetric structural power has allowed the United States to break the rules with impunity and to pass the consequent risks and pains of adjustment on to others. This has damaged the stability and prosperity of the whole world economy and has not been in the long-term best interests of the United States itself. But to persuade the reader to get to that alternative starting point, or even to consider it as a possibility, I must first elaborate a little the outline of a structural analysis that leads me to it. I propose to show that, in the four structures basic to an integrated world economy in an international society with diffuse political authorities, the underlying assumptions of much contemporary theorizing are false. False points of departure have therefore led to false theory.

Structural power

The concept of relational power is clear and consists in the ability of A to get B by coercion or persuasion to do what B would not otherwise do. The concept of structural power is less clear and requires some definition. It consists in the ability of A to determine the way in which certain basic social needs are provided. One is a lever; the other is a framework. The target of relational power, B, if it should decide not to do what is required of it by A, has to suffer the consequences determined by the other. For the target or object of *structural* power, the price of resistance is determined more by the system than by any other political authority. Structural power comes closest to the outside (that is, broadest) definition of 'regimes' in the debate that followed the Krasner (1983) collection of essays on the subject. In short, it embraces customs, usages, and modes of operation rather than the more narrow definition that stays closer to state-state agreements and state-centred institutions.

There are, in my view, four basic structures of the international political economy and each is interrelated with, and inseparable from, the other three. Although they can be described separately, it is hardly practical to disassociate any one from the other three, or to treat it in isolation from them. Power in one will tend to reinforce (though it does not always exactly coincide with) power in the others.

The four societal needs for a modern world economy are security, knowledge, production and credit. Who or what provides for these needs in a society enjoys structural power through the capacity to determine the terms on which those needs are satisfied and to whom they are made available.

Production is the basis of life and therefore the fundamental essential. But production (or wealth) cannot be enjoyed, or even produced, without order; and order requires the provision of security. Credit supplied by the financial structure is a necessary condition for all but the most basic production structures. In the highly developed, highly capitalized production structure of any industrialized economy, a decisive role is played by the provision of credit through the financial structure. But the choice of social goals and the means of reaching them is determined by the knowledge structure. The power exercised over the nature of the knowledge to be acquired, and over the means used for its storage and communication, is a necessary complement to power exercised through the other three structures. Only by considering all four can the study of economic power and political power be treated together; and only by considering all four can power exercised by the primarily economic entities be seen in the context of power exercised by the primarily political authorities. Only by structural analysis is it possible to develop theoretical propositions regarding the impact of political authority (for example, states) on economic transactions in markets, and conversely of the impact of transactions in markets upon states (Strange 1988e).

The concept of a production structure is the most familiar because it is central to a Marxist analysis of the capitalist system. Marx pointed out long ago that power in society is exercised through the relations of production. That is to say, whoever determines what shall be produced by what means and modes, and who shall work at producing on what terms, exercises structural power irrespective of the political system. It follows that a production structure can, conceptually and actually, be market-based; or it can be market-managed by monopolies, oligopolies, or vertically integrated enterprises that 'internalise' a market; or it can be command-based, in which case some political authority 'plans' the market and determines what shall be produced by what means and modes, and who shall work at producing what and on what terms.

If we analyse the world system as a production structure, we find the following features.

First, that part of the world economy responding directly to political command (which might be described as socialist if that word were not so badly abused) is the smaller part and is shrinking. Even in the avowedly socialist countries more and more production of goods and services is designed for and sold on a world market, over which the political authorities of the socialist states have little influence, even if they wished to exert it. (Gold and shipping are two exceptions.)

Second, that part of the world economy that responds entirely to market signals, and obeys the laws of supply and demand with the absolute minimum of interference by governments and other authorities, is also shrinking. Trade in primary products – food and unprocessed raw materials – is more often conducted in markets over which individual buyers and sellers have little or no capacity to determine price than is trade in manufactures and services where more prices are 'administered' in Galbraith's words. But trade in primary production constitutes a shrinking proportion of total world trade.

Third, that part of the production structure geared to purely national markets over which national authorities may if they wish exercise a choice of policies to influence the preferred combination of factors of production, the price and terms for the employment of labour, land, and capital, and the rules incumbent on employers, banks, landlords, buyers, sellers, brokers and other intermediaries, is also shrinking. The technological imperative to sell on a world market reduces the area common to all states over which national governments are able to exercise exclusive regulatory power.

Fourth, the largest part of the global production structure in raw materials, in manufacturing, and in service industries is dominated by large transnational corporations (TNCs). The TNCs account for an ever-growing proportion of world trade. This is intrafirm trade that is not subject either to the market and not necessarily affected by the trade barriers imposed by states. In this largest and fastest-growing section of the world production structure, TNCs based in the United States, plus TNCs based elsewhere but having a large part of their profit-making operations in the United States, play a dominant role. Any TNC, whatever its nationality, that hopes to keep a substantial share of the world market now finds it indispensable to operate in the territorial United States. The political authority, therefore, that most TNC executives are likely to heed and most anxious to avoid offending is that based in Washington. Some Japanese executives will still respond more readily and out of habit to Japanese political authority, but if they wish to operate on a global market, even they will find it increasingly necessary in the future to pay close attention to what goes on in Washington.

The combined effect of the above dynamic features of the contemporary production structure is to increase the asymmetric influence of some governments compared with others over what is produced, where, by whom, and on what terms. All the decisions about the regulation of market operators and intermediaries that used predominantly to be the prerogative of each national government are now shared unevenly between a few governments of the largest and richest countries – of which the government of the United States is by far the most important.

It follows that the structural power of the United States is not to be measured by the value of the goods and services produced within the territorial United States (that is, the US GNP). Nor yet is it to be measured by the value of such goods sold on (exported to) the world market. If it can be estimated at all, it is the total value of goods and services produced by large companies responsive to policy decisions taken by the US government. A good example of this is the power of the United States to restrict trade between the world market economy and the Soviet bloc. This is not exercised primarily, as recent experience shows, by bludgeoning the governments of NATO allies to conform to the COCOM list. It is exercised by the implicit (and occasionally explicit) threat of the US government to make life hard for any non-US corporation that flouts its will. Another example is the influence of US policy on the corporate strategies of major oil companies, including those like Shell or BP that are not themselves US-based.

The dominance of the US government over the financial structure of the world economy – what Peter Drucker (1986) has called the 'flywheel' of the real economy – and the enormous leverage that is exercised through this particular form of structural power is even more evident. How much credit is provided by governments, by international organizations, and by banks, and to whom, and on what terms is more important than what they produce or sell on the world markets. Whether the US decides to let loose the hounds of inflation or to bang the door of deflation is something over which the rest of the world has little control. Yet it is the world economy that is the anvil and the United States the hammer, in Lenin's apposite metaphor. The story of deregulation of banking and financial services is too long and complex to go into here but there is absolutely no disagreement today among the experts who have researched its progress over the last decade that the initial steps were every time first taken in Washington. And because of the worldwide integration of financial and money markets, because of the competition of banks in an integrated global financial system, and because of the competition of governments as hosts for financial and capital markets, it has proved impossible for any country involved in this financial structure to resist the magnetic pull of

US policy. Whether its good effects (opening new opportunities for borrowing and hedging for instance) are worth the bad effects and the risks involved is beside the point. The point is that policymaking power has rested – as it has done throughout the post-war period – with the United States. The perception that the United States has lost power to the banks or to the foreign exchange markets is only correct in the short term. As the experience of the Roosevelt administration in the 1930s showed clearly, bankers like everyone else (even insider traders) are subject to the law, and the law can be changed to bring them back under the control of the states.

The knowledge structure is the least familiar concept to scholars in international relations, even though all are familiar with the adage that 'knowledge is power'. In this short chapter there is hardly space to explain the concept in full. But just as the power to determine what shall be produced by whom and on what terms constitutes structural power in production, so the power to determine what knowledge shall be sought; how it shall be accumulated and applied; how and where knowledge once accumulated shall be stored; and to whom it shall be communicated and on what terms, constitutes another kind of structural power in world society and in the world economy (Strange 1988e).

Some of the illustrations of American dominance in the global knowledge structure that may be cited are the continued dominance of US corporations in most of the high-technology industries; the dominance of US banks in transborder data flows; the dominance of US media organizations in news and entertainment; the outward spread from the United States to the rest of the world of management, marketing, and advertising techniques; the dominance of US banks and consultancy enterprises in debt management; the dominant position of US government and US corporations in satellite communications; and the ability of US universities to attract and use scientists and academics from the rest of the world, drawing them not simply by better salaries but by better opportunities for research and exchange of information and ideas with their peers. Above all, perhaps, it is evident in the use of the American version of the English language as the world's lingua franca even for the French, the Russians and the Chinese.

Finally, there is the structural power exercised in matters of security. It is the United States, in response only to the Soviet Union, that has determined the world's dependence for its security on the balance of nuclear deterrence conveyed by an armoury of intercontinental, intermediate, and short-range missiles. This is the only global structure of them all where the United States shares power with the Soviet Union. In all the other three, Soviet structural power extends only as far as the reach of the Red Army; US structural power reaches deeply into the developing continents of Africa and South America, into Asia and the Middle East, and relentlessly even into Eastern Europe and China. This structural power over who is assured security and by what means, at what costs, and at what risk is, however, reinforced by the United States' structural power over the world's productive system, over its financial structure and the credit institutions and markets that function in it, and over the producers and communicators of knowledge in the knowledge structure.

The conclusion to be drawn from this structural analysis is that the decline of US hegemony is a myth – powerful, no doubt, but still a myth. In every important respect the United States still has the predominant power to shape frameworks and thus to influence outcomes. This implies that it can draw the limits within which others can choose from a restricted list of options, the restrictions being in large part a result of US decisions. As Wallerstein emphasizes, hegemony does not mean total power to command. It means predominance; and predominance conveys the ability to change the range within which it is reasonably possible for others to choose among various courses of action.

All that happened in the late 1970s in the aftermath of Vietnam, of Watergate, of the fall of the Shah and of the partly self-inflicted humiliation over the Tehran hostages, is that American self-confidence faltered under the leadership of a weak, tired, and shallow-minded president. The academics of the 1980s have been living in the past and figuring out theories of hegemonic stability to account for the public mood of the late 1970s. This is not, however, the first time that social scientists have behaved like generals who, overtaken by events, make elaborate preparations to fight the last war.

The other thing that has happened, and not only to the United States, is that structural change has at last severed the connection between the power of the state and its control over territory. The territorial frontiers of the state are now important only inasmuch as there is a consensus among existing, mutually recognized political authorities that regulatory power over the *consumers* living within its frontiers rests with the authorities of the territorial state. The power over the producers, and over the security, credit, and ideas available to both producers and consumers may be exercised by other authorities beyond the territory. This structural change has perforated the borders that define national societies, national defensive systems, national monetary and economic systems, and to a large extent national cultures. But the perforations operate unevenly, and certainly asymmetrically, so that the borders of the United States are far less perforated by structural change than those of others, and the United States has had more influence than others over the nature and direction of the structural change.

What is emerging therefore is a non-territorial empire with its imperial capital in Washington D.C. Where imperial capitals used once to draw courtiers from outlying provinces, Washington draws lobbyists from outlying enterprises, outlying minorities, and globally organized pressure groups. Authority in this non-territorial empire is exercised directly on people – not on land. It is exercised on bankers and corporate executives, on savers and investors, on journalists and teachers. It is also of course exercised on the heads of allied and associated governments, as successive summit conferences have clearly shown. Moreover, all the major policy trends of the 1980s that have commonly afflicted most of the developed and semi-developed countries and that have appeared to be of a national and internal character – deregulation, deflation, privatization, and so on – have been set off in the United States and have been followed by others who felt unable to resist. In all these policy areas, frontiers have been no defence against pressures emanating from the United States.

This is the major difference between the American and Soviet empires. The Soviet empire is more old-fashioned. It remains much more firmly territorial, much more dependent, like the empires of old, on a clearly defended perimeter frontier all around it, marking off those inside the empire from those outside.

The American non-territorial empire is different.

To start with, the perimeter fence around those American client states corresponding to the Soviet client states of Eastern Europe is not a rigid containing wall, preventing movement outside and enforcing conformity inside. Canada and Mexico both live in the shadow of the United States but their degree of freedom to choose is very substantially greater than that of Poland or even Hungary. Moreover, beyond the US 'backyard' of North and Central America and the Pacific and Caribbean islands, there is another American empire that really *is* non-territorial and in some respects is more like the Roman empire than the French or British empires. As in Rome, citizenship is not limited to a master race and the empire contains a mix of citizens with full legal and political rights, semi-citizens and non-citizens like Rome's slave population. Many of the semi-citizens walk the streets of Rio or of Bonn, of London or Madrid, shoulder to shoulder with the non-citizens; no one can necessarily tell them apart by colour or race or even dress. The semi-citizens of the empire are many and widespread. They live for the most part in the great cities of the non-communist world. They include many people employed by the large transnational corporations operating in the transnational production structure and serving, as they are all very well aware, a global market. They include the people employed in transnational banks. They often include members of 'national' armed forces, those that are trained, armed by, and dependent on the armed forces of the United States. They include many academics in medicine, national sciences, and social studies like management and economics who look to US professional associations and to US universities as the peer group in whose eyes they wish to shine and to excel. They include people in the press and media for whom US technology and US examples have shown the way, changing established organizations and institutions.

Because the Americans once fought a war of independence to be free of British domination, they have ever since counted themselves as among the world's anti-imperialists. They think of empire building as a peculiarly European foible in which they themselves do not indulge. They think of empires as if they were all like European empires. For this reason they find it particularly hard to abandon their embedded image of themselves as inveterate liberals and anti-imperialists, or to recognize US foreign and economic policies as in any sense the policies of an imperial power (Strange 1986f; Dale 1984; Nunnenkamp 1985).

Americans are not, of course, the only ones to nurture a delusion about themselves or to suffer the myopic inability, as Robert Burns put it, 'to see ourselves as others see us!' But in their particular case the myopia has had the side effect that it has shut scholarly inquiry off from a whole range of questions that could be of great significance for the future of the world. It has made most US scholars temperamentally rather indifferent to theoretical analysis of all aspects of the phenomenon of empire. Recent exceptions are Doyle (1986), Olson (1982) and Kennedy (1987). But even these studies have addressed the question of what it is that makes some empires decline, rather than what it is that makes other empires last.

Interest in imperialism as a phenomenon of world society already has a bias towards the negative aspects rather than the positive aspects of the subject, for which Hobson and Lenin and much subsequent Marxist writing are chiefly responsible. This has emphasized the negative causes – reasons such as the falling rate of profit on capital – for the acquisition of empires, and the negative consequences of imperialism for the inhabitants of empires and for international relations generally. The major divergence of interpretation was that between Lenin and Kautsky as to whether competition between capitalist states for imperial possessions was apt to increase the chances of war between them or, alternatively, whether their shared interest in the exploitation of human and natural resources of less economically developed parts of the world would lead them to form an implicit cooperative structure that would make it more difficult for dependent peoples to throw off their inferior, disadvantaged role in the world economy. The presumption of most writers on imperialism has been that imperialism was undesirable, so that the main policy-related issue was how to get rid of it.

Standing back a little from the literature on imperialism, it is at once apparent that it has been very narrowly based upon European experience. Certain characteristics of imperial power have been taken for granted that in fact need not apply universally, but that were characteristic of the European empires of the sixteenth to twentieth centuries. For example, it is often assumed that empires are *overseas* empires, and that they are not usually contiguous to the territory of the metropolitan power – even though it is clear that in the Russian case (under the tsars and under the soviets), and in the case of China, this is not so.

Prevailing theories also assume that the imperial power is more advanced in its economic development and in its command of technology than the areas it dominates. Again, Soviet domination of Eastern Europe, and especially of East Germany, Czechoslovakia, and Hungary contests this assumption. Soviet technology is more advanced in defence-related industry, but not in other sectors. This suggests that some US writers may be wrong who assume that the United States must lead the world in *every* sector of economic life or else resign itself to total loss of hegemonial power.

Prevailing theory also assumes that the advanced country surrounds its territorial empire with protective barriers in order to give itself a market sheltered from foreign competition. As a consequence, the prices of many goods sold to the local inhabitants are higher than they would otherwise be. Furthermore, it extracts minerals and other raw materials at low prices, thus doubly exploiting the inhabitants. By focusing exclusively on this exploitative character of territorial empires, a theory of imperialism has naturally been inclined to ask only a limited range of questions.

It seems to me that what is needed now is some fundamental reconsideration of the nature of empires; about the benefits they may confer, the risks they may modify, and the opportunities they may open up as well as the costs they may impose – on which so much attention in past theories of imperialism has concentrated. Secondly, we need some serious re-examination of the policy options open to imperial powers. (You may call them 'hegemonic powers' or 'states exercising leadership in an alliance' if labels bother you.)

The justification for pushing theoretical work in these directions is twofold. One is that imperial decline is a common source of instability and conflict in international systems. The other is that if the alternative to a power vacuum in the wake of an American empire is either a Soviet, a Japanese, or even a Chinese – or (less likely) a collective European empire – or else a collective, multipolar system, none of these would be as acceptable to the constituents as is the present American empire.

On the first point, it is a fact that the major destabilizing developments in the international system of the last hundred years have all been associated with the decline and break-up of old territorial empires. The fall of the tsarist Russian empire, of the Turkish Ottoman empire, of the Manchu Chinese empire, of the British Raj, of the French empire and even of the Belgian and Dutch empires have all been followed by quite serious conflict between the successor states or would-be states. As Denis Brogan once wrote in a book titled *The Price of Revolution* (1948), revolutionaries always overestimate the fruits of revolution and grossly underestimate the costs. There is therefore much to be said in politics and in political economy for gradualist solutions, and for gentle and gradual rather than violent change. Systematic study devoted to the development of a theory of non-territorial empires would seem to serve just this purpose.

On the second point, that an American non-territorial empire is much to be preferred to either a Soviet or a Japanese one, it seems obvious that most Europeans, Asians, and Latin Americans associate an unacceptable restriction of both political freedom and of economic freedom and enterprise with what they know of the present Soviet empire and are not keen to see it extended. Similarly, the corresponding suspicion of the resistance to a second Japanese empire in East Asia is not just a matter of bitter memories from the early 1940s.

The big difference between the Japanese and the Americans is that it is very easy to become an American and very hard to become a Japanese. Koreans who were born in Japan and have lived there all their lives are still not accepted by the native Japanese – not even as much as Turks who have lived far less long in West Germany are accepted by the native West Germans. Such is the cultural obsession with national purity that Japanese companies in Latin America do not even trust second-generation Brazilian Japanese to take managerial responsibility for running their Brazilian subsidiaries. As the British would have put it in the days of the Raj, they are considered to have 'gone native', to have lost their pure Japanese cultural status. By contract, as American semi-citizens are aware, it is not difficult for foreigners to merge into the American melting pot. And once in it, the American free enterprise culture emphasizes the opportunities of upward mobility, economically, and afterward socially. It is much easier in the United States for foreign students to work their way through college or for foreigners to buy property and establish rights of residence in the United States than in most other countries in the world. As European and especially British imperial experience showed, racial discrimination is a major handicap in running and maintaining a stable and successful empire. The Americans have less of it than most.

The absence of an alternative that is both stable and acceptable is therefore the rationale for pushing theory building in international studies toward some re-examination of those policies for governing an empire that are essential and ineluctable and those that are less essential or even counterproductive. There is no lack of historical material here to draw on. For example, it suggests that direct rule is not necessary for stable imperial government. Direct British rule in India coexisted with indirect control over the Indian princely states. They were only taken over or interfered with – as in Oudh – in cases of grossest incompetence or the most extreme strategic necessity. Even in Africa, the British managed a dual system, governing indirectly through tribal chiefs and directly through district commissioners who were sometimes almost beardless former public schoolboys given authority over hundreds of square miles of territory. Experience suggests that one of the recurrent problems for imperial powers – and one of the most difficult – has always been how much support and in what form to give to the local rulers and how much to interfere in their decision making. The United States currently faces precisely this problem both in South Korea and in the Philippines.

The evidence of history also suggests that among the policy areas requiring close imperial control are defence and communications. How the imperial armed forces protecting the empire are to be recruited, equipped, commanded, and paid for has always been a major policy question – as it is now for the United States and its NATO allies (Calleo 1987). In communications – so vital to the cohesion and control of any empire from Rome and ancient China to the US-dominated financial system of today – the question who shall have access to the means of communication, how these shall be paid for, and what they may be used for in addition to the messages of state remains a crucial one.

Students of international organizations familiar with the history of INTELSAT and MARISAT will readily appreciate the similarities of US policies to those of the Roman and Chinese empires, with their roads and pony express systems, and the British and French empires with their steamship routes, their air routes, and telegraph and telephone cable links.

Not every state is well suited to an imperial role nor to act as leader of an affluent alliance of protected states taking collective responsibility for managing the world's monetary, financial, and other economic affairs. It would seem from historical experience that two variables will make for good imperial government. One is a political philosophy that has some universal appeal to fundamental ethical principles, and which will therefore find an echo in the hearts and minds of affluent associates and less affluent 'subjects'. The other is a political system, whether formally run according to a written constitution or not, that allows the coordination of policy directed at the imperial state with other policies directed at the government of the empire. (The semi-independent status of the India Office in nineteenth-century Britain is one good example of this.)

The United States is more fortunate on the first count than on the second. It was a state inaugurated with a formal Declaration of Independence that embodied universal principles of liberty, equality and democratic control. It does still pay lip service to these ideals though there is a persistent conflict between those who believe that the principles apply primarily within the United States (and that therefore the United States is an exceptional country), and those that see the principles broadly described as political human rights as having universal validity – or at least as ultimate goals. In recent years there have been signs of growing awareness in Washington of the long-term US interest in a more stable and growing world economy and of the need to adapt US policies (for example, on development finance to the Third World) to this imperative. There are therefore some grounds here for optimism.

The outlook for change in the US political system is less favourable. The constitution (whose bicentenary was recently celebrated with such piety and devotion) was obviously admirably adapted to prevent tyranny and ensure freedom for a developing country on the periphery of the world system. A matter for serious consideration now is how it could be adapted and improved for the future in such a way as to enable the United States to avoid the blind unilateralism, the violent changes of foreign and financial policy, and the short-sighted selfishness of its commercial policies that have marked recent years.

Even more difficult are the central political questions of legitimacy and hegemonial power as understood by Gramsci. A common weakness of most territorial empires is the risk of allowing rivalry to develop between military and civil authority.

Dependence on the military for the defence of the territorial frontier has always threatened the political stability of constitutional empires – as the example of Julius Caesar in the early Roman empire showed. It seems that concentrated military power corrupts more quickly to the detriment of civil society within an empire. The American non-territorial empire certainly has the strength of an efficient communications system. The very fact that it *is* non-territorial ought to make it possible to curb the power of the military within it because, although power in the security structure is one source of strength for the United States, it is not by any means the only one. The military interest is balanced by industrial and financial interests, as in Britain's nineteenth-century empire, and this may well be a source of strength.

A reasonable hypothesis for such a theory might be that a non-territorial empire will remain strong and stable as long as there are shared interests between the dominant centre and important sections of society in the peripheral parts of the empire. These shared interests would maintain a sort of internal balance of power preventing disintegration. This at least seems to be a conclusion that could be drawn from the history of federal states in recent times. In all of these there is a latent danger of secession, jeopardizing the cohesion of the state. Think of Bavaria in the Federal Republic of Germany, of Québec in Canada, or the deep South in the United States. Earlier on, there were other examples, like Bohemia in the Hapsburg empire. In each case, coercive power was more effective when it was tempered with placatory concessions. But equally, coercive power has sometimes to be used to prevent secession or unilateralist revolt. An instance was when the Australian Commonwealth government had to act forcefully in the 1930s to prevent New

South Wales – the largest and richest of the states of the Australian federation – from defaulting on its foreign debt. Or when the Indian government more recently has had to use force to prevent secession by the Sikhs. The result of a lack of such coercive authority can be seen in the failed East African federation – and possibly in the future – in Yugoslavia after Tito.

A theory of non-territorial empire would seek to ask the political questions of which problems were the same as in territorial empires, and which are likely to be different. And it would ask – though from a totally different point of departure – some of the same economic questions as those posed by students of 'interdependence'. How, for instance, can an international banking system be effectively managed without the risk of panic or collapse? Or, how can a Keynesian policy of demand management be effectively developed to stabilize a flagging world economy? These are questions that will find no answers so long as they are approached from a state-centric point of view. Only by assuming the existence of a non-territorial empire may we be able to find the way in which policy could be moved.

It would seem to me that the recognition by US scholars of the full implications of the structural power of the United States would lead in many interesting new directions and would produce many more constructive and creative ideas for policymakers than the present obsolete, state-centric, territory-bound debates that ignore some of the fundamental changes that have taken place in the world political economy in the last twenty-five years.

11
'States, Firms and Diplomacy' 1992

ō33
F23 Fo2

Four stops on the London Underground will take you from the London Business School in Regent's Park to the London School of Economics off the Strand. Yet for 30 years the two institutions might have been separated by a Berlin Wall, so minimal was the communication between them, so divergent the matters that interested their professors, so diverse the discourses of their students. Each was openly dismissive, but secretly jealous, of the other.[1]

This article presents the findings of a rare venture in collaboration between writers from both institutions, a professor of international business and a professor of international relations, resulting in a recent book (Stopford and Strange 1991).[2] Our research led us to shared beliefs that went beyond the primary focus of the book to identify structural factors in the world economy. Three propositions will be advanced here. First, that many seemingly unrelated developments in world politics and world business have common roots and are the result in large part of the same structural changes in the world economy and society. Second, that partly in consequence of these same structural changes, there has been a fundamental change in the nature of diplomacy. Governments must now bargain not only with other governments, but also with firms or enterprises, while firms now bargain both with governments and with one another. As a corollary of this, the nature of the competition between states has changed, so that macroeconomic management and industrial policies may often be as or even more important for governments than conventional foreign policies as conventionally conceived. The third proposition follows from the second, and concerns the significance of firms as actors influencing the future course of transnational relations – not least for the study of international relations and political economy.

Structural change

Most commentators on international affairs have in our opinion paid far too little attention to structural change, particularly to change in the structure of production in the world economy.[3] Our recent work argues that most of the recent changes in world politics, however unrelated they may seem on the surface, can be traced back in large part to certain common roots in the global political economy. We see common driving forces of structural change behind the liberation of Central Europe, the disintegration of the former Soviet Union, the intractable payments deficit of the United States, the Japanese surpluses, the rapid rise of the East Asian newly industrialized countries, and the U-turns of many developing country governments from military or authoritarian government to democracy, and from protection and import substitution towards open borders and export promotion.

These common driving forces of change, in brief, are the accelerating rate and cost of technological change, which has speeded up in its turn the international-ization of production and the dispersion of manufacturing industry to newly industrialized countries; increased capital mobility, which has made this dispersion of industry easier and speedier; and those changes in the structure of knowledge that have made transnational communications cheap and fast and have raised people's awareness of the potential for material betterment in a market economy. These common roots have resulted, at the same time and in many countries, in the demand for democratic government and for the economic flexibility that is impossible in a command economy.

This perception of the power of universal structural change came from looking in detail as we did at the processes of bargaining between host governments and foreign firms in three developing countries, Brazil, Malaysia and Kenya. The bargaining in question related mainly to the terms on which the firms could operate and would invest in a particular venture within the country. We interviewed government officials and corporate executives of foreign firms in the three countries.

The firms we interviewed were working in a variety of sectors of business and were of various national origins. Though the study was based on case studies and attention to detail at the micro level, while we were struck first by the diversity of states' responses to global changes, certain common trends were rather clearly visible in the relations between states and firms, especially foreign firms. The pressures on both firms and governments appeared to be very similar across all three countries. These pressures were forcing both the host governments and the foreign firms to compete more and more actively for world market shares, and in so doing to reach new modes of accommodation with one another.[4] It seemed clear to us that these pressures arose from structural changes in the global market economy that were not always obvious either to area specialists or to writers on corporate management or development economics.

Technological change, mobile capital, transborder communications

Most obvious of the structural changes acting as the driving force on firms and governments alike were those in the technology of industrial and agricultural production; related to them were changes in the international financial structure. The accelerating pace of technological change has enhanced the capacity of successful producers to supply the market with new products and/or to make them with new materials or new processes. At the same time product and process lifetimes have shortened, sometimes dramatically. Meanwhile, the costs to the firm of investment in R&D, research and development – and therefore of innovation – have risen. The result is that all sorts of firms that were until recently comfortably ensconced in their home markets have been forced, whether they like it or not, to seek additional markets abroad in order to gain the profits necessary to amortize the investments in time to stay up with the competition when the next techno-logical advance comes along. It used to be thought that internationalism was the preserve of the large, privately owned Western 'multinational' or transnational corporations. Today, thanks to the imperatives of structural change, these have been joined by many smaller firms, and also by state-owned enterprises and firms based in developing countries. Thus it is not the phenomenon of the transnational corporation that is new, but the changed balance between firms working only for a local or domestic market, and those working for a global market and in part producing in countries other than their original home bases.

Besides the accelerating rate of technological change, two other critical developments contributed to the rapid internationalization of production. One was the liberalization of international finance beginning perhaps with the innovation of Eurocurrency dealing and lending in the 1960s, and continuing unchecked with the measures of financial deregulation initiated by the United States in the mid-1970s and early 1980s (Strange 1976d; 1986f). As barriers went down, the mobility of capital went up. The old difficulties of raising money for investment in offshore operations and moving it across the exchanges vanished. It was either unnecessary for the transnational corporations to find new funds, or they could do so locally.

The third contributing factor to internationalization has often been overlooked – the steady and cumulative lowering of the real costs of transborder transport and communication. Without them, central strategic planning of far-flung affiliates would have been riskier and more difficult, and out-sourcing of components as in car manufacture would have been hampered.

Broader perspectives

These structural changes have permeated beyond finance and production to affect global politics at a deep level. They have, for instance, significantly affected North–South relations. The so-called Third World no longer exists as a coalition of developing countries ranged, as in UNCTAD (the UN Conference on Trade and Development), in opposition to the rich countries. Developing countries are now acutely aware that they are competing against each other, the laggards desperately trying to catch up with the successful newly industrialized countries. The trans-national corporations' search for new markets was often a major factor leading them to set up production within those markets. Sometimes this was done for cost reasons. Other times it was done simply because the host government made it a condition of entry. The internationalization of production by the multinationals has surely been a major factor in the accelerated industrialization of developing countries since the 1950s. For it is not only the Asian newly industrialized countries whose manufacturing capacity has expanded enormously in the last two or three decades, but also countries like India, Brazil, Turkey and Thailand.

At the same time, the internationalization of production has also played a major part in the U-turn taken in economic policies by political leaders in countries as diverse and far apart as Turkey and Burma, Thailand and Argentina, India and Australia. Structural change, exploited more readily by some than others, has altered the perception of policy-makers in poor countries both about the nature of the system and the opportunities it opens to them for the present and the future. In the space of a decade, there has been a striking shift away from policies of import-substitution and protection towards export promotion, liberalization and privatization.

It is no accident that the 'dependency school' writers of the 1970s have lost so much of their audience. Not only in Latin America (where most of this writing was focused), we see politicians and professors who were almost unanimous in the 1970s in castigating the multinationals as agents of American imperialism who now acknowledge them as potential allies in earning the foreign exchange badly needed for further development.

Nor, we would argue, is the end of the Cold War, the détente in East–West relations and the liberation of Central Europe from Soviet rule and military occupation to be explained by politics or personalities alone. Here too there are ways in which structural change has acted, both at the level of government and the bureaucracy, and at the popular level of consumers and workers.

In the production structure, even in the centrally planned economies industrialization has raised living standard from the levels of the 1930s and 1940s, at least for the privileged classes of society. Material progress has not been as fast as in the market economy, but in the socialist countries as in Latin America or Asia, the ranks have multiplied of a middle class of managers, professional doctors, lawyers, engineers and bureaucrats, many of whom are significantly better educated than their parents. With this *embourgeoisement* has come greater awareness of what is going on in other countries, and of the widening gap between living standards in the affluent West and their own.

In the world market economy, competition among producers has lowered costs to consumers and widened their choice of goods, while raising their real incomes. Under the pressures of shortening product life-cycles, heavier capital costs and new advances in technologies, rivalry among producers has unquestionably contributed to material wealth for the state as well as for consumers. Witness the spread down through income groups of cars, colour TV, washing machines, freezers, video recorders, telephones, personal computers. In any Western home, a high proportion of these consumer goods carry the brand-names of foreign firms.

By contrast, the Soviet consumer has suffered the deprivation consequent on the economy's insulation from the fast-changing global financial and production structures. But the information about what others enjoyed in the West could not altogether be kept from people even in the Soviet Union, let alone in Central Europe. The revolution in communications, and thus in the whole global knowledge structure, helped to reveal the widening gap between standards of living for similar social groups under global capitalism and under socialism.

At the same time, the new bourgeoisie, aware of the inefficiencies of the command economy, saw that economic change was being blocked by the entrenched apparatus of centralized government and could only be achieved through political change and wider participation. While the burden of defence spending certainly played a part in both East and West in furthering détente and making possible the liberation of Central Europe, political change was accelerated within the socialist countries by the rise of a new middle class and their perception of the gap in living standards and of the apparent inability of centrally planned systems to respond to the structural change in technologies of production.

We would argue that similar structural forces also lie behind the worldwide trend to democratic government and the rejection of military and authoritarian rule. In short, people have become better off and better educated and are making their material dissatisfaction and their political aspirations strongly felt. We would argue that this wave of political change has the same universal roots, whether in Greece, Portugal or Spain, in Turkey, or in Burma, Brazil or Argentina.

Structural change has also played a major part in the much discussed relationship between the United States and Japan. American multinationals in the 1950s and 1960s were the first to respond in large numbers to the opportunities opened up by the internationalization of production. Indeed much early analysis – Servan-Schreiber's famous *défi américain* for example (1967) – even perceived the move as an essentially American phenomenon. The natural result of moving so much production offshore was the decline of manufacturing as a source of employment in the territorial United States, together with a rise in the American trade deficit – for which many firms based in the United States but locating production offshore were no less responsible than firms based in Japan or Europe. Twenty years later, in the 1970s and 1980s, the Japanese firms began a similar exodus – to the United States and to East Asia, rather less to Europe until 1992 loomed on the horizon.

Once understood in terms of structural change, it looks as though the imbalance in US–Japanese payments may be due more to a difference in the timing of the exodus of firms going abroad to expand production than to inherent or cultural differences between Americans and Japanese. If so, the imbalance is likely to be much more temporary than some commentators have suggested. Already Malaysia, after a period in which heavy imports of Japanese capital goods produced a marked deficit in trade with Japan, is finding in Japan its best market for manufactures produced by Malaysian affiliates of Japanese firms.

Two new sides to diplomacy

State–firm diplomacy

The net result of these structural changes is that there now is greatly intensified competition among states for world market shares. That competition is forcing states to bargain with foreign firms to locate their operations within the territory of the state, and with national firms not to leave home, at least not entirely. We observed from our case-studies at the micro level in three developing countries that this bargaining produces partnerships or alliances between host-state and firm, which may be of long or short duration, but which are based on the exchange of benefits and opportunities to enhance either party's success in the competition for world market shares. This bargaining, which was the main focus of our research, constitutes a new dimension of diplomacy.

Again and again we found that the transnational firm has command of an arsenal of economic weapons that are badly needed by any state wishing to win world market shares. The firm has, first, command of technology; second, ready access to global sources of capital; third, ready access to major markets in America, Europe and, often, Japan. If wealth for the state, as for the firm, can be gained only by selling on world markets – for the same reason that national markets are too small a source of profit for survival – then foreign policy should now begin to take second place to industrial policy; or perhaps, more broadly, to the successful management of society and the efficient administration of the economy in such a way as to outbid other states as the preferred home to the transnational firms most likely to win and hold world market shares.

While the bargaining assets of the firm are specific to the enterprise, the bargaining assets of the state are specific to the territory it rules over. The enterprise can operate in that territory – even if it just sells goods or services to people living there – only by permission and on the terms laid down by the government. Yet it is the firm that is adding value to the labour, materials and know-how going into the product. States are therefore competing with other states to get the value-added done in their territory and not elsewhere. That is the basis of the bargain.

Firm–firm diplomacy

A third dimension, equally the product of the structural changes noted earlier, is the bargaining that goes on between firms. This too may lead to partnerships or alliances in which, while they may be temporary or permanent, each side contributes something that the other needs, so that both may enhance their chances of success in the competition for world market shares. Firms involved in this third dimension of diplomacy may be operating in the same sector (as in aircraft design, development and manufacturing) or in different sectors (where, for instance, one party may be contributing its expertise in computer electronics, the other in satellite communications).

For scholars of international relations, both new dimensions are important. The significance of the state–firm dimension is that states are now competing more for the means to create wealth within their territory than for power over more territory (Strange 1990c). Power, especially military capability, used to be a means to wealth. Now it is more the other way around. Wealth is the means to power – not just military power, but the popular or electoral support that will keep present ruling groups in their jobs. Without this kind of support, even the largest nuclear arsenals may be of little avail. Nowadays, except perhaps for oilfields and water resources, there is little material gain to be found in the control of more territory. As Singapore and Hong Kong have shown, world market shares – and the resulting wealth – can be won with the very minimum of territory. Even where, as in Yugoslavia or the

Soviet Union, there is a recurrence of conflict over territory, the forces behind it are not solely ethnic nationalism of the old kind. Many Slovenes, Croats, Russians or Georgians want to wrest control over their territory from the central power because they believe they would be able to compete better in the world economy on their own than under the control of their old federal bosses. Autonomy is seen as a necessary condition for economic transformation and progress.

Successfully managing society and economy

Having got control over territory, government policy-makers may understand well enough what is needed to bargain successfully with foreign firms to locate with them. But they may not always be able to deliver. For though the forces of structural change affect everyone, even the old centrally planned economies, the capacity of governments to respond are extremely diverse.

We were struck in our research by the wide variation between our three countries in the policies they felt willing and able to follow. There was no denying the multiple constraints on any Kenyan government attempting, for example, to overcome the handicap of African illiteracy, or even to effect radical reform of an inflated and featherbedded bureaucracy sufficiently to make the country attractive to new foreign firms. Existing firms in Kenya were hanging on only so long as they were protected from competition, whether local or foreign. But at that point the absence of tough competition itself became a handicap. Meanwhile, debt problems and political constraints sometimes made it hard even to adopt the obvious policies of reform, such as abandoning price controls.

Brazil, by comparison, though it has had bigger debt problems, has a bigger home market, and when it came to negotiating with foreign firms it had more room to manoeuvre in shifting from market-reserve protectionism to export-promoting pragmatism. It has been able to play chicken-games with the IMF in a way no African country, dependent on official government loans and support from the international organizations, has been able to match.

It is Malaysia, curiously, which has the best record of growth of the three, and which also has been most liberal in its policies toward many (though not all) foreign investors.[5] This liberality, we found, was not wholly due to Asian sagacity. Historical accident, now all but forgotten, played a part. Recall that for five years after 1948 Malaya (as it was then still called) was under attack from Chinese-backed communist guerrillas. Though this civil war was eventually won, Tunku Rahman's sense of the country's vulnerability led him to make a unique bargain with Britain. In return for British military aid and protection, independent Malaysia would remain in the sterling area, making substantial contributions to the common pool of monetary reserves with its dollar-earning exports of tin and rubber. With this monetary dependence on London went a cautious and conservative style of monetary management, and a liberal attitude to British businesses in the country. From that time on, Malaysia never once put controls on the right of foreign firms to transmit profits or even capital abroad. Nor did it impose punitive taxes, even though both profits and capital gains were high. These terms, added to the reassuring presence of British troops, meant there was no exodus of foreign capital after independence such as Kenya experienced, nor any wild indulgence in foreign borrowing such as Nkrumah's Ghana went in for. Malaysia carried on with this open, liberal policy long after the demise of the old sterling area in the late 1960s, even though the beneficiaries in the 1970s and 1980s were mostly Japanese or American rather than British.

There can be little doubt that these policies contributed substantially to comparatively high rates of investment by foreign firms, and in turn to high rates of economic growth: 7.3 per cent a year in the period 1965–80. (Though less than Brazil's average of 8.8 per cent in the same period, Malaysia's growth was less vulnerable to the hard times of the 1980s: while Brazil's average then fell below 3 per cent, Malaysia's held up at over 4.5 per cent. Exports continued growing at a phenomenal rate of over 9 per cent a year, and by 1988, 45 per cent of these by value were manufactures.)

This is not to say, of course, that policies towards foreign firms were or are the only factor. Malaysia's wider range of policy options compared with Kenya's was certainly helped by a high rate of domestic savings – 36 per cent of GDP in 1988 – and by past moderation in foreign borrowing. The exigencies of debt-servicing suffered by Brazil and Kenya made it harder for them both to fight inflation and to resist the fatal temptation to resort to distorting and ineffective price controls.

So the diversity of government responses to structural change usually reflects the policy dilemmas peculiar to the government of that society. But precisely because of increased integration in the world market economy, it is more and more difficult for governments to 'ring-fence' a particular policy so that implementing it does not directly conflict with, perhaps negate, some other policy. For instance, it is no good Kenya luring foreign investors into a free export-processing zone if at the same time the administration of import licences to economize on foreign exchange prevents potential exporters from replacing spare parts quickly enough to keep up the flow of output.

Contemplation of the diversity of host-country policies in monetary management, trade and competition policy very soon brings home the fact that there are no short cuts and no magic tricks in wooing foreign firms. However, some general advice is still possible. One piece of advice is obviously to pinpoint the policy dilemmas where objectives clash. Another is to cut out the administrative delays and inefficiencies that bedevil the work of local managers. In Kenya, for example, one really striking success story was to be found in a sector where government intervention and control had been minimal, in the growing and export of flowers and pot-plants. Another good piece of advice, already stressed in the growing literature on the management of international business, is to break up monopolies and enforce competition among producers. Michael Porter (1990), for example, has rightly stressed the importance of fierce rivalry between local firms unprotected by trade barriers from competing imports.[6] On the basis of our work we would agree that Brazilian growth has certainly been hampered not only by featherbedded state monopolies, but also by the power given to the big business associations of local and foreign producers in some key sectors of industry.

But useful as such analyses as Porter's have been, they have rather left out the political element, both domestic and global. The diversity of government responses which so struck us is surely due not only to mulish stupidity or ignorance of the keys to success. Governments are, after all, political systems for the reconciliation of conflicting economic and social, and sometimes ethnic, interests. Moreover, the global structural changes that affect them all do so very differently, sometimes putting snakes, sometimes ladders in their path. Some small boats caught by a freak low tide in an estuary may escape grounding on the mud by alert and skilful management; others may be saved by luck. Our research suggests that the crucial difference between states these days is not, as the political scientists used to think, that between 'strong' states and 'weak' ones, but between the sleepy and the shrewd. States today have to be alert, adaptable to external change, quick to note what other states are up to. The name of the game, for governments just as for firms, is competition.

Firms as diplomats

Our third general point – the importance of firms as major actors in the world system – will be obvious enough to leaders of finance and industry. They will not need reminding that markets may be moved, governments blown off course and balances of power upset by the big oil firms, by the handful of grain dealers, by major chemical or pharmaceutical makers. It will come as no surprise to them that the game of diplomacy these days has two extra new dimensions as well as the conventional one between governments.

But while I have scratched the surface of one of these – the bargaining between firms and governments – I have not said much about the third, bargaining between firms. This deserves to be the subject of a whole new research programme. Examples have recently multiplied of firms which were and may remain competitors but which under the pressures of structural change have decided to make strategic or even just tactical alliances with other firms in their own or a related sector of business (Mytelka 1991). In the study of international relations it is accepted as normal that states should ally themselves with others while remaining competitors, so that the bargaining that takes place between allies is extremely tough about who takes key decisions, how risks are managed and how benefits are shared.

The implications for international relations analysis of the three-sided nature of diplomacy are far-reaching. The assertion that firms are major actors is at odds with the conventions of international relations as presently taught in most British universities and polytechnics. The standard texts in the subject subscribe to the dominant 'realist' school of thought, which holds that the central issue in international society is war between territorial states, and the prime problematic therefore is the maintenance of order in the relations between these states.[7] This traditional view of international relations also holds that the object of study is the behaviour of states towards other states, and the outcome of such behaviour *for states*: whether they are better or worse off, less or more powerful or secure.

Transnational corporations may be mentioned in passing, but they are seen as adjuncts to or instruments of state policy.[8]

Our contention is that transnational corporations should now be put centre stage; that their corporate strategies in choosing host countries as partners are already having great influence on the development of the global political economy, and will continue increasingly to do so. In common with many contemporary political economists, our interest is not confined to the behaviour of states or the outcomes for states. Who-gets-what questions must also now be asked – about social groups, generations, genders, and not least, about firms and the sectors in which they operate. Ten years from now we anticipate that the conventions and limitations of what has sometimes been called the British school of international relations will be regarded as impossibly dated, its perceptions as démodé as 1950s fashions. This is not to say, of course, that there are no lessons to be learned by economic ministries and corporate executives from the diplomatic history of interstate relations. Only that the study of international relations must move with the times, or be marginalized as a narrow specialism.

There are three issues, in our understanding, in the state–firm relationship that deserve much closer expert attention than they have so far received. One issue is how and why governments choose firms as partners; a second is the specifics that are bargained over, and who is likely to have the upper hand on any one of them; the third relates to the nationality of firms. The question here is not so much what internationalized production does to the state, but what it does to the national identity and behaviour of the transnational firm.

1. Why governments choose firms as partners

As to the first, not the least attribute of the shrewd state is the ability to choose the right partners among firms. Depending on sectors, markets and circumstances, this may be a leading firm or a follower. There are pros and cons either way. Similarly, firms have difficult choices to make about which markets to contest, where to locate what elements of production, research and financing, and how to manage their offshore operations. Our point simply is that before either government or firm gets to the point of bargaining over the terms and conditions under which the firm operates, both have to make strategic choices about their partners. Governments therefore need to be well advised on the relative strengths and weaknesses of different firms. As much attention should be paid to the corporate history, character and decision-making habits of major transnational firms as international relations specialists have been used to paying to nation-states.

2. Knowing your allies

Second, the advice 'Know your enemy' applies also to allies and partners. In bargaining over specific issues between host governments and firms, each side needs a clearer understanding than they often have of the other's long-term objectives, its bargaining strengths and weaknesses. Thus in order to achieve your own prime objective, it may be well worthwhile making concessions on some other subjectively minor issue.

A recurrent issue, for example, is exports. So many countries are either burdened with debt-service charges or have ambitious development programmes needing imports of foreign capital goods that firms that make extra efforts to increase export sales will be especially welcome. Subsidies – such as Brazil offers under its Befiex cheap-credit, low-tax programme – are an indication of such a wish. On the other hand, subsidies are rarely decisive in corporate strategies. When General Motors, to the fury of the US Trade Representative's Office, took a Brazilian export subsidy for a particular product line, its objective was to undercut labour costs in Detroit and to consolidate its position in the potentially very large and competitive Brazilian market. The subsidy was just an added bonus.

Another common issue – witness the Franco-British squabble over whether Nissan cars made in Britain are British or Japanese – is domestic content: what proportion of the final product is made up of locally produced components. For developing countries, this determines the important question of how much spillover among small local enterprises can be expected from the presence of a multinational. But it is not only developing countries that bargain hard with foreign firms on whether the local content of a product should be 60 or 75 per cent of the value added. A major US concern in the US–Canada Free Trade Agreement was to make sure that Japanese cars produced in Canada conformed to (higher) American domestic content requirements if they were not to incur tariff barriers.

The industrialized countries are less concerned about how much foreign firms are prepared to spend on training local workers. But for developing countries – especially those who have experienced the exploitation of young girls on the assembly lines of export-processing zones – it is an important question. Even though managers may suspect that not all workers they train will stay with the company, it may be a price worth paying to gain access to the market. If the market is potentially large and the global competition severe, a training programme may reap long-term dividends that exceed the cost.

The same may be said of firms' willingness to throw into the package substantial contributions to local health services or environmental clean-up programmes. One Italian construction company operating in Africa automatically sends out a small field hospital, properly staffed and supplied, with every construction job it undertakes. To this are welcomed not only its own local workers, but anyone in need. Presumably it has found this practice a good investment in government–firm diplomacy.

Japanese companies are sometimes praised and envied by Europeans for their more open, less class-ridden styles of management. But their exclusivist, not to say racist, habits of restricting senior management jobs to Japanese and keeping out the indigenous workforce may prove a handicap in the long run. In Brazil, some Japanese firms reportedly would not consider even Brazilian Japanese as foremen. They were perceived as having 'gone native'.

In Central Europe and the former Soviet Union, as in Asia, another contested issue will be the location of research centres and the employment foreign firms are prepared to offer to locally trained and educated science workers. Companies that have come to think that 'not invented here' rules out research work by their overseas affiliates may be losing important opportunities for beating the competition.

All the issues briefly outlined here pose questions for research on the bargaining process between governments and foreign – and sometimes also domestic – firms; and most of them are rather more significant for the firm than the value of tax breaks or subsidies.

3. National identity and transnational firms

The third and rather more abstract issue concerns the nationality of firms, and therefore the validity of policies based on discrimination between 'one of ours' and 'one of theirs'. While it is true that US-based firms rarely admit non-Americans to their main board – they are more likely to appoint a statutory woman or a black American – nevertheless the behaviour of firms and their vital interests cannot always be predicted from the country where they are registered and have their headquarters. Northern Telecom is Canadian-based and controlled, but its US operations are more important than its operations in Canada. In firms like General Motors or Volkswagen, their geographically dispersed operations create tensions within the company that are essentially political rather than economic and which alter the relations of management to the home state. Academics who are interested in the phenomenon of nationalism should pay much closer attention to current change affecting multinationals.

For governments, and for the way they are organized and staffed, both new dimensions of diplomacy have far-reaching implications. Governments may find that they need to make radical changes in their foreign ministries – or else drastically to cut them down to size and importance. They may need to be more open to short-term entrants from industry or finance, and to recruit new staff with business experience or technical and scientific qualifications. The British government in particular may need to think hard about the lessons of its relationship with Nissan, Honda and Sony. While British firms were axing jobs and cutting back in the summer of 1991, Nissan was expanding, offering new job opportunities in a formerly depressed region. The prejudices of Mme Cresson, of some American congressmen and of some British trade unionists against Japanese firms cannot bear rational assessment of the national interest. A European state's best ally among firms may just as easily be American or Japanese as European.

To sum up. Much more analytical work is needed on firm–firm bargaining as well as on state–firm bargaining in all its multivariant forms. It needs recognizing that both types of bargaining are interdependent with developments in state–state bargaining (the stock in trade of international relations), and that this in turn is interdependent with the other two forms of transnational diplomacy. In the discipline of management studies, corporate diplomacy is becoming at least as important a subject as analysis of individual firms and their corporate strategies for finance, production and marketing. In the study of international relations, an interest in bargaining is already beginning to supplant the still-fashionable analysis of international regimes (eg. Grosse 1989).[9]

A focus on bargaining, and the interdependence of the three sides of diplomacy that together constitute transnational bargaining, will necessarily prove more flexible and better able to keep up with change in global structures. No bargain is for ever, and this is generally well understood by anyone with hands-on experience of negotiation. The political art for corporate executives, as for government diplomats, is to devise bargains that will hold as long as possible, bargains that will not easily be upset by changes in other bargaining relationships. This is true for political coalitions between parties, or between governments and social groups, such as labour; and it is equally true for bargains between governments and foreign firms, and between firms and other firms. The multiplicity of variables in the pattern of any one player's interlocking series of bargains is self-evident.

A final point about the interlocking outcome of transnational bargaining relates to theories of international relations and political economy. Social scientists like to think that the accumulation of more and more data, the perfecting of analytical tools and their rigorous application according to scientific principles will some day, somehow, produce a general theory to explain political and economic behaviour. They are a bit like peasants who still believe there is a pot of gold buried at the end of the rainbow despite their repeated failures to track it down. Today, the complexity of the factors involved in each of the three forms of transnational bargaining, and the multiplicity of variables at play, incline us to deep scepticism about general theories. Not only are economics – *pace* the economists – inseparable from the real world of power and politics, but outcomes in the global political economy, the product of this complex interplay of bargains, are subject to the great divergences that we have observed.

12
'Who Governs? Networks of Power in World Society', 1994

For
D72

I recently heard Professor Kenneth Waltz lecture in London on the international order after the end of the Cold War. I found the experience rather depressing. According to Professor Waltz, the problematic for world society was still the preservation of peace between the great powers. All that had happened in the last three-quarters of a century was that, with the collapse of the Soviet empire at the end of the 1980s, we were back, more or less, where we were in, say, 1910. The twentieth century had come full circle, back to an unstable, multipolar world order. In place of the bipolar balance between the two superpowers and their respective alliances, there were four or five great powers – the United States, Europe, Japan, China and possibly a revived Russia – just as before 1914 there had been Germany, France, Russia, Britain, and, possibly, the weakening Austrian and Ottoman empires.

I propose in this paper to contest this rather narrowly 'international relations' perception of the problem of world order. I think there are a great many – mostly younger – scholars in Asia, Europe and America who share my dissatisfaction with this perspective on world affairs. They feel, almost instinctively, that it is old-fashioned and myopic and probably also misleading, but they are not always clear about why they should feel this way. For that reason, it may be worth offering for discussion and criticism my own explanation of the reasons why it is misleading and why, therefore, students of world affairs should be encouraged to adopt a political economy instead of a narrowly international relations approach. To do so, I shall have to go back to some of the basic questions of political theory – like how to think about Power, and what is the nature of Politics. These questions may seem rather abstract and far from the focus of this colloquium, but I beg your patience and indulgence and promise to be as brief and as clear on these points as possible. They are necessary to the next stage of the argument which is about the nature of the real networks of power in the international system today and their relevance to the major issues of politics in a world market economy and a materialist world society. These issues are much wider than the simple question of peace or war among the more powerful nation-states. In the next century, I shall argue, the stability and viability of world society as we know it today is more likely to be jeopardised by economic, financial and environmental disorders than by military conflict between the great powers. I can then conclude with some more practical, policy-oriented propositions in answer to Lenin's pertinent – and perennial – question, 'What is to be done?'

In parenthesis, this argument is indirectly critical not only of the realist school in International Relations but also of a more contemporary body of opinion to be found in the United States and Japan, and to some extent in Europe. I am referring to those engaged in the debate about competition between the Triad. They are more often economists than political scientists and are joined by experts like Michael Porter or Kenichi Ohmae from management and business schools. Their common assumption is that world order is under potential threat of worsening conflict between the three major trade 'blocs' – North America, Europe and East Asia, led respectively by the United States, Germany and Japan. I shall also have something to say about this debate and the weakness of some of its economic and political assumptions.

The nature of politics

The Waltzian view of international relations is based on the fundamental assumption that international politics are fundamentally different from domestic politics. All the classic realist writers – Morgenthau, Bull, Holsti, even Aron – share this assumption. The difference between international society and national society, they insist, is that in the former there is no over-riding authority endowed with a monopoly of violence and therefore able to maintain order and a rule of law. The major political issue in international society, therefore, is how to preserve some minimal order and to prevent or minimise the risk of war between states who refuse to accept any higher authority, especially when it comes to questions of national security in what Bull described as an 'anarchical' society (i.e. one lacking government). Whereas, in national society, the issues of politics are much more complex, as any first-year student of political science is made to realise. They concern the multiple responsibilities of government and the various institutions of government – legislative, judicial, administrative. States therefore differ, as students of comparative politics learn, in the extent to which governments are given responsibility for managing the economy, for ensuring equity among social classes, for safeguarding the rights of individuals and for providing for the defence of national territory and for conducting relations with the rest of the world. They differ, too, in the manner in which they choose to discharge their responsibilities and the institutional framework they choose to discharge those responsibilities. They choose a federal or a centralised, a parliamentary or a presidential system of government. Some – like the United States – favour a system based on the separation of powers, aiming at a balance between the legislative, judicial and executive arms of government, while others – like Britain or Japan – favour a system in which governments are constrained only by the authority of parliament. And behind the constitutional facade, students of politics are also taught to look for the real networks of power – the party bosses, the big business associations, the major state or privately owned enterprises, the labour unions, the 'hidden' organisations whether illegal and criminal like the Italian Mafia, or legal but secret like the freemasons, the Catholic Church or certain influential families – within which the real decisions are taken even before they pass through the formal institutions of the state.

To sum up, the limits set to the study of politics within the state are defined by the list of issues of a political nature that someone, somehow decides, and by the nature of the authority through whom those decisions are taken. Politics, in short, are not simply what politicians do. Politics occur whenever some individual or group of individual has to find ways of getting the support of others in order to achieve some objective. Politics, therefore, occurs outside as well as within the state – inside firms, inside parties, inside cities, inside universities, inside sports organisations, for instance. If politics is – in Lasswell's classic definition of the subject – about who gets what, where and how, then in any study of politics we have to look first for the contested issues – the 'what' – and then for the sources, of authority and the processes by which these issues are decided. If each of us – students, professors, factory workers or secretaries, managers or shopkeepers – asks ourselves the question, Who or what, governs my daily life? There are very few people in the world who can honestly say that in every respect and on every matter, 'I do.' Figuring out the who, or what, governs which issues is the job of the political economist.

It is my contention that we now have to apply all these general principles concerning the nature of politics to the world economy and a world society. We certainly have a global financial system operating 24 hours a day around the clock and regardless of national frontiers. Communication systems – think of Internet, or ham radio, or satellite TV – are global and images and ideas very quickly spread across the world and influence local debates and local outcomes. The fate of firms depends increasingly on what they sell (or buy) abroad, rather than on what they sell locally. The growth of world trade constantly outruns the growth of production.

To confine the study of world politics to the single issue of peace or war between states cannot possibly be justified in such a world. One of the questions that intrigued Raymond Aron throughout his long and productive life was one that transcended the bounds of traditional international relations. It was whether the industrialisation of the economies of the great powers and their increasing involvement in world trade was making them more, or less, warlike and aggressive. Aron was not sure. But it seems to me that, despite the temptations and risks inseparable from the sophisticated weapons developed with industrial technology, the governments of all the major states today have to deal with materialist societies. These societies are increasingly rejecting war with other major states as too dangerous an option. They will, I think, continue to do so. It is not as Comte, and Aron, hoped, that increased trade across frontiers generates harmony in international society. It often generates more conflict than cooperation. But people on both sides want economic growth and the wealth it brings to themselves and their families. They know that trade is the necessary means to achieving greater wealth, while war fatally interrupts trade and war puts not only living standards but life itself at risk. Young people everywhere are no longer sure that, whatever the cause, it is always sweet and proper, as the Roman motto said, to die for one's country.

That is one big change since the first half of this century. The other results from the greatly increased cost and technological sophistication of the means of making war. The assumption of traditional theories of international relations was that each state – at least, each great power – had the means of making war under its own control. Peace or war, and therefore international order, was thus a matter of international relations between states. This is no longer the case. Today, we can recognise that the issue of international order and security is inseparable from the political economy of the world market for armaments to fight the wars. The specialist in strategic studies, therefore, has to take into account who, or what, governs access to that market before he or she can analyse the factors affecting the outcome of even a local conflict like the Iran–Iraq war. The agenda even of those professionally engaged in conducting relations with other governments is no longer limited to questions of foreign and defence policy. The staff or Foreign Ministries are engaged in bargaining over trade relations, exchange rates and many other matters besides foreign and defence policy. And they share the work with the staff of other ministries – of finance, economics and trade, health and welfare, the environment, education and justice.

And their negotiations are by no means the sole deciding factor when it comes to outcomes. As John Stopford and I have argued in a recent book, diplomacy these days is a trilateral matter (Stopford and Strange 1991). That is to say, the old diplomacy between professional diplomats representing their respective governments is now only part of the story of international, or transnational bargaining. It is accompanied by what we called the new diplomacy – the bargaining that goes on between foreign firms and host governments – Matsushita and Malaysia, for example, or Fujitsu and Britain – and the bargaining that goes on between big firms who need to collaborate on research or combine forces to influence governments or international organisations or who need to settle disputed matters of marketing and distribution or of property rights.

The nature of power

But before we get further into the difficult question of what are the main issues in world politics – or international political economy as I would prefer to describe it just because it really does concern so many predominantly economic issues – if they are not simply issues of order and peace and war, we have to consider carefully another basic question of all social science – what is the nature of power in human relations, and how do we discover who has it? If we are to try and analyse the sources of authority over a much longer list of issues than just the peace/war issue, we cannot avoid getting to the bottom of this question of power. As long as the only, or at least the dominant, question in international studies was the peace/war question, we could take for granted that it was governments, the managers of the nation-states, that exercised the power over it. We needed to look no further simply because their monopoly of legitimate violence, their control over the armed forces of the state, gave them the authority to make war, to invade another state's territory and to resist or to give in to invading forces from another country. Once we try to decide who or what has the power to decide outcomes in a much longer list of who-gets-what issues, we have to stop and think harder about two things. First, we have to think how we know where power lies. What do you look for if you want to know who has power? Second, we have to think about how power is exercised. How, in reality, do the strong prevail over the weak, and get their own way in these wider issues of world politics?

On both basic questions, there is a vast literature in political and social theory, and I do not propose to go into every aspect of it here. Let me just indicate, quite briefly, the answers which others have found and which seem to me to be relevant to inter-national studies in a post-Cold War, highly interdependent global political economy.

On the first question, who has power, we should look at objectives and outcomes. If Government X wants an airport built and local people don't want it built and the outcome is that the airport is built, we can conclude that Government X has power and the locals do not. If, on the other hand, the outcome is that Government X gives up the idea and either extends other airports or builds elsewhere, we can conclude that the locals, somehow, exercised power. An example of the first is Narita airport. An example of the second is the third London airport at Wing, near my home, which was never built (and which no one consequently has ever heard of) because organised but spontaneous local opposition was so strong that the government changed its mind and expanded Heathrow and Stansted and Luton instead.

The point of this illustration is to show that much discussion of power in inter-national politics and in national politics mistakes the shadow for the substance. In other words, writers have been tempted to look at resources under the command of the powerful, at their capabilities, not at the outcomes which those resources may or may not achieve. This is especially so in international politics where scholars like Klaus Knorr have written books about the power of nation-states that go through a catalogue of the military and material resources of states to determine which are the more powerful – but often end up by admitting that the sums do not always add up. The Germans in 1940, for instance, were endowed with fewer planes and men and other weapons than the French but they had a better strategic plan and more will to win so that they overran France with relative speed and ease.

In domestic politics, political scientists have had a different temptation. It was to look at the institutions of the state and to assume that command of the institutions conferred power. This was only ever true as long as that command was sustained by a social consensus that gave legitimacy to the authority of those in charge of the institutions. If the British people decide in future – as I think they may well do – that they do not want a monarchy, or only want one with much restricted rights and privileges, then that is the end of the constitutional powers of the monarchy in British politics. Or take another example. Constitutionally, the German Bundesbank is an independent arm of government. But the outcome of a contest in 1990 between the federal chancellor and the Bundesbank over the rate at which the old DDR currency would be exchanged for the D-mark was that the Bundesbank lost. Those – especially those in Europe today – who extol the advantages of central bank autonomy and believe that constitutional change will reallocate power over monetary and fiscal outcomes should ask again the basic question, how do you know who has power?[1]

On the second question, how the strong prevail over the weak, we have to abandon right away the answer found in some old textbooks of international relations. It was that A has power over B if A is able to get B to do what B would not otherwise do. This assumes that power is exercised only by direct coercion or bribery. The strong are able either to threaten the weak with the consequences of non-compliance, or to reward them handsomely for doing what they want. At least some political theorists have moved on from this first 'level' of power (Cox, Furlong and Page 1985; Dahl 1984; Lukes 1974; 1986). Power is also exercised, they say, at a higher level when the strong can rule out any objectives the weak may have in mind by just keeping it off the agenda, excluded from the issues recognised as needing political debate and decision. An example in international political economy would be the success of the G24 over the G77 in the matter of international action to stabilise commodity prices. At this second level, power is also exercised by the strong when they decide on adding issues to the agenda for debate and decision. Even more so, when they act indirectly to affect the structures through which outcomes are settled. This may mean determining how an international organisation functions – weighted voting in the IMF for instance. Or it may mean deciding how a market is regulated or not regulated. Once the market – for steel, say, or T-shirts or diamonds, is in operation, those who want to buy and sell it have to accept the conventions and rules of that market and will often be powerless to change them. This is what I would call structural, as opposed to the first kind, relational, power. And in my view, it is both more important and a more effective source of power for the strong, including the United States, than direct coercive power. That was supposed to be the message of the short text I wrote introducing students to international political economy as I defined it (Strange 1988e).[2]

But more than this structural power that is decisive in matters of security, production and finance for instance, the political theorists recognise a third 'level' at which power is exercised by the strong over the weak, and which I have rather loosely described as the realm of ideas, or an important part of the knowledge structure in the international political economy. At this level, the strong implant their ideas, even their self-serving ideology, in the minds of the weak, so that the weak come to sincerely believe that the value-judgments of the strong really are the universally right and true ones. The acceptance by intellectuals in the ex-socialist countries of central Europe, for instance, of the idea that the less the state intervenes in the market economy the better, that protection of local firms is always against the national interest, and that keeping inflation to a minimum is always the first priority for the central bank, is all a classic instance of power exercised through the knowledge structure.

Key issues for world society

On the basis of the two theoretical propositions outlines above, we can now ask, first, what are the main political issues for world society today, and second, who has the power to determine the outcome on these issues. Recall that the first theoretical proposition was that politics involves more than governments and therefore includes enterprises and all sorts of non-state sources of authority. And the second was that power can be, and is, exercised on three levels – directly, structurally and through influencing other people's belief-systems.

When it comes to choosing the main political issues in world society today, I look for the answers more in economic history than in neoclassical or liberal economic theory. This tells me that in the past national societies based on a market economy have been fatally damaged – even destroyed beyond recognition – when political authority failed to discharge any of three basic responsibilities. One was certainly the responsibility to provide security – law and order within the society and defence against attack from without. No market economy can prosper if persons and property are not assured some reasonable degree of security. When the Netherlands became a cockpit or battleground for Europe in the seventeenth and early eighteenth centuries, the Dutch lost their economic and financial leadership to England.

Another was the responsibility to maintain stable money. A market economy has to use money. To grow, it has to have an efficient system of credit-creation in which producers and traders have confidence. Unstable money – as in runaway inflation – can soon destroy that confidence and undermine the foundations of society. That happened, say the historians, in Germany in 1923, and in China in the mid-1930s when the silver-based currency was replaced by the uncontrolled issue of paper money.[3] But the converse can also be destructive; if the system fails to create credit because capitalists lose confidence in the prospects for investment, you get economic depression, unemployment and, often social unrest and political upsets. In the 1930s depression in Europe, only the toughest, most repressive governments survived: Mussolini in Italy, Salazar in Portugal and Stalin in the Soviet Union. Everywhere else, the incumbent parties lost power. The failure then of governments in the leading economies to keep the flow of foreign capital going to the indebted countries – Australia, Argentina, Japan, Latin America – after the crash of 1929, and the failure of the World Economic Conference of 1933 – gave early warnings of the need for counter-cyclical action on an international and not just a national scale. Keynesian pump-priming was tried in several countries, even the United States. But against the forces of a global depression even Roosevelt's New Deal made little impact on the depression; there were still 13 million Americans out of work when the war started.

I would conclude from this that financial management to avoid both depression and inflation, to maintain an even flow of credit – not too much, nor too little – to sustain the continued growth of the world economy is a major political issue and a major responsibility which only authority and not the market – and certainly not the banks – can fulfil.

By comparison, the issue of rules for international trade is comparatively minor. For most of the post-war period, these rules have been few, have been riddled with exceptions, and the basic principle behind them – non-discrimination – has been repeatedly broken and ignored. GATT has been a useful forum, but while tariff barriers have come down as a result of successive multilateral Rounds, other barriers – as the Japanese know only too well have gone up. Bilateral bargaining over trade, in which the outcome is determined more by political muscle than by free trade principles, has become the norm.

World trade – and more particularly world trade in manufactures – has nevertheless continued to thrive and grow. The simple reason is that firms trade, not governments. And despite the barriers and aggravations created by governments, the imperative need for firms to sell abroad as well as at home if they are to survive against the competition of other firms has made sure that trade went on growing year after year. For these reasons, I have repeatedly argued that the importance of a successful conclusion of the Uruguay Round has been greatly exaggerated; that whether or not agreements can be reached on the contested issues – and I doubt if they can – the future of the world economy depends far more on the future management of finance than it does on the liberalisation of trade. Because protectionism damages your health, governments themselves will hesitate before going too far or for too long down that road. Because industries are increasingly interdependent, the producers who favour protectionism are increasingly opposed by other producers who do not relish the handicap of paying more than their global competitors for indispensable components of their products.

For these reasons, the resolution of trade conflicts between the major industrialised countries is not a serious issue of post-cold war politics. Trade diplomacy – as between the US and Japan or the EC and Japan – may continue to be conducted with acrimony and mutual accusations of 'unfair' practice. But the protagonists will be rather like chimpanzees who make 'threat faces' at each other until one or the other backs away, and who rarely harm each other in any serious way. Nor is there any serious risk of the world splitting into three warring trade blocs. All of the big transnational enterprises have interests in each of the three so-called blocs. Without controls over capital flows, or over the transfer of technology, governments are powerless to fight serious trade wars against each other.

If trade liberalisation has generally been over-emphasised of late as a burning issue, economic development has probably faded too much from the public view. The North–South gap was a great issue between rich and poor countries in the 1960s and the 1970s. The gap has not disappeared. Even though some poor people and some poor countries have done well, others (in Africa especially but also in parts of Latin America) are poorer than ever and their prospects grim indeed. If only because transport and communications systems are lowering the physical barriers preventing people moving into the rich countries, creating problems within them instead of far away, the welfare issues of hunger, poverty and untreated disease must be surely added to the list. Because the major obstacle is often more political than economic – the inefficiency, corruption and indifference of ruling elites – international agencies like the IMF and the World Bank already face the dilemma that their task is incompatible with respect for the principles of non-intervention in the affairs of supposedly sovereign states. It is a dilemma which is likely to become more, not less acute in the future.

For the third basic responsibility of authority – the responsibility to preserve the ecological base for the physical environment of the economy – we have to look further back into history, to ancient Mesopotamia, what today we call the Middle East – or West Asia, according to our geographical perspective. A succession of early civilisations there (and in Sri Lanka) thrived on the basis of an environment artificially improved by elaborate systems of irrigation. When these eventually collapsed from neglect, the region fell back into poverty and political instability. Most other parts of the world had more favoured, equable climates and soils and could withstand the modest changes brought about by the primitive or intermediate technology of the human inhabitants.

The first two responsibilities were recognised by the classical writers on political economy like Adam Smith. Smith is remembered for arguing that the state should stop strangling the market with mercantilist and other restrictions. Just as strongly, he also argued that, for the economy to prosper, the state had to look after the Defence of the Realm and the Value of the Currency. In his time, Nature could still take care of herself. The environmental responsibility of authority only returns to prominence, and today on a global scale, with the massive use of fossil fuels and of industrial chemicals.

Others may disagree, but I would argue that the financial and the environmental responsibilities of authority in the world market economy will in future be more crucial than the responsibility for security. There are two reasons for saying this. One is historical: that in the early phases of capitalism, the very insecurity of society in a political system of constantly warring states – especially in Europe – gave rise to the competitive, territorial nation-state. The imperative need to defend each realm against intruders justified strong government, and gave it the necessary legitimacy. Strong government was thus able to impose domestic order, build the economic infrastructure and regulate and nurture trade, banking and investment to the benefit of the economy and society. Governments in England did better than most at discharging these tasks and England prospered earlier and, at first, more than most.

The other reason has already been referred to above and has to do with technology, though it is also in a sense historical. In recent times, the technology for defence has become very costly. It has also become very destructive. The costs and the risks of major war between industrial countries have escalated exponentially. At the same time, prosperity has given a voice to more and more sections of society, sections that have good reason to like peace and prosperity and to fear the risks and costs of war. Prosperity no longer depends on amassing more and more territory. There is no incentive for making war on neighbours, as Japan did on China in the 1930s or Germany did on Poland. Prosperity depends on the enterprises in a country being able to gain and hold world market shares.[4]

Thus the responsibility of authority for security has to be re-examined. If the danger of major war between the advanced industrial powers – primarily, the

United States, Japan, and Europe – and also among the newly industrialised countries like India and Pakistan, Brazil and Chile, Korea and Taiwan is, as I believe, greatly diminished, then perhaps the world market economy does not need universal, 'perpetual peace' – or even a system of effective collective security against aggression. Recent experience in the Middle East, Yugoslavia and the former Soviet republics – not to mention the Falkland islands – suggests that perhaps the world economy and society can manage pretty well despite these outbreaks of violence and insecurity. Of course, the places where violence erupts will not attract as much investment, foreign and local, and will not prosper as much as quieter places. But economic life will go on around them and elsewhere without too much notice being taken. Northern Ireland – a violent and insecure province of the United Kingdom for the last 25 years or more – has suffered in lost jobs and low investment despite government aid. But it has had little effect on either the British or the Irish Republic's economies. In short, let us not assume, with Professor Waltz, that because preventing major war between great powers was the main issue of world politics in the twentieth century that it will also be the major issue for the twenty-first century.

Networks of power

I began this paper with the declaration of belief, first, that in the next century the stability and viability of world society as we know it today is more likely to be jeopardised by economic, financial and environmental disorders than by military conflict; and, second, that to see how these issues are being, and might be, addressed and managed, we needed to look beyond the world of states to discern the real networks of power over outcomes. What, more precisely, are these networks of power?

At this stage, I can only suggest what I think they look like and how they have affected, and will in future affect the major issues of international finance, development and the environment that I have identified. To go further, we need, I believe, to do much more research, research that necessarily crosses disciplinary boundaries and certainly goes beyond the concerns of traditional studies in international relations.

For a start, I have three hypotheses, all of which are open to discussion. The first is that states in general have lost the authority they once had over markets. As markets have become increasingly global, and as the production of firms has been geared to selling on a world market, and consequently dispersed over several national economies at once, so firms everywhere, *even in the United States*, pay less attention to the direct, first-level power exercised by governments and more attention to the markets. But these markets are not neutral. They do not function in a political vacuum. The rules under which they operate are subject to the second-level structural power of, primarily, the United States, but also of certain non-state authorities which differ from sector to sector. They may include the big banks and insurance companies. They may include inter-industry cartels or 'special relationships' between major firms. The authority of the US over so many world markets is dominant, even after the end of the Cold War, mainly because the US has the single largest and richest domestic market that is also subject – unlike the market of the European Community – to a clear single set of rules; and also because – unlike the Japanese market – it is more open both to imports and to foreign investors. The openness to foreign firms is both historical – the nineteenth century dependence on British investors – and accidental, to the extent that foreign firms, Japanese and European, have been forced by rising US protectionism against foreign imports to locate production with the country. Inevitably, then, they become vulnerable to policies determined in Washington.

It also helps US predominance that the international organisations like the IMF, the World Bank, the OECD and the GATT which were created when Germany and Japan were defeated and powerless after the Second World War were designed to institutionalise American structural power and to proclaim and preserve American preferences and political and economic ideas – power, that is, at the third level of ideas, values and belief systems.

A consequence of this shift in the balance of power between states and markets is that the equality of sovereign states – always a fiction of international lawyers – has become even more of a fiction. In other words, my second hypothesis is that the asymmetry of power over outcomes between the United States on the one hand and other major states on the other has increased; and at the other end of the rank order of states, the weak ones have got even weaker in relation to the rich and strong. This is to be seen very clearly in the influence exerted through their Structural Adjustment Programmes by the World Bank and the IMF over the governments of poor indebted countries in Africa. The IMF even exerts substantial influence over much bigger indebted countries like Brazil or India and over the indebted countries of central Europe.

Nor are these the only international agencies that are, at the least, sharing some of their authority with national governments. In Europe, the federalist dreams of a United States of Europe may have faded somewhat in the last two years, and for obvious reasons. But in such matters as competition policy, agricultural protection and even environmental regulation, the European Community's bureaucracies are taking some responsibilities away from national governments. The European Court, especially, has overruled national policies on a number of matters.[5]

For whatever reason, a suspicion is growing – at least in Europe if not in Japan – that the nation-state is suffering some sort of decline or loss of legitimacy. People do not seem to have the respect they used to have for their heads of government – think of Munroney in Canada or Major in Britain. Political leaders still make promises – to the unemployed, the old, the sick. But no one believes they can keep them. The old justification for deference to your government, its symbols and its representatives was that it both protected you from foreigners and provided its citizens with a social security cushion against hard times. Now it is doubtful whether it can do either, and even whether it can find the means to resolve its own fiscal problems. Regional authorities, in Europe and elsewhere, are increasingly challenging the authority of central government.

The third hypothesis is that as power has become more dispersed, away from the sovereign state that was supposed to be the unit of analysis of international society, so some of the functions of authority are not being properly discharged by anybody. Power has evaporated, like steam. No one is entirely in charge, not even the United States.

This is really an answer to the declinist school of writers in the United States, with whom I have never agreed. Not only did they choose poor indicators of the supposed loss of power by the United States, they also tacitly assumed a zero-sum game between states. If the US lost, some other state must have gained. Because Japanese firms were pushing US firms out of certain markets – steel, ships, consumer electronics and semiconductors – Japan must be gaining the power that the US had lose. But this totally ignored the structural power in security, finance and knowledge especially that the United States still exercised. Moreover, the game was not a zero-sum game between national governments. As explained above, all states were losing power to markets. The plight of workers and firms tied to production inside the territorial United States was to a large extent the consequence of policies pursued by successive US Administrations from Truman's onwards. Tragedy, as always in human affairs, was mostly self-inflicted. It was the US which had insisted on an open world market economy – open to trade in goods and services, open to investment and therefore subject to mobility of capital if not of labour. If the US government found itself unable to control the market, it was a monster, a Frankenstein, that it had itself created. The American response, since the late 1960s, was to act – not as the benevolent, self-denying hegemon that the system (and Kindleberger's original Hegemonic Stability Theory) required – but as an irresponsible, self-serving, even malevolent one when it came to 'punishing' the Asian countries it blamed for its own troubles.

According to the theory, the system required the hegemon to maintain the stability of the key international currency. But, beginning with the Vietnam War, US government allowed the unchecked piling-up of dollar reserves with foreign central banks – reserves that were financing deficits the US was unwilling to rectify by spending less or taxing and saving more. The theory also required an uninterrupted outflow of capital from surplus countries to developing ones. But in the 1980s, US policies reversed the flow so that Latin American capital flowed northwards instead of the reverse, while the Japanese and other surpluses that might have sustained economic growth in the developing countries were drawn to the United States where the return on capital was higher than at home and the political risk less than in the Third World.

The one bright spot – for poor people, at least – in the picture of the world economy of the last decade has been the result not of government action, but of corporate decisions. The shift of manufacturing capacity from established industrialised countries – America, Europe, Japan – to developing countries has raised growth rates in the favoured host countries to levels undreamt of by official donors of foreign aid. In short, the multinationals have come to the rescue at least of some developing countries. Their authority over the location of production, as well as over the direction of technological innovation, is undisputed.

What is to be done?

This is a big question and I cannot claim to have the answer. I do observe, however, that the declinist school of scholarship in the United States is itself in decline. Recognition of the extent of American structural power is beginning to dawn, only partly as a result of American success in launching the Gulf War and getting others to pay – perhaps even overpay – for it. To be sure, American unilateralism in military and commercial affairs is still very much alive – as the UN exercise in Somalia and the air strike against Baghdad last June, or the sudden imposition of punitive steel tariffs last March, demonstrated. But on the other hand, the U-turn of American policy on aid to Russia and the ex-socialist countries, and the concern over financial re-regulation, showed a return to some sense of responsibility for financial leadership.

What needs to be done – as Delors and many Japanese leaders realise – is for more concerted diplomacy between the non-American members of the Group of Seven. This would add the weight of expressed foreign public and informed opinion to that of the more enlightened sections of the American political community. In this, academics have an important part to play. I hope that before too long the close ties already in existence between US and Japanese scholars and universities on the one hand, and US and European scholars and universities on the other, will be matched by much closer and denser ties between Japanese and European scholars and universities.

Only so can we hope to develop a perspective on major issues of international political economy that is more broadly based, both in terms of national perspectives on common problems and how to manage them and in terms of the underlying assumptions about power and politics that would free us of some of the myopic limitations of the traditional study of foreign policy and international relations.

Section IV
Engagements

Introduction and Commentary

Given Susan Strange's view that many of the problems of international policy making stemmed from a misrecognition of how the international economy actually worked, it is hardly surprising that another major theme to which she returned again and again was shortcomings in the academic analysis of international relations. In the twenty-seven years that separates the first from the last of the pieces in this section, Strange continued to criticise and fume at the conceptual and analytical lapses which she detected throughout International Relations (IR) and International Economics. Never afraid to be outspoken, and driven by her own frustration with what she read, Strange repeatedly returned to the offensive in this intertextual engagement. Utilising her extensive knowledge of the financial sector, international trade and transnational relations, as well as her belief in the necessity of 'value sensitive' analysis, Strange identified significant lacunae in the approaches adopted by the mainstream of IPE, IR and International Economics. While always friendly to the radicals, Strange attempted to pursue her own fight from within the discipline rather than from the critical territory outside its (self-policed) borders. In this sense, Strange represents an important bridge between the radical left-field of IPE and the mainstream at which its critique is aimed, although much of her work continues to defy easy classification.

The first selection is probably her best-known, and arguably most significant article, in which she first called for the development of International Political Economy as a modern, separate discipline. She identified a major void between the study of international relations and international economics. Her work on transnational relations and international monetary relations at Chatham House had led her to conclude that a new approach, IPE, was needed to deal with the major problems that beset the international economy and the international polity. Without such a discipline IR and International Economics would be doomed to irrelevance. This powerful statement sets out what became a major part of her advocacy over the next thirty years.

In the second selection, we have included an early discussion of her structural power theory, which she would then develop over the next thirteen years to its major statement in *States and Markets* (Strange 1988e). This built on her interest in 'the market' as a form of power, and clearly illustrates the analytical problems that she grappled with as she became increasingly concerned with the inadequacy of conventional IR analyses of power. The misrecognition of the reality of the international political economy by conventional IPE is also the core argument of the third selection. This is the piece most frequently cited by US academics, partly because it is familiar, having appeared in what US IPE scholars often consider to be 'the' definitive volume on regimes and regime theory, and partly because it was the token critical piece included therein. It is a classic Strange *critique*: she argues that there are a number of crucial shortcomings in regime theory, and these collectively not only diminish the centrality of regimes (most of the really important issues, she notes, are not covered by a regime), but reduce 'regimes' to an ideological concept designed to serve the interests of US power.

The fourth selection outlines Strange's development of a critical ontology based on her conviction that it is not sufficient merely to argue that the state has lost power; what is it that has replaced the power of the state? The linking together of territory, state, authority and economy enabled her to identify a shift in authority from the territorial state to other actors, including markets, in the global political economy. Strange contextualised this argument in a discussion of 'realism' and her perception of the reality of power in the late twentieth century. For Strange the real test of any academic work was how it dealt with the developing (and changing) reality of the global political economy.

13

'International Economics and International Relations: A Case of Mutual Neglect', 1970

The purpose of this article is to put forward a proposition which, if accepted as correct, seems to me to be of rather major importance to the academic study of international relations. It concerns the unequal pace of change in the international political system and in the international economic system, and the effects of this unequal rate of change on the international society, and on the relations of states with one another.

These changes have gone very largely unnoticed. There are two possible reasons why this has been so. Partly, they have crept up on us rather quickly in the last decade or so. And partly, many academics engaged in international relations, politics and history in these years have been absorbed and preoccupied with arguments about theory and methodology which have focused, far too exclusively, in my view, on the political and strategic relations between national governments, to the neglect of all else.

I believe that this neglect is already apparent from the state of the literature on international economic relations, and that it will become even more evident as time passes. There are some questions which are vital to the coherence and relevance of our view of the world to which we – the teachers and writers, that is, of international relations, politics, history, law and organisation – shall soon badly need the answers, but answers which, equally, we cannot safely leave to others to provide. The situation is also responsible, I believe, for a growing and as yet rather ill-defined uneasiness in the universities – or at least, in some of them – about the adequacy of international relations courses and about the gap between international relations and international economics. But it is one thing for a busy academic to be aware of a neglected void, and another to know how best it should be filled. To these practical questions I shall come later.

When I try to put in precise terms my basic proposition, from which the rest follows, I do not find it all that easy. For it is apt to sound as though I am only repeating the banal platitude that we are all closer together economically than we used to be. But what I have in mind is more specific than the increase in economic interdependence and interaction. It is that the pace of development in the international economic system has accelerated, is still accelerating and will probably continue to accelerate. And that, in consequence, it is out-distancing and out-growing the rather more static and rigid international political system. Many economists and some bankers and the executives of international companies, observing this outgrowing process, are inclined to assume that the political system will have, as it were, to catch up: that it, too, is bound to change its character and become less firmly based than it was (and is) on the unit of the individual state and government. I am not persuaded of this. I can only see that in certain respects it will have to adapt and find adjustment mechanisms and synchronising devices – as it has before. How far these devices will substantially change the nature of the political system and the behaviour of states is, of course, the key question.

Three kinds of change

There seem to be three main kinds of change which the developing international economy has brought about and which directly affect international relations.

First, there are the direct effects on states of their common involvement in the expanding international economic network. Richard Cooper (1968), subdividing again, finds three different ways in which states are affected. One is by what he calls the 'disturbance' effects – the increase in the disturbance, originating externally in some other part of the international economy, of some important part of the domestic economy – whether it is the level of employment, of prices, of interest rates, or of the country's monetary reserves.

Second, there are the hindrance effects, when the mutual sensitivity of national economies to each other slows down or diminishes the effectiveness of national economic policies – as when a credit squeeze and tight money policy which is intended to dampen domestic demand pulls in foreign funds which will tend (unless sterilised, insulated or counteracted) to frustrate the policy-makers' intentions.

And third, there are competitive or what used to be called 'beggar-my-neighbour' policies, by which states seeking to serve their own national economic interests (as by trying to control overseas investments, or by trying to regulate mergers and takeovers) coincidentally damage the national economic interests of other states, and thus risk creating new sources of international conflict.

Indirectly, all these changes have produced two kinds of response in the behaviour of states which therefore constitute a dynamic element in international politics as well as in economics. One response is cooperative, the other defensive, and I am not foolhardy enough to guess which is the predominant. The co-operative response produces a steady expansion in international economic co-operation and organisation. 'The central problem,' to quote Cooper again, 'is how to keep the manifold benefits of extensive international economic intercourse free of crippling restrictions while at the same time preserving a maximum degree of freedom for each nation to pursue its legitimate economic objectives'. Let us leave aside the political observation that it is never so easy to get governments to agree on which objectives are 'legitimate' and which are not. The point here is that the expanding and pervading international economy is now the major innovative influence in the field of international organisation. Swaps, Special Drawing Rights, recycling of short-term funds, and a number of other recent devices invented by co-operative official minds, or adapted and restyled by them from the blueprints produced by idealistic reformers, were all in a sense forced upon governments, because there seemed no alternative way for them to continue to co-exist within the same economic system without losing some of its benefits.

The defensive response, however, has also been important. No contemporary analysis of state behaviour in international relations would be complete that did not recognise this and try to account for it. It follows logically that as governments tend to increase their concern with domestic welfare, including economic welfare, they will have to devise and to adopt new defensive weapons to protect this welfare should it be threatened or jeopardised from outside.

This is a big and complex subject. But perhaps one specific example will illustrate what I have in mind. The six governments of the EEC once upon a time proclaimed their intention to extend and increase their monetary co-operation with the ultimate objective of a common currency. But in practice, the pressures of the last ten years upon their respective central banks have led them to do almost the opposite. They have had to devise new weapons which a monetary economist sees as 'a material enrichment in the craft of central banking' (Katz 1969), but which research also makes clear were motivated by the desire to attain domestic economic goals '*even when such policies conflicted with the requirements of international balance*' (my italics). As Katz says, 'Central bankers in our generation have not been prepared to watch passively as international influences disturb the internal economy without regard to domestic priorities.'

The other general effect of these developments of the international economy is one of those differences of degree so great as to be a difference of kind. I do not count as changes in the political system the swapping of roles among the actors in the system, the relative rise or fall of different states or the rearrangement of states in looser or closer groupings, or in new multipolar instead of bipolar patterns, and so forth. But it seems to me that the shape or structure of international society must be materially affected by a pronounced trend towards lopsided development. That is to say, when the economic system so favours the increasing wealth of a minority of developed national economies over the majority of less developed ones that it produces a list to port, so to speak, in the political system, then this can count as a political as well as an economic change. The label 'populist', attached first, I think, by Robert Cox (1969) to the states on the wrong side of the divide, is in this context an apt one, for it underlines the point that the growing inequality has produced a new basis of political alignment in international society – not strategic, nor religious, nor cultural, nor ideological – the consequence of which for the operation of that system neither we nor the economists can yet foresee.

The state of the literature

My next point is that the study of international relations, in most universities at the present time – and not only in this country, is not keeping up very successfully with the changes I have tried very briefly to outline. Instead of developing as a modern study of international political economy, it is allowing the gulf between international economics and international politics to grow yearly wider and deeper and more unbridgeable than ever. This dichotomy is well reflected in the current state of the literature dealing with this middle ground – or perhaps I should say middle void – between the two, whether you call it the economic aspects of international relations or that large part of international economics that is susceptible and sensitive to political considerations.

From the international relations side of the void has come only a meagre contribution, except in certain specialised fields. Two such fields that come to mind are studies of international economic organisations, where a useful beginning has been made. I do not count in this context the 'company history' type of books written by international organisation-men, but such critical, analytical works, for example, as William Diebold's study of the Schuman Plan (1959) or Michael Kaser's of Comecon (1967). The other is what could loosely be described as area studies – where it is so immediately and evidently impossible, in any serious analysis of international relations between pairs of groups of countries, to divorce the economic and political aspects. I have in mind, for example, such studies as Richard Gardner's *Sterling-Dollar Diplomacy* (1969), recently reissued (1980), Dennis Austin's study of *Britain and South Africa* (1966), Trevor Reese's recent book on *Australia, New Zealand and the United States* (1969), Arthur Hazelwood's *African Integration and Disintegration* (1967), or Miriam Camps' *European Unification in the Sixties* (1966).

What is noticeably missing from the picture are more general studies of international economic relations – whether of problems or issue areas – treated analytically, with the political analysis predominating over the economic analysis.

These general questions have so far been very much left to the economists. And admirable and distinguished as their work undoubtedly is, it seems to me that when looked at from a critical international relations point of view it has shortcomings that perhaps are unavoidable, given the nature of the discipline. To put it bluntly, the literature contributed to the void by the economists suffers, first from a certain partiality for some aspects and questions over others, and secondly from a certain political naiveté in its conclusions. The partiality is shown particularly to the questions concerning international trade and international payments and to the mechanistic questions which they raise. With trade and payments, part of the fascination is probably explained by the opportunities for mechanistic analysis – roughly, how it works and what happens in the economic mechanism – and the availability of quantifiable data that can be subjected to model calculations.

It also happens that the study of economics is led and dominated by the United States, and that the national interests of the United States, both political and economic, are much concerned with both subjects – not only from a narrow national point of view, but also as what I would call the Top Currency country which by definition has a special concern with the preservation of order and stability in the international economic system. The result of this partiality in the economists' contributions is that what I might call the foreign economic policy analysis side of the subject has been seriously neglected. Gardner Patterson's book on discrimination in international trade (1966) and Gerard Curzon's on multilateral commercial diplomacy (1965) are valuable, but they are not enough. They do not make up for the lack of a substantial literature on the theory of international political economy – not applied or descriptive international economics but a political theory of analysis and explanation. The result is that great gaps are left wide open to be occupied by popular myth and legend.

Why, for example, has there never been a general political study of international loans and debts to match, for later periods, Herbert Feis' *Europe, The World's Banker*? Why is the subject of economic warfare so neglected? Apart from the pre-war Chatham House study on sanctions, and Klaus Knorr's somewhat abortive attempt to get to the bottom of war potential, the only real contribution has been from Professor Medlicott (1952; 1959), an international historian. Again, though the political role of the oil companies has come in for some attention by Edith Penrose (1968) and others (Hartshorn 1967; Tugendhat 1968), the role of other large enterprises in international situations of conflict or association has had short shrift since the happy muck-raking days of the Left Book Club. Significantly, perhaps, some of these gaps left by the university economists have tempted distinguished, non-university academics. I am thinking, for example, of two distinguished ex-financial journalists – Andrew Shonfield (1969) and Fred Hirsch (1969) – both of whom have pioneered new ground.

My other criticism is that the economists' contributions to the study of international economic relations have shown political naïveté. Too often they write on international economic problems as though political factors and attitudes simply did not exist, and could be brushed aside as some kind of curious quirk or aberration of dim-witted politicians. When the economists tell you that it is all just a matter of *will*, of summoning up the necessary will-power, does it not remind you of those who used to say and write so glibly, forty-odd years ago, that the League of Nations would be fine and all international problems could be resolved if only the members showed the necessary will to make the system work? Yet only recently, the Pearson Committee (Pearson 1969) came up with the same kind of conclusion about aid and development. The problems are new, but the responses are the same old 'infantile internationalism' – if I may be allowed a perverted Leninism. Even Professor Cooper, whom I quoted earlier, is also inclined to lapse into the tell-tale Conditional Mood and to assume, despite a measure of pessimism, that the economic co-operation required to avoid catastrophe and conflict is no different in kind (i.e., intrudes no more into perceived national interests) from the international co-operation required to control epidemics (1968: 279).

The bias of economics towards an over-optimistic view of international relations is not, perhaps, so surprising. In the first place, it tends as a discipline to exaggerate the rationality in human behaviour. Economic theory continues to assume it about economic choices, even when descriptive economics has shown how often the rationality is qualified and decisions influenced by non-economic considerations. How much more has international economic history shown that political choices on economic policies have seldom been motivated by carefully reasoned assessments of quantifiable economic costs and benefits, but rather by political aims and fears, and sometimes by totally irrelevant considerations and irrational emotions.

Indeed, the only thing I have ever found really dismal about the science is its habit of reducing individuals to units of a statistic, and then of jumping to the assumption in its model-making that at all times these units are fully inter-changeable with one another. It is hardly necessary to warn any political scientist, let alone a politician or political journalist, of the dangers of allowing these intellectual habits to influence judgment about the behaviour of states in inter-national society.

In short, the state of the literature is that it is inadequate and under-developed, from the political side, and lop-sided and subject to an optimistic and, I should personally judge, a dollar-biased skew on the economic side.

The damage to international relations

These weaknesses in the literature are more than just a regrettable omission, an unfortunate, missed opportunity. Unless they are soon made good, they are likely to be increasingly damaging and disabling to the whole study of international relations. If my initial assumptions are valid about the pressures which a fast-growing international economy is exerting on a more rigid international political system, it seems to me we shall soon need rather urgently to have a theory of inter-national economic relations, a political theory which is consistent with whatever other sort of theory of international relations we individually find most satisfactory. If we do not somehow develop one, it seems to me that any work we do on the other frontiers of the subject, in theory, in foreign policy analysis, in strategic studies and in international organisation – even, indeed, in area studies – risks a damaging loss of contact and consistency with the real world of policy-making.

At the very least, perhaps, we can agree that there are a number of key questions in this middle ground between politics and economics to which we badly need the answers. Or – lowering our sights still more – that there are areas of *terra incognitia* in which it would be helpful to us all if someone were to do some explanatory digging and to apply some careful thought.

One such area is integration theory. It is true that Ernst Haas (1965) and others have made efforts to find a theoretical framework consistent with contemporary problems and situations. In European studies, especially, it was and is important to know at what point co-ordination and harmonisation of national policies became irreversible integration of a new multistate community, and to find some means of recognising this point. Perhaps if more attention had been paid earlier on to such general 'theoretical' questions of international economic integration, there would have been fewer among us to be taken in by the assertion made by the

Brussels EEC Commission that adoption of a Common Agricultural Policy ruled out all possibility of divergent exchange rates.

Similar questions arise with a number of international economic organisations, whose real achievements we are in no position to assess or to fit into our other theories until we have tried to do more fundamental work on the nature of international economic relations in that issue area.

Out of a number of possibles let me pick three specific questions to which we badly need the answers.

It is now believed that the volume of Eurodollars is now about as big, at some $40 billion, as the domestic money supply of each of the larger European states. And it is agreed that the market in Eurodollars is an international money market, unlike any national money market in that there is no lender of last resort and no authority capable of controlling the supply or exercising supervision over it. Extrapolating the trend even at a much shallower upward angle in the 1980s and 1990s, what does this do to the financial capability of governments? Some guidance from a coherent political theory of international currencies is urgently needed.

Again, we are all familiar with the propaganda of some of the leading multinational corporations – working in the vanguard of the capitalist revolution against the outworn shibboleths of nationalism, and all that. But we do not have to believe everything that IBM tell us to see that the activities of multinational corporations could upset some conventional ideas about the international political as well as economic system. So long as the theory of international trade, resting on the law of comparative costs, seemed to accord with reality, there was at least a close coincidence between the structural form of the subject-matter of international economics and of international politics. The units were more or less the same. But what are the implications for the political system if the theory of international trade has to be replaced, as some American economists are now insisting, by a theory of international production? The calculation that international production (i.e., the output of companies operating abroad) is growing at twice the rate of the GNP of the US domestic economy, and at this rate will equal the aggregate of all national GNP's by the year 2000, should surely concern students of international relations no less than it does the companies themselves.

A third poser is the place in our conceptual framework (to use the posh phrase) of the recent growth in rule-making, standard-setting and market management undertaken wholly or partly extra-governmentally. A feature of this dynamic international economy is the pressures it exerts across frontiers on those with economic interests either in common or in opposition. I am thinking of such phenomena as the Berne Union of Credit Insurers which began, at least, extra-governmentally; of IATA negotiations on air fares; of informal arrangements to share the UK market for cheese, butter and bacon; of moves towards international negotiation of wage agreements directly between the unions and the managements. Two more examples from the past year are the International Association of Bond Dealers which responded to the lack of any inter-state supervision of the highly active Eurobond market by deciding to agree on its own ground rules. Another was the intrusion into negotiations on conventions covering oil pollution à la Torrey Canyon of the

London insurance industry and the tanker-owners. The final agreement depended not only on governments but on the willingness of the hard-bargaining insurers to pay out up to $10 million in compensation for a single disaster, and on the willingness of the tanker-owners to submit to auto taxation to produce a fund – known, rather endearingly I think, as 'Tovalop' (tanker owners' voluntary organisation of oil pollution).[1]

The practical question

When it comes to the practical question of how best the teaching of international relations can respond to the new demands made upon it by the accelerating spread and growth of the international economy, I doubt if there is a single valid answer. I certainly have not the qualifications to give it. There has been far too little in the way of experiment and trial of alternative solutions by which to judge. In British universities, the explanation is given that departments are too small, and budgets too constrained, for such pioneering. But even in the best-heeled universities in the United States, surprisingly little has been done in this direction.

Some discussions that have recently been held among interested British academics, first at the Bailey Conference[2] in London last January and then at Chatham House, have shown that there is not only a wide measure of shared concern about the problem, of dissatisfaction with present arrangements, but also of uncertainty about how best to change them. It seems to be quite widely agreed that there is now an area of international studies which requires familiarity with three kinds of economic knowledge – with economic theory and the concepts and methods necessary to it; with the functioning of economic mechanisms and institutions, both national and international, and with economic history. There is also agreement on the poverty of the literature, and on the prospectively growing need for university courses, whether of a general or a regional 'area study' type, to introduce subject-matter, with an added political ingredient, from what is now known as international economics.

The most common solution to the problem has been, and still is, the parallel course or joint degree, simply because it is the easiest and most feasible. One of the oldest and best-known British examples has been the Oxford P.P.E. (Politics, Philosophy and Economics) degree. The London BSc. (Economics) has similarly, and rather more flexibly than the Oxford model, tried to combine the disciplines of politics and economics, and, for specialists in international relations, some law and history as well. A more recent variation is the Cambridge Social Science Tripos, and there are other examples at a number of British universities.[3]

In each case, the chief weakness of the parallel course solution is that it inevitably tends to develop divergence rather than confluence of the component parts. The economics taught by the economists and the politics or international relations (and come to that the philosophy) have less and less relevance to one another, rather than more and more. Nor is any very serious attempt made from either side to relate the courses to one another. The economists do not even try to deal with the political aspects of international economic relations and international economic problems; and few political scientists even try to explore the economic dimension of international politics or diplomacy. The economic historians are perhaps alone in attempting some sort of synthesis, and it is a pity for everyone that they are so few and comparatively far between.

Another point of fairly general agreement is that a grounding in basic economics is now needed for any serious student of international relations, and that it is better begun at an early stage. It is not only that the jargon of economics, or political science, becomes more and more alien to the ear of the other discipline – though, regrettably, this is quite an important consideration, but the habits and processes of thought are different. If students are not introduced quite early on to the intellectual exercises of both, they are apt to get too mentally stiff and unbending to take easily to them later.

Beyond the elementary stages, however, many international relations teachers would be as unhappy as I am to see the developing study of international economic relations left to the economists. The occasional brilliance of a politically astute general does not invalidate the old saying about war being too serious a matter to be left to the generals in the plural. Nor does the enlightenment sometimes shed by one brilliant economist make up for the overall effect of economists in the mass.

It follows that, at some stage, departments of political science, of international history or international relations (and, indeed, the centres or schools of area studies) will have to take their courage in both hands and attempt to build their own bridges across the gulf. The parallel course leaves it to the students to do this for themselves. But students, especially undergraduates, are by definition absorbed in absorbing, and this sort of innovative bridge-building is a pretty strenuous creative activity to ask of them. Not much help is to be expected from the economists. Most international relations teachers complain very bitterly in private about the difficulties they have experienced in getting the economists to meet them half-way or to undertake any serious collaboration on this middle ground. It must be said here that there have been and are some honourable and much appreciated exceptions to the generalisation – Professor James Meade and the late Eli Devons are two often mentioned, and there are a fair few among the younger generation of economists. But most of the rest manage to convey the impression that they regard consorting with other social scientists as a form of intellectual slumming. On the whole, they are blissfully and amazingly unaware of their own lack of judgment and expertise in political analysis, or of any subjective or professional bias that afflicts them – much more unaware, certainly, than the teacher of international relations is likely to be of his or her own inexpertise in economics.

Such bridge-building will be easier to do, and bridging courses easier to design and conduct, if it is somewhat specialised – by period, by region or by issue-area. The politics of international economic aid or the problems of regional economic co-ordination are familiar examples. But I think it would be regrettable if some of the larger departments did not have a shot at more general courses. After all, we are not, most of us, very good historians; we do not know as much as we should about international law, about sociology, political theory and a large number of other things. But we do in practice attempt to teach students some part of them. Why not international economic relations?

The aim it seems to me is twofold. Primarily, in my view, it is to start off a new generation of bridge-builders better able than the older and middle-aged teachers to meet the economists on equal terms, to make a respectable and serious contribution to the literature, and better able, in their turn, to enlighten and instruct the generation now still at school.

There is also surely some broader political responsibility. It is true that the Foreign Office in Britain – rather noticeably more so than the American State Department – is inclined to show a lordly disdain for, and disinterest in, the academic study of international relations. There are a number of possible reasons for this attitude, some good and some bad, which need not be gone into here. But now, as a result of the accelerating international economy, and the changes which economic inter-dependence are bringing about, new questions concerning the nature of the national interest are constantly cropping up. Some are perhaps really old questions in a new form; some really are unfamiliar. And most countries, rich and strong, and poor and weak, are trying to answer them. Do we, for example, want more or less foreign investment? Of what kind, and how do we treat it? How big a payments surplus do we aim for? Is it a help or a handicap to operate a financial centre as large and volatile as London? What is a reasonable rate of inflation, a tolerable burden of foreign debt? The answers so far found, in Britain at least, have either fudged long- and short-term considerations, or have been given out of a stock of conventional and rather dusty ideas from our vanishing past. Officials have been too busy, politicians and the moguls of the mass media too afraid of unpopularity, to give much thought to finding new ones. There is little doubt in many minds, though, that the stock badly needs replenishing and refurbishing. Possibly the practitioners of foreign policy might pay more attention to the academics if they had something relevant and coherent to say on questions as crucial as these. For the latter building intellectual card-houses and playing academic word-games is not enough.

14
'What is Economic Power, and Who Has It?' 1975

for

The double question is prompted by a growing dissatisfaction with the apparent inability of most conventional theories of international politics and economics to offer any coherent explanation of certain recent events and developments. For instance it is widely thought that the growing power of the multinational companies, the Arabs' raising the price of oil, the intermittent refusal of Europe to follow the United States' lead on some international issues like monetary reform and trade arrangements, that these and other straws in the wind suggest that there has been some redistribution recently of the balance of economic power in the world at the expense of the United States, and at the expense of governments in general and governments of developed countries in particular. It therefore seems of some topical importance to attempt first to explain the source of much current confusion about the nature and significance of economic power in international affairs and second to offer a suggested framework that may incorporate enough of both the political and economic dimensions of international affairs to count itself a proposition in political economy.

The question, 'What is economic power, and who has it?' is not just academic. It is surely relevant to many of the great issues concerning the future prospects for mankind and for human society that we find ourselves facing with such uncertainty and apprehension. For instance, it is a sort of joker, or factor of indeterminate quality, in any estimate we make of future relations between the superpowers. An answer to it will also be implicit in any guess about the future capacity of the international economic order to overcome the dangers of both deepening recession and mounting inflation. It must also count in our judgement and anticipations concerning future relations between rich countries and poor ones.

Even for narrowly professional reasons, the question seems to me to deserve more academic attention than it has received in recent years. In many universities, the difficulties of communication between students and staff, in the social sciences especially, are made worse because the radical young think they have a pat answer to the question and are puzzled at the indifference of their teachers and resentful of their failure even to discuss it.

But when we look to conventional theories of international economics and international politics as to how economic power may be defined and assessed so that we can better judge the consequences of contemporary change, we find neither is very helpful. Both it seems to me are inhibited – one might almost say immobilized – by intellectual corsets that they themselves have chosen to wear.

International political theories have been restricted in their approach to economic power chiefly by two basic assumptions. The most important of these is that the international system is dominated by the relations between states – effectively, between governments. It is interstate relations, of conflict and co-operation, that are the stuff of international politics and provide the framework for all other international studies. Now, though there is some truth in this, it is by no means the whole truth – as the recent attention paid to what is loosely called 'transnational relations' has clearly shown. Writers like Nye and Keohane (1972), Bergsten (1973), Camps (1974), Diebold (1972), Kaiser, Calleo, Schmitt, and others have all, from different starting points, agreed on the contention that the growing interdependence created by the expansion of the international economy (especially since the end of World War II) has brought into prominence as 'high politics' whole new areas of policy in which states have the choice of finding new ways of hanging together if they are not to hang separately. In this interdependent world it follows that the greatest threat to the autonomy and integrity of states – for some states and at some times – may be, not the threat of external aggression by another state, but the subtle, silent, and insidious permeation of national societies by trans-national actors. By their permeability, societies may be split, class from class, region from region, town from country; and transnational actors may either destroy whatever national unity was the basis of the political authority of the state, or else, perhaps by bolstering the power of an elitist group, frustrate reasonable aspirations for non-violent change and reform within national society. In either case, the prime influence on the national political situation has been external, that is to say international, but the source of influence has not been another government.

In different degrees, I think most of the writers on transnational relations I have mentioned (and a good many others) would agree that their contentions fundamentally challenge much of the existing framework of international political theory, while others, less convinced, regard the study of transnational relations as a sort of embroidery, or additional embellishment, on the basic model. The reason for thinking (as I do) that it fundamentally challenges conventional political theory is clear when one looks at the way in which economic power is commonly treated. It is well summed up, for example, in the introduction by Fred Northedge to a recent volume of essays, *The Use of Force in International Relations*. Distinguishing force from power – not always an easy task if one includes the threat of force as well as the overt physical use of it – Northedge rightly states that in political studies power usually means 'the capability of a person or group to make his or its will felt in the decision-making process of another person or group ... A state may be said to have power in the international system when another state recognizes that it cannot be ignored when issues have to be determined' (1974: 12). The emphasis, as in the great majority of university courses on international politics, is still on interstate impacts and reactions. The basic model is of a system made up of states, in each of which a political system coincides with a national economic system which it is the responsibility of the political authority to order, direct in the national interest, and adjust to the extent that by political process it is decided that it does not automatically provide for the socially desirable qualities of stability and justice.

The absurd consequences of this self-imposed corset can be readily seen in the recent attempt by Klaus Knorr (1973) to analyse the relation of power to wealth in the international system. This study starts by accepting the conventional model of that system as a collectivity of states; there is then a sort of inevitable logic that limits all subsequent analysis to the conscious use of economic weapons by governments in relations with other governments. Thus, the premise is adopted that just as armed forces provide the state with an influence base for supplying security to (or detracting it from) other states, so wealth gives the state an influence base from which to use either rewards or threats to achieve its own objectives or to impose its will on other states. There is, it is true, an early reference in the study to the dilemmas of states in a position of 'patronal leadership' (Knorr 1973: 27–9) (i.e., something less than imperial and more than hegemonical leadership) which touches tangentially on the question of power over and within the world economy. But, for the rest, the book makes economic power follow the exemplar of military power and interprets it almost exclusively in the capacity either to coerce other states (aggressive economic power) or to defend the state against coercion by others (defensive economic power). This is to accept two limiting assumptions at once – the neoclassical assumption that power is unimportant in the politically vital key issue-areas of international investment, trade, and money, as well as the assumption of interstate politics that relations between governments are the only ones that really matter. The result is to exclude from the analysis any exercise of market power that is not deliberately undertaken to weaken or coerce other states but only to secure income gains (Knorr 1973: 77). Apart from the fact that it is not always easy objectively to separate one from the other – as in the case of Arab oil strategies – the excuse given, that market power receives analysis elsewhere in theories of international trade, is a rather lame one. The further exclusion follows logically enough – that 'commercial or quasi-commercial exchanges do not involve economic power so long as benevolence or malevolence is absent' – an assertion that is hardly realistic when applied to the international trade in arms or aircraft, for example, or to Soviet trade arrangements with the countries of the Council for Mutual Economic Assistance, or indeed to most of the bilateral trade-and-investment deals made in the last eighteen months between oil producers and oil consumers. Moreover it shows great naiveté to assume that one can easily and objectively decide when benevolence or malevolence is absent in interstate relations – as witness, for example, the bitter arguments about the part played by the United States credit blockade in the fall of Allende in 1972.[1]

Similarly, the Knorr approach to economic power entirely excludes concern with the consequences of state actions that are undertaken to satisfy a domestic interest and – still more important – all actions of the dominant economy in an international system that are not deliberately and intentionally taken with a foreign policy aim in mind. Indeed, far from 'building outward' from Kindleberger's pioneering *Power and Money*, as Benjamin Cohen asserts in the preface, Knorr has rather, by comparison with Kindleberger, retreated into a narrower, more abstract, and less realistic world.

Before we leave the shortcomings of international political theory to deal with those of international economic theory, the second and subsidiary stumbling block in the political approach to economic power should also be briefly mentioned. It is less obvious but I believe not unimportant.

It starts with the strong focus in the study of international politics on the phenomenon of conflict. Now there are good historical reasons for this focus which, in this Journal, I do not need to spell out. We are all familiar with the way in which the pendulum of mood in international studies has swung from the optimism of the League of Nations period to the pessimism of the post-Hitler Morgenthau period – if I may be allowed that shorthand for the 'power politics' school of writers – and back again for some scholars (following the lead given by Boulding and Richardson, for example) to an interest in the potentiality for harmony and conflict resolution in the relations between states. Many teachers of international politics have never gone all the way in either direction and have now reached the point where they visualize interstate relations as containing a capacity for both conflict and harmony and responding with either according to the general political environment. As Joseph Frankel, for example, has put it, interstate relations can be conducted along a continuum from total harmony at one end to total conflict at the other (1973: 35–52).

The limitation which to my mind this view imposes on analysis of actual situations is that it tends to imply that at any moment of time the degree of conflict or harmony between states can be read off, like barometric pressure, indicating the precise mix of suspicious wariness or grudging co-operation with which each state approaches the other in response to an external environment. In the highly interdependent, mutually vulnerable world that we see about us, this seems to me misleading. There can (now, especially) be high simultaneous readings of conflict and of harmony. Deep mutual fear and suspicion in one issue-area of international politics can coexist with extensive co-operation and co-ordination in others. One has only to study the range of Soviet–American relations in the recent period of détente to see this. I am particularly impressed by the results of some recent work we have been doing at Chatham House on the history of international economic relations between developed countries in the 1960s. Gaullist France, for example, in relative conflict with the United States over defence policies in the Western alliance was nevertheless (and contrary to much popular mythology on this subject, notably in the United States) pulling punches in the monetary field, despite a deep opposition to what France saw as the strong American bias in the international monetary order. The point of broader relevance here is that there is in a growing number of high politics issue-areas of international politics a strong perception of underlying common interest in the preservation of some sort of order that inhibits the full expression of opposition to the particular form taken by that order or to particular aspects of it. In other words there is much more similarity than there used to be in international politics to the government-and-opposition model of domestic politics than to the old 'have/have not', 'status-quo states/revolutionary state' confrontations model of interstate politics. This is important to any understanding of the realities of economic power. It suggests that while a balance of power may be thought of as beneficial in the old interstate system model – because it inhibits conflict – it may be thought a bad thing in the international economic order if (as in a perfect balance of party strength in a parliamentary system) the distribution of power is so exactly balanced that it inhibits effective action by anyone.

If I have spent rather long on explanation of the shortcomings of international politics theories in analysing economic power it is not because international economic theory has done any better. Indeed, it is possible even today for students to go through quite long and advanced courses in economics without hearing the word 'power' mentioned (save in a very specialist sense) or at least without being asked to consider how economic processes are affected by the distribution of economic power. By and large it is assumed not to exist, and if it does exist, not to make any material difference to economic analysis. As K.W. Rothschild put it,

> As in other important social fields, we should expect that individuals should struggle for position; that power will be used to improve one's position in the economic 'game'; and that attempts will be made to derive power and influence from acquired economic strongholds. Power should, therefore, be a recurrent theme in economic studies of a theoretical or applied nature. Yet if we look at the main run of economic theory over the past hundred years we find that it is characterized by a strange lack of power considerations. (1971: 7)

Rothschild's explanation for this neglect is partly intellectual – that economists have understandably preferred a closed framework of analysis such as is offered by the competitive equilibrium model – within which it is possible to find logical consistence; and partly historical and socio-political – that it was both easier and more socially acceptable to build on an existing (and impressive) intellectual structure than to strike out into more dangerous unknown territory. Whatever the reasons, the result has been that the 'main run' of neoclassical economics has regarded economic power as quite separate from the datum of economic analysis, and has always been inclined to blame exogenous political factors and considerations for any policy choices taken contrary to the conclusions of that analysis.[2]

The only challenges to this rather astonishing separation of economic power from analysis of economic processes have come from the Marxists and from certain special branches of economics – notably labour and development economics. (This is a generalization unfair to several distinguished economists, such as J.K. Galbraith and Charles Kindleberger in North America, Nicholas Kaldor and E. Phelps-Brown in Britain, and Francois Perroux in France.) Of these, the Marxists have tended to go to the opposite extreme from the neoclassical economists and to argue that economic and political power were one and the same thing and inextricable from each other. Because the normative concern of Marxists has been much more with change in national societies than with change in international society, they have entered into much hot debate with the sociologists – especially those like Dahrendorf, Aron, and Giddens who were concerned with class structures – but much less so into debate about international politics or economics. It is here, in fact, in the analysis of the international system that the Marxist assumptions about the identity of economic and political power are most open to question – indeed, are downright unhelpful when it comes to explaining something like the role of Japan, the proverbial economic giant, political pygmy, in recent economic diplomacy.

Where the Marxist approach has made some obvious impact on non-Marxist thinking is in development economics. Here the Marxist emphasis on the constraints imposed on political choices by the nature of the productive system coincides in part with the development economists' perception of the dilemmas facing the governments of developing countries who have to exist in a world market economy dominated by the consumption, investment, and production patterns of the rich industrialized countries and especially of the United States. However, important as development issues are in international political debate and in international studies, they are only one aspect of the international economic system. That system, for better or worse, is effectively managed – so far as it is at all – by the rich countries not the poor ones and neither development economics nor the Marxist contribution to it help us much when it comes to understanding the role of economic power within and between the rich countries.

A major challenge – but one that has generally gone unnoticed in international studies – has come from the analysis of the labour market in economic systems. Here it is particularly obvious that the inequality of economic power can and does have a significant effect on economic outcomes. In earlier times, the weakness of unorganised hungry men seeking jobs by which to feed their families in negotiating with long-pocketed employers over the price of labour made nonsense of the equilibrium models showing the interactions of demand and supply. Now, sometimes, the boot is on the other foot and (as in newspaper production) it is the employers producing a perishable commodity who are most vulnerable and the printing unions that have extra bargaining power. The conclusion, however, is much the same. As a Dutch labour economist, Jan Pen, explained, the outcome of wage bargaining is decided according to a complex of factors affecting the ability of either side to bargain: 'All those factors which are summarized under the heading of the ability to bargain determine the result of the exercise of power' (Pen 1959).

Pen's starting point, which seems worth hanging on to, is that there is no sensible way of defining economic power other than to regard it as that form of power which is derived from an economic relationship. Since most economic questions are notoriously political, and almost all political questions involve some economic consideration, one cannot describe issues any more as 'purely economic', or as 'purely political'. Both are both. One can separate, however, power derived from a military relationship (e.g., an agreement to defend another state in case of attack), power derived from an ideological relationship (e.g., an acknowledgement of another state's vision of the good society as being more right than a third's), and power derived from the economic relationships – whether of buyer and seller, lender and borrower, producer and processor, processor and consumer, investor and entrepreneur, employer and employee, and so forth.

Each of these economic relationships is characterized by some sort of balance of power; and the balance is apt to shift from side to side and from time to time according to circumstances. In each case, the process of deciding the balance, and therefore the outcome, is essentially a bargaining process. And as labour economists see plainly, anything affecting that bargaining process must contain an element of economic power.

In labour/management bargaining it is clear that the bargaining process in any instance must be much affected by two external factors. One is the state of the market for labour, specifically in the industry and generally in the economy, whether the economic climate is expansionary or deflationary and whether the course of economic development favours this industry or form of employment or that. As Pen put it, 'there are close links between the form of the market and power' (1959: 97). The second factor is the surrounding context of rules or laws, particularly labour laws but also laws regarding the rights and protection of private property, the public provision of social security, and other matters. The scope of any bargain, therefore, is defined first by a certain economic structure and secondly by a primarily political structure. Only when these two limits have been set can one go about explaining the specific bargain – why a particular union has secured one kind of wage contact, for example, rather than one that is less or more favourable to the interests of its members.

Of course, there may be interaction between the bargainers and the groups or organizations responsible for the limiting structures. Employers may have a significant influence on the economic structure, either in general or by their economic management of particular industries. Unions may exert (as through the Labour party in Britain they have often exerted) a significant influence on the political structure, increasing their power in the bargaining process by ensuring that the political structure guarantees the right to strike and the right to strikers to picket peacefully and to enjoy unemployment benefit.

With some important modifications, we can perhaps apply this method of analysis to answer the original question: 'What is economic power in the international system and who has it?'

In the first place, we have in the international system an economic structure, a certain pattern of production, of the use and transfer of factors of production (labour and capital) and of exchange of raw materials, semi-finished and finished goods and services, and a certain pattern of distribution for consumption. Outside the centrally directed economies of China and the Soviet bloc, the predominant influence shaping this structure and set of patterns is unquestionably that of the United States economy and, after that, the economies of the dozen or so richest countries that account for the bulk of GNP, world trade and consumption. It is not only that the wealthiest consumers exercise the most 'votes' in a market economy, but also that over time a series of investment decisions to satisfy perceived demand has been taken expressing a certain order of preference for particular goods and services. For example, the European economy expressed a strong demand for spices and for salt in the Middle Ages; later for bullion, for sugar, tea, coffee, and tobacco, for cotton and grain, then for palm oil, meat, and other products. Now, the accumulated choices expressed by past investment decisions have given us an international economic structure that puts more resources into putting men on the moon than into the provision of general medical care, more into the production of five-seat automobiles than 500-seat hover trains, more into television than desalinization, more into energy-prodigal production than energy-saving production. One result has been a demand for Middle East petroleum that has accelerated so fast as to bring into prospect the ultimate exhaustion of even the vast reserves of fossil fuels – a prospect which in turn has persuaded the members of the Organization of Petroleum Exporting Countries (OPEC) that they must make hay while the oilfields flow.

This is a pattern of demand which people in the United States and other rich countries sometimes tend to imply – to the intense annoyance of the Third World – was ordained by God or History as part of the datum of the human condition. Rather, it is the product of the economic structure; and the economic power to influence and direct the course of that world economic development lies predominantly with the rich countries and with the large multinational enterprises and banks that have grown out of these economies. Neoclassical economic theory, of course, justifies it on the grounds that it approximates 'the efficient allocation of resources' but ignores the fact that the criteria for judging efficiency are variable and subjective.

In the second place, the scope of bargains struck in the international system is defined by a political structure. This is where there is most divergence between economic power in the international market economy and in the labour market. The great majority of wage negotiations – notwithstanding some small essays in international bargaining in recent years – are made inside one well-defined political system dominated by one defined political authority, whereas, in the international system, there is for the most part no single political authority presiding over the bargains struck on access to raw materials, access to capital markets, access to labour or technology, or any other economic transaction.

Here, the rules of the game include some national rules, some international rules, some private rules – and large areas of no rules at all. (This is a fact of the real world often overlooked in much study of proliferating international organization.) Moreover, the international 'rules', so-called, are themselves the subject of a continued bargaining process between national governments. What appeared in, say, 1965 to be fairly well-defined rules for the operation of the international monetary system concerning, for example, exchange rates between national currencies, the role of gold, and other matters no longer hold good in 1975. A bargaining process, for example, between France and the United States involving energy (i.e., oil market) policies as well as monetary policies had finally brought the Americans, late in 1974, to concede that official gold reserves should be revalued at market price. In the same way a bargaining process, initiated by the United States in August 1971 and protracted over the next four months, finally decided the terms on which the dollar should be devalued in relation to other currencies. In this process the market itself can be an effective actor, requiring action by governments and altering the balance of economic power between them.

A further important point is that the weight to be attached – that is, the influence exerted on operators – to the national rules of different states is highly unequal. It also varies from issue-area to issue-area. The rules made by Switzerland, for example, are quite influential in the international monetary issue-area – and also in the matter of migrant labour in Europe – but not at all in the military issue-area or the international market for armaments. The strength of rules made collectively by the OPEC states on the rate of output of oil is very important in the energy issue-area, but these countries have very little power to influence the rate of world inflation and the consequent price of manufactures – a situation that has been likened to selling oil for blocks of ice that are being stored in a hothouse. But the rules made by the United States – and made in response for the most part to *domestic* political pressures and *domestic* economic and social needs – are almost always much the most important set of national rules affecting operators in international markets. Consider the attention paid by all multinationals, whether they are United States-based or German-, Dutch-, Swedish-, or British-based, to United States antitrust legislation – particularly now that it is becoming an area of administrative activity again. Consider the international repercussions of interest-rate policies pursued by the Federal Reserve Board, of air transport rulings given by the Civil Aeronautics Board, of stock market regulations enforced by the Securities Exchange Commission. They are all much more influential on operational bargaining processes than the rules laid down by another nation-state, or even by another group of states such as the European Community. This is why there is so much pessimism about the prospects for international agreement and co-operation on the difficult subject of non-tariff barriers to free non-discriminatory international trade. The NTBs raised against invasion of the American market are so much stronger and more effective than those protecting any other less important market.

Nor, finally, must we overlook rules made by non-governmental agents. In quite a few international markets the most important rules regarding access, whether to resources or to markets, will be those made by a cartel or informally worked out within a small oligopolistic group of large multinational enterprises – like the aluminium companies, for example. The objections raised in UNCTAD against the political framework around the international shipping business are directed not against an intergovernmental body, or against any national government, but against the shipping conferences of the operators.

In short, the nature and the source of the impact, of primary bargaining processes regarding the regulation of markets on the secondary bargaining processes at the operational level is going to vary quite widely in the international system, not only from country to country but from market to market. Whereas one can roughly generalize about the effect of the political framework on all wage bargaining in a given national economy, it is almost impossible to do so about the effect of the political framework on (for example) relations between producer states and consumer states, between rich and poor countries. General theories regarding the nature and distribution of economic power will have to be treated with extreme caution.

The more so because the sum of regulations – intergovernmental, national, quasi-official, and private – applied to any market is a further variable. Here is another sense in which there is a balance of power to be analysed afresh in each situation: the balance between public political authority and private economic enterprise. To explain the point as briefly as possible, it is evident that in any market economy the political authorities take certain conscious decisions about the ends, means, and extent of market regulation and intervention, not only for political distributive reasons but also weighing freedom and growth against risk and instability. There is no such thing in reality as laissez-faire. Even the maintenance of order, the punishment of fraud and extortion, the provision and management of a monetary medium, the barest ring-holding measures are all minimal interventions in the operations of a completely 'free' market. In practice, most governments in most markets go a great deal further, seeking to limit risks of loss and to avert collapse, disorder, and the general loss of confidence that these bring with them.

In many areas or aspects of the international economy, this is the sense in which it is correct to say that there has been – as a result of growing integration and inter-dependence – a shift in the balance of economic power between political authority and economic enterprise. The loss of economic power that governments complain of in relation to multinational enterprise is of a different order than the loss of power by one operator to another or by one rule-maker to another. It is not – as the aggrieved protestations of innocence by multinationals indicate – so much that power has been filched from them as that the processes and structures through which political authority is exercised to ensure order and stability in markets and to enforce some measure of 'fairness' have failed to keep pace with changes in the scale of the market and in the scale of operations and transactions. The Eurodollar market is only one very obvious and glaring example among many of international regulations having to run harder and harder to keep us in the same spot.

The sum of these observations can therefore by quite briefly stated. Economic power is exercised in the international system at four different levels or stages. It is first exercised by the rich economies (including their governments) on the structure of the world market economy – the pattern of investment, production, trade and consumption. As the market grows, so does their influence on the world beyond, on the Second World and on the Third World.

Second, it is exercised by governments acting together and after political bargaining to erect a framework of minimum rules for the maintenance of stability, order and justice in the world market economy. In the necessary bargaining process to arrive at agreement on these rules the government of the largest national market remains by far the most influential. How hard it will have to bargain with 'the opposition' will depend on the measure of consent forthcoming from the opposition for the existing framework of rules and, second, on the power of the opposition to oppose effectively – a function in large part of its unity at any given moment on a given issue.

Third, economic power is exercised by national governments through the formulation of national rules governing access to factors of production, credit and markets, and other fundamental questions affecting economic enterprise and economic transactions. As before, the national government with the largest domestic market and which is the home state for the largest number of multinational enterprises responsible for global strategies of production will exercise the greatest economic power. To the extent that a non-governmental framework of rules governs economic activity, it will be by tacit permission of this government. Conflict of national rules will arise when less important governments find it necessary to increase their intervention in contradiction to that of the dominant power.

Fourth, economic power is exercised at the operational level on both sides of every actual economic transaction, by buyer and sellers, creditors and debtors. The balance of economic power in each transaction will be expressed in the outcome of the bargaining process. The rate of change in demand or supply, in technology or organization, and the power to adjust to change will be other powerful factors affecting the outcome.

It follows from this that the sense of lost power which, as indicated at the beginning, is currently sensed in the United States is not entirely unjustified. Influence at the first level (and subsequent levels) will wane as economic growth decelerates in a time of recession. Influence on intergovernmental regulation will decline if either the opposition's dissatisfaction or its organized unity of purpose increases. The influence of national rules at the third level may be counterbalanced by opposing national rules – as in the case of recent Australian or Canadian codes governing foreign investment – to fill perceived shortcomings in the international framework. And fourthly, some change in the balance of power over particular transactions is always possible and will be most painful for those least able to adjust to it.

This suggests that the most keenly felt loss of economic power – that is for the United States at present the loss of bargaining power over the terms of supply of oil – is probably, in the long run, the least important. In fact, at each of the four levels at which a bargaining process takes place, the economic power, effective or latent, of the United States is still far the greatest of any other state. There is no significant diminution of its capacity to regulate and direct if it should choose to use it. What the rest of us are witnessing, it seems, is much more a loss of the will to do so, a loss of the taste for bargaining with others to achieve a desired end – perhaps of a failure of vision of what might be achieved before the end of the century in the way of a more just and stable as well as a richer and more orderly international political economy.

15
'Cave! Hic Dragones:[1] A Critique of Regime Analysis', 1982

for

The purpose of this relatively brief article is rather different from that of others in this volume. Instead of asking what makes regimes and how they affect behaviour, it seeks to raise more fundamental questions about the questions. In particular, it queries whether the concept of regime is really useful to students of international political economy or world politics; and whether it may not even be actually negative in its influence, obfuscating and confusing instead of clarifying and illuminating, and distorting by concealing bias instead of revealing and removing it.

It challenges the validity and usefulness of the regime concept on five separate counts. These lead to two further and secondary (in the sense of indirect), but no less important, grounds for expressing the doubt whether further work of this kind ought to be encouraged by names as well-known and distinguished as the contributors to this volume. The five counts (or 'dragons' to watch out for) are first, that the study of regimes is, for the most part a fad, one of those shifts of fashion not too difficult to explain as a temporary reaction to events in the real world but in itself making little in the way of a long-term contribution to knowledge. Second, it is imprecise and woolly. Third, it is value-biased, as dangerous as loaded dice. Fourth, it distorts by overemphasizing the static and underemphasizing the dynamic element of change in world politics. And fifth, it is narrow-minded, rooted in a state-centric paradigm that limits vision of a wider reality.

Two indirect criticisms – not so much of the concept itself as of the tendency to give it exaggerated attention – follow from these five points. One is that it leads to a study of world politics that deals predominantly with the status quo, and tends to exclude hidden agendas and to leave unheard or unheeded complaints, whether they come from the underprivileged, the disfranchised or the unborn, about the way the system works. In short, it ignores the vast area of non-regimes that lies beyond the ken of international bureaucracies and diplomatic bargaining. The other is that it persists in looking for an all-pervasive pattern of political behaviour in world politics, a 'general theory' that will provide a nice, neat, and above all simple explanation of the past and an easy means to predict the future. Despite all

209

the accumulated evidence of decades of work in international relations and international history (economic as well as political) that no such pattern exists, it encourages yet another generation of impressionable young hopefuls to set off with high hopes and firm resolve in the vain search for an El Dorado.

Not wishing, however, to be entirely destructive, I conclude the article by suggesting an alternative and, to my mind, more valuefree, more flexible, and more realistic approach to the study of what I take to be everyone's underlying concern – which is, 'where (and how) do we go from here?' This approach is both to the 'left' of most of the other contributors and to the 'right' of some who would call themselves liberal internationalists.

It is to the 'left' of the majority in that it starts from a frankly structuralist perception of the international system (in the sense in which Marxists and neo-Marxists use the word structuralist). This does not mean the political system dominated by territorial states but the structure of a world economy in which the relationships between those states are largely determined by the relations of production and the other prevalent structural arrangements for the free movement between states of capital, knowledge and goods (but not labour) that make up a world market economy.

And it is to the 'right' – as they would see it – of most liberal internationalists in that it is sceptical of the achievements to be expected of international organizations and collective decision making, that is, it is realist in the sense of continuing to look to the state and to national governments as the final determinants of outcomes.

Five criticisms of the concept of regimes

A passing fad?

The first of my dragons, or pitfalls for the unwary, is that concern with regimes may be a passing fad. A European cannot help making the point that concern with regime formation and breakdown is very much an American academic fashion, and this is reflected in the fact that all the other contributors to this volume work in American universities. They share a rather striking common concern with the questions posed about regimes. A comparable group in Europe – or in most other parts of the world, I would suggest – would have more diverse concerns. Some would be working on questions of moral philosophy, some on questions of historical interpretation. (Europeans generally, I would venture to say, are more serious in the attention they pay to historical evidence and more sensitive to the possibilities of divergent interpretations of 'facts'.) Europeans concerned with matters of strategy and security are usually not the same as those who write about structures affecting economic development, trade, and money, or with the prospects for particular regions or sectors. Even the future of Europe itself never dominated the interests of so large a group of scholars in Europe as it did, for a time, the American academic community. Perhaps Europeans are not generalist enough; perhaps having picked a field to work in, they are inclined to stick to it too rigidly. And conversely, perhaps Americans are more subject to fads and fashions in academic inquiry than Europeans, more apt to conform and to join in behind the trendsetters of the times. Many Europeans, I think, believe so, though most are too polite to say it. They have watched American enthusiasm wax and wane for systems analysis, for behaviouralism, for integration theory, and even for quantitative methods indiscriminately applied. The fashion for integration theory started with the perceived US need for a reliable junior partner in Europe, and how to nurture the European Communities to this end was important. The quantitative fashion is easily explained by a combination of the availability of computer time and the finance to support it and of the ambition of political scientists to gain as much kudos and influence with policy makers as the economists and others who had led the way down the quantitative path. Further back we can see how international relations as a field of study separate from politics and history itself developed in direct response to the horrors of two world wars and the threat of a third. And, later, collective goods theories responded to the debates about burden-sharing in NATO, just as monetarism and supply-side economics gained a hearing only when the conditions of the 1970s cast doubts on Keynesian remedies for recession, unemployment, and inflation.

The current fashion for regimes arises, I would suggest, from certain, somewhat subjective perceptions in many American minds. One such perception was that a number of external 'shocks', on top of internal troubles like Watergate and Jimmy Carter, had accelerated a serious decline in American power. In contrast to the nationalist, reactionary response of many Reaganites, liberal, internationalist academics asked how the damage could be minimized by restoring or repairing or reforming the mechanisms of multilateral management – 'regimes'. A second subjective perception was that there was some sort of mystery about the uneven performance and predicament of international organizations. This was a connecting theme in Keohane and Nye's influential *Power and Interdependence*, which struck responsive chords far and wide.

But the objective reality behind both perceptions was surely far less dramatic. In European eyes, the 'decline' arises partly from an original overestimation of America's capacity to remake the whole world in the image of the USA. In this vision, Washington was the centre of the system, a kind of keep in the baronial castle of capitalism, from which radiated military, monetary, commercial, and technological as well as purely political channels carrying the values of American polity, economy, and society down through the hierarchy of allies and friends, classes and cultural cousins, out to the ends of the earth. The new kind of global empire, under the protection of American nuclear power, did not need territorial expansion. It could be achieved by a combination of military alliances and a world economy opened up to trade, investment, and information.

This special form of non-territorial imperialism is something that many American academics, brought up as liberals and internationalists, find it hard to recognize. US hegemony, while it is as non-territorial as Britain's India in the days of John Company or Britain's Egypt after 1886, is still a form of imperialism. The fact that this non-territorial empire extends more widely and is even more tolerant of the pretensions of petty principalities than Britain was of those of the maharajahs merely means that it is larger and more secure. It is not much affected by temporary shocks or setbacks. Yet Americans are inhibited about acknowledging their imperialism. It was a Frenchman who titled his book about American foreign policy *The Imperial Republic* (Aron 1974).

Moreover, Americans have often seemed to exaggerate the 'shocks' of the 1970s and the extent of change in US–Soviet or US–OPEC relations. Nobody else saw the pre-1971 world as being quite so stable and ordered as Americans did. Certainly for Third-Worlders, who had by then lived through two or three recent cycles of boom and slump in the price of their country's major exports – whether coffee, cocoa, tin, copper, sugar or bananas – plus perhaps a civil war and a revolution or two, the 'oil-price shock' was hardly the epoch-making break with the stable, comfortable, predictable past that it seemed to many Americans. If one has been accustomed for as long as one can remember to national plans and purposes being frustrated and brought to nothing by exogenous changes in the market, in technology or in the international political situation between the superpowers – over none of which your own government has had the slightest control – then a bit more disorder in a disorderly world comes as no great surprise.

To non-American eyes therefore, there is something quite exaggerated in the weeping and wailing and wringing of American hands over the fall of the imperial republic. This is not how it looks to us in Europe, in Japan, in Latin America or even in the Middle East. True, there is the nuclear parity of the Soviet Union. And there is the depreciated value of the dollar in terms of gold, of goods, and of other currencies. But the first is not the only factor in the continuing dominant importance to the security structure of the balance of power between the two superpowers, and the second is far more a sign of the abuse of power than it is of the loss of power. The dollar, good or bad, still dominates the world of international finance. Money markets and other markets in the United States still lead and others still follow; European bankrupts blame American interest rates. If the authority of the United States appears to have weakened, it is largely because the markets and their operators have been given freedom and licence by the same state to profit from an integrated world economy. If Frankenstein's monster is feared to be out of control, that looks to non-Americans more like a proof of Frankenstein's power to create such a monster in the first place. The change in the balance of public and private power still leaves the United States as the undisputed hegemon of the system.[2]

To sum up, the fashion for regime analysis may not simply be, as Stein suggests, a rehash of old academic debates under a new and jazzier name – a sort of intellectual mutton dressed up as lamb – so that the pushy new professors of the 1980s can have the same old arguments as their elders but can flatter themselves that they are breaking new ground by using a new jargon (1982: 300). It is also an intellectual reaction to the objective reality.

In a broad, structuralist view (and using the broader definition of the term) of the structures of global security, of a global credit system, of the global welfare system (i.e., aid and other resource transfers) and the global knowledge and communications system, there seems far less sign of a falling-off in American power. Where decline exists, it is a falling-off in the country's power and will to intervene with world market mechanisms (from Eurodollar lending to the grain trade) rather than significant change in the distribution of military or economic power to the favour of other states. Such change as there is, has been more internal than international.

The second subjective perception on the part of Americans that I wish to address is that there is some mystery about the rather uneven performance in recent times of many international arrangements and organizations. While some lie becalmed and inactive, like sailing ships in the doldrums, others hum with activity, are given new tasks, and are recognized as playing a vital role in the functioning of the system. I would personally count the GATT, FAO and UNESCO in the first group, the World Bank and the regional banks, the BIS and IMCO in the second. The IMF holds a middle position: it has largely lost its universal role but has found an important but more specialized usefulness in relation to indebted developing countries.

The mixed record of international organizations really does need explaining. But Americans have been curiously reluctant, to my mind at least, to distinguish between the three somewhat different purposes served by international organizations. These can broadly be identified as *strategic* (i.e., serving as instruments of the structural strategy and foreign policy of the dominant state or states); as *adaptive* (i.e., providing the necessary multilateral agreement on whatever arrangements are necessary to allow states to enjoy the political luxury of national autonomy without sacrificing the economic dividends of world markets and production structures); and as *symbolic* (i.e., allowing everybody to declare themselves in favour of truth, beauty, goodness, and world community, while leaving governments free to pursue national self-interests and to do exactly as they wish).

In the early postwar period, most international organizations served all three purposes at once. They were strategic in the sense that they served as instruments of the structural strategies of the United States. Also, they were often adaptive in that they allowed the United States and the other industrialized countries like Britain, Germany, France and Japan to enjoy both economic growth and political autonomy. Finally, many organizations were at the same time symbolic in that they expressed and partially satisfied the universal yearning for a 'better world' without doing anything substantial to bring it about.

In recent years the political purposes served by institutions for their members have tended to be less well balanced; some have become predominantly strategic, some predominantly adaptive, and others predominantly symbolic. This had happened because, where once the United States was able to dominate organizations like the United Nations, it can no longer do so because of the inflation of membership and the increasing divergence between rich and poor over fundamentals. Only a few organizations still serve US strategic purposes better than bilateral diplomacy can serve them; they are either top-level political meetings or they deal with military or monetary matters in which the US still disposes of predominant power. In other organizations the tendency toward symbolism, expressed in a proliferation of Declarations, Charters, Codes of Conduct, and other rather empty texts, has strengthened as the ability to reach agreement on positive action to solve real global problems has weakened. This applies especially to the

United Nations and many of its subsidiary bodies, to UNCTAD, IDA and many of the specialized agencies. The one growth area is the adaptive function. The integration of the world economy and the advance of technology have created new problems, but they also have often enlarged the possibility of reaching agreement as well as the perceived need to find a solution. Such predominantly adaptive institutions are often monetary (IBRD, IFC, BIS) or technical (ITU, IMCO, WMO).

Imprecision

The second dragon is imprecision of terminology. 'Regime' is yet one more woolly concept that is a fertile source of discussion simply because people mean different things when they use it. At its worst, woolliness leads to the same sort of euphemistic Newspeak that George Orwell warned us would be in general use by 1984. The Soviet Union calls the main medium for the suppression of information *Pravada* (Truth), and refers to the 'sovereign independence of socialist states' as the principle governing its relations with its East European 'partners'. In the United States scholars have brought 'interdependence' into general use when what they were describing was actually highly asymmetrical and uneven dependence or vulnerability. In the same way, though more deliberately, IBM public relations advisers invented and brought into general and unthinking use the term 'multinational corporation' to describe an enterprise doing worldwide business from a strong national base.

Experience with the use of these and other, equally woolly words warns us that where they do not actually mislead and misrepresent, they often serve to confuse and disorient us. 'Integration' is one example of an overused word loosely taken to imply all sorts of other developments such as convergence as well as the susceptibility of 'integrated' economies to common trends and pressures – a mistake that had to be painstakingly remedied by careful, pragmatic research (Hu 1981).

'Regime' is used to mean many different things. In the Keohane and Nye formulation ('networks of rules, norms and procedures that regularize behaviour and control its effects') it is taken to mean something quite narrow – explicit or implicit internationally agreed arrangements, usually executed with the help of an international organization – even though Keohane himself distinguishes between regimes and specific agreements. Whereas other formulations emphasize 'decision-making procedures around which actors' expectations converge', the concept of regime can be so broadened as to mean almost any fairly stable distribution of the power to influence outcomes. In Keohane and Nye's formulation, the subsequent questions amount to little more than the old chestnut, 'Can international institutions change state behaviour?' The second definition reformulates all the old questions about power and the exercise of power in the international system. So, if – despite a rather significant effort by realist and pluralist authors to reach agreement – there is no fundamental consensus about the answer to Krasner's first question, 'What is a regime?', obviously there is not going to be much useful or substantial convergence of conclusions about the answers to the other questions concerning their making and unmaking.

Why, one might ask, has there been such concerted effort to stretch the elasticity of meaning to such extremes? I can only suppose that scholars who by calling, interest, and experience are themselves 'internationalist' in aspiration, are (perhaps unconsciously) performing a kind of symbolic ritual against the disruption of the international order, and do so just because they are also, by virtue of their profession, more aware than most of the order's tenuousness.

Value bias

The third point to be wary of is that the term regime is value-loaded; it implies certain things that ought not to be taken for granted. As has often happened before in the study of international relations, this comes of trying to apply a term derived from the observation of national politics to international or to world politics.

Let us begin with semantics. The word 'regime' is French, and it has two common meanings. In everyday language it means a diet, an ordered, purposive plan of eating, exercising and living. A regime is usually imposed on the patient by some medical or other authority with the aim of achieving better health. A regime must be recognizably the same when undertaken by different individuals, at different times, and in different places. It must also be practiced over an extended period of time; to eat no pastry one day but to gorge the next is not to follow a regime. Nor does one follow a regime if one eats pastry when in Paris but not in Marseilles. Those who keep to a diet for a day or two and abandon it are hardly judged to be under the discipline of a regime.

Based on the same broad principles of regularity, discipline, authority and purpose, the second meaning is political: the government of a society by an individual, a dynasty, party or group that wields effective power over the rest of society. Regime in this sense is more often used pejoratively than with approval – the 'ancient regime', the 'Franco regime', the 'Stalin regime', but seldom the 'Truman' or 'Kennedy' regime, or the 'Attlee' or 'Macmillan', the 'Mackenzie King' or the 'Menzies' regime. The word is more often used of forms of government that are inherently authoritarian, capricious, and even unjust. Regimes need be neither benign nor consistent. It may be (as in the case of Idi Amin, 'Papa Doc' Duvallier or Jean-Bedel Bokassa) that the power of the regime is neither benign nor just. But at least in a given regime, everyone knows and understands where power resides and whose interest is served by it; and thus, whence to expect either preferment or punishment, imprisonment or other kinds of trouble. In short, government, rulership and authority are the essence of the word, not consensus, nor justice, nor efficiency in administration.

What could be more different from the unstable, kaleidoscopic pattern of international arrangements between states? The title (if not all of the content) of Hedley Bull's book, *The Anarchical Society*, well describes the general state of the international system. Within that system, as Bull and others have observed, it is true that there is more order, regularity and behaviour, and general observance of custom and convention than the pure realist expecting the unremitting violence of the jungle might suppose. But by and large the world Bull and other writers describe is characterized in all its main outlines not by discipline and authority, but by the absence of government, by the precariousness of peace and order, by the dispersion not the concentration of authority, by the weakness of law, and by the large number of unsolved problems and unresolved conflicts over what should be done, how it should be done, and who should do it.

Above all, a single, recognized locus of power over time is the one attribute that the international system so conspicuously lacks.

All those international arrangements dignified by the label regime are only too easily upset when either the balance of bargaining power or the perception of national interest (or both together) change among those states who negotiate them. In general, moreover, all the areas in which regimes in a national context exercise the central attributes of political discipline are precisely those in which corresponding international arrangements that might conceivably be dignified with the title are conspicuous by their absence. There is no world army to maintain order. There is no authority to decide how much economic production shall be public and how much shall be privately owned and managed. We have no world central bank to regulate the creation of credit and access to it, nor a world court to act as the ultimate arbiter of legal disputes that also have political consequences. There is nothing resembling a world tax system to decide who should pay for public goods – whenever the slightest hint of any of these is breathed in diplomatic circles, state governments have all their defences at the ready to reject even the most modest encroachment on what they regard as their national prerogatives.

The analogy with national governments implied by the use of the word regime, therefore, is inherently false. It consequently holds a highly distorting mirror to reality.

Not only does using this word regime distort reality by implying an exaggerated measure of predictability and order in the system as it is, it is also value-loaded in that it takes for granted that what everyone wants is more and better regimes, that greater order and managed interdependence should be the collective goal. Let me just recall that in an early paper at the very outset of this whole project, the editor asked these questions:

'Was the 1970s really a period of significant change? Was it an interregnum between periods of stability? Does it augur a collapse or deterioration of the international economic system? Did the system accommodate massive shocks with astonishing ease or were the shocks much less severe than has been thought?

'These,' he went on, 'are perplexing questions without obvious answers, for the answers to these questions are related *to the most fundamental concern of social theory: how is order established, maintained and destroyed?'*[3]

Krasner's common question here is about order – not justice or efficiency, nor legitimacy, nor any other moral value. In an international political system of territorial states claiming sovereignty within their respective territories, how can order be achieved and maintained?

The questions people ask are sometimes more revealing of their perceptions of what is good or bad about a situation and of their motives, interests, fears, and hopes than the answers they give. Yet there is a whole literature that denies that order is 'the most fundamental concern' and that says that the objectives of Third World policy should be to achieve freedom from dependency and to enhance national identity and freer choice by practicing 'uncoupling' or delinking or (yet another woolly buzz-word) by 'collective self-reliance'.

Now, these ideas may be unclear and half-formed. But in view of the Islamic revival and the newfound self-confidence of several newly industrialized countries (NICs), it would be patently unwise for any scholar to follow a line of inquiry that overlooks them. Let us never forget the folly of League of Nations reformers, busily drafting new blueprints while Hitler and Mussolini lit fires under the whole system. Should we not ask whether this too does not indicate an essentially conservative attitude biased toward the status quo. Is it not just another unthinking response to fear of the consequences of change? Yet is not political activity as often directed by the desire to achieve change, to get more justice and more freedom from a system, as it is by the desire to get more wealth or to assure security for the haves by reinforcing order?

Too static a view

The fourth dragon to beware is that the notion of a regime – for the semantic reasons indicated earlier – tends to exaggerate the static quality of arrangements for managing the international system and introducing some confidence in the future of anarchy, some order out of uncertainty. In sum, it produces stills, not movies. And the reality, surely is highly dynamic, as can fairly easily be demonstrated by reference to each of the three main areas for regimes considered in this collection: security, trade and money.

For the last thirty-five years, the international security regime (if it can be so called), described in this volume by Jervis, has not been derived from Chapter VII of the UN Charter, which remains as unchanged as it is irrelevant. It has rested on the balance of power between the superpowers. In order to maintain that balance, each has engaged in a continuing and escalating accumulation of weapons and has found it necessary periodically to assert its dominance in particular frontier areas – Hungary, Czechoslovakia and Afghanistan for the one and South Korea, Guatemala, Vietnam and El Salvador for the other. Each has also had to be prepared when necessary (but, fortunately, less frequently) to engage in direct confrontation with the other. And no one was ever able to predict with any certainty when such escalation in armaments, such interventions or confrontations were going to be thought necessary to preserve the balance, nor what the outcome would be. Attempts to 'quick-freeze' even parts of an essentially fluid relationship have been singularly unsuccessful and unconvincing, as witness the fate of the SALT agreements, the European Security Conference, and the Non-Proliferation Treaty.

In monetary matters, facile generalizations about 'the Bretton Woods regime' abound – but they bear little resemblance to the reality. It is easily forgotten that the original Articles of Agreement were never fully implemented, that there was a long 'transition period' in which most of the proposed arrangements were put on ice, and that hardly a year went by in the entire postwar period when some substantial change was not made (tacitly or explicitly) in the way the rules were applied and in the way the system functioned. Consider the major changes: barring the West European countries from access to the Fund; providing them with a mutlilateral payments system through the European Payments Union; arranging a concerted launch into currency convertibility; reopening the major international commodity and capital markets; finding ways to support the pound sterling. All these and subsequent decisions were taken by national governments, and especially by the US government, in response to their changing perceptions of national interest or else in deference to volatile market forces that they either could not or would not control.

Arrangements governing international trade have been just as changeable and rather less uniform. Different principles and rules governed trade between market economies and the socialist or centrally planned economies, while various forms of preferential market access were practised between European countries and their former colonies and much the same results were achieved between the United States and Canada or Latin America through direct investment. Among the European countries, first in the OEEC and then in EFTA and the EC, preferential systems within the system were not only tolerated but encouraged. The tariff reductions negotiated through the GATT were only one part of a complex governing structure of arrangements, international and national, and even these (as all the historians of commercial diplomacy have shown) were subject to constant revision, reinterpretation, and renegotiation.

The trade 'regime' was thus neither constant nor continuous over time, either between partners or between sectors. The weakness of the arrangements as a system for maintaining order and defining norms seems to me strikingly illustrated by the total absence of continuity or order in the important matter of the competitive use of export credit – often government guaranteed and subsidized – in order to increase market shares. No one system of rules has governed how much finance on what terms and for how long can be obtained for an international exchange, and attempts to make collective agreements to standardize terms (notably through the Berne Union) have repeatedly broken down.

The changeable nature of all these international arrangements behind the blank institutional facade often results from the impact of the two very important factors that regime analysis seems to me ill-suited to cope with: technology and markets. Both are apt to bring important changes in the distribution of costs and benefits, risks and opportunities to national economies and other groups, and therefore to cause national governments to change their minds about which rules or norms of behaviour should be reinforced and observed and which should be disregarded and changed.

Some of the consequences of technological change on international arrangements are very easily perceived, others less so. It is clear that many long-standing arrangements regarding fishing rights were based on assumptions that became invalid when freezing, sonar and improved ship design altered the basic factors governing supply and demand. It is also clear that satellites, computers, and video technology have created a host of new problems in the field of information and communication, problems for which no adequate multilateral arrangements have been devised. New technology in chemicals, liquid natural gas, nuclear power and oil production from under the sea – to mention only a few well-known areas – is dramatically increasing the risks involved in production, trade and use. These risks become (more or less) acceptable thanks to the possibility of insuring against them. But though this has political consequences – imposing the cost of insurance as a kind of entrance tax on participation in the world market economy – the fact that no structure or process exists for resolving the conflicts of interest that ensue is an inadequately appreciated new aspect of the international system.

Technology also contributes to the process of economic concentration, reflected in the daily dose of company takeovers, through the mounting cost of replacing old technology with new and the extended lead-time between investment decisions and production results. Inevitably, the economic concentration so encouraged affects freedom of access to world markets and thus to the distributive consequences in world society. The nationalist, protectionist, defensive attitudes of states today are as much a response to technical changes and their perceived consequences as they are to stagnation and instability in world markets.

Since the chain of cause and effect so often originates in technology and markets, passing through national policy decisions to emerge as negotiating postures in multilateral discussions, it follows that attention to the end result – an international arrangement of some sort – is apt to overlook most of the determining factors on which agreement may, in brief, rest.

The search for common factors and for general rules (or even axioms), which is of the essence of regime analysis, is therefore bound to be long, exhausting, and probably disappointing. Many of the articles in this volume abound in general conclusions about regimes, their nature, the conditions favouring their creation, maintenance and change, and many of the generalizations seem at first reading logically plausible – but only if one does not examine their assumptions too closely. My objection is that these assumptions are frequently unwarranted.

State-centredness

The final but by no means least important warning is that attention to these regime questions leaves the study of international political economy far too constrained by the self-imposed limits of the state-centred paradigm. It asks, what are the prevailing arrangements discussed and observed among governments, thus implying that the important and significant political issues are those with which governments are concerned. Nationally, this is fairly near the truth. Democratic governments have to respond to whatever issues voters feel are important if they wish to survive, and even the most authoritarian governments cannot in the long run remain indifferent to deep discontents or divisions of opinion in the societies they rule. But internationally this is not so. The matters on which governments, through international organizations, negotiate and make arrangements are not necessarily the issues that even they regard as most important, still less the issues that the mass of individuals regards as crucial. Attention to regimes therefore accords to governments far too much of the right to define the agenda of academic study and directs the attention of scholars mainly to those issues that government officials find significant and important. If academics submit too much to this sort of imperceptible pressure, they abdicate responsibility for the one task for which the independent scholar has every comparative advantage, the development of a philosophy of international relations or international political economy that will not only explain and illuminate but will point a road ahead and inspire action to follow it.

Thus regime analysis risks overvaluing the positive and undervaluing the negative aspects of international cooperation. It encourages academics to practice a kind of analytical *chiaroscuro* that leaves in shadow all the aspects of the international economy where no regimes exist and where each state elects to go its own way, while highlighting the areas of agreement where some norms and customs are generally acknowledged. It consequently gives the false impression (always argued by the neo-functionalists) that international regimes are indeed slowly advancing against the forces of disorder and anarchy. Now it is only too easy, as we all know, to be misled by the proliferation of international associations and organizations, by the multiplication of declarations and documents, into concluding that there is indeed increasing positive action. The reality is that there are more areas and issues of non-agreement and controversy than there are areas of agreement. On most of the basic social issues that have to do with the rights and responsibilities of individuals to each other and to the state – on whether abortion, bribery, drink or drug pushing or passing information, for example, are crimes or not – there is no kind of international regime. Nor is there a regime on many of the corresponding questions of the rights and responsibilities of states toward individuals and toward other states.

In reality, furthermore, the highlighted issues are sometimes less important than those in shadow. In the summer of 1980, for example, INMARSAT announced with pride an agreement on the terms on which US-built satellites and expensive receiving equipment on board ship can be combined to usher in a new Future Global Maritime Distress and Safety System, whereby a ship's distress call is automatically received all over a given area by simply pressing a button. For the large tankers and others who can afford the equipment, this will certainly be a significant advance; not so for small coasters and fishing boats. In the same year, though, millions died prematurely through lack of any effective regime for the relief of disaster or famine. Meanwhile, the Executive Directors of the International Monetary Fund can reach agreement on a further increase in quotas, but not on the general principles governing the rescheduling of national foreign debts.

Moreover, many of the so-called regimes over which the international organizations preside turn out under closer examination to be agreements to disagree. The IMF amendments to the Articles of Agreement, for example, which legitimized the resort to managed floating exchange rates, are no more than a recognition of states' determination to decide for themselves what strategy and tactics to follow in the light of market conditions. To call this a 'regime' is to pervert the language. So it is to call the various 'voluntary' export restrictive arrangements bilaterally negotiated with Japan by other parties to the GATT 'a multilateral regime'. Since

1978 the Multi-Fibre 'Agreement', too, has been little more, in effect, than an agreement to disagree. Similarly, UNESCO's debate on freedom and control of information through the press and the media resulted not in an international regime but in a bitter agreement to disagree.

One good and rather obvious reason why there is a rather large number of issues in which international organizations preside over a dialogue of the deaf is simply that the political trend within states is towards greater and greater intervention in markets and greater state responsibility for social and economic conditions, while the major postwar agreements for liberal regimes tended the other way and bound states to negative, non-interventionist policies that would increase the openness of the world economy.

In a closely integrated world economic system, this same trend leads to the other aspect of reality that attention to regimes obscures, and especially so when regimes are closely defined, in this volume by Young and others, as being based on a group of actors standing in a characteristic relationship to each other. This is the trend to the transnational regulation of activities in one state by authorities in another, authorities that may be, and often are, state agencies such as the US Civil Aeronautics Authority, the Department of Justice or the Food and Drug Administration. There is seldom any predictable pattern of 'interaction' or awareness of contextual limitations to be found in such regulation.

Other neglected types of transnational authority include private bodies like industrial cartels and professional associations or special 'private' and semi-autonomous bodies like Lloyds of London, which exercises an authority delegated to it by the British government. This club of rich 'names', underwriters, and brokers presides over the world's largest insurance and reinsurance market, and consequently earns three-quarters of its income from worldwide operations. By converting all sorts of outlandish risks into costs (the premiums on which its income depends), Lloyds plays a uniquely important part in the smooth functioning of a world market economy.

By now the limits on vision that may be encouraged as a secondary consequence of attention to regimes analysis have been implied. The aspects of political economy that it tends to overlook constitute the errors of omission that it risks incurring. I do not say that, therefore, *all* regime analyses commit these errors of omission; I can think of a number that have laboured hard to avoid them. But the inherent hazard remains. They should not have to labour so hard to avoid the traps, and if there is a path to bypass them altogether it should be investigated.

I shall suggest where this path might be discovered after a word about the second indirect reason for scepticism about the value of regime analysis. This is that it persists in the assumption that somewhere there exists that El Dorado of social science, a general theory capable of universal application to all times and places and all issues, which is waiting to be discovered by an inspired, intrepid treasure-hunter. I confess I have never been convinced of this; and the more I know of political economy, the more sceptical I become. If (as so many books in international relations have concluded) we need better 'tools of analysis', it is not because we will be able to dig up golden nuggets with them. Those nuggets – the great truths about human society and human endeavour – were all discovered long ago. What we need are constant reminders so that we do not forget them.

Outline of a better alternative

My alternative way of analysing any issue of international political economy, which is likely to avoid some of these dragons, involves extending Charles Lindblom's useful clarifying work on *Politics and Markets* (1977) to the world system. Whether one chooses to apply it to sectors of the world economy or to the structures of that system, it suggests many much more open-ended and value-free questions about the relationship between authorities and markets and about the outcomes of their interaction than does regime analysis.

It thus allows serious questions to be posed for research or discussion about any issue, whether they are of interest to governments or not. Moreover, it does not take markets as part of the data, but accepts that they are creations of state policies – policies that affect transactions and buyers and sellers, both directly and indirectly, through the part played by markets in shaping basic structures of the world system such as the security structure, the production structure, the trade and transport structure, the credit and money structure, the communication and knowledge structure, and (such as it is) the welfare structure.

It involves asking a series of questions, none of which in any way pre-judges the answers. It is therefore equally adaptable to the concerns and interests of conservatives and radicals, to scholars far to the right or far to the left, or to those who want only to move more freely in the middle ground between extremes.

Not only does it liberate inquiry from the procrustean limits set by ideology, it also breaks the confining limits set when regime analysis identifies an international regime with the existence of a particular international agency or bureaucracy. Patients often abandon a regime but do not feel it necessary to eliminate the doctor; international institutions are seldom wound up, however useless. Indeed, the continued existence of the 'doctors' on the international scene and the fairly widespread abandonment of regular regimes by the 'patients' seems to me precisely what has been happening in the international political economy in the latter half of the 1970s. There has been a rather marked shift from multilateral arrangements around which actors' expectations (more or less) converged toward bilateral procedures, negotiations, and understandings.

This shift took place in the security structure, as Jervis explains, at a relatively early date in recognition of the limited distribution of capacity to wreak global destruction by nuclear weapons and delivery systems. It can be seen gathering speed from Cuba and SALT I onwards and spilling over in the 1970s into other issues such as food. Moreover, on one important aspect of the security structure, the sale or transfer of arms to other states, there never have been any effective multilateral arrangements. Bargains have always been bilateral.

This bilateralism in security matters has recently become common in other fields. In trade, for example, the most recent report from the GATT had this to say:

While the rules of the GATT continued to exert considerable influence on policy conduct, there is no denying that infractions and circumventions of them have tended to multiply ... That there has not been more open violence to the rules is also partly explained by the increasing resort to privately agreed and officially tolerated if not promoted, restraints on trade and competition. Developments in such important industrial sectors as steel, automobiles, synthetic fibres and perhaps other petrochemicals exemplify this tendency. (GATT 1981: 11)

In matters of investment for future production, too, the most notable achievements of recent years have not come through multilateral or general processes but through an aggregation of a great deal of piecemeal bargaining. Most of the key bargains have been struck between governments (and not only governments of developing countries) and large manufacturing or processing enterprises, some state-owned, some private, some syndicates of both. Since these arrangements will radically affect future relations of production in the world economy and the relative economic prospects of states and their governments, they cannot be ignored with impunity.

Thus, asking what are the key bargains that have been made – or could conceivably be made in the future – and how they have affected outcomes will reveal rather more about the real levers of power in the system than attention to regimes. For in that system, now that transnational transactions have become so important, three points are worth noting. First, the bargaining partners often dispose of very different kinds of power; for example, one has the political power to refuse access to a market, the other the power to refuse to transfer technology. Second, each of them is vulnerable to a different kind of risk, as it might be of a palace revolution on one side or a corporate takeover on the other. So that, thirdly, the bargain struck is apt to consist of a highly variable mix of political and economic benefits conferred and opportunities opened up. Bargains will reflect both the positive goals the parties severally wish to achieve and the negative risks and threats from which they want to find some security.

In trying to draw a map of interlocking, overlapping bargains the researcher will often be drawn far beyond the conventional limits of international politics or international economics. Most likely, the map will have to include bargaining situations and their outcomes within national political economies. To illustrate the point, take Cohen's examination in this volume of the international monetary regime. He interprets this almost exclusively as concerning the regulation of exchange rate behaviour. Yet his own most recent work (Cohen and Basagni 1981) implicitly acknowledges the fundamental importance of (national) banking regulation in shaping the world's monetary system. He would probably agree that the major change in the 1970s was not the rather marginal shift from intermittently flexible fixed rates to generally managed floating rates but rather the shift in the balance of influence in international capital markets from public authorities and agencies to private operators – a shift reflected in the changing debt patterns of most NOPEC countries.

Drawing bargaining maps will therefore reveal the domestic roots of international arrangements, and tell us more about what is likely to be permanent and what will probably prove ephemeral about them.

Whether the purpose is analytical description or normative prescription, the exercise will also leave far more open the question of what values the existing pattern or bargaining has produced or what values might conceivably emerge from future patterns or bargaining. Paying more attention to values would raise our vision above the horizons set by governments and their (often limited and short-sighted) perceptions of national interest; it would allow us to include those perceived by classes, generations, and other transnational or sub-national social groups. The bias of regime analysis can be corrected by attention to the determining basic structures of the international political economy, the structures of security, money, welfare, production, trade and knowledge. Each of these raises the question, 'How to achieve change?', which is surely no less important than the question, 'How to keep order?'

The *dynamic* character of the 'who-gets-what' of the international economy, moreover, is more likely to be captured by looking not at the regime that emerges on the surface but underneath, at the bargains on which it is based. By no means all of these key bargains will be between states. For besides those between states and corporate enterprises, or between corporations and banks, there will be others between corporations and labour unions, or between political groups seeking a common platform on which to achieve political power. Having analysed the factors contributing to change in bargaining strength or weakness, it will be easier then to proceed to look at the outcome with less egocentric and value-biased eyes.

What is the net result and for whom, in terms of order and stability, wealth and efficiency, justice and freedom; and in terms of all the opposite qualities – insecurity and risk, poverty and waste, inequity and constraint? These, it seems to me, are much more fundamental political questions, and imply an altogether broader and less culture-bound view of world politics, than the ones addressed in this volume.

16
'Territory, State, Authority and Economy: A New Realist Ontology of Global Political Economy' 1997

In one of Tom Stoppard's serious-but-funny plays, titled *Travesties* (1974), three well-known men all found themselves in a Zurich library in the middle of the First World War. Each epitomised a transition between an old, disappearing world and a new, as yet unrealised one. In politics, Lenin was in transition between nineteenth-century capitalism and revolutionary socialism; in literature, James Joyce was a literary revolutionary, experimenting with a transition to a new form of descriptive writing. And in art, Tristan Tzara, founder of Dada, was in transition between nineteenth-century realism (however modified by the Impressionists) and the abstract art forms of the twentieth century. The play is also about conflicting perceptions of identity; of what is reality and what is a travesty of reality; and what is, and is not, revolutionary.

Today, the social sciences which developed during the past hundred years on the assumption of a world divided politically, socially and broadly speaking economically, by the frontiers between the authority of one state and its neighbours, is at a similar moment of transition and uncertainty. We share, I believe, an awareness that the old world is fast disappearing. Its assumptions can no longer be taken for granted. We are in transition to a new global political economy – but we are not yet sure in what essential way the new will be different from the old. We are equally unsure which assumptions are still valid and which now need to be queried.

The aim of this chapter is to look beyond the present transition, by proposing a new theoretical perspective for the study of world politics and economies in general and of multilateralism in particular. (I take multilateralism to have the *Oxford English Dictionary* meaning 'many-sided', with no assumption that states, or their governments, are the only authorities to constitutes the sides.) This perspective is based on the more holistic methodology developed in *States and Markets* (Strange 1988e) and in other work in international political economy

(Stopford and Strange 1991). It seeks to escape the state-centred limitations inherent in the conventional realist paradigm which has dominated the study of international law, international organisation and international relations since the late 1930s. At the same time, it is fearful of throwing out the baby with the bathwater. That is to say, while acknowledging change in the role, function and authority of the state in the global political economy, we must still cling to the realities of power, whether derived from the imperatives of a market economy that is now worldwide, or from the state-based international political system, from the authority of non-state actors and institutions or from the authority of states.

The changing nature of authority, and its location in the world of the 1990s has to be the starting point for any truly realist evaluation of the potential for future change in the political economy of the world today. We may reject the ontology of those conventional ideas that go under the label 'Realist'. But we cannot escape reality. However much we may want to change the world for the better, idealism is merely fantasy unless founded on realism.

The essence of *realism* as I understand it is the acknowledgement that outcomes, even in matters of trade and finance, cannot be properly analysed (*pace* the economists) in disregard of the distribution of power. There are two main kinds of power; relational and structural. Though any actor or institution may exercise both kinds at once, they are conceptually distinct. Relational power does not have to be 'legitimate' in any sense. Structural power does. By structural power, I mean power over the way things are done and the beliefs sustaining the way things are done. This may be in the provision of security, in the provision of credit, the production and marketing of goods and services, or the formulation and dissemination of ideas and information. To the extent that international institutions, states, firms and people accept the realities of structural power, it is implicitly legitimated. It then becomes 'authority'. Authority can be exercised by the International Monetary Fund (IMF), by creditor banks in negotiating debt rescheduling, or by firms choosing new locations for production and employment.

I shall begin with a brief critique of the chief models, or perceptions, of the global political economy that have prevailed in the post-war period. All of them, I maintain, have put undue emphasis on politics and on the role of governments and not enough on economics and the role of markets. I shall then, again briefly, put the case for an alternative political economy analysis of structural change in the last half-century or so, one which seeks to escape the limitations of the politics-of-international-economic-relations approach which has dominated much academic research and teaching in recent years. From this structural perspective, it becomes clear that the close coincidence in modern times of three things – political authority; economic activity and exchange; and geographical territory – no longer holds. Their growing divorce justifies the notion of a post-Westphalian international system.

The point of structural analysis is not to eliminate or discount the importance of the state. Indeed, such analysis makes clear that global structures – the way things are done – are largely shaped and formed – and have always been so – by the authority of powerful states. And within each of the four primary global structures – of Security, Production, Finance and Knowledge – there is room for subsidiary national structures of authority through which certain limited modifications of the global structure can be introduced or maintained. This truth is reflected by current discussion of rival capitalisms, all variations on the dominant market economy or business civilisation, but each showing significant differences in how the relation of authority to market forces is managed (Albert 1991; Hart 1992; Thurow 1993). Moreover, even within each national structure – Japanese, German, British, Korean or whatever – there is again room for enterprise structures of authority through which, again, various modifications of both the global structure and the national structure can be introduced. The nearest analogy would be the painted Russian dolls, each one inside another. The largest doll is the global structure; the smallest the family or even the individual.

When we say that the system has changed, reducing the authority of state over territory and over economy within that territory, it is only a start. The question of how it has changed and what it has become is still unresolved: where does authority over economy and society reside, if not – or not so much – in each individual territorial state? I shall therefore suggest how the question might be answered in terms of (1) the increased asymmetry of state authority; (2) the growing authority of enterprises; (3) the authority of other transnational social institutions; and lastly, (4) the authority of intergovernmental organisations (IGOs) and non-governmental organisations (NGOs). This latter part is thus – and necessary so – somewhat tentative since this essay is more in the nature of a research proposal, a programme for future work, than the finished results of past research and analysis.

Theory and reality

The great advantage of studying international relations or world politics is that it concentrates the mind – as the study of international economics does not – on questions of power. I believe the distinction has to be made between relational and structural power. Others have further distinguished coercive power from bargaining power and both from the persuasive power of ideological dominance (Lukes 1974; van der Pijl 1984). These are all useful aids to clearer thinking about power. They help us to have some better, more realistic perceptions of how change has affected where power has gone when governments and their citizens perceive that their powers are more constrained than they used to be. Without this diagnostic analysis, we cannot proceed to prescription. We cannot even define the problematic. Until we know where authority lies – who governs in the broadest possible sense – we cannot decide whether, as a result of integration in one world market economy, the problematic is how to arrest a tendency to greater dependence for some – and therefore greater dominance by others. Or, whether the problematic is how to close the widening gap between intensifying global problems (of security, environmental damage, inequality and so on) and the declining ability of governments through international organisation or diplomacy to achieve consensus, and through consensus to act. The basic definition of the problematic seems to me, therefore, to lie at the heart of our debate.

The deficiency of theories in international economics has been their disregard of – even indifference to – power. This has led to a concentration of economic advantages rather than political ones, on profit-seeking motivation rather than power-seeking or security-seeking motivation. The corresponding deficiency of most theorising in international relations/world politics has been the opposite. IR theorists have concentrated on political relations, on political motivations and goals, showing a massive indifference to economic forces, to markets and market operators.

Reflect that most of the prevailing models of the global political economy have put their main emphasis on the political element, on the role of states and inter-governmental organisations. A more truly realist view suggests a different model in which the sources of dynamic change have been technological, financial and economic rather than political. For example, for the last 40 years, what might be called the Cold War model of the world economy prevailed in Western literature. In this, the political and military rivalry between the US and USSR was mirrored by a competition between rival economic systems. Each offered a runway, to use Walt Rostow's phrase, by which poor countries could take off from poverty to affluent development. Each superpower, using a mixture of aid and ideology, wooed to their side the politically non-aligned, mixed-economy countries of Asia, Latin American and Africa. Many developing countries chose to be as uncommitted to either development model as they were non-aligned militarily or politically. The world economy thus reflected a three-way *political* division between the American camp, the Soviet camp and the uncommitted so-called Third World.

By the 1960s, an alternative model appeared but one which also put the emphasis on political factors. This portrayed the world divided North–South rather than East–West. And the explanation lay in the political failure of the affluent North, epitomised by the Organisation for Economic Cooperation and Development (OECD), to make up for the inherently unequal results of capitalist development and international trade by providing the poor with the generous aid and preferential market access which would give them a fairer share of the world's wealth. The explanation for the allegedly widening North–South gap was essentially political. While within capitalist states, the need to secure social cohesion to preserve the state in an anarchical system had impelled the ruling class to use political authority to modify the rich–poor gap with the provision of public goods, trade protection and transfer payments, in the global economy, there was no such compelling reason to preserve social cohesion, to build in Gramscian terms a *blocco storico*. Hence the failure of the Brandt Commission to make much impact on those international organisations supposed to be concerned with development and poverty but in fact politically dominated by the indifferent rich.

Now, with the end of the Cold War, we are asked to believe in yet another essentially political model of the world economy – what is becoming known as the Triad Model. Now that there is no longer a socialist camp of states opposed to capitalism and the forces of the market, it is said, the looming danger is that the world economy will increasingly be threatened by division into three rival trading blocs – a North American (possibly in time a Western Hemisphere) bloc, a European Community (possibly in time an EC–European Free Trade Area (EFTA)–central

European) bloc, and a Japanese-dominated East Asian–Pacific bloc. This political model goes beyond saying that, as noted above, there are national or regional variations on the capitalist authority–market relationship. It says they are bitter rivals and will engage in trade wars, manipulated by governments.

Once again, political theory is in danger of ignoring economic reality. The modifications introduced to the global structures – Japanese exclusionism towards foreigners, European protectionism, American discriminatory unilaterialism – all these are practised within the commonly accepted structures of the global political economy. The economic reality is that despite protection, trade discrimination and the agreement of governments to form regional trading associations, world trade through the 1980s continued to grow faster than trade within them. The reason for this lies in structural changes which I come to in a moment. The lessons of economic history, overlooked by the extreme political version of the Triad Model of warring blocs, are that the only effective regional blocs that ever existed in the past were those where trade discrimination by tariffs or QRs (quantitative restrictions) was reinforced by exchange controls over mobile money. Thus the sterling bloc and the franc zone of the 1950s did affect trading patterns – but nevertheless coincided with a big surge in the volume of world trade. In the 1930s, the only effective trading bloc was the German Sperrmark system, through which mutual discrimination by Germany in favour of Balkan exports, and by the Balkan countries in favour of German exports was backed by very strict exchange controls, imposed even before the advent of the Nazis in order to husband suddenly scarce foreign exchange.

Parenthetically, one can point to a possibly unconscious ideological bias in this Triad Model – at least in the form it has been propounded in the United States. It alleges that economic danger derives from political rivalry between the US, Japan and the EC. And it justifies American self-defence with strategic trade policies against the other two rival blocs. Sustained by neo-classical economics, it exonerates the market and capitalism and puts the blame for the alleged threat to growth and prosperity on governments, and their failure to provide a 'level playing field'. But the reality to be found in trade statistics – true realism – tells us that firms trade, not governments, and that the alleged blocs are not at all exclusive, that the danger is grossly exaggerated and that – in effect – the Uruguay Round has been an elaborate charade, brilliantly stage-managed by Ms Carla Hills, President Bush's US Trade Representative. Its purpose from the first was not to outlaw all trade barriers, but to break down the barriers to trade in services (the sectors where US banks and insurance companies were strong traders) and to make the Europeans change the means by which they protected their farmers. The divide-and-rule strategies adopted toward the Cairns Group, toward the Brazil–India axis on trade in services, and toward the debt-ridden developing countries were all such as to allow the US to remain free unilaterally to protect its own markets by means of VERs (voluntary export restrictions) while opening up those of others by means of VIEs (voluntary import expansion measures). It could do this by using the bargaining power derived from control over access to the large, rich North American market combined with the institutionalised dominance of multilateral organisation (Tussie and Glover 1993).

Structural change

The argument so far has been that realist theories of change in the international political economy have been guilty of over-emphasis on political factors, and on political structures. And that this had led to some very dubious conclusions about present predicaments and about the problematic for the future. It is now time to leave the negative part of the argument and put the positive one. This is that structural changes in technology, finance and information and communications – all affecting the world economy more than world politics – have been much more important in altering the basic relationship in any political economy – that between authority and market.[1] So, because the rapid integration of the world economy has so far outgrown the relatively static international political system, the locus of authority over markets which once were predominantly national, bounded by national territorial frontiers, but now are transnational, even global, is no longer consistent with the political map of the world divided into discrete territorial states.

The first and most obvious structural change that has created this dissonance between world politics and world economy is in science and technology. These changes have transformed – and are continuing every day to transform, the global production structure – that is, what is produced, by what combination of factors, where and by whom, for whom and on what terms. Any schoolchild know that the products of today are vastly different from those of 30, 60, 90 or 150 years ago. There is surely no need to elaborate the point that this is where structural change has been greatest. Moreover, the speed of this kind of change has accelerated and is still accelerating. As it accelerates, so does the rate of change in the organic composition of capital, that is, the ratio of capital costs to the costs of land, labour and raw materials.

In everyday language, this means that for an enterprise in a market economy subject to such technological change to remain competitive with its rivals, it has to spend more on capital every time it incorporates technological change either in the product or in the process. Some of that spending can be financed from past profits, or by borrowing or issuing stock. But these sources are exhaustible. To stay up with the leaders, profits must be reaped from a wide a market as possible. Selling only to the locals, on a national market will not produce enough profits quickly enough to warrant investing in the next product change or process change.

This is where economics and management theory have misled us. Attention was misdirected to the attractiveness for the enterprise of reducing, by internalising, transaction costs. This, they argued, explained why firms were drawn to export, then to produce and sell offshore, why they had to grow from national firms to transnational corporations (TNCs), how Vernon's product cycles were set in motion.[2] While not untrue, the transaction costs logic was not a sufficient explanation. Only the accelerating pace of technological change and the ever-changing capital costs of keeping up with technological change explained why firms did not so much choose as they were forced to sell on world markets.

The consequences for production of structural change in science and technology were, of course, reinforced by structural changes in finance and in transport and communications. I have argued that it is in finance that structural change has proceeded fastest (Stopford and Strange 1991: 40). Very rapidly, nationally-centred credit systems have yielded to a single trans-global system of integrated financial markets. 'The balance has shifted from a financial structure that was predominantly state-based with some transnational links to a predominantly global system in which some residual local differences in markets, institutions and regulations persist as vestiges of a bygone age' (Stopford and Strange 1991: 41).

The greater mobility of capital within this global system has made it unnecessary for TNCs to invest abroad by moving money for direct investment from one currency and one territorial state to another. Easier and better to raise capital locally, or to let a local partner do so; which is why figures of foreign direct investment (FDI) flows are generally conceded to be irrelevant as indicators of change in international production (Oman 1984). Better indicators may be the figures on international and intercontinental air transport and telephone/telefax communication – essential to corporate managers in the direction and supervision of geographically scattered operations.

So much, in brief, for the causes of the internationalisation of production. Its consequences are, for our purposes, more important. In the last five years, almost every government, even including Cuba and Burma, has changed its policies toward foreign firms, easing controls, speeding up administrative decisions, opening the national market. The implication is clear: where governments once claimed power and authority over the economic destiny of national society they are now acknowledging that progress in industrialisation and the raising of (at least some if not all) living standards requires them to make alliances with foreign-owned firms (FOFs). They may still be able to choose among rival firms – but the firms too are choosing between rival host countries, and whichever firms a government chooses, those firms enter a bargaining relationship with them; 'I'll increase your exports but you give me government contracts/tax breaks/a place in the local cartel if not exclusive access and so on.' They are allies, partners, not subordinates. Such firms in general, and the successful entrants in particular, come to share authority over what kind of production, where it will be located, what restrictions it will accept or refuse, how its employees are paid and treated and so on, and so on.

We can observe the same diminution of the authority of national government resulting from changes already mentioned in the financial structure. Most central banks as the national lenders of last resort to commercial banks counted on their authority over the national financial and credit creating system. Now it is not only the central banks of indebted countries who are obliged to share authority – with the international financial institutions dominated by the G7, with the markets and with the more powerful of the market operators. Because of the mobility of capital and the rivalry of states as borrowers, the latter have the authority to reward or to punish according to their judgement of how any government manages its money supply, its fiscal deficit, its foreign debts, or through deregulation of cosy banking cartels, improves the efficiency of its banks and its local credit markets.

Some observers will argue that these structural changes have destroyed rather than transferred authority; that it is not that firms and banks have acquired authority, but that the sum of authority has shrunk. It has evaporated rather than moved. For the time being, this must remain an open question, to which research may be able to offer at least a hypothetical answer.

The other major consequence is perhaps more significant for the international organisations. Structural changes have increased the asymmetry of power between states. A few – notably, in my view, the United States – have acquired extra-territorial authority that they did not have before. Of the others, some have suffered marginal, other substantial loss of autonomous authority within their territorial limits. It is not difficult to find examples of both extreme changes.

Yet the basic assumption of international law, and of most international organisations, especially the United Nations, is that all states have equal rights, and all have equal status in an international court. That has always been a fiction, but one which for certain purposes could be maintained. My contention is that it has become substantially less tenable as a result of structural change increasing the asymmetry of authority, and – coincidentally – a tendency to admit mini-states as equal members of the UN. The last and most preposterous suggestion is that the Republic of San Marino, not much more than a castle and a few tax-free shops and houses on top of a rock in eastern Italy, should be admitted as a member of the United Nations. When institutions depart too far from the underlying distribution of structural power, they cease to be taken seriously by those who possess such power. At its inception in 1945, the United Nations was so designed by then great powers that it did at least partially reflect asymmetries of power, allotting only to the five permanent members of the Security Council the right of veto.

If, now, we recognise that structural power has been, first enhanced, and second, redistributed as a result of change in (especially) the production structure, the financial structure and the knowledge structure, it would seem that the problematic for multilateralism is how institutions and mechanisms can be adapted so as to reflect these changes.

Some, no doubt, will see that statement as advocating a legitimisation of the power of a transnational capitalist class (Gill 1990), of what I have called the global business civilisation (Strange 1990c). But recognising the reality of power, whether structural or relational, does not necessarily imply approval. Refusing to recognise the realities of power merely leads to mistaken remedies. Persisting with institutions that totally fail to reflect power structures, therefore, is to condemn them to impotence and irrelevance. A realistic reform in line with the changed distribution of structural power would at least have a better chance of taking effective action on global problems. Who can doubt, for example, that the reformed parliamentary system of nineteenth-century Britain – reflecting as it did the rise of new capitalist class and a shift of structural power within the society – was more capable by the end of the century of responding to the need for educational and social reforms than the corrupt parliamentary system of the previous century?

To recapitulate, I have made three fundamental assumptions so far. First, that structural power in the political economy is more significant than relational power. Second, that the changes in the nature and distribution of structural power as between states and non-states institutions, including firms, are more significant in the long run than changes in relational power – such as that between the United States and the former Soviet Union. And, third, that the problematic for multilateral organisations is how best to adapt in response to such changes. Having laid out the assumptions and the underlying argument, it is now time to clarify a little the concepts of power and legitimate authority in the context of political economy (as distinct from politics *tout court*). The way will then be clear to propose a research programme which would put flesh on the bare bones of the general theory.

Power and authority

To clarify the relation between authority and economy, it is helpful to start with the notion of state as the source of authority over social and economic relations, over society and economy. Unfortunately, we cannot easily generalise about the relation of state to economy without grossly distorting reality to fit a Procrustean bed of our own preconceptions of what that relationship is and ought to be. We must allow for the reality of divergence. Let us conceive therefore of a max–min continuum running from a maximalist role of the state toward the economy at one end to a minimalist role at the other. Between each extreme, it would be possible to plot how particular authorities have managed specific aspects of the economy. In some cases, state authority has supplanted the market – state monopolies of alcohol or tobacco or of postal services are common examples. Or state authority has intervened to set mandatory rules for market operators – health standards, safety standards, labour conditions for example. In addition, most states have supplied the market with certain infrastructural public goods, beginning with the institutions of public order – laws, police, courts and prisons – and continuing with the provision of a currency for exchange relations. State responsibility will also often extend to building and maintaining roads and ports, schools and hospitals. By taking each of these roles or responsibilities of state authority, we can build a framework with which to analyse the relation of authority, whether state or non-state, to economy and society in the world market economy.

The first prerequisite for all economic activity is security, the provision of minimal law and order, defining and protecting property rights whether those of the state, the enterprise or the individual. Only within the framework of social order can wealth be created (Olson 1993). Wealth creation – the production process – starts however with innovation, whether of product or process. The maximalist state (or the totally integrated TNC) exercises authority in the production structure by taking total control over R&D – as, for instance, the Soviet state did in Solzhenytsin's *Gulag* research centre on voice recognition. The minimalist state leaves innovation to competition in a free market, without even giving legal protection to intellectual property rights.

The next step in economic activity is investment, followed by production and distribution. At each stage, the maximalist state authority – or within the large enterprise, the managing authority – takes sole responsibility for making choices, taking decisions which, inevitably have social consequences. The minimalist state leaves as much as it can – or as much as it dares for its own social and economic security – in investment, production and distribution to the market. But (as even neoclassical economists are beginning to realise) this seldom means leaving *everything* to the market.

Then, as mentioned above, there are public goods – such as the provision of security, law and order – which markets habitually fail to provide, but which are so fundamentally necessary to the functioning of a market economy that they must therefore be provided by authority of some kind. The more developed the economy, the more complex its industrial development and its financial institutions and markets, the longer the list of indispensable public goods. It comes to include provision of public goods like the infrastructure for a system of transport and communication, or the prudential rules to preserve the financial structures from abuse and damaging instability. If the state does not provide these public goods, some other authority must or the economy suffers.

The same holds good in principle for the functioning of the world market economy. Lacking a central authority, it still needs some authority that will provide a minimum of public goods, and the minimum of legal rules and systems of enforcement necessary to protect property rights and the reliability of contracts. The crucial questions for multilateralism are just which public goods are indispensable for the efficient functioning of a market economy; and what is the minimum degree of intervention in the market by authority which is prudentially necessary? To answer these questions, the idea of a hypothetical minimalist state may help to show the bare minimum of public goods required and the bare minimum of legal rules necessary. While there are some responsibilities of authority which the minimalist state may safely delegate to others or may farm out by licensing, there are others which historically all governments have found it necessary to retain. Discerning which these responsibilities are, may help indicate to us, for the world market economy, the lowest common denominator of intervention by states (or by other coexisting authorities) in the market that experience has found to be prudentially necessary.

Identifying the minimalist issues of authority–market intervention will also serve to help us distinguish those issues where intervention is necessary and those where the intervention of authority is only optional. The same approach, or method of analysis, may help us to highlight those recent changes in the exercise of authority where power has been.

- transferred from one state to another
- transferred by one or more states to a multilateral organisation
- shared between the state and a non-state authority
- exercised exclusively by a non-state authority
- exercised by no one

As all this is somewhat abstract, let me illustrate with a few examples. In a maximalist state, such as Cuba or pre-1989 Czechoslovakia, the security, law and order necessary to the production of wealth was provided in large part by another state – the Soviet Union, controlled as it was by the Communist Party. In the world market for diamonds, the authority of De Beer's, sustained by the Republic of South Africa, has (and has had for the last 100 years or more) the authority over the production, distribution and hence the market price, of diamonds. Its authority did not extend however to the production of artificial diamonds which it shared with the government of the former Soviet Union. In that rather important part of the world market economy that deals with petroleum, authority over innovation, production and distribution is shared between states, major oil enterprises (state and privately-owned), and (intermittently) an intergovernmental organisation or bargaining forum, the Organisation of Petroleum Exporting Countries (OPEC).

The ignominious and scandalous collapse of the Bank of Commerce and Credit International or of the Robert Maxwell empire are two cases where authority and supervision, such as might have been exercised in a closed national system by a central monetary authority as lender-of-last resort clearly were lacking. It is generally agreed among financial experts and international economic lawyers that opening the world market economy by liberalising trade and removing barriers to the movement of money has created no-go areas, where no single political authority is effectively in charge.

One could go on. The list does suggest, however, what a number of scholars in international political economy (IPE) have recognised, that the inconsistency of the authority/market nexus in the world system across sectors or products is so great that the questions can only be answered, if at all, at the sectoral level. It is impossible to generalise about the locus and reach of authority over the market as between, say, steel, nuclear power plants, textiles, coffee, toys, air transport, insurance, drugs, small arms, telecommunications or biogenetics.

A programme for research

I make no apology for this rather lengthy explanation of the theoretical perspective and the methodological approach which are fundamental to my proposed research. Without either some guiding theory and some clear methodology, a plan to dig out the details of the role of non-state authority in the world system might seem merely bizarre and eccentric, even irrelevant to problems of multilateralist reform and the improvement of world order. I repeat, however, that until we have a better perception of what regulatory role is played and by whom, of what public goods are provided by states and by non-state actors, we cannot accurately assess the extent and nature of the problematic.

I am not the first to see the present order as approximating more to that of mediaeval Europe than to the 'black box' model assumed in many texts on international relations (Bull 1977). In medieval Europe, markets functioned under systems of rules, but the authority behind the rules was widely dispersed. It was shared between princes – but princes with very unequal command of resources –

the Church, the professional guilds, and the local lords of the manor (Braudel 1979). What we do not know today, or can perceive only very vaguely, is how authority over world society and economy is shared, where it resides, and over what issues, if no longer so predominantly with the governments of each territorial state.

Tentatively, I see the work as manageable under several headings, each of which can be posed as a question.

Asymmetries of power. How much authority over economy and society has been appropriated by one (or more than one) state from other states? The perception outside the United States that the extra-territorial reach of that country has extended further and deeper into other societies and economies is strong and widespread. It relates not only to the administration of criminal justice – arresting people outside the United States for trial in the United States, for example. It also relates to adjudication on product and manufacturing liability, and the safe conduct of, for example, air traffic. It relates, through such measures as the Super 301 clause to the determination of what trade practices should be judged 'unfair'. Or (as over Airbus) what are unfair subsidies by other governments. If we need to know who-governs-what, we cannot overlook such asymmetries. If the research cannot produce an exhaustive account of all the asymmetries, it can perhaps indicate, through some examples, the main issues raised for multilateralism.

Firms as hierarchies. How far do enterprises, especially transnational firms, act as self-contained political institutions acting within the system of states but in large measure independently of it? They can be compared with medieval religious orders which, while operating under the formal umbrellas of papal and princely authority, nevertheless functioned as largely autonomous hierarchies for the accumulation of capital, the organisation of production, the administration of justice and the provision of welfare. Now that so many TNCs operate inside a number of national economies and societies, they too come to share some of the functions of political authority with governments. Work on the complexity of firm–state bargaining suggests that the political character of enterprises – which may differ in practice just as widely as the political character of states – is an important variable in the deter-mination of outcomes for individuals, regions, countries, continents, classes, genders, generations.

Firms as authorities. How far do some enterprises act as authorities for other enterprises? This is a slightly different question from the previous one. There are a growing number of enterprises whose command of expertise and whose knowledge of the international economy and world markets is so much greater than that of most national bureaucracies that they are 'recruited' as adjuncts or agents of state authority. Accountancy firms like Price Waterhouse or Peat Marwick are good examples. Law firms, bond and share-rating agencies, research centres whether of large banks and security houses or universities exercise a growing degree of influence through their actual or perceived expertise.

International bureaucracies. These are widely perceived as having authority somewhat independent of the will of their constituent member-states. The European Community, in particular, because of its constitution and because of divisions between governments, has increased its administrative reach into regions, firms, distribution systems and society in the member states. The same applies at least in developing countries to the bureaucracies of the World Bank, the IMF and other development banks. While it would be too large a task to analyse all the evidence on this, it may be useful to provide a summary of the conclusions reached in the relevant specialised literature.

Non-governmental international bureaucracies. Their role in world affairs seems to be growing, again probably because of specialisation and specialist knowledge not possessed by governments. For example, there is the London Club of commercial creditors of developing countries which, with the Paris Club of official creditors, has been party to rescheduling negotiations with individual debtor countries on a case-by-case basis. There are also self-regulating transnational NGOs like that which makes rules for the marketing of international bonds, including Eurobonds. The extent and the functioning of this sub-state level of transnational authority calls for examination. Not since the 1930s have scholars in international relations paid much attention to the influence of international cartels and business associations. Yet in the European Community, there is no question but that policy is influenced by Eurofer in steel, by Eurotextil in textiles, Eurochem in chemicals. What is, and is not, subject to such ancillary authorities?

Professional associations. Mostly the professions are each organised in some inter-national body which is responsible for organising meetings for the exchange of information and ideas among specialists from international lawyers to dentists, medical specialists, sportsmen and women, journalists, publishers, political scientists, economists, local government officers, environmental movements, electronic engineers and so forth. Yet the cumulative influence of some of the key associations on epistemic communities, and thence through governments on inter-national regimes, is a growing factor in determining the kind of order, the prioritisation of some values over others, the ascendancy of some epistemic communities over others in the way in which the international political economy is managed.

Public opinion. What role should be attached today to world public opinion, especially when it is allied with television? There are plenty of cases where public opinion can be, and has been, manipulated and moulded by state control over the media. But there are also certain issues, especially environmental ones, where it is more independent. It may be subject not even to the epistemic communities of specialist experts sometimes credited with generating international regimes by pushing governments into coordinated regulation. I can think of two recent instances of public opinion acting independently of states and of scientific authority. One concerns the dumping of nuclear waste at sea, now prohibited under the London Convention. Here the specialists were largely unconcerned. But they were not trusted nor believed by influential sections of public opinion. Another was the US pressure group on behalf of AIDS victims which opposed the government's decision to refuse visas to AIDS victims for a conference in Boston to follow up on the 1991 meeting in Florence. Like cartels, the power of world public opinion has generally been downplayed in the international relations literature. Is it time to reconsider it?

Summing up, the research programme as envisaged at present is more a collection of signposts for future investigation and discussion than a proposal to assemble a coherent set of data. Yet it is essentially contesting Rosenau's perception of a dual world (Rosenau 1997) – the old international relations one of states and a parallel one of great complexity. Complexity, I concede. But the interaction of state, non-state authority, society and economy takes place within one world but in different ways, at different levels, and with vastly different outcomes for economic actors and for social groups. To move beyond observing that it is all very complex, very turbulent, very confusing, I believe it is necessary to identify the issues in which authority intervenes in the market along the kind of max–min continuum suggested above. By this device, it may be possible to figure out who intervenes and with what consequences.

Secondly, I believe that the identification of non-state authority in firms, in international bureaucracies, in NGOs, in professional and other transnational associations is necessary in order to recognise the role they play in social and economic development within and between countries.

Lastly, I hypothesise that such a research programme will suggest that the problematic for multilateralism is both how to cope with the growing asymmetry between dominant forces and interests and dependent groups and interests, and how to achieve consensus on a far broader range of authority/market issues than the international system organised on the basis of states has so far managed.

Section V
Conclusions?

Introduction and Commentary

In this last section we present just one article. This was Strange's final piece of completed work, and surveying the world at the end of her life she was far from impressed. Strange had travelled a long way from her stint as Washington correspondent for the *Observer* but in many ways the failures of the international system remained familiar, as did the limitations of conventional state-based analysis. Once again refusing to adopt a neutral or value-free approach to the problems of our world, Strange argues (nearer than ever to the critical theory of Robert Cox) that the only reason to think about the international system is to think about ways in which it can 'changed or superseded'. While Susan Strange constantly argued for the value-engagement of social scientists, looking around her, at the financial, environmental, social and political problems on the eve of the new millennium, she could not hide her disappointment with the way the system continued to fail, yet managed to survive. The values which drove much policy making and mainstream IPE were not her values, and while we are sure she never lost hope, in this final essay there is a clear sense of frustration. She believed at the end of her life that she had been unable to significantly move the agenda of study so that the problems she perceived so clearly could have been confronted in a way which might have started to avoid the continual repetition of the failures of Westphalia.

17
'The Westfailure System', 1999

From a globalist, humanitarian and true political economy perspective, the system known as Westphalian has been an abject failure. Those of us engaged in international studies ought therefore to bend our future thinking and efforts to the consideration of ways in which it can be changed or superseded. That is the gist of my argument.

The system can be briefly defined as that in which prime political authority is conceded to those institutions, called states, claiming the monopoly of legitimate use of violence within their respective territorial borders. It is a system purporting to rest on mutual restraint (non-intervention); but it is also a system based on mutual recognition of each other's 'sovereignty' if that should be challenged from whatever quarter.

But while we constantly refer to the 'international political system' or to the 'security structure' (Strange 1988e; Cox 1997), this Westphalian system cannot realistically be isolated from – indeed is inseparable from – the market economy which the states of Europe, from the mid-seventeenth century onwards, both nurtured and promoted. To the extent that the powers of these states over society and over economy grew through the eighteenth, nineteenth and twentieth centuries, they did so both in response to the political system in which states competed with other states (for territory at first but later for industrial and financial power) and in response to growing demands made on political authority as a result of the capitalist system of production and its social consequences. The label 'capitalist' applied to the market-driven economy is justified because the accumulation of capital, as the Marxists put it, or the creation and trading in credit as I would describe it, was the necessary condition for continued investment of resources in the new technologies of agriculture, manufacture and services (Germain 1997). As I put it in *States and Markets*, the security structure and the production, financial and knowledge structures constantly interact with each other and cannot therefore be analysed in isolation. The point is 'kids-stuff' to social and economic historians but is frequently overlooked by writers on international relations.

When I say that the system has failed, I do no mean to say that it is collapsing, only that it has failed to satisfy the long-term conditions of sustainability. Like the empires of old – Persian, Roman, Spanish, British or Tsarist Russian – the signs of decline and ultimate disintegration appear some while before the edifice itself collapses. These signs are to be seen already in the three areas in which the system's sustainability is in jeopardy. One area is ecological: the Westfailure system is unable by its nature to correct and reverse the processes of environmental damage that threaten the survival of not only our own but other species of animals and plants. Another is financial: the Westfailure system is unable – again, because of its very nature – to govern and control the institutions and markets that create and trade the credit instruments essential to the 'real economy'. The last area is social; the Westfailure system is unable to hold a sustainable balance between the constantly growing power of what the neo-Gramscians call the transnational capitalist class (TCC) and that of the 'have-nots', the social underclasses, the discontents that the French call *les exclus* – immigrants, unemployed, refugees, peasants, and all those who already felt that globalisation does nothing for them and are inclined to look to warlords, Mafias or extreme-right fascist politicians for protection. The point here is that until quite recently the state through its control over the national economy, and with the fiscal resources it derived from it, was able to act as an agent of economic and social redistribution, operating welfare systems that gave shelter to the old, the sick, the jobless and the disabled. This made up for the decline in its role – in Europe particularly – as defender of the realm against foreign invasion. Now, however, its ability to act as such a shield and protector of the underprivileged is being rapidly eroded – and for reasons to which I shall return in a while.

In short, the system is failing Nature – the planet Earth – which is being increasingly pillaged, perverted and polluted by economic enterprises which the state-system is unable to control or restrain. It is failing Capitalism in that the national and international institutions that are supposed to manage financial markets are progressively unable – as recent developments in east Asia demonstrate – to keep up with the accelerating pace of technological change in the private sectors, with potentially dire consequences for the whole world market economy. And it is failing world society by allowing a dangerously wide gap to develop between the rich and powerful and the weak and powerless.

The fact that the system survives despite its failures only shows the difficulty of finding and building an alternative. No one is keen to go back to the old colonialist empires. And though Islam and Christian fundamentalism make good sticks with which to beat the Western capitalist model, the myriad divisions within both make any kind of theocratic-religion alternative highly improbable. So the old advice, 'Keep hold of nurse, for fear of worse' is still widely followed even while faith in her skill and competence is more than a little doubted.

The symbiosis of two systems

To understand how and why the political system based on territorial states and the economic system based on markets and profit came to grow together so closely that they are inseparable the one from the other, a little historical perspective is essential. As I said earlier, this is kids-stuff to historians and sociologists, but perhaps not so much so to many students of international politics.

Recall that the European state in the latter half of the seventeenth century was almost without exception dynastic, supported by and supporting a land-owning class deriving wealth from agriculture and passing its wealth down by rights of inheritance. The Treaty of 1648 removed one major source of conflict and instability – religion – but did nothing to stop conflict over the major source of revenue by farming. It would be hard to imagine a political economy further removed from the national economies of the twentieth century.

The major difference between the system then and now, in my opinion, concerns the role of money in the state system. In the late seventeenth century, although states issued coins, they had little control over the choice of the medium of exchange preferred by traders – even within their own national territory, let along beyond it. The benefits to be derived from seignorage were therefore limited; adding lead to silver coins was common but yielded little extra to state revenues. Thus the opportunities for states to manipulate money for their own advantage were minimal.

Almost coincidentally, the big breakthrough for states came at the turn of the century with the introduction of a new kind of money – state promises-to-pay.[1] Two Scots, John Law and William Patterson, both saw that by this means money could be created with which to replenish the resources of the state by issuing pieces of paper carrying the 'guarantee' of the monarch. In France, the venture ended in disaster from over-issue of shares and the disgrace of John Law. The Bank of England only just escaped the same fate by passing the management of the state debt to the South Sea Company.[2] But by the end of the eighteenth century, the idea had caught on. Soldiers could be recruited and wars could be fought on credit; the American War of Independence was funded thus, and Napoleon paid his *Grande Armée* with the issue of assignats – promises to pay said to be guaranteed by the value of French land – but ultimately worthless.

In short, the creation of credit by governments and banks could (and did) boost trade and production in the market economy – but it also allowed the abuse of the system by states. The list of sovereign defaulters on state debt in the nineteenth century was a long one (Feis 1964). Yet although some economic growth – in the American West especially – was generated by the discovery of new supplies of specie metals, most of it was owed to the creation of credit by banks and by governments (Triffin 1964). Led by Britain and the Bank of England, the developed countries all evolved their own regulatory systems and set up central banks as lenders of last resort to ensure that banks observed prudential rules in creating credit. Britain also passed laws to ensure that the state too behaved prudentially. The Bank Charter Act of 1844 put strict limits on the right of British governments to expand the money supply – limits only raised when war broke out in 1914. The result was that the value of the pound sterling in terms of gold remained unchanged for a century, thus creating the first stable international money. In the United States, the Federal System was established belatedly in 1913 only after the shock of the 1907 financial crisis.

These safeguards gave way before the onslaught of a global political system embroiled in the First World War. The Russians on one side and the Germans on the other paid for the war more than most by printing paper. As in Napoleonic times, states in the Westfailure system made desperate by the whip of war practiced financial deception on their own and other people. The practice was the Achilles' heel of the market economy. But the history of credit creation clearly showed the symbiosis of the political system of states and the economic system of markets. The entrepreneurs in the market economy needed the security, the law and order, and the state paraphernalia of courts, property rights, contractual rules and so forth to let market forces function with confidence in the other party, whether buyer or seller, creditor or debtor. Equally, the governments of states came to depend on the financial system that private entrepreneurs had developed to create credit. Before the eighteenth century, heads of state did occasionally borrow from bankers – the Medici were unusual in running their own bank. But it was only after 1700 that the practice took hold of borrowing from society by issuing paper money or government promises-to-pay. By the twentieth century, government debt had grown to the point where the financial system had become indispensable for the conduct of state business.

The three failures

Let us start with the failure to manage this credit-creating system of finance. Up to summer 1997, the conventional wisdom was that states and their intergovernmental organisations between them were well able to supervise, regulate and control the banks and other institutions that created and traded in credit instruments – from government bonds to securitised corporate paper to derivatives.[3] This was the message of a much-praised study by Ethan Kapstein (1994). While national regulatory systems in each of the major developed economies functioned at the state level, the International Monetary Fund (IMF) and the Bank for International Settlements in Basle (BIS) functioned at the transnational level. This two-level, belt-and-braces system of governance could take care of any problems arising in the markets. But in the course of 1997, events in east Asia cast serious doubt on this comforting conclusion. The turmoil that hit the Malaysian, Indonesian and Thai currencies and stock exchange prices came out of a clear blue sky. Neither of those international regulatory institutions had foreseen or warned against such a contingency. As the turmoil spread and grew, the first rescue packages proved insufficient to restore even minimal confidence and had to be substantially increased. The common factor in all the stricken economies was an influx of mobile short-term capital, too much of which went in ill-considered speculative loans or in unproductive real-estate investments. Prime Minister Mahomed Mahathir of Malaysia blamed George Soros and other foreign speculators who had moved their funds out of the country as quickly as they had taken them in. But it was soon apparent that national regulations over the banks and over short-term capital movements in each of the east Asian countries (Taiwan excepted) had been totally inadequate. The admonitions to embrace financial liberalisation that came from Washington and the IMF had been taken altogether too literally.

But it is not just that the national systems and the international financial organisations were equally unprepared for the shocks of summer and autumn 1997. The case against Kapstein's comfortable conclusions concerns much more (a) the inadequacy of both the BIS and the IMF as global regulators; and (b) the inadequacy of *all* national systems of financial regulation (Strange 1998f: chapters 8 and 9). To be fair to Kapstein, it only became apparent after he had done his study that the Basle system of capital-adequacy rules devised by the Cooke Committee in the 1980s and subsequently elaborated was not after all really effective. In its 1997 report the BIS more or less admitted as much and, making a virtue out of necessity, announced that in future the supervisory responsibility would rest with the banks themselves. Now, as the Barings story had shown, trusting the poachers to act as gamekeepers was an unconvincing strategy. The bosses at Barings neither knew nor wanted to know what Nick Leeson was up to. Barings' survival under acute international competition made them glad of the profits while discounting the risks he was taking. And even in the most prudent of banks these days, the complexities of derivative trading are often beyond the comprehension of elderly managers.[4]

As for the IMF, its competence to coerce Asian governments into supervising and reforming their banking and financial systems is open to grave doubt. The IMF is used to negotiating with states (especially Latin American ones) over sovereign debts. Its officials – mostly economists – have no experience that helps them catch out wily and secretive bankers when they lie or cover up their business. Moreover, as the record in Kenya, for example, shows, IMF economists have no leverage when it comes to obdurate dictators protecting their corrupt and clientelist power structures. The problem with Suharto is above all political, not technical. The same is true of the African debt problem. Everyone, including the IMF, now agrees that rescheduling old debt in the Highly Indebted Poor Countries (HIPCs) is only making the problem worse, not better. But the IMF and World Bank are unable to force the creditor governments into the necessary agreement on whose debt should be wiped out and by how much (Mistry 1996).

As for the declining effectiveness of national systems of financial regulation and control, this may be less evident to Americans than it is to Europeans, and Japanese. The German, French, British and Japanese systems function very differently. But all are currently being undermined by the technological innovations in financial dealing and the almost-instant mobility of capital across borders and currencies (Strange 1998f: chapter 8). A dangerous gap is therefore opening up between the international institutions that are unable and unwilling to discipline the banks, the hedge and pension fund managers and the markets, and the national systems of supervision and control whose reach is not long enough nor quick enough to prevent trouble. Eric Helleiner has argued that supervisors now have the technical know-how to trace funds as they move about the global financial system. True, but only far too slowly and with too much painstaking effort; not fast enough nor regularly enough to protect the system (Santiso 1997). So long as tax havens provide a refuge for wrongdoers, from drug dealers to corporate tax-evaders and heads of state who regard their country's aid funds as personal property, the national regulators' hands are tied.

The environmental failure

I have put the financial failures of the state-based system first because my recent research has convinced me that it is the most acute and urgent of the current threats-without-enemies. If we do not find ways to safeguard the world economy before a succession of stockmarket collapses and bank failures eventually lands us all in a 20-year economic recession – as the history of the 1930s suggests it might – then no one is going to be in a mood to worry overmuch about the long-term problems of the environment.

On the other hand the environmental danger is much the most serious. The planet – even the market economy – could survive 20 years of slow economic growth. But if nothing is done to stop the deterioration of the environment then the point might come with all these dangers when it is too late. The destructive trend might have become irreversible. Nothing anyone could do then would stop the vicious circle of environmental degradation, and it would be the Westfailure system that brought it about and prevented remedial and preventive action. Why? Because the territorial principle which lies at the heart of it proclaims that the territorial state is responsible for its own land – but not for anyone else's.

There are three distinct kinds of environmental danger. But for each, it is not the lack of technical knowledge, nor the appropriate policy measures that is lacking. It is the ability of the Westfailure system to generate the political will to use them. One is the destruction of the ozone layer. This is mainly attributed to the release of CFC gases from aerosols and other sources. As the 'hole' in the ozone layer grows larger, the protection from the sun given by the earth's atmosphere is weakened with serious atmospheric and climatic consequences. Another environmental problem is caused by carbon dioxide and sulphur pollution of the air. Some of this pollution comes from industry. But a lot comes from cars – cars that use petrol or diesel for fuel. Third, there is the depletion of the planet's resources – primarily of water, shrinking the acreage available for cultivation. Secondarily, there is the depletion of forests – not only rainforests – bringing unforeseeable climatic consequences, and also the depletion of species of plants, fish and animals, upsetting ecological balances that have existed for millennia.

With each of these environmental dangers, it is not hard to see that it's the state, with its authority reinforced by the mutual support provided by the Westfailure system, that is the roadblock, stopping remedial action. One consequence of the principle can be seen in the indifference of British governments to the acid rain carried by prevailing westerly winds to Scandinavian forests; or the indifference of US governments to the same kind of damage to Canadian forests. Another can be seen in the impasse reached at the Rio and Kyoto intergovernmental conferences on the environment. European and Japanese concerns left the United States substantially unmoved when it came to stricter controls over CFC gases. Nothing much has changed since. The agreements at the Kyoto conference in 1997 were more cosmetic than substantial. And when it comes to the pollution danger, the biggest *impasse* is between the developed countries and China. Pressure on Beijing from the United States and others to slow down the consumption of fossil fuels for the sake of the environment is met with the question, 'If we do, will you pay?' After all, they argue, the environmental dangers you perceive today were the result of your past industrialisation, not ours. Why should you expect us to be more environmentally aware today than you were yesterday? With our growing population, we cannot afford – unless, of course, you are prepared to pay – to slow down our growth to keep the air pure and the water unpolluted. Only rarely, as when Sweden offered to contribute funds to Poland to pay for tougher environmental rules on Polish coal and chemical plants, is the Westphalian territorial principle set aside. But Sweden is rich, was directly damaged by Polish pollution and could justify the transfer on grounds of self-interest. China and the rest of the developing countries are a far bigger nut to crack. So long as the Westfailure system persists, Nature will be its victim.

As Andrew Hurrell commented in a recent review, 'the pitfalls outweigh the promise by a very considerable margin' when it comes to transmuting short-term transfers into well-institutionalised long-term commitments on environmental matters (1997). Hurrell also quotes one of the concluding chapters in the book. 'The studies of environmental aid in this volume paint a rather dark picture. Constraints on the effectiveness of environmental aid seem more pronounced than windows of opportunity.'

The social failure

The third Westphalian failure is social, or social and economic. The discrepant and divergent figures on infant mortality, on children without enough to eat, on the spread of AIDS in Africa and Asia, and on every other socio-economic indicator tell the story. The gap between rich countries and very poor ones is widening, and so is the gap between the rich and poor in the poor countries and the rich and poor in the rich countries (Kothari 1993). It is not that we do not know the answer to socio-economic inequalities; it is redistributive tax and welfare measures and what Galbraith called countervailing power to make good the tendency of capitalism to private affluence and public penury, and to booms followed by slumps. But applying that answer to world society is frustrated by the Westfailure system, so closely tied in as it is with the 'liberalised' market economy. If national Keynesian remedial policies are made difficult by the integrated financial system – as Mitterand found out so painfully in 1983 – transnational Keynesian policies are practically inconceivable. We have had one demonstration of this in central Europe in the early 1990s. Here was a case, if ever there was one, for a second Marshall Plan to prime the pump for a rapid transition from state-planning to an open, competitive and therefore productive market economy. But the Reagan and Bush administrations were ideologically unsympathetic and the Germans too self-absorbed in their own unification to bother about the fate of their nearest neighbours. Indifference, whether to central Europe or to Africa, is not just a matter of the selfish, conservative mindsets that Gerald Helleiner recently parodied in verse:

The poor complain. They always do. But that's just idle chatter. Our system brings rewards to all, at least to all that matter.[5]

It is actually an inevitable result of the symbiosis between a world market economy and a state-based political system in which those with political authority are inherently unable to see that socio-economic polarisation is not in anyone's long-term interest. It is not just that the underprivileged may riot and loot as in Los Angeles in the 1980s or Jakarta today, or that they may pass their own new epidemic diseases to the rich, or wage terrorist campaigns under the guise of religious *jihads*. It is that socio-economic inequality becomes intolerable if people believe it will get worse, not better. They can bear deprivation and hardship if they believe that their children's lot will be better than theirs. Moreover, a flourishing market economy needs new customers, with money to spend, not homeless beggars and starving African farmers. America would not be what it is today without the millions of penniless immigrants that constantly expanded the mass market for its manufactures.

What is to be done?

The two commonest reactions to the three failures of the system I have briefly described are either to deny the failures and to defend the dual capitalism–state system in panglossian fashion as the best of all possible post-Cold War worlds, or else fatalistically to conclude that, despite its shortcomings there is nothing that can be done to change things. Only quite recently has it been possible to detect the first tentative indications of a third response. It is to be heard more from sociologists than from international relations writers, perhaps because sociologists tend to think in terms of social classes and social movements rather than in terms of national-states. As a recent collection of essays around the theme, 'The Direction of Contemporary Capitalism' shows, there is little consensus among them either about current trends or about possible outcomes (Chitty 1997). A good deal of this thinking has been inspired by the rediscovery of Antonio Gramsci and his concepts of hegemony, the historic bloc and social myths that permit effective political action. A common assumption is that the present system is sustained by the power of a transnational capitalist class (TCC).

I have no doubt that such a class exists and does exert its power over the market economy and the rules – such as they are – that govern it. Nearly a decade ago, I referred to it as the dominant 'business civilization' (Strange 1990c). I think Gill was mistaken in seeing evidence of its power in the Trilateral Commission, which was more a club of well-meaning has-beens than an effective political actor, a mirror rather than a driver. But he was right in spotlighting the emergence of a transnational interest group with powerful levers over national governments including that of the United States and members of the European Union. Recent research in telecommunications, trade negotiations concerning intellectual property rights and a number of other spheres where international organisations have been penetrated and influenced by big-business lobbies all point to the existence of such a TCC. Yet to call it a class suggests far more solidarity and uniformity than in fact exists. The more I look into the politics of international business, the more I am struck by the growing divide between big business – the so-called multinationals – and the people running and employed by small and medium business enterprises. These enjoy few of the perks and privileges of the big corporations yet have to conform to the rules and agencies created by them. For them, globalisation is something to be resisted, if only because it so blatantly tramples on the democratic principles of accountability and transparency.

The environmental issue area is a good example of the fissures in the TCC. On the one side are the big oil companies, the giant chemical combines, the vested interests of the car manufacturers and associated businesses. On the other are firms in the vanguard of waste disposal and clean-up technologies and interestingly – the transnational insurance business (Haufler, 1997). Fear of the vast claims that might be made against their clients on environmental grounds is putting insurers increasingly in opposition to the polluters. Their opposition, of course, is predicated on legal systems that are sensitive to public opinion. The power of the latter meanwhile is also evident in the growing sensitivity of some elements in business to shareholders and consumers.

Thus, the notion tentatively posited by some of the neo-Gramscians that while there is some sort of TCC there is also an emerging global civil society is not lightly to be dismissed. To quote Leslie Sklair:

> No social movement appears even remotely likely to overthrow the three fundamental institutional supports of global capitalism ... namely, the TNCs, the transnational capitalist class and the culture-ideology of consumerism. Nevertheless in each of these spheres there are resistances expressed by social movements. (Sklair 1997: 534)

Similarly, Rodolfo Stavenhagen, writing on 'People's Movements, the Antisystemic Challenge' in the collection of essays edited by Bob Cox (Stavenhagen 1997: 34), finds the growth points of a nascent transnational opposition, or counterforce to Sklair's three institutional supports sustaining the Westfailure system. Not only, he says, are such social movements non-governmental, they are popular in the widest sense of that world; they are alternative to established political systems, and therefore often at odds with national governments and political parties and they seek 'to attain objectives that would entail alternative forms of economic development, political control and social organisation'.

In his introduction to this collection of essays, Cox does not predict the imminent demise of the 'fading Westphalian system'. The future world, he observes, 'will be determined by the relative strength of the bottom-up and top-down pressures'. The big contest may be a long one and no one should underestimate the power of big business and big government interests behind these top-down pressures. Yet at the same time there is no denying that as Cox says, 'people have become alienated from existing regimes, states and political processes'. Witness the recent amazing, unforeseen turn-out – a quarter of a million in Paris and the same in London – in anti-government marches by country dwellers of every class and occupation. Everywhere, in fact, politicians are discredited and despised as never before. The state is indeed in retreat from its core competences in security, finance and control over the economy; and this retreat is not inconsistent with its proliferating regulation of many trivial aspects of daily life (Strange 1996b). The new multilateralism Cox predicts 'will not be born from constitutional amendments to existing multilateral institutions but rather from a reconstitution of civil societies and political authorities on a global scale building a system of global governance from the bottom up' (Cox 1997: xxvii).

For international studies, and for those of us engaged in them, the implications are far-reaching. We have to escape and resist the state-centrism inherent in the analysis of conventional international relations. The study of globalisation has to embrace the study of the behaviour of firms no less than of other forms of political authority. International political economy has to be recombined with comparative political economy at the sub-state as well as the state level. It is not our job, in short, to defend or excuse the Westphalian system. We should be concerned as much with its significant failures as with its alleged successes.

Notes

Chapter 1

1. We will follow the academic convention that reference to the academic study or discipline will be in upper case letters, viz.: International Political Economy, International Relations, while reference to the subject is indicated by lower case, the international political economy, international relations.
2. See, for instance, Strange (1950a).
3. Typically the work of Robert Gilpin (1987).
4. For a synthesis of this view and the assertion that it actually forms the basis of IPE, see Krasner (1996) and Keohane (1989).
5. See also Ronen Palan (1999).
6. Biersteker focuses on specifically on 'theory' but his analysis is equally applicable to all knowledge of IPE.
7. Although she never fully worked through the implications of this epistemological commitment, see May (1996); Palan (1999); Tooze (2000).
8. This appeared as *The Sterling Problem and the Six* (Strange 1967c).
9. The three chapters of *Strange Power* (Lawton, Verdun and Rosenau, 2000) by Amy Verdun, Benjamin Cohen and Geoffrey Underhill, which deal with her account of the financial sector offer an excellent overview of this aspect of Strange's work.

Chapter 4

1. See also Salant and Vaccara (1961).
2. *The Economist*, September 25, 1965.
3. The amount of preference varies by category of goods. On cotton fabrics, the general British tariff is over 18 per cent, the Commonwealth tariff over 10 per cent; on miscellaneous manufactures, the general tariff is nearly 20 per cent, the Commonwealth under 3 per cent, on general clothing and fabrics other than cotton, the Commonwealth tariff is between 15 and 17 per cent, the general one between 23 and 26 per cent.
4. For some interesting material and arguments on this point, see Schumacher (1965).

Chapter 5

1. This is what the Mitterrand government in France decided when it took no action against Breton farmers incensed by imports of British meat. A contrary decision in 1984 by the Thatcher government in Britain to resist the miners' refusal to accept pit closures has proved immensely costly – according to one estimate it was running after six months into £4 billion.
2. For an interesting account of the predicament and policies of a debtor country at that time, see O'Connell (1983).
3. The assertion is also made by Commonwealth Secretariat that 'protectionism ... can have repercussions on all aspects of policy and affect international relations profoundly' (Commonwealth Secretariat 1982: 89).
4. Arthur Dunkel is also admiringly quoted as saying: 'There is no salvation outside a generally applied system of multilateral rules, and every departure from the rules, however temporary or exceptional it is intended to be, helps to create (sic) the system and to

destroy the confidence which governments and businessmen should be able to repose in it' (Commonwealth Secretariat 1982: 105).

5. Belassa, nevertheless, still subscribes to the bicycle theory of multilateral negotiations on trade policies. See also, Bergsten and Cline (1983).
6. An extreme instance of practice diverging from (socialist) theory is the agreement of China to allow the 3M Corporation to set up a 100 per cent wholly owned subsidiary in Shanghai.
7. For a contrary view that finds Keohane's hegemonic stability theory less persuasive than my own explanation of 'surplus capacity', see, Cowhey and Long (1983).
8. See also, McKeown (1983).
9. For a good, realistic summary see, Rangarajan (1984).

Chapter 6

1. There is an extensive literature on the origin and development of Eurocurrency markets, though rather less on financial innovation in the period 1975 to the present. For the former, note the bibliography in my *Casino Capitalism* (Strange 1986f). For the latter, see Dale (1984) and de Cecco (1987).
2. John Plender, 'Mad, Mad World of Banking'. *Financial Times* 28 January 1989.
3. Hence the big debate on protection for manufacturing and the role of service jobs in the US economy. See, Aaronson and Aho (1985); Cohen and Zysman (1987).
4. As N. Jequier remarks, 'The absence of imperial design does not mean that [action] is without imperial consequences' (Dedijer and Jequier 1987: 237).
5. *The Economist,* 24 December 1988, p. 14.

Chapter 7

1. I am indebted to Soichi Enkyo of the Bank of Tokyo for this important distinction. See Enkyo (1990).
2. A key move by the US authorities in 1975, for instance, was the deregulation of fixed commissions for stockbrokers buying or selling shares for their clients.
3. It was indeed some time before expert observers – notably Paul Einzig, Jacques Polak, and Ed Bernstein – even took note of its existence.
4. *The Economist* World Banking Survey, 2 May 1992, pp. 10–11.
5. *Ibid.* The pessimistic remark quoted was by Robert Litan.
6. *Ibid.*
7. See successive issues of the GATT *Annual Report on International Trade* for the statistical evidence for this statement. The rather large literature on third world debt also tells the same story (e.g. Nunnenkamp 1985; Moffitt 1984; Congdon 1988, and many others).
8. The basic argument about the reasons why the system is rather more vulnerable than most people realise is set out in Strange (1986f).
9. There is an ample literature on the subject. Shorter and more accessible titles are Tew (1988), Cohen (1977), Walter (1991), Holm (1991).
10. In the 1950s, in fact, the IMF's Executive Board changed this rule to allow drawings to be made in respect of deficits on *capital* account as well. This was done on the initiative of the United States to help Britain.
11. The term was first used then in a discussion of the declining role of sterling in world finance.
12. A Concordat was the name usually given to agreements between a state and a non-state institution, like the 1929 agreement between Mussolini and the Catholic Church in Italy.
13. For an exposition of why political economists should address these questions, and how such an approach differs from that of conventional international relations, which emphasize the importance of international order, while conventional liberal economics emphasizes the importance of wealth and the efficient allocation of resources to produce it, see *States and Markets* (Strange 1988e), chapters 1 and 2.

Chapter 8

1. My own work, *Casino Capitalism* (Strange 1986f) came out after Gilpin's big textbook. It evolved from earlier work on the pound sterling (Strange 1971c) and on international monetary and financial history in the 1960s (Strange 1976d). Its basic assumptions were the same as Gilpin's and it suggested some proto-theoretical hypotheses about the causes and consequences of Gilpin's 'virtual revolution'.
2. Waltz' first and in the long run most influential work, *Man, the State and War* (Waltz 1959) posed the basic question whether wars were caused by human nature, by the character of states claiming territorial sovereignty or by the system of states which ensured competition between them for power and wealth. As Waltz concluded, 'war will be perpetually associated with the existence of separate sovereign states ... there exists no consistent reliable process of reconciling the conflict of interest that inevitable arise among similar units in conditions of anarchy' (Waltz 1959: 238). His later book, *Theory of International Politics* (Waltz 1979) did not alter his basic realist assumptions, nor his essentially state-centric conception of world politics. (See his 1998 interview, Waltz 1998.)
3. See, for example, Dyer and Mangasarian (1989); Smith (1985); Smith and Booth (1995); Smith, Booth, and Zalewski (1996); Groom, and Light (1994); Brown (1992); Guzzini (1998).
4. For the Asian perspective on the crisis, see Higgott (1998).
5. This was explained in *Casino Capitalism*, which also discusses the criticism of the Oxford economist, S.H. Frankel and the connection with Georg Simmel's philosophical analysis of the role of money in society (Strange 1986f). The previous chapter had also referred to the seminal work of Frank Knight in distinguishing between actuarial risks which could be calculated and business risks which were, essentially, bets in the dark which often resulted in loss rather than profit to the entrepreneur.
6. See Cain and Hopkin (1993: Volume 1, 153–60) on which I have drawn heavily for this paragraph. Their study of the changing role for the City of London in British domestic and foreign policy, and the emergence of what they call the 'gentlemanly capitalists' in London as the driving force behind British imperialism is a fine exercise in multidisciplinary international political economy based on detailed and perceptive use of historical material.

Chapter 9

1. See, for example, R.O. Keohane (1984), which goes to great pains to explain the simpler versions of game theory. Also D. Snidal (1985) who follows a comprehensive review of the theory with the cautious verdict that game theory is 'a useful beginning rather than a reliable conclusion'.
2. 'Domesticism' is the term used by Henry Nau in his exchange with Fred Bergsten (Nau and Bergsten 1985). 'Unilateralism' is used by Pat Sewell (1986).
3. Walt Rostow (ironically in agreement with much neo-Marxist analysis) has also emphasized the global and systemic rather than the narrowly domestic causes of the interwar depression, see Rostow (1979) and other works.
4. The trend has been followed in many university courses on international relations. See Little and McKinlay (1986), and the earlier *Readings* for an Open University World Politics course, edited by Little, Shackleton and Smith (1981). See also, Brown (1985) and Staniland (1985).
5. See also his antecedents, Braudel (1986) and Perroux (1948).
6. An argument often made in Europe, e.g. Junne (1984).
7. W. Dekker, in a speech to European Management Forum, Davos, Switzerland, February 1986.

8. A common mistake is to suppose the oil companies ever entirely dominated the market in that they set oil prices, or that they lost power when OPEC, in alliance with the market, briefly did so. The oil companies' prime purpose is profit, and in making profits out of oil, US companies still lead.

9. The United States now holds resources in other currencies, but only because it is more convenient and less risky should the Federal Reserve Bank of New York decide (as in 1986–87) to buy dollars in order to arrest a decline in their value.

10. Note that in banking parlance loans owed to a bank are assets.

11. See also C. Hamelink (1983).

12. See for example the analysis of policymaking processes in I.M. Destler (1986). On this point, Snidal observes that when hegemony is exercised in ways that do not benefit the weaker states, they will chafe under the domination and may work for the demise of the hegemon. But in security and finance, their weakness will inhibit their opposition (1985).

13. Even Keohane, who gives a peculiarly favourable account of the IEA, concluded that rule-oriented solutions were proposed but not implemented (1984: 234).

14. M. Hudson noted earlier, 'The US strategy was to act first, to render the trade patterns of foreign countries a function of its own trade controls' (1977: 135). A chapter entitled, 'America's Steel Quotas Herald a New Protectionism', gives detailed evidence for this statement.

Chapter 11

1. This intellectual apartheid can also be found, perhaps in less acute form, in other European countries besides Britain. In the United States, where business schools have always been more highly valued by universities, the focus has often been largely confined to US-based firms and their experiences overseas, which can be very different from those of Japanese, European or Asian firms.

2. John Stopford is Professor of International Business at the London Business School; Susan Strange was Montague Burton Professor of International Relations at the London School of Economics 1978–88.

3. Peter Drucker (1989) is the most notable exception. Among others, note: Cerny (1990); Dosi and Freeman (1988); Dunning (1985); Freeman, Sharp and Walker (1991); Ohmae (1985).

4. The notion of *national* comparative advantage in much current economic analysis tends to obscure the fact that, in the real world today, comparative advantage tends to be firm-specific more than state-specific. Moreover, the nature of the comparative advantage is apt to vary considerably from sector to sector.

5. In those sectors where, for political reasons, the government wished to encourage Malay-owned enterprises in order to counterbalance the economic dominance of Chinese, regulation either kept foreign firms out or laid down very strict rules about ownership and employment. Such sectors were mostly where production was for the local market.

6. See also a recent report for the National Bureau of Economic Research, Washington DC (Levinshon n.d.) using data from the experience of Turkish firms since the liberalizing policies adopted after 1984.

7. Hedley Bull (1977) is explicit on the point. See also Bruce Miller (1981) and a much used text, Joseph Frankel (1969).

8. Some well-known texts on international politics – Holsti (1972), for instance – do not even mention multinationals. Even Robert Gilpin (1987) devotes fewer than 30 out of 400 pages to them.

9. In our view, regime analysis has always been weak on dynamics. This approach sees change in international regimes, whether in trade, money, ecology or any other issue-area, as taking place only periodically and in steps, not progressively and continuously all the time. And far too much weight is attached to rules and codes agreed (but not

always observed) by governments. In trade, for example, the investment-related flows generated by the firms we talked to will carry on unaffected by the ultimate fate of the Uruguay Round negotiations between governments. Yet scholars and journalists continue to pay undue attention to inter-governmental negotiations. In monetary matters, though the IMF certainly has a role as far as debt-trapped governments are concerned, its 'regime' has been undergoing perpetual change since the 1960s and it bears little relation now to the blueprint of Bretton Woods.

Chapter 12

1. An instructive recent study on this is Marsh (1992).
2. In retrospect, I see that the title *States and Markets* was misleading because the book was about the relations of *authority* in general to markets and not just the relation of state authority to markets. Most other texts in IPE are about the politics of inter-national (i.e. interstate) economic relations, which limits the subject much more narrowly to those matters that are of concern to governments.
3. An interesting early example of the unconscious exercise of structural power by the United States. The Silver Purchase Act of 1934, intended as a lifeboat to rescue the Rocky Mountain silver producers, promised to buy silver at a price above the world market. This unintentionally drew silver from all over the world to the US Treasury, thus shrinking the monetary base in China and Latin America and at first imposing deflation on already depressed economies, followed by inflation as governments resorted to issuing uncontrolled amounts of paper money.
4. The argument is more extensively developed in Stopford and Strange (1991). It was also made in an essay I wrote on change in the international system in the 1980s (Strange 1990c).
5. For more on this, two recent books are instructive, Tsoukalis (1993) and Marsh (1992).

Chapter 13

1. *The Economist*, 6 December 1969, pp. 91–3.
2. The Twelfth S.H. Bailey Conference on the university teaching of international relations, held at the London School of Economics, 1 and 2 January 1970.
3. As a result of the meetings mentioned earlier, it is proposed to make a collection at Chatham House of course outlines and bibliographies which might be of use to university departments contemplating change or further development in this field.

Chapter 14

1. For details, see the controversy started by Petras and LaPorte (1972) and continued in articles by Paul E. Sigmund (1974a; 1974b). Judgement as to whether the shrinkage of foreign credit or the shortcomings of Allende's economic management were most to blame for the internal economic and political failures of the Chilean regime must, in the last resort, be subjective.
2. As, for example, Harry Johnson's analysis that although the first-best policy choice for a state by 'purely' economic criteria might be free trade, a measure of mercantilism in national policies can be defended on second-best grounds that preserving a political national interest is a public good.

Chapter 15

1. The title translates as 'Beware! Here be dragons!' – an inscription often found on pre-Columbian maps of the world beyond Europe.

2. For a more extended discussion of this rather basic question, see Strange (1982c) and Calleo (1980).
3. Stephen D. Krasner, 'Factors Affecting International Economic Order: A Survey', mimeo (July 1979), the earliest draft of Krasner (1982).

Chapter 16

1. This is where the title, *States and Markets,* chosen for brevity, was fundamentally misleading. It gave the impression that the nexus was between government and market, government being whoever controlled the machinery of state. Whereas the text actually argued that while markets responded to economic change, the manner of their operation, the rules governing those who operated in them were set by authorities – which might be state, but might equally be churches, guilds, cartels, banks, professional bodies, the leaders of fashion, the media and so on. Markets, in short, always existed within a context set by authority, or by a multiplicity of authorities.
2. For a short statement of the product cycle theory, see Vernon (1966).

Chapter 17

1. Veseth (1990) has argued that this was first tried in fourteenth-century Florence. He may be right but it was a political trick not widely copied.
2. The full story is entertainingly told by Galbraith (1975).
3. Derivatives are contracts to purchase or sell *derived* from some real and variable price. This can be anything from the yen–dollar exchange rate, the price of frozen orange juice or the debt of governments or business enterprises. Derivative trading has grown at a rate of 40 per cent a year since 1990 and by 1995 according to the IMF was valued at nearly $50 *trillion* a year, or twice world economic output.
4. A 1997 survey of opinion in the City of London found that most people – bankers included – regarded bad management at the banks as the no. 1 threat to the stability of the system (CSFI 1997).
5. [Editors' note: we have been unable to trace the source for this quote from the original citation given by Strange; Helleiner (1994) in Kenen]

Bibliography of the Academic Works of Susan Strange

(1949) 'Palestine and the UN' in: *Yearbook of World Affairs: 1949* (London: Stevens): 151–68.

(1950a) 'Truman's Point Four' in: *Year Book of World Affairs: 1950* (London: Stevens): 264–88.

(1950b) *Point Four. Helping to Develop Half a World* (Peacefinder Series: 7) (London: United Nations Association).

(1951) 'The Schumann Plan' in: *Yearbook of World Affairs: 1951* (London: Stevens): 109–30.

(1953) 'The Atlantic Idea' in: *Yearbook of World Affairs: 1953* (London: Stevens): 1–19.

(1954) 'The Economic Work of the United Nations' in: *Yearbook of World Affairs: 1954* (London: Stevens): 118–40.

(1955a) 'British Foreign Policy' in: *Yearbook of World Affairs: 1955* (London: Stevens): 35–53.

(1955b) 'International Trade' in: Wilfrid Eady, Bertrand de Jouvenel and Susan Strange *Money and Trade* (A Background Special) (London: Batchworth Press): 56–77.

(1956) 'Strains on NATO' in: *Year Book of World Affairs: 1956* (London: Stevens): 21–41.

(1957) 'Suez and After' in: *Year Book of World Affairs: 1957* (London: Stevens): 76–103.

(1958) 'The Strategic Trade Embargoes: Sense or Nonsense' in: *Year Book of World Affairs: 1958* (London: Stevens): 55–73.

(1959a) 'The Commonwealth and the Sterling Area' in: *Year Book of World Affairs: 1959* (London: Stevens): 24 –44.

(1959b) *The Soviet Trade Weapon* (London: Phoenix House).

(1961) Review of: J.L. Allen *Soviet Economic Power* (Washington: Public Affairs Press, 1960), *Economica* 28, 109 (February): 98–9.

(1962) 'Changing Trends in World Trade' in: *Year Book of World Affairs: 1962* (London: Stevens): 139–58.

(1963) 'Cuba and After' in: *Year Book of World Affairs: 1963* (London: Stevens): 1–28.

(1966) 'A New Look at Trade and Aid' *International Affairs* 42, 1 (January): 61–73.

(1967a) 'Debts, Defaulters and Development' *International Affairs* 43, 3 (July): 516–29.

(1967b) 'The Sterling Question' in: Anthony Moncrieff (editor) *Britain and the Common Market 1967* (London: British Broadcasting Corporation): 43–50.

(1967c) *The Sterling Problem and the Six* (London: Chatham House/PEP).

with Geoffrey Goodwin (1968) *Research on International Organisation* (Social Science Research Council Review of Current Research: 2) (London: Heinemann Educational, for the Social Sciences Research Council).

(1969) 'The Meaning of Multilateral Surveillance' in: Robert W. Cox (editor) *International Organisation: World Politics, Studies in Economic and Social Agencies* (London: Macmillan): 231–47.

(1970a) 'International Economics and International Relations: A Case of Mutual Neglect' *International Affairs* 46, 2 (April): 304–15.

(1970b), 'International Money Matters', *International Affairs*, 46, 4 (October): 737–43.

(1970c) 'The Politics of International Currencies' *World Politics* 23, 2 (Fall): 215–31.

(1971a) 'Sterling and British Policy: A Political View' *International Affairs* 47, 2 (April): 302–15.

(1971b), 'The United Nations and International Economic Relations' in: Kenneth J. Twitchett (editor), *The Evolving United Nations: A Prospect for Peace* (London: Europa Publications for The David Davies Memorial Institute of International Studies): 100–19.

(1971c) *Sterling and British Policy* (London: Oxford University Press).

(1972a) Review of: R.J. Barber *The American Corporation: Its Power, Its Money, Its Politics* (New York: Dutton, 1970) *International Journal* 27, 2 (Spring): 308–9.

(1972b) 'The Dollar Crisis 1971' *International Affairs* 48, 2 (April): 191–216.

(1972c) 'International Economic Relations I: The Need for an Interdisciplinary Approach' in: Roger Morgan (editor) *The Study of International Affairs: Essays in Honour of Kenneth Younger* (London: RIIA/Oxford University Press): 63–84.

(1972d) 'The Multinational Corporation and the National Interest' in: James Barber (editor) *Decision making in Britain* Open University, D203, Block VII, External Relations (Milton Keynes: Open University): 165–78.

(1974a) 'Arab Oil and International Finance' *The Ditchley Journal* 1 (October): 10–23.

(1974b) 'IMF: Monetary Managers' in: Robert W. Cox and Harold K. Jacobson *et al. The Anatomy of Influence: Decision Making in International Organisation* (New Haven: Yale University Press): 263–97.

(1974c) 'International Business and the EEC' in: James Barber (editor) *The European Economic Community* Open University (Post-experience course) P933, Block II, National and International Impact (Milton Keynes: Open University): 82–95.

(1975a) 'What is Economic Power, and Who has it?' *International Journal* 30, 2 (Spring): 207–24.

(1975b) 'The Financial Factor and the Balance of Power' in: James Barber, Josephine Negro and Michael Smith (editors) *Foreign Policy: Policy Making and Implementation* Open University, D332, Block III, International Politics and Foreign Policy (Milton Keynes: Open University): 35–46.

with Richard Holland (1976), 'International Shipping and the Developing Countries', *World Development*, 4, 3 (March): 241–51.

(1976a/b) 'The Study of Transnational Relations' and 'Who Runs World Shipping?' *International Affairs* 52, 3 (April): 333–45; 346–67.

(1976c) 'Interdependence in the International Monetary System' in: Ernst-Otto Czempiel and Dankwart A. Rustow *The Euro-American System. Economic and Political Relations between North America and Western Europe* (Frankfurt: Campus Verlag/Boulder: Westview Press): 31–49.

(1976d) *International Monetary Relations* [Volume 2 of Andrew Shonfield (editor) *International Economic Relations in the Western World 1959–71* (London: Oxford University Press)].

(1977) Review of Robert O. Keohane and Joseph S. Nye (1977) *Power and Interdependence: World Politics in Transition* (Boston: Little Brown) and Edward L. Morse (1976) *Modernization and the Transformation of International Relations* (New York: Free Press, 1976), *International Affairs*, 53, 2 (April): 270–3.

(1979a) 'The Management of Surplus Capacity: Or How Does Theory Stand Up to Protectionism 1970s Style?' *International Organisation* 33, 3 (Summer): 303–35.

(1979b), 'Debt and Default in the International Political Economy' in: Jonathan David Aronson (editor), *Debt and the Less Developed Countries* (Boulder, CO: Westview Press): 7–26.

(1980) 'Germany and the World Monetary System' in: Wilfrid L. Kohl and Georgio Basevi (editors) *West Germany: A European and Global Power* (Lexington: Lexington Books): 45–62.

(1981a) 'Reactions to Brandt. Popular Acclaim and Academic Attack' *International Studies Quarterly* 25, 2 (June): 328–42.

(1981b) 'The World's Money: Expanding the Agenda for Research' *International Journal* 36, 4 (Autumn): 691–712.

with Roger Tooze (editors) (1981) *The Politics of International Surplus Capacity* (London: Allen and Unwin).

(1982a) '*Cave! Hic Dragones*: A Critique of Regime Analysis' *International Organisation* 36, 2 (Spring): 337–54.

(1982b) 'Looking Back – But Mostly Forward' *Millennium. Journal of International Studies* 11, 1 (Spring): 38–49.

(1982c) 'The Politics of Economics: A Sectoral Analysis' in: Wolfram F. Hanrieder (editor) *Economic Issues and the Atlantic Community* (New York: Praeger): 15–26.

(1982d) 'Still an Extraordinary Power: America's Role in the Global Monetary System' (Paper 3) (with discussants section) in: Raymond E. Lomra and Willard E. Witte (editors) *The*

Political Economy of International and Domestic Monetary Relations (Ames: Iowa State University Press): 73–93 [discussion: 94–101; Rejoinder, Susan Strange: 101–2].

(1982e) 'Europe and the United States: The Transatlantic Aspects of Inflation' in: Richard Medley (editor) *The Politics of Inflation: A Comparative Analysis* (New York: Pergamon Press): 65–76.

(1983a) Review of: C.F. Bergsten *The World Economy in the 1980s – Selected Papers* (Toronto: D.C. Heath, 1981) *International Journal* 38, 2 (Spring): 355–6.

(1983b) 'The Credit Crisis: A European View' *SAIS Review* (Summer): 171–81.

(1983c) 'Structures, Values and Risk in the Study of the International Political Economy' in: R.J.Barry Jones (editor) *Perspectives on Political Economy* (London: Francis Pinter Publishers): 209–30.

(1984a) 'The Global Political Economy, 1959–1984' *International Journal* 39, 2 (Spring): 267–83.

(1984b) 'GATT and the Politics of North–South trade' *Australian Outlook* 38, 2 (August): 106–10.

(editor) (1984c) *Paths to International Political Economy* (London: Allen and Unwin).

with D.P.Calleo (1984d) 'Money and World Politics' in: (1984c).

(1984e) 'What about International Relations?' in: (1984c).

(1985a) 'Protectionism and World Politics' *International Organisation* 39, 2 (Spring): 233–59.

(1985b), 'Protectionism – why not?', *The World Today*, 41, 8–9 (August–September): 148–50.

(1985c) 'The Poverty of Multilateral Economic Diplomacy' in: Geoff Berridge and Anthony Jennings (editors) *Diplomacy at the United Nations* (London: Macmillan Press – now Palgrave Macmillan): 109–29.

(1985d) 'International Political Economy: The Story So Far and the Way Ahead' in: W. Ladd Hollist and F. LaMond Tullis (editors) *An International Political Economy* (International Political Economy Yearbook No.1) (Boulder: Westview Press): 13–25.

(1985e) 'Interpretations of a Decade' in: Loukas Tsoukalis (editor) *The Political Economy of International Money: In Search of a New Order* (London: RIIA/Sage Publications Ltd): 1–43.

(1986a), 'The Bondage of Liberal Economics' *SAIS Review* (Winter–Spring): 25–38.

(1986b) 'Supranationals and the State' in John A. Hall (editor) *States in History* (Oxford: Basil Blackwell): 289–305.

(1986c), 'Politics, Trade and Money' in: Loukas Tsoukalis (editor), *Europe, America and the World Economy* (Oxford: Basil Blackwell for the College of Europe): 243–55.

(1986d), 'Reaganomics, the Third World and the Future' in: R.Gauhar (editor) *Third World Affairs 1986* (London: Third World Foundation for Social and Economic Studies): 65–72.

(1986e), 'comment' [on David T. Llewellyn 'The International Monetary System Since 1972: Structural Change and Financial Innovation': pp. 14–47] in: Michael Posner (editor), *Problems of International Money, 1972–85* (Washington DC: IMF/London: ODI): 44–5.

(1986f) *Casino Capitalism* (Oxford: Blackwell Publishers) [reprinted, Manchester: Manchester University Press, 1997].

(1987) 'The Persistent Myth of Lost Hegemony' *International Organisation* 41, 4 (Autumn): 551–74.

(1988a) 'The Persistent Myth of Lost Hegemony: Reply to Milner and Snyder ['Lost Hegemony?']' *International Organisation* 42, 4 (Autumn): 751–2.

(1988b) 'The Future of the American Empire' *Journal of International Affairs* 42, 1 (Fall): 1–17.

(1988c), 'Defending Benign Mercantilism' (Review essay) *Journal of Peace Research* 25, 3 (Autumn): 273–7.

(1988d) 'A Dissident View' in: Roland Bieber, Renaud Dehouse, John Pinder and Joseph H.H. Weiler (editors) *1992: One European Market? A Critical Analysis of the Commission's Internal Market Strategy* (Baden-Baden: Nomos Verlagsgesellschaft): 73–6.

(1988e) *States and Markets* (London: Pinter Publishers).

(1989a) 'International Political Economy. Reuniting Three Fields of Intellectual Endeavour' *Liberal Education* 75, 3 (May/June): 20–4.

(1989b) 'Towards a Theory of Transnational Empire' in: Ernst-Otto Czempiel and James N. Rosenau (editors) *Global Changes and Theoretical Challenges: Approaches to World Politics for the 1990s* (Lexington: Lexington Books): 161–76.

(1989c) 'I Never Meant to Be An Academic' in: James Kruzel and James N. Rosenau (editors) *Journeys Through World Politics: Autobiographical Reflections of Thirty-four Academic Travellers* (Lexington: Lexington Books): 429–36.

(1989d) 'The Persistence of Problems in EC–US Relations: Conflicts of Perception?' in: Jürgen Schwarze (editor) *The External Relations of the European Community, in Particular EC–US Relations* (Contributions to an international colloquium, organised by the European Policy Unit of the European University Institute held in Florence on 26–27 May 1988), (Baden-Baden: Nomos Verlagsgesellschaft): 109–18.

(1990a) 'Finance, Information and Power' *Review of International Studies* 16, 3 (July): 259–74.

(1990b) 'Economic Linkages 1967–87' in: Robert O'Neill and Raymond John Vincent (editors) *The West and the Third World: Essays in Honour of J.D.B. Miller* (Basingstoke: Macmillan Academic and Professional, 1990 – now Palgrave Macmillan): 224 –1.

(1990c) 'The Name of the Game' in: Nicholas X. Rizopoulos (editor) *Sea Changes: American Foreign Policy in a World Transformed* (New York: Council on Foreign Relations Press): 238–73.

(1990d) *Europe 1992 – Some Personal Observations* (SAIIA occasional paper) (Johannesburg: South African Institute of International Affairs).

(1991a) 'Big Business and the State' *Millennium: Journal of International Studies* 20, 2 (Summer): 245–50.

(1991b) 'An Eclectic Approach' in: Craig N. Murphy and Roger Tooze (editors) *The New International Political Economy* (International Political Economy Yearbook No. 6) (Boulder: Lynne Rienner Publishers): 33–49.

with John M. Stopford (1991) *Rival States, Rival Firms: Competition for World Market Shares* (Cambridge: Cambridge University Press).

(1992a) 'States, Firms and Diplomacy' *International Affairs* 68, 1 (January): 1–15.

(1992b) 'Ethics and the Movement of Money: Realist Approaches' in: Brian Barry and Robert E. Goodin (editors) *Free Movement. Ethical Issues in the Transnational Migration of People and Money* (Hemel Hempstead: Harvester Wheatsheaf): 232–47.

(1992c) *Traitors, Double Agents or Rescuing Knights? The Managers of Transnational Enterprises* [Working Paper for] Table Ronde No. 4 'Les Indivdus dans la Politique Internationale' Association Francaise de Science Politique, Quatrieme Congres.

(1993) 'The Transformation of the World Economy' in: Lidija Babic and Bo Huldt (editors) *Mapping the Unknown: Towards a New World Order. Yearbook of the Swedish Institute for International Affairs 1992–1993* (London: Hurst and Co. [for the SIIA]): 43–9.

(1994a) 'Wake Up, Krasner! The World *Has* Changed' *Review of International Political Economy* 1, 2 (Summer): 209–19.

(1994b) 'Who Governs? Networks of Power in World Society' *Hitotsubashi Journal of Law and Politics* (Special Issue): 5–17.

(1994c) 'Finance and Capitalism: The City's Imperial Role Yesterday and Today' *Review of International Studies* 20, 4 (October): 407–10.

(1994d) 'The Power Gap: Member States and the World Economy' in: Frank Brouwer, Valerio Lintner and Mike Newman (editors) *Economic Policy Making and the European Union* (London: Federal Trust): 19–26.

(1994e) 'From Bretton Woods to the Casino Economy' in: Stuart Corbridge, Ron Martin and Nigel Thrift (editors) *Money, Power and Space* (Oxford: Blackwell): 49–62.

(1994f) 'The "Fall" of the United States: Peace, Stability, and Legitimacy' in: Geir Lundestad (editor), *The Fall of Great Powers: Peace, Stability, and Legitimacy* (Oslo: Scandinavian University Press and Oxford: Oxford University Press): 197–211.

(1994g), 'Foreword' in: Ronen P. Palan and Barry Gills (editors), *Transcending the State–Global Divide: A Neostructuralist Agenda in International Relations* (London: Lynne Rienner Publishers): vii–viii.

(1994h) 'Global Government and Global Opposition' in: Geraint Parry (editor) *Politics in an Interdependent World. Essays Presented to Ghita Ionescu* (Aldershot: Edward Elgar Publishers): 20–33.

(1994i) 'The Structure of Finance in the World System' in: Yoshikazu Sakamoto (editor) *Global Transformation: Challenges to the State System* (Tokyo: United Nations University Press): 228–49.

(1994j) 'Rethinking Structural Change in the International Political Economy: States, Firms and Diplomacy' in: Richard Stubbs and Geoffrey R.D. Underhill (editors) *Political Economy and the Changing Global Order* (Basingstoke: Macmillan Press – now Palgrave Macmillan): 103–15.

(1994k), *States and Markets* (second edition) (London: Pinter Publishers).

(1995a) 'The Defective State' *Daedelus* 124, 2 (Spring): 55–74.

(1995b) 'European Business in Japan. A Policy Cross-roads?' *Journal of Common Market Studies* 33, 1 (March): 1–25.

(1995c) 'The Limits of Politics' *Government and Opposition* 30, 3 (Summer): 291–311.

(1995d) '1995 Presidential Address: ISA as a Microcosm' *International Studies Quality* 39, 3 (September): 289–95.

(1995e) 'Political Economy and International Relations' in: Ken Booth and Steve Smith (editors) *International Relations Theory Today* (Cambridge: Polity Press): 154–74.

(1996a) 'A Reply to Chris May' *Global Society* 10, 3 (September): 303 –5.

(1996b) *The Retreat of the State. The Diffusion of Power in the World Economy* (Cambridge: Cambridge University Press).

(1997a) 'The Erosion of the State' *Current History* 96 (613) (November): 365–9.

(1997b) 'Territory, State, Authority and Economy. A New Realist Ontology of Global Political Economy' in: Robert W. Cox (editor) *The New Realism: Perspectives on Multilateralism and World Order* (Basingstoke: Macmillan Press – now Palgrave Macmillan/United Nations University Press): 3–19.

(1997c) 'The Future of Global Capitalism; or Will Divergence Persist Forever?' in: Colin Crouch and Wolfgang Streeck (editors) *The Political Economy of Modern Capitalism. Mapping Convergence and Diversity* (London: Sage): 182–91.

(1997d), 'An International Political Economy Perspective' in: John H. Dunning (editor), *Governments, Globalization, and International Business* (Oxford: Oxford University Press): 132–45.

(1997e) 'The Problem of the Solution? Capitalism and the State System' in: Stephen Gill and James H. Mittelman (editors) *Innovation and Transformation in International Studies* (Cambridge: Cambridge University Press): 236–47.

(editor) (1997f) *Globalisation and Capitalist Diversity: Experiences on the Asian Mainland* (Florence: European University Institute/Robert Schuman Centre).

(1998a) 'Who are EU? Ambiguities in the Concept of Competitiveness' *Journal of Common Market Studies* 36, 1 (March): 101–14.

(1998b) 'The New World of Debt' *New Left Review* 230 (July/August): 91–114.

(1998c) 'International Political Economy: Beyond Economics and International Relations' *Economies et Soceiétés* 34, 4: 3–24.

(1998d) 'Globaloney?' (review essay) *Review of International Political Economy* 5, 4 (Winter): 704–11.

(1998e), 'Why Do International Organisations Never Die?' in: Bob Reinalda and Bertjan Verbeek (editors), *Autonomous Policy Making by International Organisations* (London: Routledge): 213–20.

(1998f) *Mad Money* (Manchester: Manchester University Press).

(1998g), *What Theory? The Theory in Mad Money* (CSGR Working Paper No. 18/98) (Coventry: University of Warwick/Centre for the Study of Globalisation and Regionalisation).

(1999) 'The Westfailure System' *Review of International Studies* 25, 3 (July): 345–54.

(2000) 'World Order, Non-State Actors, and the Global Casino: The Retreat of the State?' in: Richard Stubbs and Geoffrey Underhill (editors) *Political Economy and the Changing Global Order* (Second Edition) (Oxford: Oxford University Press): 82–90.

Bibliography of Works Referenced

Aaronson, J. and Aho, M. (1985) *Trade Talks: America Better Listen* New York: Council on Foreign Relations.

Aglietta, M. (1990) *Savings, Financial Innovations and Growth* Brussels: Centre for European Policy Studies.

Albert, M. (1991) *Capitalisme contre capitalisme* Paris: Seule.

Aron, R. (1958) 'War and Industrial Society' The Stevenson Lecture, London School of Economics.

Aron, R. (1974) *The Imperial Republic: The US and the World 1945–1973* Englewood Cliffs, NJ: Prentice Hall.

Arrighi, G. (1982) 'A Crisis of Hegemony' in S. Amin *et al*. *Dynamics of Global Crisis* London: Macmillan – now Palgrave Macmillan.

Ashworth, W. (1962) *A Short History of the International Economy since 1850* (Second Edition) London: Longman.

Austin, D. (1966) *Britain and South Africa* London: Royal Institute for International Affairs/Oxford University Press.

Bagehot, W. (1875) *Lombard Street* (Sixth Edition) London: H.S. Kity.

Belassa, B. (1983) 'The End of a Liberal Era' *SAIS Review* (Summer–Fall): 133–42.

Bergsten, C.F. (1973) *The Future of the International Economic Order. An Agenda for Research* Lexington, Mass.: Lexington Books.

Bergsten, C.F. and Cline, W. (1983) 'Trade Policy in the 1980s: An Overview of the Problem' in: W. Cline (ed.) *Trade Policy in the 1980s* Washington DC: Institute for International Economics.

Biersteker, T.J. (1993) 'Evolving Perspectives on International Political Economy: Twentieth Century Contexts and Discontinuities' *International Political Science Review* 14, 1: 7–33.

Block, F. (1977) *The Origins of International Economic Disorder* Berkeley: University of California Press.

Braudel, F. (1979) *Civilisation matérielle, économie et capitalisme xve–xxiiie siècle* Paris: Armand Colin.

Braudel, F. (1986) *Le Méditerranée et le Monde Méditerranéen a l'époque de Phillipe* Paris: Armand Collin.

Brown, B. M. (1985) *Models in Political Economy* London: Frances Pinter.

Brown, C. (1992) *International Relations Theory: New Normative Approaches* Hemel Hempstead: Harvester.

Buchan, D. (1993) *Europe: the Strange Superpower* Dartmouth: Aldershot.

Bull, H. (1977) *The Anarchical Society: A Study of Order in World Politics* London: Macmillan.

Bull, H. (1983) 'The International Anarchy in the 1980s' *Australian Outlook* 37 (December): 127–31.

Cafruny, A. (1985) 'The Political Economy of International Shipping: Europe vs. America' *International Organisation* 39, 1 (Winter): 79–199.

Cain, P. and Hopkin, A. (1993) *British Imperialism: Innovation and Expansion* (Volume one) New York: Longman.

Calleo, D. (1980) 'Inflation and American Power' *Foreign Affairs* 59, 4 (Spring): 781–812.

Calleo, D. (1982) *The Imperious Economy* Harvard: Harvard University Press.

Calleo, D. (1987) *Beyond American Hegemony: The Future of the Atlantic Alliance* New York: Basic Books.

Camps, M. (1966) *European Unification in the Sixties: From the Veto to the Crisis* New York: Council on Foreign Relations/McGraw-Hill.

Camps, M. (1974) *The Management of Interdependence* New York: Council on Foreign Relations.

Camps, M. and Diebold, W. Jnr (1983) *The New Multilateralism. Can the World Trading System be Saved?* New York: Council on Foreign Relations.

Carr, E.H. (1939) *The Twenty Years Crisis* London: Macmillan.

Casson, M. (ed.) (1983) *The Growth of International Business* London: George Allen and Unwin.

de Cecco, M. (ed.) (1987) *Changing Money: Financial Innovation in Developed Countries* Oxford: Blackwell.

Centre for the Study of Financial Innovations [CSFI] (1997) *Banana Skins* London: CSFI.

Cerny, P. (1990) *The Changing Architecture of Politics: Structure, Agency and the Future of the State* London: Sage.

Chandler, A. (1977) *The Visible Hand* Cambridge, Mass.: Harvard University Press.

Chitty, A. (1997) *The Direction of Contemporary Capitalism* (Special issue: *Review of International Political Economy*, 4, 3 (Autumn)) London: Routledge.

Cline, W. (1984) *Exports of Manufacturers from Developing Countries: Performance and Prospects for Market Access* Washington DC: Brookings.

Cohen, B. (1977) *Organising the World's Money: The Political Economy of International Monetary Relations* New York: Basic Books.

Cohen, B. and Basagni, F. (1981) *Banks and the Balance of Payments: Private Lending in the International Adjustment Process* Montclair, NJ: Allenheld Osmun.

Cohen, S.S. and Zysman, J. (1987) *Manufacturing Matters: The Myth of the Post-Industrial Economy* New York: Basic Books.

Commonwealth Secretariat (1982) *Protectionism: Threat to International Order. The Impact on Developing Countries* London: Commonwealth Secretariat.

Congdon, T. (1988) *The Debt Threat: The Dangers of High Interest Rates for the World Economy* Oxford: Blackwell.

Cooper, R. (1968) *The Economics of Interdependence: Economic Policy in the Atlantic Community* New York: McGraw-Hill/Council on Foreign Relations.

Corden, W.M. (1984) *The Revival of Protectionism* (Occasional Paper: 14) New York: Group of Thirty.

Cowhey, P. and Long, E. (1983) 'Testing Theories of Regime Change: Hegemonic Decline or Surplus Capacity?' *International Organisation* 37, 2 (Spring): 157–88.

Cox, A., Furlong, P. and Page, E. (1985) *Power in Capitalist Societies: Theories, Explanations and Cases* Brighton: Wheatsheaf.

Cox, R.W. (ed.) (1969) *International Organisation: World Politics* London: Macmillan.

Cox, R.W. (1981) 'Social Forces, States & World Orders: Beyond International Relations Theory' *Millennium: Journal of International Studies* 10, 2 (Summer):126–55.

Cox, R.W. (1987) *Production, Power and World Order: Social Forces in the Making of History* New York: Columbia University Press.

Cox, R.W. (ed.) (1997) *The New Realism: Perspectives on Multilateralism and World Order* Basingstoke: Macmillan – now Palgrave Macmillan.

Curzon, G. (1965) *Multilateral Commercial Diplomacy* London: Michael Joseph.

Curzon, G., Curzon, V., Ray,G. Shonfield, A. and Warley, T.K. (1976) *Politics and Trade* [volume 1 of Shonfield, A. (ed.) *International Economic Relations of the Western World 1959–1971*] London: Oxford University Press/Royal Institute of International Affairs.

Cutler, C. (2000) 'Theorising the "No-Man's Land" Between Politics and Economics' in: T.C. Lawton, A.C. Verdun and J.N. Rosenau (eds) *Strange Power: Shaping the Parameters of International Relations and International Political Economy* Aldershot: Ashgate Publishing.

Dahl, R. (1984) *Modern Political Analysis* (4th Edition) Englewood Cliffs: Prentice- Hall.

Dale, R. (1984) *The Regulation of International Banking* London: Woodhead- Faulkner.

Dedijer, S. and Jequier, N. (eds) (1987) *Intelligence for Economic Development* Leamington Spa: Berg.

Destler, I.M. (1979) *The Textile Wrangle: Conflict in US–Japanese Relations, 1969–71* Ithaca: Cornell University Press.

Destler, I.M. (1986) *American Trade Politics: System under Stress* Washington DC: Institute of International Economics.

Destler, I.M. and Henning, C.R. (1989) *Dollar Politics: Exchange Rate Policymaking in the United States* Washington DC: Institute for International Economics.

Dhar, S. (1983) 'United States Trade with Latin America: Consequences of Financing Constraints' *Federal Reserve Bank of New York Quarterly Review* 8, 3 (Autumn).

Diebold, W. (1959) *The Schuman Plan: A Study in Economic Cooperation 1950–1959* New York: Council on Foreign Affairs/Praeger.

Diebold, W. (1972) *The United States and the Industrial World: American Foreign Policy in the 1970s* New York: Council on Foreign Relations/Praeger.

Dombrowski, P. (1998) 'Haute Finance and High Theory: Recent Scholarship on Global Financial Relations' *International Studies Quarterly* 42, Supplement 1: 1–28.

Dosi, G. and Freeman, C. (eds) (1988) *Technical Change and Economic Theory* London: Pinter.

Doyle, M. (1986) *Empires* Ithaca: Cornell University Press.

Drucker, P. (1986) 'The Changing World Economy' *Foreign Affairs* 64, 4 (Summer): 768–91.

Drucker, P. (1989) *The New Realities* London: Mandarin.

Dunning, J. (ed.) (1985) *Multinational Enterprises: Economic Structure and International Competitiveness* Chichester: Wiley.

Dunning, J. and Pearce, R.D. (1985) *The World's Largest Industrial Enterprises 1962–1983* London: Macmillan – now Palgrave Macmillan.

Dyer, H.C. and Mangasarian, L. (eds) (1989) *The Study of International Relations: The State of the Art* London: Macmillan – now Palgrave Macmillan.

Eatwell, J. (1998) 'International Financial Liberalisation; The Impact on World Development' United Nations Office of Development Studies, UNDP, working paper, New York: United Nations.

Enkyo, S. (1990) 'Financial Innovation in the US, UK and Japan' Unpublished Thesis, University of London.

Feddersen, H. (1986) 'The Management of Floating Exchange Rates: The Case of the D-Mark-Dollar Rate 1873–1983' Unpublished PhD Thesis, European University Institute, Florence.

Feis, H. (1964) *Europe, the World's Banker 1870–1914* New York: Council on Foreign Relations/A.M. Kelley.

Feyerabend, P. (1993) *Against Method* (Third Edition) London: Verso.

Finlayson, J. and Zacher, M. (1981) 'The GATT and the Regulation of Trade Barriers: Regime Dynamics and Functions' *International Organisation* 35, 4 (Autumn): 561–602.

Frankel, J. (1969) *International Politics, Conflict and Harmony* London: Penguin.

Frankel, J. (1973) *International Politics, Conflict and Harmony* (Revised edition) Harmondsworth: Penguin.

Freeman, C. (1991a) 'Networks of Innovators: A Synthesis of Research Issues' *Research Policy* 20, 5 (October): 499–514.

Freeman, C. (1998) 'The East Asian Crisis: Technological Change in the World Economy' *Review of International Political Economy* 5, 3 (Autumn): 393–409.

Freeman, C., Sharp, M. and Walker, W. (eds) (1991) *Technology and the Future of Europe: Global Competition and the Environment in the 1990s* London: Pinter.

Freeman, C. and Soete, L. (1994) *Work for All or Mass Unemployment? Computerised Technical Change into the Twenty First Century* London: Pinter.

Freeman, C. and Soete, L. (1997) *The Economics of Industrial Innovation* (Third Edition) London: Pinter.

Frieden, J. (1987) *Banking on the World: The Politics of American International Finance* New York: Harper and Row.

Friedman, M. and Schwarz, A. (1963) *A Monetary History of the United States 1867–1960* Princeton, NJ: Princeton University Press.

Fukuyama, F. (1996) *Trust: The Social Virtues and the Creation of Prosperity* London: Penguin.

Funabashi, Y. (1988) *Managing the Dollar from the Plaza to the Louvre* Washington DC: Institute of Economics.

Galbraith, J.K. (1975) *Money – Whence it Came and Where it Went* London: Andre Deutsch.

Galbraith, J.K. (1980) *The Great Crash, 1929* London: Deutsch.

Gardner, R. (1969) *Sterling-Dollar Diplomacy in Current Perspective: The Origins and Prospects of Our International Economic Order* (New expanded edition) New York: McGraw-Hill.

Gardner, R. (1980) *Sterling-Dollar Diplomacy in Current Perspective: The Origins and Prospects of Our International Economic Order* (New expanded edition) New York: Columbia University Press.

General Agreement on Tariffs and Trade [GATT] (1981) *International Trade 1980–81* Geneva: GATT.

General Agreement on Tariffs and Trade [GATT] (1982) *International Trade 1981–82* Geneva: GATT.

General Agreement on Tariffs and Trade [GATT] (1983) *International Trade 1982–83* Geneva: GATT.

Germain, R. (1997) *The International Organisation of Credit: States and Global Finance in the World Economy* Cambridge: Cambridge University Press.

Gill, S. (1986) 'US Hegemony: Its Limits and Prospects in the Reagan Era' *Millennium* 15, 3 (Winter): 311–38.

Gill, S. (1990) *American Hegemony and the Trilateral Commission* Cambridge: Cambridge University Press.

Gilpin, R. (1975) *US Power and the Multinational Corporation: The Political Economy of Foreign Direct Investment* New York: Basic Books.

Gilpin, R. (1987) *The Political Economy of International Relations* Princeton NJ: Princeton University Press.

Groom, J. and Light, M. (eds) (1994) *Contemporary International Relations: A Guide to Theory* London: Pinter.

Grosse, R. (1989) *Multinationals in Latin America* London: Routledge.

Guzzini, S. (1998) *Realism in International Relations and International Political Economy* London: Routledge.

Haas, E.B. (1965) *Beyond the Nation-state: Functionalism and International Organisation* London: Oxford University Press.

Hamelink, C. (1983) *Finance and Information* Norwood, NJ: Ablex.

Harris, S. (1948) *The European Recovery Program* Cambridge, Mass.: Harvard University Press.

Hart, J. (1992) *Rival Capitalists: International Competitiveness in the United States, Japan and Western Europe* Ithaca: Cornell University Press.

Hartshorn, J. (1967) *Oil Companies and Governments* (Second revised edition) London: Faber.

Haufler, V. (1997) *Dangerous Commerce: Insurance and the Management of International Risk* Ithaca: Cornell University Press.

Hazlewood, A. (1967) *African Integration and Disintegration: Case Studies in Economic and Political Union* London: Royal Institute of International Affairs/Oxford University Press.

Herz, J. (1951) *Political Realism and Political Idealism* Chicago: University of Chicago Press.

Higgott, R. (1998) 'The Politics of Economic Crisis in East Asia: Some Long Term Implications' Centre for the Study of Globalisation and Regionalisation, working paper 02/98.

Hirsch, F. (1969) *Money International* (Revised Edition) Harmondsworth: Penguin.

Holm, E. (1991) *Money and International Politics* Copenhagen: Academic Press.

Holsti, K. (1972) *International Politics* (2nd edition) Englewood Cliffs: Prentice Hall.

Holsti, K. (1985) *The Dividing Discipline: Hegemony and Diversity in International Theory* London: Allen and Unwin.

Holsti, K. (1998) 'The Problem of Change in International Relations Theory' Paper for the ISA-ECIR conference, Vienna (September).

Hu, Yao-so (1981) *Europe Under Stress* London: Royal Institute of International Affairs/Butterworths.

Hudson, M. (1977) *Global Fracture* New York: Harper and Row.

Hughes, H. and Krueger, A. (1983) 'Effects of Protection on Developing Countries' Exports of Manufactures' [Association of Manufacturers?] (mimeo, January 1983).

Hurrell, A. (1997) 'Review of R.O. Keohane and M.A. Levy *Institutions for Environmental Aid* (1996)' *International Studies Quarterly*, Supplement 2 (November): 292–3.

Inoguchi, T. and Okimoto, D. (1988) *The Changing International Context* (The Political Economy of Japan: 2) Stanford: Stanford University Press.

Jonsson, C. (1987) *International Aviation and the Politics of Regime Change* London: Pinter.

Junne, G. (1984) 'Das amerikanische Rustungsprogramm: ein Substitut für Industriepolitik' *Leviathan* 13.

Junne, G. (1985) 'Developments in Biotechnology' mimeo, University of Amsterdam.

Kapstein, E. (1994) *Governing the Global Economy* Cambridge, Mass.: Harvard University Press.

Kaser, M. (1967) *Comecon: Integration Problems of the Planned Economies* (Second, Revised Edition) London: Oxford University Press/Royal Institute of International Affairs.

Katz, S. (1969) 'External Surpluses, Capital Flows and Credit Policy in the EEC 1958–1967' International Finance Section, Department of Economics, Princeton University.

Kennedy, P. (1987) *The Rise and Fall of the Great Powers: Economic Change and Military Conflict, from 1500 to 2000* New York: Random House.

Kenwood, A.G. and Lougheed, A.L. (1999) *The Growth of the International Economy 1820–2000* (Fourth Edition) London: Routledge.

Keohane, R.O. (1984) *After Hegemony* Princeton, NJ: Princeton University Press.

Keohane, R.O. (1989) *International Institutions and State Power* Boulder: Westview Press.

Keohane, R.O. and Milner, H.V. (1996) *Internationalization and Domestic Politics* Cambridge: Cambridge University Press.

Keohane, R.O. and Nye, J.S. (1977) *Power and Interdependence: World Politics in Transition* Boston: Little, Brown.

Keynes, J.M. (1936) *The General Theory of Employment, Interest and Money* London: Macmillan.

Kindleberger, C. (1967) 'The Politics of International Money and World Langauge' *Princeton Essay in International Finance* Princeton, NJ: International Finance Section, Department of Economics, Princeton University.

Kindleberger, C. (1973) *The World in Depression, 1919–1939* London: Allen Lane.

Kindleberger, C. (1978) *Mania, Panics and Crashes: A History of Financial Crises* New York: Basic Books.

Kindleberger, C. (1987) *Marshall Plan Days* Boston: Allen and Unwin.

King, G., Keohane, R.O. and Verba, S. (1994) *Designing Social Enquiry* Princeton, NJ: Princeton University Press.

Knorr, K. (1973) *Power and Wealth: The Political Economy of International Power* New York: Basic Books.

Knutsen, T. (1992) *A History of International Relations Theory* Manchester: Manchester University Press.

Kothari, R. (1993) *Growing Amnesia: An Essay on Poverty and the Human Consciousness* New York: Viking.

Krasner, S. (1978) *Defending the National Interest* Princeton: Princeton University Press.

Krasner, S. (1982) 'Structural Causes and Regime Consequences: Regimes as Intervening Variables' *International Organisation* 36, 2 (Spring): 185–205.

Krasner, S. (ed.) (1983) *International Regimes* Ithaca, NY: Cornell University Press.

Krasner, S. (1985) *Structural Conflicts* Berkeley: University of California Press.

Krasner, S. (1996) 'The Accomplishments of International Political Economy' in S. Smith, K. Booth and M. Zalewski (eds) *International Theory: Positivism and Beyond* Cambridge: Cambridge University Press.

Krauthammer, C. (1986) 'The Newest Challenge to the Reagan Doctrine: The Poverty of Realism' *New Republic* 194, 7 (February): 14–17.

Laitin, D. (1982) 'Capitalism and Hegemony: Yorubaland and the International Economy' *International Organisation* 36, 4 (Autumn): 687–713.

Landes, D. (1998) *The Wealth and Poverty of Nations* New York: W.W. Norton.

Lawson, F. (1983) 'Hegemony and the Structure of International Trade Re-assessed: A view from Arabia' *International Organisation* 37, 2 (Spring): 317–37.

Lawton, T.C. and Michaels, K.P. (2000) 'The Evolving Global Production Structure: Implications for International Political Economy in: T.C. Lawton, A.C. Verdun and J.N. Rosenau (eds) *Strange Power: Shaping the Parameters of International Relations and International Political Economy* Aldershot: Ashgate Publishing.

Lawton, T.C., Verdun, A.C. and Rosenau, J.N. (eds) (2000) *Strange Power: Shaping the Parameters of International Relations and International Political Economy* Aldershot: Ashgate Publishing.

Lessard, D. and Williamson, J. (1987) *Capital Flight: The Problem of Policy Responses* Washington DC: Institute for International Economics.

Levinshon, J. (n.d. [1990?]) 'Testing the Import-as-Market-Discipline Hypothesis' Washington: National Bureau of Economic Research.

Lewis, W.A. (1970 [1949]) *Economic Survey 1919–1939* London: Allen and Unwin.

Lindblom, C.E. (1977) *Politics and Markets: The World's Political-Economic Systems* New York: Basic Books.

Little, R. and McKinlay, R.D. (1986) *Global Problems and World Order* London: Frances Pinter.

Little, R., Shackleton, M. and Smith, M. (1981) *Perspectives on World Politics: A Reader* London: Croom Helm.

Lukes, S. (1974) *Power: A Radical View* London: Macmillan.

Lukes, S. (ed.) (1986) *Power* Oxford: Blackwells.

McKeown, T. (1983) 'Hegemonic Stability Theory and Nineteenth-Century Tariff Levels in Europe' *International Organisation* 37, 1 (Winter): 73–91.

MacLean, J. (2000) 'Philosophical Roots of Globalisation and Philosophical Routes to Globalisation' in R. Germain (ed.) *Globalisation and its Critics. Perspectives from Political Economy* Basingstoke: Macmillan – now Palgrave Macmillan.

Majone (1994) 'Understanding Regulatory Growth in the European Community' EUI Working Paper 94/7, Florence: European University Institute.

Marris, S. (1985) *Deficits and the Dollar: The World Economy at Risk* Washington DC: Institute for International Economics.

Marsh, D. (1992) *The Bundesbank: The Bank that Rules Europe* London: Heinemann.

Matthews, R.C. (1982) *Slower Growth in the Western World* London: Heinemann.

May, C. (1996) 'Strange Fruit': Susan Strange's Theory of Structural Power in the International Political Economy, *Global Society,* 10, 2 (Spring): 167–89.

Medlicott, W.M. (1952/1959) *The Economic Blockade* (History of the Second World War: United Kingdom Civil Series) London: HMSO/Longmans.

Melman, S. (1970) *Pentagon Capitalism: The Political Economy of War* New York: McGraw-Hill.

Meyer, F.V. (1978) *International Trade Policy* London: Croom Helm.

Michalet, C.A. (1976) *Le capitalisme mondiale* Paris: PUF.

Miller, J.D.B. (1981) *The World of States: Connected Essays* London: Croom Helm.

Miller, J.D.B. (1986) *Norman Angell and the Futility of War* London: Macmillan – now Palgrave Macmillan.

Milward, A. (1981) 'Tariffs as Constitutions' in: Susan Strange and Roger Tooze (eds) *The Politics of International Surplus Capacity* London: Allen and Unwin.

Milward, A.S. (1984) *The Reconstruction of Western Europe 1945–51* London: Methuen.

Ministry of Overseas Development (1965) *Overseas Development: The Work of the New Ministry* London: HMSO.

Minsky, H. (1982) *Can it Happen Again? Essays on Instability and Finance* New York: M.E. Sharpe.

Mistry, P. (1996) *Resolving Africa's Multilateral Debt Problem* The Hague: Fondad.

Moffitt, M. (1984) *The World's Money: International Banking from Bretton Woods to the Brink of Insolvency* London: Michael Joseph.

Morawetz, D. (1981) *Why the Emperor's New Clothes are Not Made in Colombia: A Case Study in Latin American and East Asian Manufactured Exports* New York: Oxford University Press/World Bank.

Morgenthau, H. (1954) *Politics Among Nations* (second edition) New York: McGraw-Hill.

Myrdal, G. (1970) *Objectivity in Social Research* London: Duckworth.

Mytelka, L. (ed.) (1991) *Strategic Partnerships: States, Firms and International Competition* London: Pinter.

Naylor, R. (1987) *Hot Money and the Politics of Debt* New York: Linden Press/Simon and Schuster.

Nau, H. and Bergsten, F. (1985) 'The State of the Debate: Reagonomics' *Foreign Policy* 59 (Summer 1985): 132–53.

Nitzan, J. (1998) 'Differential Accumulation: Towards A New Political Economy of Capital' *Review of International Political Economy* 5, 2 (Summer): 169–216.

Northedge, F.S. (ed.) (1974) *The Use of Force in International Relations* London: Faber.

Nunnenkamp, P. (1985) *The International Debt Crisis of the Third World: Causes and Consequences for the World Economy* Brighton: Wheatsheaf.

Nye, J. S. (1990) *Bound to Lead: The Changing Nature of American Power* New York: Basic Books.

Nye, J.S. and Keohane, R.O. (eds) (1972) *Transnational Relations and World Politics* Cambridge, Mass.: Harvard University Press.

O'Connell, A. (1983) 'Argentina under the Depression: Problems of an Open Economy' (mimeo) Buenos Aires: Instituto Torcuato Di Tella.

Odell, J. (1986) 'Growing Conflict and Growing Cooperation in Trade Between Latin America and the United States' in: K. Middelbrook and C. Rico (eds) *The United States and Latin America in the 1980s: Contending Perspectives on a Decade of Crisis* Pittsburgh: Pittsburgh University Press.

Ogata, S. (1988) 'Japan and the Asian Development Bank' (mimeo) paper for IPSA congress, Washington DC.

Ohmae, K. (1985) *Triad Power: The Coming Shape of Global Competition* New York: Free Press.

Olson, M. (1965) *The Logic of Collective Action: Public Goods and the Theory of Groups* Cambridge, Mass.: Harvard University Press.

Olson, M. (1982) *The Rise and Decline of Nations: Economic Growth, Stagflation and Social Rigidities* New Haven: Yale University Press.

Olson, M. (1993) 'Dictatorship, Democracy and Development' *American Political Science Review* 87, 3 (September): 567–76.

Oman, C. (1984) *New Forms of International Investment in Developing Countries* Paris: OECD.

Organisation of Economic Cooperation and Development [OECD] (1965) *Fiscal Incentives for Private Investment in Developing Countries* Paris: OECD.

Palan, R. (1999) 'Susan Strange 1923–1998: A Great International Relations Theorist' *Review of International Relations* 6, 2 (Summer): 121–32.

Paoli, L. (1997) 'The Pledge of Secrecy; Culture, Structure and Action of Mafia Associations' Unpublished PhD Thesis, European University Institute, Florence.

Parboni, R. (1981) *The Dollar and its Rivals* London: Verso.

Patterson, G. (1966) *Discrimination in International Trade: The Policy Issues 1945–65* Princeton: Princeton University Press.

Pavitt, K. and Soete, L. (1982) 'International Differences in Economic Growth and the International Location of Innovation' in: H. Giersch (ed.) *Emerging Technologies: Consequences for Economic Growth, Structural Change and Employment* Tübingen: J.C.B. Mohr.

Pearson, L.B. [chairman] (1969) *Partners in Development. Report of the Commission on International Development* London: Pall Mall.

Pen, J. (1959 [1971]) 'Wages and Collective Bargaining' [extract] in: K.W. Rothschild (ed.) *Power in Economics* (Penguin Modern Economics Readings) Harmondsworth: Penguin.

Penrose, E. (1968) *The Large International Firm in Developing Countries: The International Petroleum Industry* London: George Allen and Unwin.

Perroux, F. (1948) *Le Capitalisme* Paris: Presses Universitaires de France.

Petras, J.F. and LaPorte, R. (1972) 'Can We Do Business with Radical Nationalists? (2): Chile: No' *Foreign Policy* No. 7 (Summer): 132–58.

van der Pijl, K. (1984) *The Making of an Atlantic Ruling Class* London: Verso.

Polk, J., Merster, I.W. and Veit, L.A. (1966) 'US Production Abroad and the Balance of Payments: A Survey of Corporate Investment Experience' New York: National Industrial Conference Board.

Popper, K. (1969) *Conjectures and Refutations* (Third Edition) London: Routledge and Kegan Paul.

Porter, M. (1990) *The Competitive Advantage of Nations* New York: Free Press.

Rangarajan, L. (1984) 'The Politics of International Trade' in S. Strange (ed.) *Paths to International Political Economy* London: Allen and Unwin.

Ray, J.E. (1995) *Global Politics* (6th Edition) Boston: Houghton Mifflin.

Reese, T. (1969) *Australia, New Zealand and the United States: A Survey of International Relations 1914–1968* London: Royal Institute of International Affairs/Oxford University Press.

Rosenau, J (1997) 'The Person, the Household, the Community and the Globe: Notes for a Theory of Multilateralism in a Turbulent World' in: R.W. Cox (ed.) *The New Realism: Perspectives on Multilateralism and World Order* Basingstoke: Macmillan – now Palgrave Macmillan.

Rostow, W.W. (1979) *The World Economy. History and Prospect* Austin: University of Texas Press.

Rothschild, K.W. (ed.) (1971) *Power in Economics* (Penguin Modern Economics Readings) Harmondsworth: Penguin.

Rueff, J. (1972) *The Monetary Sin of the West* New York: Macmillan.

Ruggie, J. (1993) 'Territoriality and Beyond: Problematising Modernity in International Relations' *International Organisation* 46, 1: 139–74.

Russett, B. (1985) 'The Mysterious Case of Vanishing Hegemony; or Is Mark Twain Really Dead?' *International Organisation* 39, 2 (Spring): 207–31.

Sakamoto, Y. (ed.) (1994) *Global Transformation: Challenges to the State System* Tokyo: United Nations University Press.

Salant, W.S. and Vaccara, B.N. (1961) *Import Liberalization and Employment* Washington: Brookings Institution.

Santiso, J. (1997) 'Wall Street face a la crice mexicaine' (CEPII working paper) Paris: Center d'Etudes Prospectives a l'Information Internationales.

Schumacher, E.F. (1965) 'Social and Economic Problems Calling for the Development of Intermediate Technology' Paris: UNESCO.

Schumann, F. (1937) *International Politics* (2nd Edition) New York: McGraw-Hill.

Schwarzenberger, G. (1941) *Power Politics* London: Jonathan Cape.

Sen, G. (1983) *Military Origins of Industrialization and International Trade Rivalry* New York: St Martin's Press – now Palgrave Macmillan.

Servan-Schreiber, J.J. (1967) *Le défi américain* Paris: Denoël.

Sewell, P. (1986) 'The Congenital Unilateralism and Adaptation of American Academics' paper for the annual conference of the American Political Science Association (September).

Shelp, R.K. (1981) *Beyond Industrialisation: The Ascendancy of the Global Service Economy* New York: Praeger.

Shinkai, Y. (1988) 'The Internationalisation of Finance in Japan' in: T. Inoguchi and D. Okimoto (eds) *The Political Economy of Japan: Volume 2. The Changing International Context* Stanford: Stanford University Press.

Shonfield, A. (1969) *Modern Capitalism* (Second, Revised Edition) London: Oxford University Press/Royal Institute of International Affairs.

Sigmund, P.E. (1974a) 'The "Invisible Blockade" and the overthrow of Allende' *Foreign Affairs* 52, 2 (January): 322–40.

Sigmund, P.E. (1974b) 'Less Than Changed' *Foreign Policy* 16 (Fall): 142–56.

Sklair, L. (1997) 'Social Movements for Global Capitalism: The Transnational Capitalist Class in Action' *Review of International Political Economy* 4, 3 (Autumn): 514–38.

Smith, S. (ed.) (1985) *International Relations: British and American Perspectives* Oxford: Blackwell.

Smith, S. and Booth, K. (eds) (1995) *International Relations Theory Today* London: Polity.

Smith, S., Booth, K. and Zalewski, M. (eds) (1996) *International Theory: Positivism and Beyond* Cambridge: Cambridge University Press.

Snidal, D. (1985) 'The Limits of Hegemonic Stability Theory' *International Organisation* 39, 4 (Autumn): 579–614.

Soros, G. (1987) *The Alchemy of Finance: Reading the Mind of the Market* London: Wiedenfeld and Nicolson.

Spero, J. E. (1980) *The Failure of the Franklin National Bank: Challenge to the International Banking System* New York: Council on Foreign Relations/Columbia University Press.

Staniland, M. (1985) *What is Political Economy?* New Haven: Yale University Press.

Stavenhagen, R. (1997) 'People's Movements: The Antisystemic Challenge' in: R.W. Cox (ed.) *The New Realism: Perspectives on Multilateralism and World Order* Houndmills: Macmillan – now Palgrave Macmillan.

Stein, A. (1982) 'Coordination and Collaboration: Regimes in an Anarchic World' *International Organisation* 36, 2 (Spring): 299–324.

Stein, A. (1984) 'The Hegemon's Dilemma: Great Britain, The United States and International Economic Order' *International Organisation* 38, 2 (Spring): 355–86.

Story, J. (2000) 'Setting the Parameters: A Strange World System' in: T.C. Lawton, A.C. Verdun and J.N. Rosenau (eds) *Strange Power: Shaping the Parameters of International Relations and International Political Economy* Aldershot: Ashgate Publishing.

Story, J. and Ingo, W. (1997) *Political Economy of Financial Integration in Europe: The Battle of the Systems* Manchester: Manchester University Press.

Tew, B. (1988) *The Evolution of the International Monetary System 1945–1986* (4th Edition) London: Hutchinson.

Thurow, L. (1993) *Head to Head: The Coming Economic Battle Among Japan Europe and America* London: Brealey.

Tooze, R. (1984) 'In Search of International Political Economy' *Political Studies* 32, 4: 637–46.

Tooze, R. (2000) 'Ideology, Knowledge and Power in International Relations and International Political Economy' in: T.C. Lawton, A.C. Verdun and J.N. Rosenau (eds) *Strange Power: Shaping the Parameters of International Relations and International Political Economy* Aldershot: Ashgate Publishing.

Triffin, R. (1964) *The Evolution of the International Monetary System* Princeton, NJ: Princeton University Press.

Triffin, R. (1991) 'IMS – International Monetary System – or Scandal?' (Jean Monnet Chair Lecture) Florence: European University Institute.

Tsoukalis, L. (1993) *The New European Economy* (Second Edition) Oxford: Oxford University Press.

Tugendhat, C. (1968) *Oil, The Biggest Business* London: Eyre and Spottiswoode.

Tumlir, J. (1983) 'The World Economy Today: Crisis or New Beginning?' *National Westminster Quarterly Review* (August): 26–44.

Tussie, D. and Glover, D. (eds) (1993) *The Developing Countries and World Trade Policies, and Bargaining Strategies* Boulder: Lynne Rienner.

United Nations [UN] (1963) 'Measures for the Expansion of Markets of the Developed Countries for Exports of Manufactures and Semi-manufactures of Developing Countries' in: *World Economic Survey* New York: United Nations.

United Nations Centre on Transnational Corporations [UNCTC] (1979) 'Transborder Data Flows' New York: United Nations.

Uno, S. (1988) '"Engine for Development": Japan – ASEAN Cooperation toward Peace and Stability' *Speaking in Japan* 9, 95 (November).

Vernon, R. (1966) 'International Investment and International Trade in the Product Cycle' *Quarterly Journal of Economics* 80: 190–207.

Vernon, R. (1977) *Storm Over the Multinationals* Cambridge: Harvard University Press.

Versluysen, E. (1981) *The Political Economy of International Finance* Farnborough: Gower.

Veseth, M. (1990) *Mountains of Debt: Crisis and Change in Renaissance Florence, Victorian Britain and Post-war America* Oxford: Oxford University Press.

Volcker, P. and Gyohten, T. (1992) *Changing Fortunes: The World's Money and the Threat To American Leadership* New York: Times Books.

Wallerstein, I. (1984) *The Politics of the World Economy: The States, the Movements and the Civilisations* Cambridge: Cambridge University Press.

Walter, A. (1991) *World Power and World Money: The Role of Hegemony and International Monetary Order* London: Harvester Wheatsheaf.

Walters, R.S. (1983) 'America's Declining Industrial Competitiveness: Protectionism, the Marketplace and the State' *Political Studies* 16, 1 (Winter): 25–33.

Waltz, K. (1959) *Man, The State and War* New York: Columbia University Press.

Waltz, K. (1979) *Theory of International Politics* New York: McGraw-Hill.

Waltz, K. (1998) 'Interview with Fred Halliday and Justin Rosenberg' *Review of International Studies* 24, 3 (July): 371–86.

Wilcox, C. (1949) *A Charter for World Trade* New York: Macmillan.

Wolfe, A. (1977) *The Limit of Legitimacy: Political Contradictions of Contemporary Capitalism* New York: Free Press.

Yamamura, K. and Yasuba, Y. (1988) *The Political Economy of Japan: Volume 1. The Domestic Transformation* Stanford: Stanford University Press.

Subject Index

Compiled by Sue Carlton

Name Index

Compiled by Sue Carlton

284